D0882749

HANDBOOK OF PREVENTION AND INTERVENTION PROGRAMS FOR ADOLESCENT GIRLS

HANDBOOK OF PREVENTION AND INTERVENTION PROGRAMS FOR ADOLESCENT GIRLS

Edited by

Craig Winston LeCroy
Joyce Elizabeth Mann

John Wiley & Sons, Inc.

HV
1425
.H36
2008

This book is printed on acid-free paper. ∞

Copyright © 2008 by John Wiley & Sons, Inc. All rights reserved.

Published by John Wiley & Sons, Inc., Hoboken, New Jersey.
Published simultaneously in Canada.

Wiley Bicentennial Logo: Richard J. Pacifico

No part of this publication may be reproduced, stored in a retrieval system, or transmitted in any form
or by any means, electronic, mechanical, photocopying, recording, scanning, or otherwise, except as
permitted under Section 107 or 108 of the 1976 United States Copyright Act, without either the prior
written permission of the Publisher, or authorization through payment of the appropriate per-copy
fee to the Copyright Clearance Center, Inc., 222 Rosewood Drive, Danvers, MA 01923,
(978) 750-8400, fax (978) 646-8600, or on the web at www.copyright.com. Requests to the
Publisher for permission should be addressed to the Permissions Department, John Wiley &
Sons, Inc., 111 River Street, Hoboken, NJ 07030, (201) 748-6011, fax (201) 748-6008 or online at
http://www.wiley.com/go/permissions.

Limit of Liability/Disclaimer of Warranty: While the publisher and author have used their best efforts
in preparing this book, they make no representations or warranties with respect to the accuracy or
completeness of the contents of this book and specifically disclaim any implied warranties of
merchantability or fitness for a particular purpose. No warranty may be created or extended by sales
representatives or written sales materials. The advice and strategies contained herein may not be
suitable for your situation. You should consult with a professional where appropriate. Neither the
publisher nor author shall be liable for any loss of profit or any other commercial damages, including
but not limited to special, incidental, consequential, or other damages.

This publication is designed to provide accurate and authoritative information in regard to the subject
matter covered. It is sold with the understanding that the publisher is not engaged in rendering
professional services. If legal, accounting, medical, psychological or any other expert assistance is
required, the services of a competent professional person should be sought.

Designations used by companies to distinguish their products are often claimed as trademarks. In all
instances where John Wiley & Sons, Inc. is aware of a claim, the product names appear in initial capital
or all capital letters. Readers, however, should contact the appropriate companies for more complete
information regarding trademarks and registration.

For general information on our other products and services please contact our Customer Care
Department within the U.S. at (800) 762-2974, outside the United States at (317) 572-3993 or
fax (317) 572-4002.

Wiley also publishes its books in a variety of electronic formats. Some content that appears in print
may not be available in electronic books. For more information about Wiley products, visit our website
at www.wiley.com.

ISBN 978-0-471-67796-3

Printed in the United States of America.

10 9 8 7 6 5 4 3 2 1

$55.00

Midwest

112/108

In memory of Lee LeCroy.

—Craig

To my Ava May, for little Boo: that yours may
be the less-traveled road.

—All my love, Joyce

Contents

Preface ——————————————————————————

Young girls today live a difficult reality: they are confronted by many pressures, from feeling they must be beautiful to be liked to coping with life-threatening behaviors such as anorexia or substance abuse. In fact, many professionals believe that girls are more oppressed today than in the recent past. This reality is, perhaps, best captured by Mary Pipher's statement from her book, *Reviving Ophelia: Saving the Selves of Adolescent Girls* (Ballantine Books, 1994): "[Girls are] coming of age in a more dangerous, sexualized, and media-saturated culture." And in contrast to the popular media, which have done a good job of describing many of the concerns facing young girls today, attention to these issues from the professional milieu has been lacking. And therein lies the primary purpose of this book: to fill that gap, by presenting exemplary programs that were designed to promote and strengthen positive functioning and address problematic realities of the adolescent female.

We believe that ensuring a better future for adolescent girls involves, first, developing and, then making available, the resources they and their families need to navigate these difficult years. Such resources may come in any form, from a simple program organized by a parent or interest group, to promote better information, services, and programs for adolescent girls, to a major task force for change. As exemplified by the various programs described in the chapters of this book, clearly no one program will turn the tide; rather, it will be the cumulative effect of many types of programs that will ultimately lead to the better future we all want for adolescent girls. It is our hope that this book will inspire more efforts to develop new programs, involve more young girls, and, eventually, generate enough force to change their future.

We believe this book will be of keen interest to a broad range of professionals who are working to design protective measures and reduce risk factors for adolescent girls. Direct practitioners such as social workers, psychologists, teachers, youth development workers, and school principals will find the practical format used to describe the programs valuable in their work. Many of these programs can be developed and implemented in various settings: schools, YWCAs, youth camps, after-school programs, mental health agencies, and youth agencies.

More, we hope readers will be inspired to implement one of these programs, or design their own programs, or encourage others to become involved in the effort to offer more and better services to adolescent girls. We also challenge readers to become advocates for programs designed specifically to meet the needs of teen girls. Ideally, the issues we address in this text will help to raise awareness and, subsequently, serve as a launch pad for further work. Thus, we intend this book also to serve as a resource for researchers and practitioners who are studying gender-specific programs.

When we began this undertaking, we naively assumed that the widespread interest in the issues, needs, and developmental obstacles faced by adolescent girls would make compiling a handbook of programs devoted to them an easy task. It proved to be much more difficult than we had imagined. In fact, we learned there simply are not that many gender-specific programs to be found for teen girls. As it turned out, although the term *gender-specific* may be commonly used, and discussed theoretically, the programmatic reality is far from what we had imagined. For example, we could not find enough literature for a chapter on a gender-specific program for girls with depression—even though, as is well known, depression is overrepresented in girls, and those suffering from it have a depressed cognitive thought process and ruminate in ways that can be cognitively destructive. It is only recently that a few individuals have started to think about how gender-specific programs might benefit girls with depression—or, better, prevent depression from developing. And this is just one example; efforts are even less developed in other areas of concern for adolescent girls.

We look forward to the second edition of this book because much work is still required to develop, test, and disseminate programs that can have a positive influence on young adolescent girls.

Craig Winston LeCroy
Joyce Elizabeth Mann

Acknowledgments —————————————————

We heartily thank the contributors to this book for forging ahead and beginning the process of making gender-specific programs a reality.

We would also like to acknowledge the excellent staff at John Wiley & Sons, Inc., who have helped us with this book, in particular: Peggy Adams Alexander who helped bring the book into existence with her long-term encouragement; Isabel Pratt who kept the project going; and Lisa Gebo, who recently picked up the reins and helped us finish this important undertaking.

Finally, we extend our appreciation to adolescent girls, whose cause prompted the creation this book, and with whom these programs were developed, and for whom this book was ultimately written. We further extend our appreciation to you, the reader, as you work to build a better future for adolescent girls.

Thank you all.

C. W. L.
J. E. M.

Contributors

Akua Anima Ansu, MPH
School of Public Health
University of Illinois—Chicago
Chicago, Illinois

Nikia D. Braxton, MPH, CHES
Department of Behavioral Science and
    Health Education
Rollins School of Public Health
Emory University
Atlanta, Georgia

Tara M. Chaplin, PhD
Department of Psychology
University of Pennsylvania
Philadelphia, Pennsylvania

Jacqueline Corcoran, PhD
Associate Professor
School of Social Work
Virginia Commonwealth University
Alexandria, Virginia

Ralph DiClemente, PhD
Candler Professor; Associate Director
Prevention Science
Emory Center for AIDS Research for
    Behavioral Science
Atlanta, Georgia

David L. DuBois, PhD
Associate Professor
Institute for Health Research and Policy
University of Illinois—Chicago
Chicago, Illinois

Diane L. Elliot, MD
Professor of Medicine
Division of Health Promotion and
    Sports Medicine
Oregon Health and Science University
Portland, Oregon

Jane E. Gillham, PhD
Department of Psychology
Swarthmore College
Swarthmore, Pennsylvania

Linn Goldberg, MD
Professor of Medicine
Head of the Division of Health
    Promotion and Sports Medicine
Oregon Health and Science University
Portland, Oregon

John Hamilton, MD
Permanente Medical Group
    of California
Sacramento, California

Simona Haqq, MSW
Big Brothers Big Sisters of
    Metropolitan Chicago
Chicago, Illinois

Beth Hossfeld, MFT
Associate Director
Girls Circle Association
Mill Valley, California

Craig Winston LeCroy, PhD
Professor
Tucson Component
Arizona State University
School of Social Work
Tucson, Arizona

Daniel le Grange, PhD
Director of the Eating Disorders Program
Assistant Professor of Psychiatry
University of Chicago
Chicago, Illinois

Velia G. Leybas, MSW
National Center of Excellence in
    Women's Health
and
Arizona Hispanic Center of Excellence
University of Arizona
Tucson, Arizona

James Lock, MD, PhD
Department of Psychiatry
Division of Child and Adolescent
    Development
Stanford University
Stanford, California

Jane Phillips, PhD
Program Director and
    Director of Social Services
Millwood Hospital
Arlington, Texas

Julia Pryce, PhD
Institute for Health Research
    and Policy
University of Illinois—
    Chicago
Chicago, Illinois

Erin Reeves, BA
Institute for Health Research
    and Policy
University of Illinois—
    Chicago
Chicago, Illinois

Karen Reivich, PhD
Department of Psychology
University of Pennsylvania
Philadelphia, Pennsylvania

Amelia C. Roberts, PhD
School of Social Work
University of North Carolina—
    Chapel Hill
Chapel Hill, North Carolina

Jessica Sales, PhD
Rollins School of Public Health
Emory University
Atlanta, Georgia

Bernadette Sanchez, PhD
Department of Psychology
DePaul University
Chicago, Illinois

Heather Shaw, PhD
Oregon Research Institute
Eugene, Oregon

Adriana Silva, MS
School of Public Health
University of Illinois—Chicago
Chicago, Illinois

Naida Silverthorn, PhD
Institute for Health Research
    and Policy
University of Illinois—Chicago
Chicago, Illinois

Eric Stice, PhD
Oregon Research Institute
Eugene, Oregon

Janet Takehara, MED
Big Brothers Big Sisters of
    Metropolitan Chicago
Chicago, Illinois

Chiquitia Welch, MPA, MSSA
University of North Carolina—
    Chapel Hill
Chapel Hill, North Carolina

Gina Wingood, ScD, MPh
Associate Professor
Rollins School of Public Health
Emory University
Atlanta, Georgia

Introduction

ADOLESCENT GIRLS AND THE PATHWAY TO ADULTHOOD

CRAIG WINSTON LeCROY

The pathway for a 10- or 11-year-old girl through adolescence and into young adulthood is a long, developmental journey of approximately 8 years' duration. During this period, many girls will lose their way; most will encounter obstacles and need to retrace their steps; but in the end, many will also find themselves standing on solid ground. What can society offer these girls to assist them along the way?

This handbook offers aid in the form of a variety of means to strengthen and bolster these girls as they set out on their developmental journey. Indeed, in the years when girls are traversing this pathway, there are many ways to promote a positive transition to adulthood. This book represents an effort to collect those ways and share what is known about designing and implementing both preventive and interventive programs for adolescent girls.

THE GIRL'S MOVEMENT: A CONTEXT FOR PROGRAM DEVELOPMENT

The girl's movement, which started in the early 1990s, sparked much interest in the issues impacting adolescent girls in contemporary society. Early academic work by Gilligan (1990) and Brown and Gilligan (1992) such as *Making Connections: The Relational Worlds of Adolescent Girls at the Emma Willard School* and *Meeting at the Crossroads,* respectively, are now regarded as classics in helping to gain an understanding of the difficult issues girls face. Girls Inc. (2000), part of the Girls Clubs of America, anticipated many of the needs of adolescent girls; and in 1992, the organization outlined a "Girls' Bill of Rights," marking a critical beginning in the effort to improve the culture in which girls live. Orenstein's book, *School Girls: Young Women, Self-Esteem, and the Confidence Gap* (1994), followed—and made famous—the study by the American Association of University Women, finding that as young girls reach adolescence their self-esteem plummets.

Subsequently, girls became the topic of intensive writing, in particular picking up momentum after the publication of Mary Pipher's *Reviving Ophelia: Saving the Selves of Adolescent Girls* (1994), which struck a deep cord in American society for its apt depiction of the "girl-poisoning culture" in which young girls grow up today. Later books tackled these social issues in greater detail, among them Brumberg's *The Body Project: An Intimate History of American Girls* (1998), which chronicles the way growing up in a female body has dramatically changed over time and why it is more difficult in today's society to inhabit the female body; and Tanenbaum's *Slut! Growing Up Female with a Bad Reputation* (1999), which demonstrates how too many girls are turned into "sluts" and the imputations this powerful epithet carries.

Today, the book market in this field is well stocked with books directing parents on how to better care for their adolescent daughters, as well as self-help books directed at girls themselves. Plus there are more than 300 "zines," self-made publications created by and for girls. This underground culture was exposed by the popular book, *A Girl's Guide to Taking Over the World: Writings from the Girl Zine Revolution* (Green & Taormino, 1997). Other publications also appeared, including *New Moon: The Magazine for Girls and Their Dreams* and *Teen Voices: Because You Are More Than a Pretty Face*. These commercial-free magazines were created as alternatives to the traditional, glitzy teen magazines that promote society's messages about growing up, and which are at the heart of many of the problems adolescent girls confront (e.g., success equals being thin, attractive, sexy). More recently, the girl movement has transcended books and magazines, since the box office success of *Thirteen* (Hardwicke & Reed, 2003) and *Mean Girls* (Wiseman, Fey, & Waters, 2004).

SPECIAL RISKS FOR ADOLESCENT GIRLS

Researchers in studies of adolescence have worked for years to combat a negative stereotype about the difficulties of this age group; nevertheless, indications are that the problems faced by adolescent girls today may be getting more difficult. Indeed, contemporary adolescence is now seen as a period of far greater risk to the current and future health of young people than in the past. Specifically, female adolescents today exhibit myriad problems, among them: body dissatisfaction, rising cigarette and alcohol use, academic underachievement, sexually transmitted diseases, pregnancy, and high rates of depression and unhappiness. Worse, today's adolescent girls are exposed to risky behavior at a much earlier age than adolescents in the past. Dryfoos' (1991) survey of adolescent risk estimated that 50% of youth are at moderate to high risk for engaging in problem behavior. Experimentation with smoking, alcohol, sex, and other high-risk behaviors present concerns for the young adolescent who is not cognitively mature and may have a biologically based drive for risk taking. Young adolescents, especially, are likely to take greater risks because they are more susceptible to peer pressure, more oriented to the present than the future, and less able to regulate their emotions (Steinberg, 2004).

In particular, adolescent female development takes place in a biopsychosocial context that suggests gender-specific programs may be needed. Physical maturation is often experienced as negative for girls (Tobin-Richards, Boxer, & Petersen, 1983) and is found across cultures (Benjet & Hernández-Guzmán, 2002). Early adolescent girls are dissatisfied with their bodies and dislike changes associated with puberty (Brooks-Gunn & Paikoff, 1997; Striegel-Moore & Cachelin, 1999), factors often linked to low self-esteem (Furnham & Greaves, 1994). Thus, the likelihood of depression increases with the onset of puberty and, in fact, is the most prevalent disorder in adolescence—occurring twice as often for females as for males (Hankin & Abramson, 2002). As a direct result, as girls enter adolescence, they may be afflicted with an avoidant coping style, negative ruminations, and increased sensitivity to the opinions of others (Nolen-Hoeksema & Girgus, 1994; Seiffge-Krenke & Stemmler, 2002). Moreover, the developing female adolescent is confronted with media messages that facilitate a negative sex role image (LeCroy & Daley, 2001).

All these risk factors may interact with stressors associated with adolescence and lead to an unhealthy and difficult transition into later adolescence and adulthood. Prevention and intervention programs should address these factors in order to build effective gender-specific developmentally based interventions.

DEVELOPMENTAL CONSIDERATIONS

Development is an important factor in understanding both adolescent protective and risk factors. Early adolescence brings special biopsychosocial considerations for female adolescents, such as puberty, the transition to middle school, friendship difficulties, and body image. Middle adolescence often raises issues such as heterosexual involvement, developing sexuality and sexual identity, personal identity, and academic status. A consideration in late adolescence focuses more on career and vocational development, self-image, and the transition to adulthood. Indeed, emerging adulthood has itself become worthy of special developmental consideration (Arnett, 2004).

Program development needs a developmental perspective in order to maximize impacts; for example, depression in adolescent females often does not emerge until later adolescence (Radloff, 1991). Issues of substance abuse and sexual behavior are also linked to important developmental considerations. Therefore, programs that can key into specific developmental understandings are more likely to target the correct issue and intervene at a point when an intervention can be must useful. As our developmental understanding of girls increases, we can create more developmentally sensitive programs.

DIVERSITY

Critical to any discussion of adolescent girls is diversity: more than one third of girls between the ages of 10 and 18 in the United States are African American, Latina, Asian, Pacific Islander, American Indian, or Eskimo (Ohye & Daniel, 1999). Race, ethnicity, gender, class, and sexual identity play essential roles in the development of risk and protective factors that impact girls' lives. Indeed, ethnicity is a determinant of one's identity. For example, self-image and personal identity shape the female adolescent's life trajectory. Societal influences, media messages, economic opportunities, interpersonal relationships, and family ritual and tradition all interact with diversity.

Immigrant girls of color present another unique face of diversity, one that demands special considerations (de las Fuentes & Vasquez, 1999). Some of the challenges for this group include: fewer cultural ties, increased harassment and violence, poor educational opportunities, poverty, reduced employment, bicultural adaptation and identity, and parent-child conflict. Conversely, any discussion of diversity would be remiss if unique strengths were not also presented. Increasingly, research on diversity is examining resiliency and healthy adaptation. A number of strengths emerge, including family traditions, cultural identity, close and extended family relations, and a strong sense of community.

BUILDING PROGRAMS

The long path to the current girl's movement includes a wealth of information about girls from a variety of sources and perspectives. The issues confronting adolescent females have been well documented and presented, in research articles in peer-reviewed journals, popular books, TV specials, and movies. Social programs for girls are now in their prime, as the concerns for girls are increasingly translated into action-based remedies. What role can preventive and interventive programs play in addressing critical issues for adolescent girls? That is the question answered by this book, for which a primary goal was to survey the field and identify programs that were being used in different communities. It is hoped that the information described in these chapters will serve as a stepping stone on the journey to understanding and empowering adolescent girls.

REFERENCES

Arnett, J. J. (2004). *Emerging adulthood: The winding road for late teen through the twenties.* New York: Oxford University Press.

Benjet, C., & Hernández-Guzmán, L. (2002). A short-term longitudinal study of pubertal change, gender, and psychological well-being of Mexican early adolescents. *Journal of Youth and Adolescence, 31,* 429–442.

Brooks-Gunn, J., & Paikoff, R. (1997). Sexuality and developmental transitions during adolescence. In J. Schulenberg, J. L. Maggs, & K. Hurrelmann (Eds.), *Health risks and developmental transitions during adolescence* (pp. 190–219). London: Cambridge University Press.

Brown, L. M., & Gilligan, C. (1992). *Meeting at the crossroad.* Cambridge, MA: Harvard University Press.

Brumberg, J. J. (1998). *The body project: An intimate history of American girls.* New York: Vintage.

de las Fuentes, C., & Vasquez, M. J. T. (1999). Immigrant adolescent girls of color: Facing American challenges. In Johnson, N. G., Roberts, M. C., & Worell, J. (Eds.), *Beyond appearance: A new look at adolescent girls* (pp. 131–150). Washington, DC: American Psychological Association.

Dryfoos, J. G., (1991). *Adolescents at risk: Prevalence and prevention.* New York: Oxford University Press.

Furnham, A., & Greaves, N. (1994). Gender and locus of control correlations of body image dissatisfaction. *European Journal of Personality, 8,* 183–200.

Gilligan, C. (1990). Teaching Shakespeare's sister. In C. Gilligan, N. Lyons, & T. Hanmer (Eds.), *Making connections: The relational worlds of adolescent girls at the Emma Willard School* (pp. 6–29). Cambridge, MA: Harvard University Press.

Girls Inc. (2000). *The Girls' bill of rights.* Available from www.girlsinc.org/bill.html.

Green, K., & Taormino, T. (1997). *A girl's guide to taking over the world.* New York: St. Martin's Press.

Hankin, B. L., & Abramson, L. Y. (2002). Development of gender differences in depression: An elaborated cognitive vulnerability-transactional stress theory. *Psychological Bulletin, 127,* 773–776.

Hardwicke, C., & Reed, N. (Writers). (2003). *Thirteen* [Motion Picture]. Retrieved July 27, 2005, from www.the-numbers.com/movies.

LeCroy, C. W., & Daley, J. (2001). *Empowering adolescent girls: Building skills for the future with the Go Grrrls program.* New York: Norton.

Nolen-Hoeksema, S., & Girgus, J. S. (1994). Gender differences in depression during adolescence. *Psychological Bulletin, 115,* 424–443.

Ohye, B. Y., & Daniel, J. H. (1999). The "other" adolescent girls: Who are they. In Johnson, N. G., Roberts, M. C., & Worell, J. (Eds.), *Beyond appearance: A new look at adolescent girls* (pp. 115–130). Washington, DC: American Psychological Association.

Orenstein, P. (1994). *School girls: Young women, self-esteem, and the confidence gap.* New York: Doubleday.

Pipher, M. (1994). *Reviving Ophelia: Saving the selves of adolescent girls.* New York: Putnam.

Radloff, L. S. (1991). The use of the Center for Epidemiological Studies Depression scale in adolescents and young adults. *Journal of Youth and Adolescence, 20,* 149–166.

Seiffge-Krenke, I., & Stemmler, M. (2002). Factors contributing to gender differences in depressive symptoms: A test of three developmental models. *Journal of Youth and Adolescence, 31,* 405–417.

Steinberg, L. (2004). Adolescent brain development: Vulnerabilities and opportunities. *New York Academy of Science, 1021,* 51–58.

Striegel-Moore, R. H., & Cachelin, F. M. (1999). Body image concerns and disordered eating in adolescent girls: Risk and protective factors. In Johnson, N. G., Roberts, M. C., & Worell, J. (Eds.), *Beyond appearance: A new look at adolescent girls* (pp. 85–108). Washington, DC: American Psychological Association.

Tanenbaum, L. (1999). *Slut! Growing up female with a bad reputation.* New York: Seven Stories Press.

Tobin-Richards, M., Boxer, A., & Petersen, A. (1983). The psychological significance of pubertal change: Sex differences in perceptions of self during early adolescence. In E. J. Brooks-Gunn & A. Petersen (Eds.), *Girls at puberty: Biological and psychological perspectives* (pp. 127–154). New York: Plenum Press.

Wiseman, R. (Book Author), Fey, T. (Screenwriter), & Waters, M. (Director). (2004). *Mean girls* [Motion Picture]. United States: Paramount Pictures. Retrieved July 27, 2005, from www.the-numbers.com/movies.

Chapter 1

UNIVERSAL PREVENTION FOR ADOLESCENT GIRLS

The Go Grrrls Program

CRAIG WINSTON LeCROY

The decibel level rises as the last bell rings. Middle school students flood the hallways, their voices loud and their laughter echoing off the walls. The participants in our new after-school program find their way to the alcove near the school entrance, where we wait to meet and greet them. Slowly they trickle in, girls of a remarkable variety of shapes, sizes, skin tones, and levels of development. I think to myself that during the course of this program I hope my co-leader and I can help each of them to appreciate her uniqueness and natural vitality. (from the journal of a group leader, in LeCroy & Daley, 2005, p. 127)

Social changes in contemporary society are having an enormous impact on adolescent girls, who today are coping with a multitude of issues, such as rising cigarette and drug use, body dissatisfaction and body image disorders, academic underachievement, problems associated with sexual behaviors, and high rates of depression and unhappiness. Gender-specific programs are needed to address all these issues unique to adolescent girls. In particular, primary prevention offers one response to the growing concerns raised by many practitioners and researchers (Denmark, 1999; LeCroy & Daley, 2001a).

IMPORTANCE OF GENDER-SPECIFIC PROGRAMS

Gender-specific programs can address the biological, psychological, and social changes that take place in adolescent girls—for example, physical maturation can be a negative experience (Benjet & Hernández-Guzmán, 2002). Research has established that early in their development adolescent girls report being dissatisfied with their bodies and dislike changes associated with puberty (Brooks-Gunn & Paikoff, 1997; Striegel-Moore & Cachelin, 1999). Studies have found early maturation to be a significant risk factor for girls, relating it to: eating problems and body image disorders (Attie & Brooks-Gunn, 1989), depression and low self-esteem (Brooks-Gunn & Reiter, 1990; Fabian & Thompson, 1989), and delinquency (Caspi, 1995). Body image is often linked to low self-esteem and may account for the large percentage of girls who begin to experience depression (Furnham & Greaves, 1994). Normal, healthy girls often perceive themselves as overweight, thus developing negative body images (Berg, 1992). One study (Eisele, Hertsgarrd, & Light, 1986) found that a majority (78%) of adolescent girls aged 13 to 19 are dissatisfied with their weight; and 1 in 10 adolescent girls is at the threshold of a diagnosis for bulimia nervosa (Stice, Killen, Hayward, & Taylor, 1998). Adolescent girls also are afflicted with negative ruminations, an avoidant coping style, and increased sensitivity to the opinions of others (Nolen-Hoeksema & Girgus, 1994; Seiffge-Krenke & Stemmler, 2002). The impact of the media on this population is also worth noting because the messages delivered to these girls often translate to a negative sex role image (Wylie, 1979). All these factors support the notion that gender-specific prevention training is called for to promote a healthy transition into adulthood for adolescent girls.

An additional consideration in the development of adolescent prevention programs is that adolescence today is recognized as being more difficult and dangerous than it was in the recent past. Specifically, modern adolescents are exposed to risky behavior at a much earlier age than adolescents of the past (see, e.g., Johnston, O'Malley, & Bachman, 2002). Many youths begin experimenting with smoking, drug use, and sex during the early adolescent years (Dryfoos, 1990; Takanishi, 1993). The Office of Technology (1991) classified one fourth of all adolescents at high risk. Dryfoos (1990), in a survey of adolescent risk behavior, estimates that half of all youth are at moderate to high risk of engaging in problem behaviors. And even those young people who are not considered to be at risk may have difficulty navigating through adolescence. In sum, this is a period accurately characterized as one fraught with obstacles and barriers to healthy development.

DIRECTING INTERVENTIONS

Because of the number of considerations involved, interventions are best directed toward promoting competence and positive development, as opposed to the remediation of single problems. Several researchers (e.g., Elliott, 1993; Johnson & Roberts, 1999; Millstein, Petersen, & Nightingale, 1993) have recommended moving away from interventions for individual problems such as substance abuse, suicide, and adolescent pregnancy, suggesting instead those that focus more generally on positive adolescent development and health. These efforts have grown out of the recognition that specific problem behaviors can be better understood as a constellation of interrelated issues. Often, the goal is twofold: (1) to reduce risk factors associated with problem behaviors and (2) to promote personal and social competence leading to adaptive outcomes such as coping skills. A number of controlled trials have examined the benefits of broader interventions designed to promote general psychological well-being or to prevent substance abuse (e.g., Botvin, Schinke, Epstein, Diaz, & Botvin, 1995; Bruene-Butler, Hampson, Elias, Clabby, & Schuyler, 1997; Caplan et al., 1992; Ellickson, Bell, & McGuigan, 1993; Hawkins, Catalano, Kosterman, Abbott, & Hill, 1999), with encouraging results (Greenberg, Domitrovich, & Bumbarger, 2001). Masten (2001) calls for interventions that promote competence as well as the prevention or amelioration of symptoms and problems. Wyman, Sandler, Wolchik, and Nelson (2000) suggest the phrase "cumulative competence promotion and stress protection" to indicate how interventions can be conceptualized. However, in spite of researcher recommendations for broader prevention models, practice has lagged behind.

Kazdin (1993, p. 136) argues that "large-scale universal programs for young adolescents in the schools are important to promote positive social competence and resistance to internal and peer pressure that might lead to at-risk behavior (e.g., unprotected sex, experimentation with hard drugs, use of alcohol while driving)." It is increasingly recognized that a range of interventions are necessary to respond to the needs of adolescents. More targeted interventions will be required to respond to specific problem areas for individuals. However, preventive interventions are often the gateway for young people to access those targeted or treatment-focused interventions.

In this context, prevention may be particularly relevant to adolescent girls because access to treatment services appears biased toward boys. Moreover, treatment services are most often directed at externalizing disorders or disruptive behaviors (Kazdin, Bass, Ayers, & Rodgers, 1990), as these are disturbing to parents or teachers, who subsequently activate the referrals to treatment. Problems that can be classified as internalizing or emotional (e.g., depression, anxiety, or eating disorders) are more likely to be overlooked by those who activate the treatment process (Kazdin & Weisz, 1998). Since internalizing disorders and problems are more likely to be experienced by girls, they may not be receiving treatment resources they could benefit from.

This background of research lays the foundation for the development of a developmentally based gender-specific program for adolescent girls, an important aspect of which is to take into account their unique aspects of development (LeCroy & Daley, 2001a). For example, the Empowering Adolescent Girls Program, or Go Grrrls curriculum (LeCroy & Daley, 2001a), is informed by understanding the timing of the intervention, selection of relevant issues, and a focus on reducing identified risk factors. In this manner, the program is both developmentally appropriate and gender-specific in that it addresses some of the unique aspects of adolescent development. Table 1.1 lists the various developmental issues, the developmental process, and the program objectives for the Empowering Adolescent

Table 1.1 Developmental Issues and Process and Program Objectives for the Empowering Adolescent Girls Program

Developmental Issues	Developmental Process	Program Implementation: Empowerment Objectives
Gender role identification	At puberty, gender-intensification theory suggests gender-related expectations influence behavior.	Enhance positive messages about gender roles; promote a more positive sex-role self-image.
Body image	Adolescent girls are at risk to develop a negative body image that leads to low self-esteem, depression, body image disturbance, and eating disorders.	Promote understanding of the changes that take place during puberty. Promote positive body image and body acceptance.
Self-acceptance	In early adolescence, girls have a drop in self-esteem accompanied by increased self-criticism, negative mood states, and, for some girls, depression.	Promote a positive self-image in response to the biological, psychological, and social changes girls confront. Reduce self-criticism and promote positive mood states.
Peer relationships	Membership in the peer group is a major developmental task. Adolescents who fail to develop positive peer relationships are at greater risk for developing problems such as substance abuse and depression. Conformity and peer pressure can lead to bad choices made by young people.	Promote positive peer relationships. Build on the relational quality many girls find in friendships to strengthen positive reasons for these relationships. Encourage sharing and mutual understanding for enhanced companionship, support, and empathy.
Responsible decision making	Most adolescents in today's society will confront decisions that could have lifelong if not lethal consequences. The cognitive development of young people has important implications for adolescent risk taking.	Promote responsible decision making by teaching problem-solving skills. In conjunction with decision making, encourage personal assertiveness.
Sexuality	Girls' sexuality is a major issue because of the potential consequences associated with high-risk behaviors. As girls develop sexually, they need information and skills to prevent unwanted sex, unwanted pregnancies, and STDs.	Promote awareness and understanding of sexuality issues. Enhance responsible decision making and safe sex. Broaden girls' understanding of sex so it isn't seen only as intercourse. Address the special risks for younger girls.

Table 1.1   *(Continued)*

Developmental Issues	Developmental Process	Program Implementation: Empowerment Objectives
Accessing resources	Adolescent girls face multiple risks; fully one third are estimated to be at high or very high risk. Along with "invisible" problems (e.g., depression) adolescents vastly underutilize systems of care.	Reduce barriers to services and help prepare girls to find and accept professional help when they need it.
Planning for the future	Adolescent girls often experience a crisis in confidence that undermines their educational and career decisions in later life.	Enhance girls' achievement motivation. Build their confidence for educational and vocational aspirations. Teach a *mastery orientation* as opposed to one of *learned helplessness.*

Girls Program (also see LeCroy, 2005). The remainder of this chapter describes the cumulative results from three studies that establish the empirical support for the program.

STUDIES EVALUATING THE GO GRRRLS PROGRAM

Two studies have been conducted to evaluate the effectiveness of the Go Grrrls program. The first had a quasi-experimental design, for which we were able to recruit 54 volunteer girls from a school. They had an average age of 12.7 and were culturally diverse: 64.8% Caucasian, 18.5% mixed race, 11.1% Hispanic, 3.7% African American, and 1.9% Asian American. The groups were led by two female graduate students who had received intensive training on the curriculum. The intervention was described in a detailed curriculum (see LeCroy & Daley, 2001a). A matched group of girls from a physical education class constituted the comparison group; hence, it was a no-treatment group. The treatment groups (7 to 8 girls assigned to one of three groups) met after school for 12 weeks.

A total of six measures were used to evaluate the program:

1. Body Image Scale (Simmons & Blythe, 1987), a five-item scale
2. Gender Role Attitudes Scale (Simmons & Blythe, 1987), a three-item scale

3. Peer Esteem Scale (Hare, 1985), a 10-item scale
4. Common Beliefs Scale (Hooper & Layne, 1983) a 24-item scale
5. Depression Self-Rating Scale (Birleson, 1981), an 18-item scale
6. Help Endorsements Scale (LeCroy & Daley, 2001a) a 15-item scale

All measures, except the Gender Role Attitudes Scale ($r = .36$) obtained adequate reliability on the study sample.

The outcome results are based on a comparison of mean scores between the intervention and comparison group using a one-way analysis of covariance (ANCOVA) that used the pretest scores as a covariate. The measures were considered independent because they measured different aspects of the program.

Participants in the Go Grrrls group showed significant positive change from the pretest to the posttest on measures of irrational beliefs, help endorsements, and friendship esteem. These changes were significantly different from the control group, where no change was observed over time; and the effect sizes ranged from small to medium (see LeCroy, 2004a, 2004b, for details).

Following the promising results presented in the quasi-experimental design, the next stage in empirical testing was to conduct a randomized study. In this study, a total of 118 girls were recruited to participate. The mean age of the sample was 13.5 years old. Similar to the previous study, the sample was culturally diverse, with 62.4% Caucasian, 19.7% mixed race, 13.7% Hispanic, 2.6% Native American, and less than 2% African American. Participants were randomly assigned to either the no-treatment control group or the experimental group. Three of the measures used in the quasi-experimental study were used again: Body Image Scale, the Peer Esteem Scale, and the Help Endorsement scale. In addition, several new scales were added to examine in a more detailed manner the outcomes of the program. The new measures were:

- Assertiveness Scale (Center for Substance Abuse Prevention, 1993), a 7-item scale
- Attractiveness Scale (LeCroy & Daley, 2001a), an 8-item scale that measures girls' perceptions about attractiveness
- Girls' Self-Efficacy Scale (LeCroy & Daley, 2001a), a 9-item scale that measures girls' perceived gender role efficacy
- Self-Liking and Self-Competence Scale (Tafarodi & Swann, 1995), a 20-item scale
- Hopelessness Scale (Kazdin, Rogers, & Colbus, 1986), a 17-item scale

All measures were found to have acceptable reliabilities—.72 to .94—for the study population.

Five of the outcome measures were significant in the comparison between the Go Grrrls group and the control group. Go Grrrls' participants made significant gains beyond the control group on: body image, assertiveness, attractiveness, self-efficacy, and self-liking. Two measures, hopelessness and help endorsements, would be significant if the significance criteria were lowered to the .10 level.

More than 10 years' effort went into building the empirical base for the empowering adolescent girls program. In the initial study, the focus was on studying the implementation process and ascertaining that the curriculum was well received by the participants. Data were gathered from focus groups, observations, and interviews of program participants and group leaders. This critical data helped the program developers revise and improve the overall program. The quasi-experimental and experimental programs established the empirical foundations of the program. Future studies are needed to examine the long-term effects of the program.

OVERVIEW OF THE PROGRAM

The Go Grrrls program is a social skills training/psychoeducational program administered in a group format, which is both practical for reaching large numbers of girls and developmentally appropriate because adolescents tend to strongly value social interaction with their peers. As the girls settle into the meeting room on the first day, a large poster board sign greets them (see Figure 1.1). The sign resembles a jigsaw puzzle, with each of the seven major topic areas of the project delineated on its pieces:

1. Being a girl in today's society
2. Establishing a positive body image
3. Establishing a positive mindset
4. Establishing independence
5. Making and keeping friends
6. Talking about sex
7. Planning for the future—when it all seems like too much

Some of the group sessions (e.g., on problem solving) emphasize skill building in areas equally pertinent to boys and girls, but the examples and role-plays used to illustrate the skills emphasize girls as the major "actresses." Other sessions (e.g., on being a girl in today's society) are designed to address areas of special concern to adolescent girls. An outline of the 13 sessions is presented in Table 1.2, followed by a more in-depth description of each. The complete curriculum can be found in LeCroy and Daley (2001a).

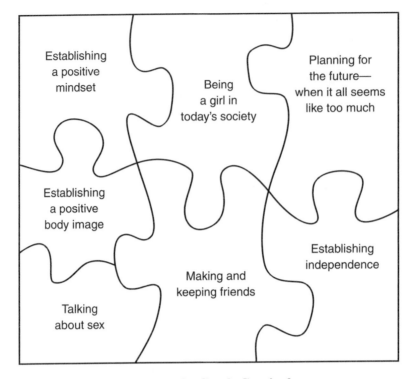

Figure 1.1   Go Grrrls Curriculum

Week 1: Being a Girl in Today's Society

Session 1: Introductory Session/Pretest

The goals for the initial session are to:

- Create a supportive atmosphere and begin building cohesiveness within the group.
- Collect baseline data for program evaluation.
- Introduce participants to group standards, such as confidentiality and respect for others.
- Introduce the program content.

The girls begin by filling out a questionnaire designed to gather background and evaluation data; then they play a name game, to loosen everyone up and help with introductions. Following the game, we help the girls establish group standards by asking them to suggest their own rules for the group. If the group-generated rules do not include important areas (such as confidentiality and its limits), the group

Table 1.2   Session Outline

Week 1: Being a girl in today's society
    Session 1: Introduction/pretest
    Session 2: Challenging media messages

Week 2: Establishing a positive body image and positive mindset
    Session 3: Addressing body image
    Session 4: Rethinking self-statements

Week 3: Making and keeping friends
    Session 5: Identifying qualities of a friend
    Session 6: Making and keeping friends

Week 4: Establishing independence
    Session 7: Problem-solving strategies
    Session 8: Assertiveness skills

Week 5: Talking about sex
    Session 9: Sex 101 and refusal skills
    Session 10: Risky business: alcohol, drugs, and unwanted sex

Week 6: Planning for the future—when it all seems like too much
    Session 11: Where to go for help
    Session 12: Visions for a strong future

Week 7: Closure
    Session 13: Closure/review/posttest

leaders bring up these subjects. Next, we introduce the program content by displaying a large poster with the Go Grrrls puzzle, shown in Figure 1.1, and encouraging each member to read one of the topics aloud. Finally, we distribute journals or Go Grrrls workbooks (LeCroy & Daley, 2001b), which the girls are instructed to use to complete brief assignments for the group and to express themselves in any way they wish. The workbooks are a tool for helping the girls incorporate what they learn into their personal lives; they also serve as a mechanism for encouraging them to continue their self-growth and discovery after the group ends.

Session 2: Challenging Media Messages

The goals of this session include:

- Identify pressures society places on girls through media messages.
- Examine perceptions about gender roles and feelings about gender.
- Help girls challenge the message that sexuality and physical image are the most important aspects of an individual and teach the girls to "talk back" to these negative influences.

This session is intended to promote awareness of the profusion of negative images of women and girls that abound in popular media, and to equip girls with the ability and confidence to critically challenge such cultural stereotypes. Group activities for this session include creating a collage culled from teen magazines, examining stereotypes presented in the media, and evaluating lyrics from recent popular songs.

Week 2: Establishing a Positive Body Image and a Positive Mindset

Session 3: Body Image

As described in the introduction, adolescent girls are likely to develop a negative body image, which tends to be related to low self-esteem and depression. Therefore, the goals of this session are to:

- Help girls accept their bodies as they are and develop a positive body image.
- Teach them that attractiveness is based on factors other than physical traits.
- Encourage girls to appreciate their unique qualities, talents, and skills.

The session begins by asking participants to discuss the reasons that developing a positive body image is important for them. We then embark on a series of image-boosting activities. In one such activity, girls are asked to make a list of five things they like about themselves, and then share these things aloud in the group. Group leaders construct a chart of their responses as they are given. The chart includes categories for physical aspects, social/personality traits, specials skills and abilities, and cognitive abilities. Discussion then centers on the fact that attractiveness is only one admirable aspect of a person. Leaders emphasize that each girl has a unique set of strengths from all of these different categories.

Session 4: Rethinking Self-Statements

An important part of the Go Grrrls program is teaching participants about the relationship between self-esteem, self-criticism, and depression. As mentioned previously, girls entering the seventh grade show a significant decline in their overall self-esteem. To address this issue, this session is designed to teach girls how they can avoid setting unrealistic standards for themselves and instead give themselves positive messages to facilitate realistic goal achievement. The goals of this session are to:

- Gain awareness of the "downward spiral"—that is, how negative self-perceptions can lead to self-criticism.
- Understand how self-criticism can lead to unhappiness and depression.

Participants complete fill-in-the-blank handouts listing their unrealistic "I should" messages. We then help them to turn these messages into "I want" statements that are more constructive. For example:

"I should" statement: I should be liked by everyone.
"I want" statement: I want to have good friends.

Finally, a description is provided of how negative thoughts tend to generate even more negative thoughts, causing a downward spiral, whereas positive self-messages tend to lead to increased confidence, in an upward spiral. This is shown in Figure 1.2.

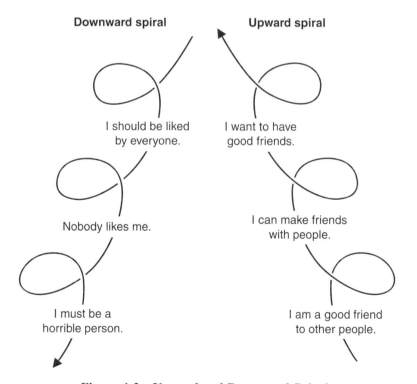

Figure 1.2   Upward and Downward Spirals

Week 3: Making and Keeping Friends

Session 5: Identifying Qualities of a Friend

Adolescents are social beings, and adolescent girls in particular seem to value close friendships. Friendship provides a social support system that helps to bolster self-esteem, lessen depression, and ameliorate hard times. The primary goals of this session are, therefore, to teach girls to:

- Focus less on being popular and more on developing intimate, satisfying friendships.
- Identify healthy qualities in friends.
- Understand friendship as a source of support.
- Learn to identify and how to avoid unhealthy friendships with girls and boys.

One of the activities during this session involves having participants brainstorm a list of qualities that a good friend might have. Each group member then fills out a "friendship want ad." A sample follows:

Seeking a new friend: I am looking for someone to talk with and go rollerblading with. I would like someone who is friendly, outgoing, and funny. I think a friend is someone who you can tell secrets to, so I have to be able to trust you.

Group leaders collect these ads and then randomly redistribute them. Each girl must then write a response to the friendship ad they receive. A sample response to the ad above might read:

I am a very active person and would enjoy rollerblading. I agree with you about wanting a friend you can trust. In the past I have had friends I trusted, but then found out they told my other friends things I did not want shared. I promise to be a person you can trust. I like to talk about boys! And right now I am having a lot of trouble with my Mom. Let's meet and see what happens.

Again, the intent is to move girls away from a focus on popularity.

Session 6: Making and Keeping Friends

Making and keeping friends requires a high level of social skills, so goals of this session are to:

- Teach friendship skills.
- Give group members an arena in which they can practice these skills.

Group leaders help girls to, first, identify and, then, practice using tools to start conversations (e.g., making eye contact, asking someone a question, and saying something positive about another person). We also discuss and practice how to communicate positive feelings and deal with friction when it arises between friends. In addition to role-plays, the girls brainstorm different ways to build, maintain, and mend friendships. They write these ideas down on strips of paper, which are placed in a "friendship toolbox," which they decorate and keep.

Week 4: Establishing Independence

Session 7: Problem-Solving Strategies

Often, adolescents make decisions impulsively, without considering the impact of their choices. Their decisions represent experimental attempts to acquire skills for dealing with new situations; but, unfortunately, these attempts may lead to serious consequences. Thus, session 7 is truly a skill-building session with these goals:

- Teach group members a method for solving problems.
- Encourage them to practice this method.

Group leaders also encourage members to discuss some unproductive ways that they have used in the past to try to solve problems (e.g., ignoring problems in the hope that they will just go away, or blaming someone else for the problem). Leaders then describe a five-step strategy for problem solving. Each girl receives a handout delineating this process (see Table 1.3). The group divides into two smaller groups, each of which is given a hypothetical problem to solve. For example:

> Your best, oldest friend asked you to sleep over at her house on Friday night and you told her you could. On Thursday, though, a really popular girl at school invites you (but not your friend) to her party on Friday night. What do you do?

Table 1.3   Making Decisions and Solving Problems

Here are the steps you can use for problem solving:

1. Define the problem. (What is it?)
2. Brainstorm choices. (Think of every possible solution—even silly ones! Don't criticize any of them yet.)
3. Evaluate the choices. (What are the pros and cons of each choice?)
4. Make your decision. (Select the best idea.)
5. If your decision doesn't work out, start over again at number 1.

After reviewing the steps listed in the handout, complete the following:

1. Define the problem. My problem is:

_____

_____

2. Brainstorm choices. I could:

_____

_____

3. Evaluate the choices. Put a + or – sign beside each idea above.

4. Make your decision. I decided to:

_____

_____

because

_____

_____

5. If your decision doesn't work out, start over at number 1, and try another idea.

Session 8: Assertiveness Skills

Girls are often socialized to be accommodating to others. One positive result of this socialization is that girls may acquire sensitivity to others' emotions and may develop insight into the intricacies of relationships. One potentially negative result of this socialization is that they may begin overlook or disregard their own thoughts and feelings in an effort to "keep the peace"; or, conversely, they may become frustrated when authority figures or peers do not demonstrate understanding of their needs.

Session 8, therefore, attempts to teach girls three different options for responding to situations: being assertive, passive, and aggressive. Group leaders begin by defining these terms for members, after which participants are provided with scripts depicting assertive, passive, and aggressive responses to provocative remarks or situations. They role-play these scenes for the group, and all members are asked to identify which responses are assertive, passive or aggressive. Scripts are formatted with an introduction that sets up the dialogue, and all are tailored to reflect situations that early adolescent girls are likely to face. Here's an example:

Situation 1: Introduction

One thing that really helps girls to be successful is being involved in outside activities like sports, dancing, exercise, and community work.

Sometimes when girls get to be in middle school they feel pressure to stop doing activities that they've enjoyed for many years, not because they don't enjoy them anymore but because they are afraid that their friends will think they're not cool if they keep doing them. Let's see what happens in this situation, and how being assertive can help.

Situation 1

Your ballet teacher invites you to perform at the annual dance recital. You are very excited about it, so you tell your best friend.

Person 1: Hey Linda, my ballet teacher just asked me to perform at the recital!

Person 2: You aren't really going to do it, are you? Recitals are for geeks.

Person 1 response A: No, I guess not.

Person 1 response B: Yeah, I am; and you're just jealous because you're a complete klutz.

Person 1 response C: I've worked really hard to get this chance, and I'm excited about doing it.

Week 5: Talking about Sex

Girls are usually eager to discuss sexuality by the time these sessions roll around. The Go Grrrls curriculum places an emphasis on pregnancy prevention within a broader program context that is both educational and skill based. The program includes two group meetings devoted specifically to the topic of sexuality; but it is the cumulative effect of the entire curriculum that is most likely to make a difference in a young girl's behavior. Specifically:

- The skill-building sessions included in the curriculum (assertiveness, problem solving, making and keeping friends, positive self-talk, and setting reachable goals for the future) all serve as important components in reducing the likelihood that of young girls engaging in early, unhealthy sexual activity.

- Psychoeducational components of the curriculum (confronting media messages and establishing a positive body image) boost girls' understanding of the effects of broader cultural trends on their individual lives.

Session 9: Sex 101, and Refusal Skills

Important goals of this session are to:

- Develop new knowledge about sexuality.
- Explore values and societal attitudes.
- Build confidence to decline unwanted sexual activity.

For example, we review myths versus facts about sexual activity. Leaders display posters depicting male and female reproductive organs, explain the physical act of intercourse, review the menstrual cycle, and cover other basic sexual information.

Participants are then asked to write down their questions about sexuality, or myths they may have heard about sex, then place them into an anonymous "question can." This is the highlight of the session; and, typically, after the initial round of anonymous questions have been answered, girls continue to toss new questions in the can, or simply ask them aloud as they become more comfortable with the process. After all questions have been answered, participants discuss reasons that some teens choose to have sex and others do not. Role-play activities give girls practice in using refusal skills; thereafter, community resources for obtaining birth control information and supplies are given out.

Session 10: Risky Business: Alcohol, Drugs, and Unwanted Sex

Young people are natural risk takers. Indeed, the process of growing up consists of a series of risks, as teenagers try new things. Unfortunately, some of the risks they take can have lifelong negative consequences. The goals of this session are to:

- Help girls understand the risks involved in using alcohol and other substances.
- Establish the link between substance use and impaired judgment, including the potential for unwanted sexual activity.

During this session, students brainstorm reasons that some teens choose to use substances and others choose not to. Each girl designs an advertising campaign that depicts alcohol or other drugs as glamorous; then she draws an "anti-advertisement" that responds to the first ad, debunking the glamour myth and highlighting the link between alcohol/drug use and risky sexual behaviors. Next, we play a game that demonstrates the link between substance abuse and risky behaviors, emphasizing the risk of exposure to sexually transmitted diseases (STDs). After the game, leaders explain ways to reduce the risk of exposure to STDs.

Week 6: Planning for the Future—When It All Seems Like Too Much

Session 11: Where to Go for Help

The primary goals of this session are:

- Learning that some situations require outside help.
- Recognizing when a problem is too serious to handle alone.
- Learning how and where to obtain help for serious problems.

This topic can provoke major issues for girls, so leaders must begin by reviewing confidentiality and limits to confidentiality with the group. Next, girls participate in an exercise designed to help them discern the difference between problems they can solve on their own and those for which they need to seek help. The group establishes a set of general guidelines to indicate when a problem requires outside resources to solve. The girls are then encouraged to think about the adults they trust, and to consider these adults as members on their personal resource list. Leaders then pass out the Personal Yellow Pages of community resources (health and social services, recreational activities, etc.) available to girls in their own area (obviously, these must be constructed locally). Girls can practice using the resource guides by reading through sample problems and suggesting appropriate agencies or individuals to contact in each situation. Finally, girls are encouraged to view "resource seeking" as a sign of intelligence and strength rather than a sign of weakness. Leaders should be alert during and after the session for those girls who seem ready to disclose serious problems.

Session 12: Visions for a Strong Future

Notably, when they begin the Go Grrrls program, many participants express the desire to be a model when they grow up; by the end of the sessions, they have become aware of many other possibilities, and come away with an actual plan to explore the educational requirements for becoming, for example, a physician, teacher, engineer, social worker, or physicist.

In this session, we encourage girls to set long-term educational, career, and adventure goals for themselves, and teach them how to create short-term objectives to help them achieve those goals. We also try to help the girls establish a connection to the future by having them evaluate a list of value statements about world issues (e.g., environment, education, racism) and consider ways that they might truly make a difference in the world that will be theirs. Finally, we play a "planning for the future" game, in which each girl stands in front of the group and takes a turn at drawing herself performing one of her goals, while the other members guess what goal she is drawing.

Week 7: Closure

Session 13: Closure/Review/Posttest

The goals for the final session are to:

- Review and summarize topics covered during the course of the group.
- Collect data for program evaluation.
- Provide participants with a sense of closure and accomplishment.

Group leaders begin by conducting a brief review of all of the subjects covered during the program. Girls then complete the posttest and a satisfaction survey. Next, leaders hold a graduation ceremony, during which they read each girl's name aloud, present her with a certificate, and thank her for some specific way that she contributed to the group.

The program ends with a party that usually features pizza, music, and a raffle to distribute the incentives for attendance (e.g., a portable CD player) and journal assignment completion (e.g., a gift certificate to a local mall). Finally, just before the program concludes, leaders call everyone together and thank the participants again for all of their fine efforts.

CONDUCTING A SESSION: A CLOSER LOOK

It is important to reiterate that this program was designed for all middle school girls, not just at-risk students. By the second session, the six girls in our group already seem to feel fairly comfortable with each other and with us. At this point, it is still important to build a sense of group cohesiveness, so we begin the session by asking if anyone remembers the name game we played in the opening session. "Sharp Shannon," a smart 13-year-old, declares that she does, and proceeds to reel off everyone's name, along with the positive adjective they chose to describe themselves. Other girls want to try their hand at this, too, and several complete the whole round of names. This serves as a good icebreaker activity, and the girls relax.

Lily, a bright and confident track star, has already emerged as one of the group's natural leaders. We encourage her participation because the other girls are likely to follow the lead of a respected peer. After we review each other's names, Lily volunteers to read today's topic from the large puzzle. (We begin each session by referring to the puzzle.) This ritual serves two purposes:

1. It reminds the group members of topics that we've covered previously.

2. It links the day's topic into the context of the larger program.

Lily reads, "Being a girl in today's society," aloud, and I explain that today we will be discussing some of the messages and stereotypes about women that abound in the media and popular culture.

We divide the girls into two groups by having them count off by twos. (We specifically decide to split the group using this method so that all the participants can get to know everyone better. Having smaller groups also affords a greater opportunity for leaders to interface with the girls about the topic at hand.) The groups each gather around a large sheet of poster paper that is surrounded by a collection of popular magazines, scissors, glue, and magic markers. We ask each group to construct a collage depicting media images of the so-called ideal woman. While they work on this task, we play some popular songs—not raunchy, but that nevertheless contain disparaging or controversial lyrics about a woman's role in life.

"I like this song!" Melissa says about one, while dancing around. That's fine, of course. We are not trying to stop girls from listening to popular music; rather, our goal is to teach them to *hear* negative media messages and learn to "talk back"—think critically—about what they hear.

"Yeah, it's got a great bass line," I agree, disarming the need for the girls to defend their music. "But let's check out what they're saying."

"You're supposed to be sexy," offers Eileen, a girl who has been very quiet so far. I tell her to pick a marker and write that down on the poster.

At the same time, Patti is pasting down an image of a woman standing on a scale, frowning, with the caption, "Take off ugly weight in one week." They've all gotten the spirit of the exercise, now, and they're pasting and scribbling, using different-color markers, and writing upside down, sideways, and every which way. Words such as "easy" and "hoochie mama" appear alongside images of scantily clad models; and phrases such as, "Be a perfect mom and good cook" appear alongside photos of women in traditional nurturing roles. (We deliberately laid out a wide mix of magazines and played some very specific songs to reflect these messages.)

Meanwhile, my co-leader is working with the other group, whose members also have been foraging through popular magazines and listening to the songs, constructing a collage of media stereotypes of women.

After about half an hour, we pull the two activity groups together to present their findings to one another. (We informed each group that they would present their findings to the other groups when they finished their collage.) Each group can point to and be proud of a tangible product. My group volunteers to go first.

Claire, a forthright student, speaks up first. She points to several images of supermodels, and notes that they are all tall and skinny.

Anne, a girl with East Indian ancestry, adds, "Yeah, and most of them are white, too."

"That's right," Claire continues, "and nobody has zits, and their teeth are all perfectly straight and real white."

From these responses, I understand that they are comparing *themselves* to the airbrushed images on the page. I don't point out their self-comparison, yet, as I want to let both groups share their information before we begin coming to any conclusions.

Everyone giggles when another girl in the group points out an ad included in the collage, which states: "You can even buy rubber boobs to make yourself look bigger, or a rubber butt to make yours look firmer!" As my group ends their presentation, they bow, as the other group applauds.

My co-leader's group now assembles in the front of the room. Lily begins to read from the graffiti they have scribbled while listening to the songs:

> Some stuff that we thought they are saying is, like, you've gotta be sexy . . . and you're supposed to be easy, but then you're bad, like a "hoochie mama" if you do stuff. Then you're supposed to take care of your house and your husband and kids . . . but you're supposed to wear make-up while you do.

They all nod and laugh. Even though the messages that each group presents are roughly the same, the impact of having the girls present to each other is palpable. We are not lecturing them or listing these stereotypes for them. They are declaring their revelations aloud, to each other. As the second group ends its presentation, they bow and the other group applauds their efforts.

Now it is time to discuss the implications of the girls' findings. We challenge them to come up with a list of 10 stereotypes about women they have discovered during this exercise. They eagerly grab markers and work together to list several key words and phrases. "Skinny" appears on the list, as do "big chest," "ditzy," "clueless," and "buff."

Of course, it would be simple to point out that no one really matches the absurd media ideal, but we want the girls to reach this awareness themselves. But we do guide them to the point with some open-ended questions.

"What do the magazines and music lyrics have in common?" my co-leader asks.

They review the traits, stereotyped behaviors, and roles they uncovered. Then we ask the million-dollar question: "What happens when we compare ourselves to these stereotypes?"

Until now, no one in the room has actually stated that she does this: compare herself to the stereotypes. We are reaching for a deeper understanding now, and the girls become more quiet and serious.

"Well, you feel bad. And there's stuff you can't do anything about. I mean, I know I'm never gonna be tall. Everybody in my family is short," Eileen offers.

Her comments open the door, and other group members begin to reveal more personal comparisons. One already slender girl admits that she is on a diet. The others tell her that she looks great the way she is. For the first time in this program, we have reached a true work stage.

We let these revelations unfold for as long as we can, but it is important that we don't close the session on this note, so we begin to summarize the discussion. We note that many girls and women strive to look or act like the media stereotypes; and when they cannot, they end up feeling frustrated, disappointed in themselves, and sometimes depressed. We ask them how many women they know in their real lives look or act like the so-called ideal woman from the magazines and music. No one knows any such person.

We wrap up the session with a discussion of what the girls admire about the real women in their lives—teachers, parents, aunts, or others. We discuss the fact that the media stereotypes of women are not only unattainable, but also undesirable in many ways. We close by pointing out that it's okay to want to look and feel good, but that it's more important to learn to accept who we are and what we look like.

CONCLUSIONS

Adolescent girls live in an environment that is often toxic to their healthy development. Our culture continues to portray successful and happy women as thin, long-legged, and classically beautiful. Consequently, body image problems become significant in early adolescence, and can last a lifetime. Many girls also become so obsessed with their bodies that they develop serious eating disorders. Others simply become chronically unhappy and develop feelings of depression.

Clearly, adolescent girls present unique challenges. To meet those challenges, the Go Grrrls program is designed to help girls prepare for a healthier and happier lifestyle. Using empirical studies that identify the developmental issues that impact early adolescent girls the most, a psychoeducational skills training program was designed. Based on practical instruction and skill building concepts, the program provides knowledge and skills to help girls cope with the pressures of growing up in today's culture. It promotes the positive assets of adolescent girls and addresses relevant developmental issues. In a group format designed to build social support, the program helps girls achieve these eight developmental objectives:

1. Identify an appropriate gender role.
2. Establish an acceptable body image.
3. Develop a positive self-image.

4. Develop satisfactory peer relationships.

5. Establish independence through responsible decision making.

6. Understand sexuality.

7. Learn to obtain help and find access to resources.

8. Plan for the future.

These are the critical pieces that comprise the Go Grrrls puzzle. We hope that all girls can master their developmental tasks and live healthier and happier lives.

REFERENCES

Attie, H., & Brooks-Gunn, J. (1989). Development of eating problems in adolescent girls: A longitudinal study. *Developmental Psychology, 25,* 70–79.

Benjet, C., & Hernández-Guzmán, L. (2002). A short-term longitudinal study of pubertal change, gender, and psychological well-being of Mexican early adolescents. *Journal of Youth and Adolescence, 31,* 429–442.

Berg, F. (1992, July/August). Harmful weight loss practices are widespread among adolescents. *Obesity and Health,* 69–72.

Birleson, P. (1981). The validity of depression disorders in childhood and the development of a self-rating scale: A research report. *Journal of Child Psychology and Psychiatry, 22,* 73–88.

Botvin, G. J., Schinke, S. P., Epstein, J. A., Diaz, T., & Botvin, E. M. (1995). Effectiveness of culturally focused and generic skills training approaches to alcohol and drug abuse prevention among minority adolescents: Two-year follow-up results. *Psychology of Addictive Behaviors, 9,* 183–194.

Brooks-Gunn, J., & Paikoff, R. (1997). Sexuality and developmental transitions during adolescence. In J. Schulenberg, J. L. Maggs, & K. Hurrelmann (Eds.), *Health risks and developmental transitions during adolescence* (pp. 190–219). London: Cambridge University Press.

Brooks-Gunn, J., & Reiter, E. O. (1990). The role of pubertal processes. In S. S. Feldman & G. R. Elliott (Eds.), *At the threshold: The developing adolescent* (pp. 16–53). Cambridge, MA: Harvard University Press.

Bruene-Butler, L., Hampson, J., Elias, M., Clabby, J., & Schuyler, T. (1997). The Improving Social Awareness—Social Problem-Solving Project. In G. W. Albee & T. P. Gullotta (Eds.), *Primary prevention works* (pp. 239–267). Thousand Oaks, CA: Sage.

Caplan, M., Weissberg, R. P., Grober, J. S., Sivo, P. J., Grady, K., & Jacoby, C. (1992). Social competence promotion with inner-city and suburban young adolescents effects on social adjustment and alcohol use. *Journal of Consulting and Clinical Psychology, 60,* 56–63.

Caspi, A. (1995). Puberty and the gender organization of schools: How biology and social context shape the adolescent experience. In L. J. Crockett & A. C. Crouter (Eds.), *Pathways through adolescence: Individual development in relation to social contexts* (pp. 57–74). Mahwah, NJ: Erlbaum.

Center for Substance Abuse Prevention. (1993). *Knowledge, attitude, and behavior instrument (KAB).* Unpublished manuscript.

Denmark, F. L. (1999). Enhancing the development of adolescent girls. In N. G. Johnson, M. C. Roberts, & J. Worell (Eds.), *Beyond appearance: A new look at adolescent girls* (pp. 377–404). Washington, DC: American Psychological Association.

Dryfoos, J. (1991). *Adolescents at risk: Prevalence and prevention.* New York: Oxford University Press.

Eisele, L., Hertsgarrd, D., & Light, H. (1986). Factors related to eating disorders in young adolescent girls. *Adolescence, 21,* 283–290.

Ellickson, P. L., Bell, R. M., & McGuigan, K. (1993). Preventing adolescent drug use: Long-term results of a junior high program. *American Journal of Public Health, 83,* 856–861.

Elliott, D. S. (1993). Health-enhancing and health-compromising lifestyles. In S. G. Millstein, A. C. Petersen, & E. O. Nightingale (Eds.), *Promoting adolescent health* (pp. 119–145). New York: Oxford University Press.

Fabian, L. J., & Thompson, J. K. (1989). Body image and eating disturbance in young females. *International Journal of Eating Disorders, 8,* 63–74.

Furnham, A., & Greaves, N. (1994). Gender and locus of control correlations of body image dissatisfaction. *European Journal of Personality, 8,* 183–200.

Greenberg, M. T., Domitrovich, C., & Bumbarger, B. (2001). The prevention of mental disorders in school-aged children: Current state of the field. *Prevention and Treatment, 4, Article 1.* Retrieved February 28, 2004, from http://journals.apa.org/prevention/volume4/pre0040001a.html.

Hare, B. R. (1985). *The HARE general and specific (school, peer, and home) self-esteem scale.* Unpublished manuscript.

Hawkins, J. D., Catalano, R. F., Kosterman, R., Abbott, R., & Hill, K. G. (1999). Preventing adolescent health-risk behavior by strengthening protection during childhood. *Archives of Pediatrics and Adolescent Medicine, 153,* 226–234.

Hooper, S. R., & Layne, C. C. (1983). The common belief inventory for students: A measure of rationality in children. *Journal of Personality Assessment, 47,* 85–90.

Johnson, N. G., & Roberts, M. C. (1999). Passage on the wild river of adolescence: Arriving safely. In N. G. Johnson, M. C. Roberts, & J. Worell (Eds.), *Beyond appearance: A new look at adolescent girls* (pp. 3–18). Washington, DC: American Psychological Association.

Johnston, L. D., O'Malley, P. M., & Bachman, J. (2002). *Monitoring the future: National results of adolescent drug use: Overview of key findings, 2001* (NIH Publication No. 02-5105). Bethesda, MD: National Institute on Drug Abuse.

Kazdin, A. E. (1993). Adolescent mental health: Prevention and treatment programs. *American Psychologist, 48,* 127–141.

Kazdin, A. E., Bass, D., Ayers, W. A., & Rodgers, A. (1990). The empirical and clinical focus of child and adolescent psychotherapy research. *Journal of Consulting and Clinical Psychology, 58,* 729–740.

Kazdin, A. E., Rogers, A., & Colbus, D. (1986). The hopelessness scale for children: Psychometric characteristics and concurrent validity. *Journal of Consulting and Clinical Psychology, 54,* 241–245.

Kazdin, A. E., & Weisz, J. R. (1998). Identifying and developing empirically supported child and adolescent treatments. *Journal of Consulting and Clinical Psychology, 66,* 19–36.

LeCroy, C. W. (2004a). The development and evaluation of an empowerment program for early adolescent girls. *Adolescence, 39,* 427–441.

LeCroy, C. W. (2004b). Experimental evaluation of the "Go Grrrls" preventive intervention for early adolescent girls. *Journal of Primary Prevention, 25,* 457–473.

LeCroy, C. W. (2005). Building an effective primary prevention program for adolescent girls: Empirically based design and evaluation. *Brief Treatment and Crisis Intervention, 5,* 1–10.

LeCroy, C. W., & Daley, J. (2001a). *Empowering adolescent girls: Examining the present and building skills for the future with the Go Grrrls program.* New York: Norton.

LeCroy, C. W., & Daley, J. (2001b). *The Go Grrrls workbook*. New York: Norton.

LeCroy, C. W., & Daley, J. (2005). Empowering adolescent girls: The Go Grrrls social skills training program. In C. W. LeCroy & J. Daley (Eds.), *Case studies in child, adolescent, and family treatment* (pp. 127–141). Belmont, CA: Brooks/Cole.

Masten, A. S. (2001). Ordinary magic: Resilience processes in development. *American Psychologist, 56,* 227–238.

Millstein, S. G., Petersen, A. C., & Nightingale, E. O. (1993). Adolescent health promotion: Rationale, goals and objectives. In S. G. Millstein, A. C. Petersen, & E. O. Nightingale (Eds.), *Promoting the health of adolescents: New direction, for the twenty-first century* (pp. 3–12). New York: Oxford University Press.

Nolen-Hoeksema, S., & Girgus, J. S. (1994). Gender differences in depression during adolescence. *Psychological Bulletin, 115,* 424–443.

Office of Technology, U.S. Congress. (1991). *Adolescent health: Vol. 1. Summary and policy options* (Publication No. OTAH-468). Washington, DC: U.S. Government Printing Office.

Seiffge-Krenke, I., & Stemmler, M. (2002). Factors contributing to gender differences in depressive symptoms: A test of three developmental models. *Journal of Youth and Adolescence, 31,* 405–417.

Simmons, R. G., & Blythe, D. A. (1987). *Moving into adolescence: The impact of pubertal change and school context.* New York: Aldine De Gruyter.

Stice, E., Killen, J. D., Hayward, C., & Taylor, C. B. (1998). Age of onset for binge eating and purging during adolescence: A four-year survival analysis. *Journal of Abnormal Psychology, 107,* 671–675.

Striegel-Moore, R. H., & Cachelin, F. M. (1999). Body image concerns and disordered eating in adolescent girls: Risk and protective factors. In N. G. Johnson, M. C. Roberts, & J. Worell (Eds.), *Beyond appearance: A new look at adolescent girls* (pp. 85–108). Washington, DC: American Psychological Association.

Tafarodi, R., & Swann, W. B., Jr. (1995). Self-liking and self-competence as dimensions of global self-esteem: Initial validation of a measure. *Journal of Personality Assessment, 65,* 322–342.

Takanishi, R. (1993). The opportunities of adolescence: Research, interventions, and policy. *American Psychologist, 48,* 85–87.

Wylie, R. (1979). *The self-concept theory and research* (Vol. 2). Lincoln: University of Nebraska Press.

Wyman, P. A., Sandler, I., Wolchik, S., & Nelson, K. (2000). Resilience as cumulative competence promotion and stress protection: Theory and intervention. In D. Cicchetti, J. Rappaport, I. Sandler, & R. P. Weissberg (Eds.), *The promotion of wellness in children and adolescents* (pp. 133–184). Washington, DC: Child Welfare League of America Press.

DEVELOPING FRIENDSHIPS AND PEER RELATIONSHIPS

Building Social Support with the Girls Circle Program

BETH HOSSFELD

Tell me your friends, and I'll tell you who you are.

—Assyrian proverb

Female friendship is one of the most important dimensions of a girl's life, and its influence on her well-being may be surpassed only by family relationships in her growth toward adulthood. Teachers, school counselors, and parents know only too well the consuming and complex emotional struggles girls face on a daily basis on playgrounds, in hallways, during class, on the phone, and in chat rooms. Recently, the subject of girls' friendships has received a great deal of media attention. Notably, for example, major motion pictures such as *Thirteen* (Hardwicke & Reed, 2003), *Mean Girls* (Wiseman, Fey, & Waters, 2004), and *Sisterhood of the Traveling Pants* (Brashares, Ephron, & Kwapis, 2005) grossed between $4 million and $87 million dollars in revenue (Nash, 2005). These movies offer varied perspectives and experiences about the significant role that female peer relationships play, negatively and positively, in early adolescence and adolescent development. National best sellers *Odd Girl Out: The Hidden Culture of Aggression in Girls* (Simmons, 2002) and *Queen Bees and Wannabees: Helping Your Daughter Survive Cliques, Gossip, Boyfriends, and Other Realities of Adolescence* (Wiseman, 2003), as well as the book *Girlfighting: Betrayal and Rejection among Girls* (Brown, 2003) address various gender-specific social behaviors and experiences that are both painful and common to female peer relationships throughout childhood and adolescent years. Although perspectives vary on the factors that influence girls' peer relationships, there is agreement among writers, scholars, teachers, service providers, and researchers that girls' friendships are critical in the developing adolescent's identity, behaviors, and overall health. Such stories and studies highlighting girls' peer relationships provide an opportunity to consider the common problems of female friendships through a broad sociocultural and gender lens, shifting the focus away from solely an individualistic approach.

Of particular interest in recent years has been relational aggression among girls that occurs physically (which is less common but increasing) and covertly. Cultural attention to girls' mean behaviors portrays a dark side of female peer relationships, in which girls use relationships as the vehicle with which to express anger or power through rumors, exclusion, secrets, or gossip. Statistics indicate a rapid increase in female arrests for assault incidents in both Canada and the United States during the past decades, including assaults between females (Odgers & Moretti, 2002). However, the majority of girls use relational tactics, both verbal and nonverbal, to express anger or seek to gain social power (Olweus, 1993). From a sociocultural point of view, most girls' aggressive behaviors may be covert because an obvious or direct expression of anger does not fit with notions of acceptability or attractiveness for girls—it's not nice. In addition, female oppression within Western society forces girls to compete with each other for the few prized positions of popularity that afford status and power within the social settings where girls connect, and in which there is experience of limited access to power. Lyn Mikel Brown argues that girls' anger has been ignored in our society, and that the root source behind relational aggression is a lack of genuine empowerment for girls and young women (Brown, 2003). This empowerment involves a whole set of policies, attitudes, proactive tools, and strategies that address gender, culture, race, class, and developmental needs for girls (American Association of University Women, 1994; Benard, 2004; Brown, 2003; Brown & Gilligan, 1992; Office of Juvenile Justice and Delinquency Prevention, 1998; Phillips, 1998; Pipher, 1994; Schoenberg, Riggins, & Salmond, 2003; United Way of the Bay Area, 2003; Ward, 2000).

The Relational-Cultural Theory (RCT) of female development, originally developed by Jean Baker Miller (1991) recognizes relationships as the central organizing feature in girls' development. For girls, this core component of psychological make-up shapes overall health, so that girls' healthy connections influence all other arenas of individual health (emotional, physical, spiritual, cognitive). Conversely, compromised connections have negative influence in girls' overall health. Theorists Carol Gilligan and Lyn Mikel Brown have suggested there is a critical need for girls to experience relationships in which they are able to use their voices authentically and without risk of alienation, in order to develop psychological health (Brown & Gilligan, 1992). In light of the cultural context girls live within, whereby, according to the National Youth Violence Prevention Resource Center (NYVPRC; 2005), at least 30% of youth (more than 5.7 million males and females) are experiencing some aspect of bullying, as a target or perpetrator, at any given time, use of authentic voice in peer relationships is most likely very difficult. This number does not include those youth who are actively witnessing the bullying.

In a study of students at junior high and high schools in the Midwest, 88% of students reported observing bullying at school (Hoover, Oliver, & Hazier,

1992). The difficulty in being real with one's peers is especially problematic at early adolescence, when, as statistics indicate, incidents of bullying behavior are higher (NYVPRC, 2005) and developmental and social-emotional pressures dictate a need for sameness amongst peers. These transitional years, in turn, shape girls' identities and peer relationship patterns as they proceed through adolescence. In social climates that discourage and interfere with natural self-expression within empathic and mutually supportive relationships, girls' connections weaken. In *Meeting at the Crossroads* (1992), Brown and Gilligan explain that a "crisis of connection" ensues, in which girls must either forgo expression of self and risk alienation from their own experiences and knowledge; or, if they speak their true minds, risk alienation and rejection from peers. The need to belong generally trumps the authentic voice, where emotional safety has not been established, in effect short-circuiting girls' use of their full range of internal resources (knowledge, feelings, experiences, ideas).

Key questions facing educators, practitioners, and researchers are:

- If girls' overall healthy development is indeed dependent on healthy connections with others, yet girls' peer relationships present significant forces of aggression and rejection, how can the resilient, prosocial influences of girls' friendships grow?
- What inherent strengths and capacities exist intrapersonally and interpersonally with girls that can counter hurtful interactions?
- How can professionals and concerned adults foster these strengths, and through what structures?
- If girls' development is inherently and predominantly attuned to maintaining connections, is it possible to redefine relational aggression as a learned but inadequate attempt at finding meaningful connection?

CHAPTER SCOPE

While some girls are players in the cycles of aggressive behaviors, others find themselves outside of the security that peer relationships offer due to ineffective social skills. Still other girls are more moderately able to enjoy close and rewarding friendships. Can a prosocial, relationship-focused support structure for girls enhance developmental tendencies toward connection and provide sufficient anchoring for girls within positive peer connections as a pathway toward health? This chapter presents an approach that aims to address these questions, called Girls Circle, a gender-specific, relational-cultural empowerment model for girls' healthy development within a peer support group. This approach is presented as follows:

1. First, a glimpse at current research identifies the needs of early adolescent and adolescent females for growth-promoting, positive relationship-based experiences with peers. Strengths, gaps, and differences, of other models are identified.

2. Next the chapter presents the Girls Circle philosophy and the core components that foster girls' healthy relationships: the basic format of a Girls Circle curriculum that specifically target peer friendship and facilitator methods.

3. Science-based outcomes (see addendum for additional outcomes) revealing significant positive changes for girls in self-efficacy, perceived body image, and perceived social connection follows.

Examples of activities and experiences are included throughout the chapter, as well as reflective statements about Girls Circle from both girls and facilitators. Essential considerations for programmatic success are mentioned, and implications for future development of the model, as well as broader implications based on the RCT of female development are suggested.

Peer Support: A Key Determinant in Girls' Health

Friendships have both protective and risk-promoting factors (Benard, 2004; Dekovic, 1999; Maxwell, 2002; Pleydon & Schner, 2001; Storch, Masia-Warner, & Brassard, 2003). When students in middle school do not experience reciprocal friendships, increases in depression and lower academic motivation occur (Wentzel, Barry, & Caldwell, 2004). Likewise, adolescents who are targets of either overt or relational aggression show greater levels of anxiety and loneliness (Storch et al., 2003). Feeling safe and comfortable in the environments girls inhabit is the subject of a report issued by Girl Scouts of the United States of America (Schoenberg et al., 2003). Surveys of girls' self-reports on feelings of safety reveal that "girls define safety in terms of relationships—when they trust the people around them, they feel safe." *Who* girls are with is as important as *where* girls are relating. Girls' biggest worry is being teased by others. Additionally, 45% reported that speaking in class is threatening to their emotional safety. Striking differences were noted between girls' attitudes and experiences—in academic success, ability to concentrate, quality of relationships, belief in their abilities—and between girls who feel emotionally and physically safe and those who do not. Girls who feel less emotionally safe reported fewer friends and are slower to trust peers or adults. For teens, feeling safe involves being with friends.

In a study comparing friendships and peer relationships of female juvenile offenders and nonoffenders, researchers found: (a) a significant correlation between a deviant peer group and prediction of adolescent female delinquency; and (b) girls in delinquency showed less communication and more perceived peer pressure (Pleydon & Shner, 2001). The study authors suggest that the level of self-disclosure is similar for girls in and out of delinquency, but that there is less inquiry and discussion regarding disclosures among delinquent girls. Finally, they indicate that females are more likely to conform to female peers' behaviors, even when in mixed-gender groups, and argue that interventions for female adolescents in delinquency should focus not only on individual approaches but also address peer group influences in interventions.

Peer support has been shown to have a more significant role than family support for students in middle and later adolescence (Wentzel, 1998). Girls value support from teachers and close friendships (Kilpatrick-Demaray & Kerres-Malecki, 2003). Adolescent girls perceive higher levels of support and value social support more so than boys, especially once they reach high school. Prosocial behaviors by peers showed moderating abilities on loneliness and social anxiety of students (Storch et al., 2003). Social support is described as both a buffer against life stressors as well as a factor acting to promote wellness (Vaux, 1988). Peer support influences adolescents' motivation for involvement in talent and sport activities (Patrick et al., 1999).

Current Programs Aimed at Increasing Positive Connection

Espelage and Swearer (2003) provide a comprehensive view of bullying research and peer victimization. They suggest that prevention efforts should incorporate discussions with students related to peer pressures and obstacles to resisting social forces to comply with aggressive or unkind behaviors. Leff, Power, Manz, Costigan, and Nabors (2001) reviewed the following model programs that aim to reduce student bullying behaviors toward peers:

- Promoting Alternative Thinking Strategies
- Second Step
- First Step to Success

- Anger Coping Program
- Brain Power Program

Their conclusion was that those programs that did not include relational aspects of bullying were falling short of their target goals. A Second Step, middle school/junior high program evaluation revealed significant changes, in that participating students who received the program for 2 years were less tolerant of aggression, including teasing, in their school communities (Van Schoiack-Edstrom, Frey, & Beland, 2002). The program did not change exclusionary attitudes or behaviors, however. In a study of self-esteem for early adolescent females participating in a Girl Scouts curriculum, there were no significant increases in self-esteem for girls who participated and girls who did not. Self-esteem was higher for participants in the Girl Scout curriculum, but with increasing age groups, self-esteem was found to decrease (Royse, 1998). Girl Scouts programs have traditionally served to provide socialization, leadership, and life skills experiences for girls in a gender-specific program. It is important to point out, however, that although self-esteem changes were not significant, the study measure does not address how the Girl Scouts curriculum impacts girls' relationships.

Several studies indicate that support groups within communities or schools are effective settings in which to strengthen social connection, self-esteem, and body image (Benard, 2004; Conklin, 2002; Laszlo, 2001; Waggoner, 1999). Further, programs that integrate a cultural and gender-relevant approach to prevention and intervention have been emerging over the past decade. Hudley (2001) urges researchers to address the challenges of the underserved populations when developing and implementing programs, especially children of color, urban residents, and girls. She suggests researchers consider culture as a primary factor in the health of the communities. This recognition of the significant role of culture is consistent with studies that recognize the inherent resiliency that is tapped when positive ethnic and cultural identity is emphasized (Benard, 2004; Leadbeater & Way, 1996; Ward, 2000).

One such program, Sisters of Nia: A Cultural Program for African American Girls, was evaluated for effectiveness in increasing cultural values and beliefs (Belgrave et al., 2004). Relational aggression was reduced for participants in the groups, while positive ethnic identity increased.

Another program, Go Grrrls, was evaluated for its effectiveness in empowering early adolescent girls with a developmentally appropriate curriculum that included a focus on making and keeping friends and other gender-relevant tasks toward building competencies (LeCroy, 2004). Significant positive ncreases in peer esteem, common beliefs, and helping endorsements were achieved, though body image and depression levels at posttest were not significant. The researcher suggests that the body image measurement tool may have been insufficient, or possibly the curriculum underperformed. The depression results raise questions as to whether depression can be treated successfully in an intervention program and, if so, what methods might be appropriate for young adolescents. The overall positive results of the Go Grrrls program are encouraging and suggest that prevention programs that are developmentally designed and gender-relevant, with a focus on identity, body image, mood, mastery of life skills, and positive peer relationships, are a feasible and important step toward improving girls' health.

Finally, a wellness model of health offered by Hartwig and Myers (2003) approaches girls development from a holistic, strength model. This program, Wheel of Wellness, is being applied to girls and young women in the juvenile justice system. While presented as an assessment and intervention tool for use with individuals, Wheel of Wellness incorporates resiliency factors and skills development with a proactive and positive approach, viewing girls and young women as capable of creating balance and developing competencies for successful and healthy lives. The approach is consistent with recommendations that include holistic, developmental and strength-based programs for effective gender-responsive programs for girls as described by Patton and Morgan (2001).

GIRLS CIRCLE

Overview

The Girls Circle model, a structured support group for girls from 9 to 18 years, integrates relational theory, resiliency practices, and skills training in a specific format designed to increase positive connection, personal and collective strengths, and competence in girls (Hossfeld & Taormina, 2006). It aims to counteract social and interpersonal forces that impede girls' growth and development by promoting an emotionally safe setting and structure in which girls can develop caring relationships and use authentic voices. It has been utilized in a broad spectrum of prevention and intervention settings with diverse populations and programs, serving girls since 1994. Recognized as a "promising approach" by the Office of Juvenile Justice and Delinquency Prevention in 2005, Girls Circle is emerging as a gender-specific program with outcomes and potential to positively influence the direction of social-emotional development for girls in the United States, Canada, and a growing number of countries around the world.

Girls Circle is based on the relational-cultural model of female psychology, mentioned earlier, which views girls' healthy development as stemming from a core experience of positive and caring relationships with those in her family, peer group, culture, and community. When these connections are weakened due to any number of conditions and causes, girls' well-being suffers psychologically, socially, and in all areas of growth. Girls Circle views issues related to girls' health risks such as relational deficits, violence prevention, early sexual activity, substance abuse, poor body image, self-doubt, poverty, and other concerns as factors continually affected by and influencing connections with others, especially primary relationships such as family, peers, and school communities. Within the RCT, the Girls Circle model aims to increase protective factors and reduce risk factors in adolescent girls, as defined by resiliency researchers such as Benard (2004). Such hallmarks of resiliency development in youth are: high expectations, caring and support, and meaningful participation within their communities. To this end, a key component in the model is the council-type format, with one group member speaking at a time, and with the expectation of attentive listening from other participants. This form of communication intends to increase empathy skills on the part of the listeners, as well as a mutual empathic understanding in the whole group. From the relational perspective, "the deepest sense of one's being is continuously formed in connection with others and is inextricably tied to relational movement. The primary feature, rather than structure marked by separateness and autonomy, is increasing empathic responsiveness in the context of interpersonal mutuality" (Jordan, 1997). Empathic connection is an integral aim of the Girls Circle model, to increase girls' psychological health in its entirety, including self-efficacy, social support, and body image (Steese et al., 2006).

Girls Circles are 1.5- to 2-hour sessions, held on a weekly or biweekly basis, for 8 to 12 weeks minimum, in settings such as after-school programs, schools, juvenile justice programs, group homes, recreational programs, mentoring organizations, and in individual homes and communities. Where time restrictions exist, Girls Circle can be adapted to fit a one-hour period. Each session, a group of girls of similar age and development meet with a facilitator. During this time, the girls take turns talking and listening to one another respectfully about their concerns and interests. The girls express themselves further through creative or focused activities such as role-playing, drama, journaling, poetry, drama, dance, drawing, collage, clay, and so on. Gender-specific themes and topics are introduced, which relate to the girls' lives, such as being a girl, trusting ourselves, friendships, body image, goals, sexuality, drugs, alcohol, tobacco, competition, and decision making.

Girls' positive relationships and empathic connections are fostered in the Girls Circle model through three interacting components: the six-step basic circle format, the gender-relevant curriculum, and the facilitator's methodology.

Basic Circle Format

Six steps comprise the Girls Circle format, each session includes:

1. Opening ritual
2. Theme introduction
3. Check-in
4. Activity
5. Sharing of activity
6. Closing ritual

These components are described in the following subsections and in Table 2.1.

Opening Ritual

The opening ritual is a simple action that marks the beginning of the circle and fosters a special tone, distinguishing this time and place from others in a girls' daily life. Examples: lighting a candle, making a wish, reading of a quote or passage, listening to specific song.

Theme Introduction

The theme introduction is a short description of the focus of the session activity and discussion. Examples: being included or excluded, best friends and boyfriends, and all about blame.

Check-In

Using the council format based on Native American traditions, check-in is the phase of the session during which girls have an opportunity to "check in" one at a time with the other members of the circle, to share experiences, feelings, or ideas. It is a central aspect of the Girls Circle. The council format is an ancient practice that places each member of the circle on an equal basis and in direct relationship with one another. This step may be time-limited to ensure there is sufficient time for all girls to check in and to voice concerns that may be of great importance to them, and so that other planned activities can take place. The facilitator's discretion, together with group responses, can help guide the length of time available for check-in. Should a girl have a serious matter to discuss, the time can be adjusted to allow for full expression and support.

Participants can choose the subject they wish to share, and/or complete an unfinished sentence related to the theme of the day. Examples: feelings about the theme, a high and low point of the week, using a scale of 1 to 10 to describe

Table 2.1 Basic Circle Format

1. **Opening ritual**
2. **Theme introduction**
3. **Check-in**
4. **Activity**
5. **Sharing of activity**
6. **Closing ritual**

Opening ritual	Begin the circle with an opening ritual that marks commencement of the circle process, fosters a special tone, and invites participants into the unique space and time of the circle.
Theme introduction	The introduction of the theme is presented by the facilitator and is usually a short synopsis of what is planned for the meeting. The chosen theme will usually be tied to the activity and discussed and shared in greater detail at that time.
Check-in	Check-in is a time for the girls to check in with the group and express whatever they wish, or perhaps say something about the theme. One person speaks at a time. A talking stick may be used. Respect is emphasized and given by listening. Girls are welcome to say as little or as much as they choose.
Activity	Verbal activities (discussions) and creative activities (artistic) put girls in touch with their inner experiences. It enables them to express themselves in a safe and protected environment without the danger of losing connection with others.
Sharing of activity	The sharing of the activity is when the circle reconvenes to allow time for sharing. Through careful questioning, girls can begin to share responses and feelings, interpret themes, explore commonaities, and make the connection between the theme and their experiences in the real world.
Closing ritual	The closing ritual brings a special ending to the shared experiences and sends off the members safely with a positive tone, sense of gratitude, and respect. It reflects the intimacy that has developed and unites the circle for a final moment, to bring awareness to the communal energy and heartfelt sharing.

their mood, something that happened at school, a success or a disappointment, and so on.

During check-in, there is no cross talk; rather, a "talking piece" such as a talking stick or stuffed animal is employed. Once a speaker has checked in with the group, she passes the talking piece to the person on her left, in clockwise order. The practice within the group during this time is of attentive listening. When other girls have comments or feedback about a particular participant's experiences, they wait until their own check-in time to share. Depending on time availability, the talking piece can continue to travel around the circle when members have additional reflections to state. Feedback, however, is provided only if a speaker requests or agrees to receive it, and participants are encouraged to speak from their own experience if they have a statement to make that they believe may be helpful to another participant. In this way, experience, rather than advice, is generally offered.

Activity

The activity portion of the circle allows girls to explore and express their experiences and beliefs through a variety of verbal, nonverbal, creative, and experiential mediums. Activities ideally combine both verbal and nonverbal components, in order to invite girls with a wide variety of learning styles to engage in critical thinking processes and to connect their own experiences with the topic of the session. Activities can be broadly divided into two categories: verbal and nonverbal or creative.

Verbal Activities   The verbal portion of an activity period is generally a guided discussion, typically taking place before a creative or experiential activity. Discussions tend to be left-brain or linear-oriented in style. In settings that have less than 1.5 hours for the full circle, facilitators often rotate verbal and creative activities each week, so that there is a time dedicated to discussion as well as a time dedicated to creativity. The guided discussion serves to establish relevance of the topic, explore general ideas and experiences about that topic, and identify girls' concerns and needs.

An example of a verbal activity is a guided discussion about anger and girls' relationships. In this discussion, the facilitator might ask questions or invite girls to talk about their observations and experiences about how girls show their anger to one another, and what the goals, behaviors, and outcomes might be. Additionally, the discussion might invite girls to talk about the social and cultural messages about anger and females, practices that may backfire on girls, and tools that are most helpful when girls want to manage a conflict in such a way that they feel confident, capable, and mature. The purpose of the activity is to hear the girls' experiences and to encourage peer exchange in order for the girls to develop their own best strategies, rather than to become passively "educated" by the facilitator as to best practices. Engagement and involvement are the critical goals because the resiliency-based philosophy in practice here is that the girls have the knowledge and wisdom inside them, in most instances, to resolve problems, given a listening and respectful environment that promotes such thinking and articulation.

An alternative verbal activity might be a paired activity, where girls join with a partner, discuss a topic together for varying lengths of time, then rotate partners, and discuss a related topic with another participant. Following multiple partner pair-shares, the whole group reconvenes to debrief the experience, find commonalities, raise ideas, or identify strategies for common problems.

Verbal activities offer several benefits to girls' groups. Most girls show interest in talking and want to address a variety of social and gender issues. While the council format used during check-in permits a specific time for each girl, verbal activities increase the opportunities for talking and sharing of experiences, and target topics that girls might not raise to the group, or address on their own. Further, the exchanges allow girls to hear a variety of viewpoints that are not necessarily addressed outside of the safety of the circle.

Nonverbal or Creative Activities   Creative activities put girls in touch with their inner experiences. Frequently, these approaches are right-brain-oriented activities that utilize imagery, perception, impression, space, color, imagination, or rhythm for expression. Facilitators select creative activities to enhance the exploration of the session's theme, based on the interests of the group, or follow the curriculum provided using the Girls Circle Theme and Activity Guides (see Tables 2.2 to 2.4). In the Friendship Theme Kit, for instance, one theme is "Feuds, Followers, and Fairness," in which the associated activity involves dividing girls up into small teams, providing a scenario related to peer conflict, and challenging each team to develop a resolution strategy that demonstrates respect, empathy, and fairness. Each team then performs that strategy with the whole group. The active practice of resolving a peer conflict in such a way becomes an important embodied experience for girls, enhancing verbal discussion, so that they might have a more developed option to utilize in real-life situations outside of the circle. Examples of creative activities include: role-play, mime, video creation, collage, poetry, storytelling, murals, yoga, mask making, beading, songwriting, listening to music, guided visualizations, exchanging facials, poster making, creating traditional meals, or creating affirmation mobiles. Examples of themes relevant to girls' friendships include: passive, aggressive or assertive response styles; stereotypes; inclusion/exclusion, cliques; self-care; cultural clashes; handling stress; sisterhood; heroines; getting along with others; give and take in relationships; building trust; relationship styles.

Table 2.2   Friendship Theme and Activity Guide Overview (Recommended for Ages 9 to 14; 8-Week Program)

Week	Theme	Activity
1	A friendly place	Creating group guidelines, making a poster, choosing a name
2	Being my own friend first	"The qualities I possess"
3	Being included, being left out	Pair sharing, group sharing
4	Same and different	Questions sheets, drawings
5	The whole is greater than all the parts	Minigroup posters and whole-group mural
6	Feuds, followers, and fairness	Role-plays
7	Our qualities and strengths	Chain of strengths
8	Appreciation celebration	Flower petals

Sharing of Activity

After the activity, girls reconvene in a circle and are invited to share their experience of it. Since the activities are designed to promote expression and learning about a particular theme, reflection and discussion can help girls become aware of perceptions, behaviors, or alternative options, or simply to identify feelings around the theme. This sharing period also increases group members' empathic capacities and social connections, as they listen to one another and find differences and similarities. Depending on the type of activity that occurs, the sharing of activity might be a brief group discussion, in which the facilitator asks open-ended, thoughtful questions; or it might be a time to go around the circle using the council format, as in the check-in step of the format. For example, after a role-play activity such as the peer conflict scenarios described previously, a guided group discussion may be more useful, whereas following a more individually oriented activity such as a personal collage, going around the circle might be most appropriate.

The important factor for the facilitator is to give a clear opportunity for every girl to participate, including those who might shy away from doing so. Generally, participants in these circles have varying levels of comfort or discomfort in self-disclosure. Girls are welcome to share at their own pace. Facilitators and group members may allow girls to pass if they choose, provided that the pass option is not used as a way to refuse participation. With increased experience in the consistent format of the circle, participants generally increase their self-disclosure during this process, taking risks in revealing more and

Table 2.3   Honoring Our Diversity Theme and Activity Guide Overview (Recommended for Ages 11 to 16; 12-Week Program)

Week	Theme	Activity
1	Beautiful diversity	Icebreakers, creating circle guidelines, journal decoration (Optional: Obtain video for week 3.)
2	Beyond fear	Team-building games, journaling, group discussion, and personal stories
3	Stereotype busting	"Graffiti wall," journaling; wild garden poster (Optional: video)
4	Cultural treasures	Treasure tiles, journaling
5	Heroines	Heroine "autobiography," stage readings, journaling
6	Culture clash	Physical drama/enactment, medicine wheels
7	Stress stories	"Girls' news hour," connection web
8	Sisters!	Magic coin trust exercise, discussion, group trust fall, journaling
9	Local action, part I	Yoga postures, group decision making
10	Local action, part II	Letter-writing campaign, journaling (Reminder for girls to bring excerpt or item for week 11.)
11	Soul of my culture	Expression: poetry, dance, music, art, journaling, group poem, and photo
12	Community	Meal and music, appreciations, closing circle, and journal distributions

more of themselves. In part because of this truth telling, girls begin to develop voice, deepen their bonds to one another, experience safety, and build trust within the circle.

Closing Ritual

The closing ritual is a short, simple, and important action that marks the completion of the session, recognizes the importance of the process that has occurred, and provides a positive tone for the group members as they transition out from the circle session. It unites members for a final moment to bring awareness to their group as a whole, and offers appreciation and respect to each. The closing ritual reinforces emotional safety for the girls, in effect anchoring the importance of their shared words and creative expressions within the group. This action provides closure and assists girls in feeling comfortable with what has occurred in circle and moving forward. For some groups, the opening and closing

Table 2.4 Relationships with Peers Theme and Activity Guide Overview (Recommended for Ages 13 to 18; 10-Week Program

Week	Theme	Activity
1	Connecting with each other	Creating group guidelines, commonalities bead game
2	Labels—exploring new perspectives	Vision quest game
3	Expressing myself	Guided visualization, poetry reading and writing
4	Accepting all different parts of myself	Quick writing, group poster, bowls of compassion
5	Cultivating respect	Tea ceremony
6	Romantic relationships—What is it worth to you?	Analyzing teen relationship stories, relationship definition exercises
7	Girlfights or girlfriends?	"Blame Game" talk show
8	Giving voice to feelings, part I	Journaling, feelings identification exercise, role-play
9	Giving voice to feelings, part II	"I statements"; Role plays
10	Wholeness and completion	Mandala making

rituals are identical, while for others, distinct. Examples: ringing and listening to the tone of a bell, holding hands and "passing the pulse" around the circle, each girl stating one positive affirmation or statement about herself or a compliment or hope for the girl on her left, a group statement of purpose, or a theme song.

Implementation

The basic circle format can be implemented and adapted in a full range of settings where girls convene. The six steps create a simple structure that supports the group experience with a balance of talking, listening, activity, time for spontaneous expression, as well as focused dialogue or exploration. Although the time allotment for each step may need to be adjusted according to the setting and the girls' developmental stages (e.g., younger girls might appreciate shorter check-in time and lengthier activity time while older girls might want the reverse), the model promotes adherence to the six steps as much as possible. Consistent and predictable application of the format reduces girls' anxiety and increases their security and sense of emotional safety in the circle, which, in turn, invites genuine expression.

Gender-Relevant Curriculum

The Girls Circle curriculum addresses girls' friendship development in several of the nine separate theme and activity facilitator guides (Girls Circle Association, 2007). Three of the nine guides address peer relationships comprehensively and directly. These are: Friendship with Peers, for ages 9 to 14; Honoring Our Diversity, for ages 11 to 18; and Relationships, for 14- to 18-year-olds. Furthermore, most of the additional six guides include one or more units that address peer relationships themes, while the overall content delves more specifically into other arenas of girls' lives, such as decision making about drugs, alcohol, and sexuality; identity as a female; and a specific guide dedicated to court-involved girls.

Honoring Our Diversity is a 12-week guide that assumes girls' need for opportunities to break down social, emotional, cultural, and class-based barriers toward peer understanding and peer relationships. It provides activities to engage girls in learning more about their own and their peers' cultural, social, and family backgrounds, and underscores the powerful role that ethnic, cultural, and family experiences play in shaping girls' identities. Unique and common challenges and strengths are identified, and, ultimately, an opportunity is provided to gain understanding that girls have similar needs and that unity among female peers can offer an empowering alternative to the divisive, competitive climate that prevails in most school communities.

The Relationship with Peers Guide takes the peer relationships to a more mature audience of teen girls. In it, aspects of friendliness and self-care are explored in a rich context of activities that identify and challenge patterns in which girls blame one another, hold preconceived notions and assumptions about each other, and label and box each other into roles, all of which impede empathic connection. This guide brings out these patterns, offers playful yet critical examination of these practices, and brings new and respectful patterns of relationship into practice through ceremonial rituals such as the ancient Eastern practice of a tea ceremony. Experiences such as this one demonstrate a way of relating toward one another based on practices of respect, kindness, and empathy, and consistent with the Girls Circle philosophy. To exemplify a session-by-session Girls Circle experience, an in-depth view of the Friendship Guide follows.

Friendship Guide

The Friendship Theme and Activity Guide is an 8-week plan that aims to build girls' interpersonal skills while diminishing the power of cliques and exclusionary practices. During preadolescence and early adolescence, girls' social behaviors and experiences often seem to mirror the rapid physical and emotional changes of puberty. Close friendships change, as girls become interested in exploring new styles, attitudes, friends, and behaviors. Trusted relationships shift, and a heightened sense of uncertainty, anxiety, and self-consciousness emerges as girls' developmental tasks center around peer acceptance. Frequently, secrets and whispers, shared glances, passed notes, playground territories, gossip, rumors, name-calling and teasing become common practices among fourth- through eighth-grade girls.

Following initial icebreakers, the Friendship Guide requires the group to begin the circle experience by setting up group agreements, or guidelines, that create emotional safety in the group. The principles of respect, kindness, and honesty are integral to these guidelines. The Friendship Guide encourages a tone of friendliness as an inherent expectation of the group experience. Once this fundamental expectation is established, the guide moves on through various weekly themes and activities. In week 2, girls are encouraged to look inward, to define the qualities they recognize within themselves. This activity asks girls to speak to their strengths, literally, and to make a flower with petals that display a number of their own attributes. Such an activity challenges the cultural norm that a girl should not speak positively about herself. In fact, girls typically respond initially to this exercise by saying, "I don't know," "I don't have any," or "This is weird; you're not supposed to brag." It is important for girls to understand the distinction between bragging and recognizing or acknowledging one's strengths, and this activity increases girls' capacity to do this. The activity also demonstrates the underlying philosophy that every girl has strengths and uniqueness. Another reason to ask girls to identify their strengths is to increase their attention to their own views and perceptions, to counter the exaggerated importance of the external world from which girls attempt to gain a sense of self-worth.

Next, girls address the problem caused by cliques, by talking and listening to one another in pairs, together with girls with whom they don't typically mix. Facilitators find random methods to assign partners, and girls tell each other stories about their own experiences with inclusion and exclusion. The task requires girls to talk to each other, bypassing the strict covert rules about who talks with whom. It levels the playing field, and assumes that all girls have some experiences in common, inviting understanding and promoting empathy. Further, girls' *own* stories become bridges to more genuine connection, in contrast to the common basis for connection among schoolgirls of telling stories about *other* girls. Following the paired sharing, the group reconvenes to identify individual and group observations from the experience. A guided discussion invites girls to consider the motivations of exclusionary behaviors, the impact of them on girls' sense of self, and an exploration of strategies that girls can employ to avoid exclusion and be more inclusive with one another.

The fourth session addresses the girls' diverse family experiences, recognizing differences and similarities as important aspects of developing positive peer relationships. Identifying and describing the cultural and familial influences that shape their lives, girls begin to fill in the blanks for one another about who they are as individuals. This process assists girls in transcending the pressure to look, act, and be perceived as the same as everyone else. Instead, they are encouraged to reveal traditions and interests particular to themselves. Assumptions by others in the group are challenged as well, when girls learn more about one another. Favorite meals, the meaning of certain names, family treasures—all of these aspects of girls' lives begin to show more of a girl's real life. In the middle school years, the developmental task of identity formation is taking shape. Because of the powerful need for belonging that surges in early adolescence, personal identities often take a backstage to collective or group identities. Early adolescents want to belong to a group and will sacrifice individual leanings for peer group sameness. The "same and different" focus of this fourth session, therefore, permits girls to view themselves more broadly; and because it is expected, girls have permission to show a variety of their experiences.

The fifth session encourages miniteams of girls to define the qualities and characteristics of a good friend. Each team creates and decorates a poster to identify the characteristics, then all the miniteam posters are glued or taped onto one large mural, which is decorated by the whole group. Spokespersons present their team posters, and the whole group debriefs the exercise with guided questions regarding the key aspects of a good friendship, and personal goals regarding these qualities. This session spells out the main message about what really counts to girls in a close friendship. Generally, the stated qualities include honesty, a sense of humor, caring about the other person, not going behind their back, and doing things together.

Facilitators can have the girls read or state the key points, and invite them to notice features that are not listed as important aspects of friendship, such as beautiful clothes, being popular, or a good student. These stated observations can increase girls' recognition of *what they themselves value most,* contrary to what they perceive to be of value to others.

The sixth week, Feuds, Followers, and Fairness, presents girls with a set of tools to use to successfully manage difficult peer relationship conflicts. Common problem scenarios are provided, or girls can offer their own problematic scenarios for use in the group. One scenario, for example, states:

> You learn that one friend is mad at another. Both friends seem to want you to take their side. One of them tells you to stop including the other. You want to be friends with both of them. How can you do this?

Respect, empathy, and fairness (REF) is presented as the criteria girls can use when developing a healthy and effective response to the various peer conflicts that arise. First, girls describe to the group the common reactions and behaviors girls show when situations occur. Then, small teams are once again created randomly and each team develops a two-minute role-play to demonstrate both the problem scenario and a solution that incorporates the REF criteria. The teams perform their skits to the whole group, who has been instructed to show appreciation for each team's performance. Following each skit, a brief discussion invites girls to talk about their feelings, express their views about the specific methods demonstrated, and offer their own ideas for resolving the problem. This role-play enables girls to interact directly with the peer conflict situations they face routinely at school and in extracurricular activities. But because they perceive themselves as "just acting," they are willing to try out responses they might otherwise never attempt. This experimentation allows players to voice and show alternative responses to peers. Frequently, girls need encouragement trying out the REF responses; but once they have done so, marked increase in positive and confident affect appears. The stage becomes a practice zone. Girls can end the activity by identifying a current personal situation and a response they want to apply in the coming week. Optional videotaping of these skits for additional group review can enhance skill building, as girls witness their own new responses in action.

The seventh session focuses on the strengths of the entire group. This team-building and team-honoring activity recognizes that the group is powerful because its members have strengths to share. Sets of index cards or decorative cards identify individual strengths, talents, and gifts. All of these cards are ceremoniously joined with string, becoming a chain, and hung up in the room to illustrate the collective strengths of the group. This chain visually demonstrates the uniqueness and unity of the group, girl to girl, link to link. The facilitator encourages girls to recognize and acknowledge the wide range of qualities shown on the chain, and to recognize these items as a potential source of help to each girl in the group, as the group's assets.

The eighth and final session of the Friendship Guide is an appreciation ceremony. Girls are given colored paper, scissors, and markers and pens so that they can write compliments to and appreciative comments about one another, and these are made available to girls to take home at the end of the circle. Food and beverages can be served while listening to music or sharing favorite memories. During a closing circle, girls can make individual wishes, and a collective wish can be created as well. Facilitators can acknowledge the sequence of events in the circle, and point out the relationship styles and behaviors that have shifted. Celebrations such as this are a vital part of every community, recognizing stages of growth and cohesiveness, accomplishments, and the impending completion and transition out of the group.

FACILITATOR METHODOLOGY

Girls Circle facilitators play a key role in the overall experience of the Girls Circle groups. They represent professionals and service providers in a wide spectrum of child and adolescent programs including education, youth development, substance abuse, mental health, and juvenile justice settings. Aspects of this role include:

- Preparing for the theme and activity plan each session
- Knowing and accessing professionals for consultation and referrals as needs arise for girls
- Having cultural competence
- Promoting interaction
- Developing group agreements
- Involving circle members as much as possible
- Managing difficult group dynamics

But of utmost importance is the facilitator's primary task: to protect the physical, emotional, and social safety of the group environment.

Launching Group Sessions

To start group sessions, the facilitator uses engaging icebreakers and activities that quickly create a fun, playful, relaxing, and safe atmosphere for all girls. This is essential because members of the group may or may not know each other, and are likely to have social, peer, or cultural differences. It is important from the beginning, also, that the facilitator acknowledge differences and commonalities in the group, offering an appreciation for the diversity of girls. Ideally, the facilitator shares characteristics with the girls that may include ethnicity, race, or cultural heritage, but this is not required. What is most important is that facilitators recognize their own assumptions and biases, that they are open and interested in cultural differences, and acknowledge these, and that they incorporate representations of varied female traditions and experiences, so that the girls are comfortable relating their experiences and revealing as much as they choose about themselves.

The facilitator invites the group to develop group guidelines that lay the foundation for group expectations, interactions, and behavior. Ideally, all participants contribute to creating these codes of interaction, jointly. Once a guideline is identified, such as "one person speaks at a time," the facilitator asks the group for consensus on that idea. When there are differences of opinion, the facilitator encourages the group to consider all views and needs, and to develop compromises or revised guidelines that satisfy the group. Examples of common guidelines include: respect everybody, listen to the speaker, be honest, talk from your own experience, be open-minded, keep things confidential. Facilitators invite girls to make posters, sign them, and place them in noticeable places in the room. Fully inviting group members into the process encourages girls' sense of ownership of and accountability to the group.

In addition, facilitators explain their legal and ethical responsibilities to the group, including their obligation as mandated reporters. Providing a clear and explicit policy up front helps girls know what to expect from the facilitator. This policy can also be written on a poster, which is put in a visible place in the group room. Regular reading or stating of both the group guidelines and the confidentiality and exceptions policy gives girls both clarity and security in the knowledge of the facilitator's obligations, should the information shared meet the criteria.

Handling Negative Behaviors

Particularly important in maintaining safety is the facilitator's task of addressing group members' hurtful behaviors. There are a variety of strategies facilitators may employ when responding to dynamics such as exclusion, cliques, insults, name-calling, secrecy, and other relationally aggressive or relationally oblivious behaviors. The chosen responses depend on the facilitator's judgment and knowledge of the particular situation and participants involved. Options may include: noticing and naming the observed behaviors, asking members what the intent of their actions or words are, reminding girls of their group agreements, introducing activities and discussions that target disruptive dynamics, and turning the problem over to the group for exploration and problem solving. Individual facilitators often develop unique strategies that match their personality styles, some using humor, others firm requests, and still others, nonverbal techniques.

At times, a group's configuration or a specific participant may challenge the authority of the facilitator. Experienced facilitators develop responses that blend limit setting and high expectations with neutrality and a nonshaming, nonpunitive approach. Skilled facilitators avoid power struggles, instead looking for the strengths of individual girls. When recognizing these capacities, facilitators give girls new and positive images to uphold. Girls Circle facilitators value inclusive approaches, providing important limits while taking a nonjudgmental, respectful attitude toward the girls, even—and especially—when their behavior disrupts the group. Facilitators maintain a perspective on the girls' capacities to make choices and mistakes, and to learn from these decisions. Consequences such as removing girls from the group for a session, or for good, are extremely rare, not advised, and unnecessary in most situations. From the relational perspective, girls grow and develop in relationships with others. The various manifestations of "acting out" that girls show while in group can be considered as attempts to make connections with others, however misguided by faulty beliefs and misguided learning. As in restorative justice circles, Girls Circles uphold kind, clear expectations of girls' potential and capacity to manage challenges and develop skills in and through relationships. With offerings of consistent, encouraging words and deeds, facilitators convey caring and respect for each girl's feelings. They provide acceptable choices for behavior.

Addressing Self-Disclosure

A common concern for group facilitators is the question of self-disclosure when working with youth. Given the powerful influence that these role models have on girls' lives, facilitators must pay prudent attention to the matter of self-disclosure. In general, the Girls Circle model recognizes the significance of authentic relationships between caring adults, such as the facilitators, and the girls. Facilitators must strive to express themselves genuinely, while setting limits and boundaries around personal or sensitive information. To that end, many trained facilitators use guideposts or questions for themselves when confronted with a girl's question about their personal life, history, or activities. They might ask themselves, for example:

- How will this information benefit the group?
- Am I willing to share this same information with these girls' parents?
- Is the purpose of sharing the information self-serving?

Sometimes, facilitator self-disclosure can be an important opportunity for the girls, to expand their knowledge about a situation or to reflect or consider experiences from a different lens. An example may be a situation where girls express hopelessness or discouragement about graduating from high school and having optimistic future opportunities. A facilitator could tell a story about a time she herself felt similarly, but encountered an opportunity that changed her perspective and created new possibilities.

Self-disclosure in very simple ways can also be effective when the Girls Circle is still in an early stage of trust building, not yet sure of what to share, or how much, as in during check-in. Facilitators can set an example by sharing a feeling they have, using self-expression for the purpose of assisting the group, at the same time keeping in mind the key purpose is to support the girls in developing bonds of trust and use of voice.

While avoiding self-expression to meet personal emotional needs within the group, facilitators benefit from regular self-care such as adult peer support when providing this significant service to girls.

Achieving Balance

Facilitators must balance attention to the needs of individual girls and the needs and interests of the group as a whole. They must also balance use of the particular curriculum content, activities, and themes with the energy, interest, and needs of the group members. For example, one or more girls may need extra time to talk about a specific situation, whereas the rest of the girls' interest revolves around a different topic more immediate to their day. In these instances, facilitators rely on both their own best judgment and the girls' input in deciding together where the group needs to direct its attention. When a group gets off-track or distracted, the facilitator brings the girls' focus back to the theme and activity of the session. Another challenge is that girls often want to talk at great length about a topic. The guidepost here, as in most situations, is to remain flexible, to meet the energy and interests of the group, while proceeding to offer new experiences and activities that promote girls' healthy development.

Finally, facilitators promote active listening, critical thinking, and active use of voices by involving girls in discussions. Using thoughtful questions and a discussion style, facilitators seek to hear the experiences, ideas, and observations of the group, and to encourage exchanges between members. Recognizing the powerful influences peers have when they tell their stories or share their opinions and beliefs, facilitators emphasize the importance of gathering a variety of experiences from the girls, with interest and open-mindedness. From this perspective, facilitators convey a clear message: "Your ideas matter; say more." Facilitators can express their own points of view and their concerns for girls, but in such a way as to reflect, underscore, or even challenge positions of others. They show patience, respect, and willingness to let go of the idea of being "right."

CRITERIA FOR PROGRAMMATIC SUCCESS

Successful programs within organizations are those that receive administrative support on theoretical and practical bases. Girls Circles function best when:

- Groups are time limited or closed, or there is a process for the rapid transitions in settings where girls are unable to stay for the entire 8- to 12-week period.
- There is space consistency and confidentiality.

- Consultation and support are available for regular and crisis support.
- Staff receive facilitator training, adequate preparation time, curricula, materials, and supplies.
- Staff have knowledge of community resources and are given clear policies regarding facilitator-mandated reporting responsibilities and procedures.
- Mental health and medical consultants are available for referrals.
- Transportation assistance is available for girls who need it; and snacks are a helpful addition.
- A network of support for the program and the girl participants is developed via parental consent and communications, as well as communication between service providers and host settings, such as school personnel.
- Cofacilitators have an established time for communication, planning, and debriefing.

Research-Based, Highly Valued Program

Outcomes for girls in the Girls Circle program have demonstrated significant positive changes in perceived social support, perceived body image, and self-efficacy (see Table 2.5). Additionally, girls' and facilitators' responses to feedback questionnaires reveal strong appreciation for the experience. Three studies (Irvine, 2005; Rough & Matthews, 2005; Steese et al., 2006) evaluated the effectiveness of the Girls Circle as a prevention and intervention model. In the first study, 63 girls ranging in age from 10 to 17 participated in 9 Girls Circle support groups across the United States for 10 weeks. These girls were of diverse racial-ethnic backgrounds: African American (18%), Caucasian (51%), Hispanic (21%), Asian (2%), Native American (3%), and other (5%). Girls were from urban (48%), suburban (25%), and rural (27%) areas. The girls completed the Multidimensional Scale of Perceived Social Support (Zimet, Dahlem, Zimet, & Farley, 1998), the Body Parts Satisfaction Scale (Berscheid, Walster, & Bohrnstedt, 1973), and Schwarzer's General Self-Efficacy Scale (Schwarzer & Scholz, 2000). Statistical analyses incorporating the paired-samples t-test revealed a significant increase in

Table 2.5   Outcome Study Result

Girls Circle Curriculum Dependent	Pretest Mean (SD)	Posttest Mean (SD)
Self-efficacy	27.42 (5.00)	30.55 (4.65)
Body image	107.11 (24.58)	113.11 (24.73)
Social support	58.29 (14.35)	65.06 (16.21)

$(t(53) = -5.27, p < .05)$

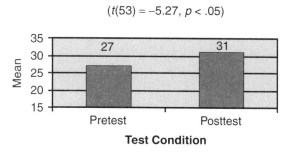

Figure 2.1   Mean Pre- and Posttest Scores of Self-Efficacy

self-efficacy scores (Figure 2.1), body image (Figure 2.2), and perceived social support (Figure 2.3). Results indicate that all three variables improved at the end of the 10-week Girls' Circle curriculum.

Self-Efficacy

Self-efficacy refers to one's belief in his or her ability to do the things necessary to achieve desired results (Bandura, 1995). Student identity and peer relationships are two key aspects of adolescent development that are greatly influenced by beliefs in one's abilities (Bradley & Corwyn, 2001). Self-efficacy is also enhanced through positive ethnic identity (Benard, 2004; Rotheram et al., 1996).

When asked to describe changes they noticed in themselves since participating in Girls Circle, middle school students in Victoria, British Columbia, said: "I have learned how to deal with my stress," "I learned how to explain how I feel," and "I learned to have patience." Following an after-school Girls' Circle experience at a middle school in southern California, one girl wrote: "I learned

$(t(53) = -2.02, p < .05)$

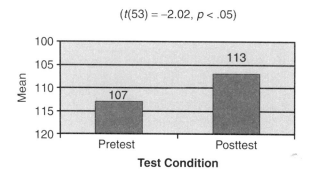

Figure 2.2   Mean Pre- and Posttest Scores of Body Image

$(t(53) = -4.07, p < .05)$

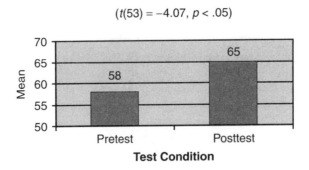

Figure 2.3   Mean Pre- and Posttest Scores of Social Support

about wiping away my inner critic and listening more to my positive side"; another wrote: "I don't down myself."

One Girls Circle facilitator, a licensed clinician and parent of a 13-year-old girl in Santa Rosa, California, hosted a Girls Circle as a parent facilitator for her own daughter and six other girls in the community, as she and other parents were concerned that the girls were rapidly losing their voices. Using the Friendship Theme and Activity Guide, the facilitator assisted the girls in discussing peer conflicts and dilemmas and developing strategies to respond to peer problems. In one example, girls reported being bothered by classmates who asked them to pass a note along to another classmate, or to show them test answers. They didn't want to pass notes or cheat but, individually, they were at a loss for an adequate response. Together they brainstormed ideas and determined they could simply say, "I don't pass notes," or "I don't share test answers" in a calm, matter-of-fact manner. The facilitator stated that, "Their own ideas were incredible; they were specific, and they reported success with their solutions. The role-plays were very powerful. [The girls] felt they could speak for themselves. Developmentally, if you get it at the right time, it doesn't take that much for them to find their voices."

Body Image

A striking result was the significant positive increase in perceived body image evident in the research because just two units of the 10-week research curriculum focused on body image. So much of a girl's identity is focused on how she looks (American Association of University Women, 1994). These results suggest that the Girls Circle body image theme and activities can promote girls' rethinking and reshaping their own ideas and expectations regarding identity and body image.

Body image is the mental representation you hold of your physical appearance. Negative body image can lead to eating disorders (Cash & Lavallee, 1997), depression, anxiety, sexual difficulties, poor self-esteem (Cash, 1990), and increased suicide risk (Eaton, Lowry, Brener, Galuska, & Crosby, 2005). Perception of your physical appearance has been consistently recognized to be the number-one factor in predicting self-esteem (Harter, 2000). Current research indicates that girls as young as 8 to 9 years of age have negative views of being overweight and high levels of body image dissatisfaction (Hill, 1993; Koff & Reirdan, 1991; Rolland, Farnhill, & Griffiths, 1997). O'Dea and Abraham's (2000) results were consistent with previous research in regard to positive changes in body image and intervention programs.

At the middle school in southern California, Girls Circle participants wrote to their facilitators (a classroom teacher and a trained parent volunteer): "I learned to love myself more and to be more appreciative of my body and myself" and "You're beautiful no matter what." Seventh-grade Girls Circle participants at a girls' camp in Pennsylvania wrote about their experiences to their facilitator, a camp counselor. After experiencing the body image theme and activities sessions, they wrote: "I will pay attention to my body and myself. I won't let people say 'you look ugly' . . . ," "I have learned to not threaten my body . . . don't go on diets," and "I learned to be kind and take care of myself."

This author's own experience facilitating dozens of Girls Circles consistently suggests that adolescent girls feel uncomfortable in their bodies, especially when receiving uninvited or unwanted stares, comments, evaluations, and overt and covert messages related to physical attractiveness or sexuality. Having a safe arena for talking about these difficult experiences is a great relief for girls because they recognize they are not alone and their feelings are shared by others. They gain an opportunity to observe the cultural conditions within which females grow up, and a chance to strengthen a positive, self-defined evaluation of their physical being.

Perceived Social Support

Social support is defined as the experience or the perception of being cared for, valued, included, and/or guided by others, especially of your family, peers, and/or community members. Social support from peers, teachers, and parents has been recognized as a protective factor for children and teens (Benard, 2004). Figure 2.3 displays significant increases in perceived social support for girls participating in the Girls Circle program.

Girls' comments regarding their social growth include: "I have become more aware of people's feelings and how to look at a situation through their eyes,"

"I've learned how to talk to different people," "I will try to stand up for other girls if they are in trouble and definitely stand up for myself; I won't let boys push me around or call me names," "[liked] the unity that we had and the openness that we had," and "I have people that I trust and understand." In the highest security detention facility for girls 12 to 22 years of age, in Ventura, California, girls participating in Girls Circle offered comments such as: "I learned that everyone goes through something during their lifetime," "I learned that it's okay to open up around others," "I really appreciate this group and I'm glad that I feel comfortable with these girls in the circle," "I can sit back and listen to girls and hear what their saying instead of judging them," and "[I learned] that I'm not alone on how I feel."

A facilitator at a juvenile detention center in Ohio writes, "It is amazing how the Girls Circle has changed the relationships among our girls. They are even talking more confidently about themselves. Where we used to hear all negative comments from some of our girls, they are starting to realize they actually do like themselves."

A residential treatment facility for girls in delinquency in Nebraska integrated the Girls Circle model into its group treatment approach. Where there had been regular physical altercations between girls prior to implementation, staff reported a drop to only one such incident in the 5 months since the Girls Circle model began. Staff also reported an increase in level of staff rapport and morale, as tensions and stress appeared to be reducing in the setting.

At the mountain camp in Pennsylvania, mentioned previously, girls utilized the REF approach from their Friendship Girls Circle experience to manage peer conflicts outside of group. In one instance, some of the girls struggled with a new camper whom they found to be mean and intimidating. The girls considered how to be true to themselves yet inclusive of the new girl. Applying the REF criteria, they discovered various opportunities and ways to see things from her perspective, show kindness, and be clear about their own limits. "They tried and tried and, gradually, through listening to her, and by talking authentically, they gained compassion," stated their facilitator.

In a replicate and extension study in 2005, 49 girls, ages 11 to 17 years, from across the United States participated in Girls Circle support groups for 10 weeks. As shown in Figure 2.4, this study found significant increases in self-efficacy and body image (Rough & Matthews, 2005).

Positive increases in perceived social support approached significant levels. The mean score for Pre-MSPSS was 65.71, with a standard deviation of 16.19, and the mean score for Post-MSPSS was 67.16, with a standard deviation of 15.33. One possible explanation is that the participants of the second study

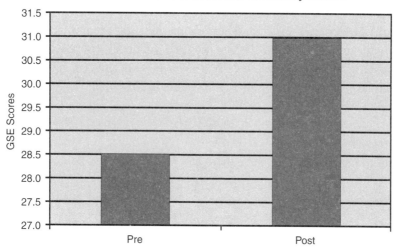

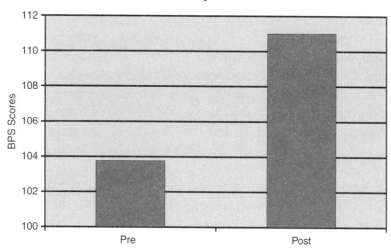

Figure 2.4   Replicate Study Results

(2005) revealed pretest scores as high as those achieved at the posttest with the initial group of girls. Perhaps the second group of girls entered the study with a higher baseline of perceived social support. Complete analysis is underway at this time.

Irvine (2005) looked at the impact of the Girls Circle model for court-involved girls in multiple juvenile justice settings nationally. Results were significant in all three areas, with more likely gains in perceived social support for girls in the legal system.

While girls' responses and feedback about their experiences cover a wide range of topics and vary according to program feedback processes, there are many common responses regarding their overall experiences. The following words might best convey what girls say about Girls Circle:

> I would tell my friends to join up [with Girls Circle] because it's so much fun and you can just be yourself. (10th grader)
>
> It's such a good feeling to come there and just relax; I can be myself there. (10th grader)
>
> I notice I understand my friends more now. (7th grader)

CONCLUSIONS

Social relationships are vital to girls' growth and development. Beyond family connections, friendships offer companionship, safety, security, social protection, motivation to participate, positive self-identity, and connection to culture and community. Close friendships can mitigate effects of hardship, scapegoating or victimization, and act as a buffer against depression, anxiety, and loneliness. Humor, shared experiences, and mutuality offer meaning and give pleasure, aspects of a balanced and healthy lifestyle. Having positive relationships, especially good friends, is of great value to adolescents, and has significant impact on overall well-being.

Although most girls have friends, friendships are highly unstable during adolescent years, and girls regularly witness or experience cliques, betrayal, exclusion, and competition for status in peer groups and with boys. Some girls are randomly assigned to outcast status, while others struggle with learning styles or personalities that are ineffective in establishing or sustaining reciprocal relationships. In and out of classrooms, girls find themselves in settings they consider emotionally unsafe. These settings are dependent on persons as much as place. When girls feel unsafe, or unwelcome, their moods, attention, confidence, body image, and academic performance, peer relationships, and development of competencies suffer. Unfortunately, most girls report feelings of concern about their emotional safety, including, and often, among each other. Girls who experience sexual and physical abuse have profound needs for environmental safety and heightened difficulties trusting others.

Emotional and physical safety are basic needs for every growing child and adolescent (Goleman, 1995). When these needs are met, girls have a greater capacity to learn; are willing to take important developmental risks; and develop skills, talents, and interests. Consequently, educational settings and institutions serving girls are turning increasingly toward approaches that address and improve emotional safety. Recognition of girls' gender-relevant, developmental needs for connection improves the outcomes for girls' health-related behaviors and experiences.

Prevention programs aimed at improving peer connections, reducing bullying, increasing positive ethnic and gender identity, and improving self-esteem have been mentioned.

Girls Circle is a research-based model that integrates gender, resiliency, and relationship-focused approaches with adolescent and early-adolescent girls across varied settings. Increases in self-efficacy, perceived body image, and social connection suggest that this model may be useful for broad prevention programs as well as targeted groups. In meaningful ways, Girls Circle promotes girls' involvement, and influences them to explore and shape their journeys through adolescence. The empowerment methods "meet" girls where they are and encourage ownership for participants. Its basic premise rests in RCT, acknowledging the significance of healthy connections as the touchstone for all development.

Girls Circle evaluations that incorporate control groups are underway. Qualitative studies and longer-term evaluations will enable assessment of Girls Circle as a prevention or intervention method over the adolescent span. The impact of the program for girls in the juvenile justice system is being evaluated for recidivism rates as well as curriculum-specific outcomes such as social connection and self-efficacy.

An important question is how to implement a Girls Circle program in large school settings, where emotional safety is of major concern to girls. Groups generally consist of 6 to 12 girls, meaning there are logistical challenges to implementing circles broadly as a prevention method; nevertheless, the setting provides the greatest potential of access for girls. As a prevention and intervention model for promoting girls' growth, Girls Circle helps girls to resolve the relational impasse: they can speak truthfully, offer and receive caring and attention, address relevant topics, experience genuine acceptance and belonging, and grow healthfully toward young womanhood.

If you have additional questions or comments about the Girls Circle model, facilitator trainings, theme and activity guides, ongoing research, consultations, and other questions, please contact:

Giovanna Taormina, Executive Director
Beth Hossfeld, MFT, Associate Director
Girls Circle Association, Project of the Tides Center
458 Christensen Lane
Cotati, CA 94931
Phone: 707-794-9477
Fax: 707-794-9938
E-mail: girlscircle@yahoo.com
Web site: www.girlscircle.com

ADDENDUM

Girls Circle is approaching a best practice gender-responsive model for working with girls in the juvenile justice system, as well as in prevention and early intervention settings. Roa, Irvine, and Cervantez (2007) evaluated the Girls Circle model in 2007, with data from 278 girls of diverse ethnicities in nineteen cities across the United States. Participant girls' data revealed significant *increases* in school attachment, communicating needs to adults, self-efficacy, body image, and peer selection satisfaction. Importantly, significant *decreases* were found in self-harming behaviors and in rates of alcohol use. Researchers concluded that Girls Circle is a promising model for girls in multiple locations (i.e. education, juvenile justice) and is a flexible model to meet the needs of a wide range of girls (i.e. girls with and without school problems, foster youth, LGBT girls, group home residents, and girls in the juvenile justice system). A new evaluation will focus on juvenile justice administrative data to understand how Girls Circle participation shapes re-offense patterns for girls in the juvenile justice system. A separate study will focus on pre- and post-participation survey data from community-based organizations serving girls in school and justice settings, analyzing participant girls' responses with those of girls in comparison groups.

REFERENCES

American Association of University Women. (1994). *Shortchanging girls, short-changing America, executive summary.* AAUW Educational Foundation.

Bandura, A. (1995). Exercise of personal and collective efficacy in changing societies. In A. Bandura (Ed.), *Self-efficacy in changing societies* (pp. 1–45). New York: Cambridge University Press.

Belgrave, F. Z., Reed, M. C., Plybon, L. E., Butler, D. S., Allison, K. W., & Davis, T. (2004). An evaluation of Sisters of Nia: A cultural program for African American girls. *Journal of Black Psychology, 30*(3), 329–343.

Benard, B. (2004). *Resiliency, what we have learned.* San Francisco: WestEd.

Berscheid, E., Walster, E., & Bohrnstedt, G. (1973). Body image: The happy American body—A survey report. *Psychology Today,* 119–131.

Bradley, R. H., & Corwyn, R. F. (2001). Home environment and behavioral development during early adolescence: The mediating and moderating roles of self-efficacy beliefs. *Merrill-Palmer Quarterly, 37*(2), 165–187.

Brashares, A. (Book author), Ephron, D. (Screenwriter), & Kwapis, K. (Director). (2005). *Sisterhood of the traveling pants* [Motion picture]. United States: Warner Bros. Retrieved July 27, 2005, from www.the-numbers.com/movies.

Brown, L. M. (2003). *Girlfighting: Betrayal and rejection among girls.* New York: New York University Press.

Brown, L. M., & Gilligan, C. (1992). *Meeting at the crossroads.* New York: Ballantine Books.

Cash, T. F. (1990). The psychology of physical appearance: Aesthetics, attributes, and images. In T. F Cash & T. Pruzinsky (Eds.), *Body images: Development, deviance, and change* (pp. 51–79). New York: Guilford Press.

Cash, T. F., & Lavallee, D. M. (1997). Cognitive-behavioral body image therapy: Extended evidence of the efficacy of a self-directed program. *Journal of Rational-Emotive and Cognitive-Behavior Therapy, 15,* 282–294.

Conklin, D. L. (2002). Feminist theory-based girls' group (Doctoral dissertation, Chicago School of Professional Psychology). *Dissertation Abstracts International, 62,* 8-B.

Dekovic, M. (1999). Risk and protective factors in the development of problem behavior during adolescence. *Journal of Youth and Adolescence, 28*(6), 667.

Eaton, D. K., Lowry, R., Brener, N. D., Galuska, D. A., & Crosby, A. E. (2005). Associations of body mass index and perceived weight with suicide ideation and suicide attempts among U.S. high school students. *Archives of Pediatric and Adolescent Medicine, 159,* 513–519.

Espelage, D. L., & Swearer, S. M. (2003). Research on school bullying and victimization: What have we learned and where do we go from here? *School Psychology Review, 32*(3), 365–383.

Girls Circle Association, A Project of the Tides Center (2007). *Girls circle facilitator activity guides.* Cotati, CA: Author. Available from www.girlscircle.com/materials.

Goleman, D. (1995). *Emotional intelligence: Why it can matter more than IQ.* New York: Bantam Books.

Hardwicke, C., & Reed, N. (Writers). (2003). *Thirteen* [Motion Picture]. Retrieved July 27, 2005, from www.the-numbers.com/movies.

Harter, S. (2000). Is self-esteem only skin deep? *Reclaiming Children and Youth, 9*(3), 133.

Hartwig, H. J., & Myers, J. E. (2003). A different approach: Applying a wellness paradigm to adolescent female delinquents and offenders. *Journal of Mental Health Counseling, 25*(1), 57–75.

Hill, A. (1993). Pre-adolescent dieting: Implications for eating disorders. *International Review of Psychiatry, 5,* 87–100.

Hoover, J. H., Oliver, R., & Hazier, R. J. (1992). Bullying: Perceptions of adolescent victims in the Midwestern USA. *School Psychology International, 13,* 5–16.

Hossfeld, B., & Taormina, G. (2006). *Girls Circle facilitator manual: Promoting resiliency in adolescent girls* (1st ed.). Cotati, CA: Girls Circle Association, A Project of the Tides Center.

Hudley, C. (2001). The role of culture in prevention research. *Prevention and Treatment, 4.* Retrieved July 26, 2005, from www.journals.apa.org/prevention /volume4/pre0040005c.html.

Irvine, A. (2005). *Girls Circle: Summary of outcomes for girls in the juvenile justice system.* Report submitted by Ceres Policy Research to the Girls Circle Association. Santa Cruz, CA: Ceres Policy Research.

Jordan, J. (Ed.). (1997). *Women's growth in diversity: More writings from the Stone Center.* New York: Guilford Press.

Kilpatrick-Demaray, M., & Kerres-Malecki, C. (2003). Importance ratings of socially supportive behaviors by children and adolescents. *School Psychology Review, 32*(1), 108–131.

Koff, E., & Reirdan, J. (1991). Perceptions of weight and attitudes towards eating in early adolescent girls. *Journal of Adolescent Health, 12,* 307–312.

Laszlo, A. M. (2001). Effects of group intervention on the self-esteem of sixth and seventh grade girls. *Dissertation Abstracts International: Section B: Sciences and Engineering, 6,* 6140.

Leadbeater, B. J., & Way, N. (Eds.). (1996). *Urban girls: Resisting stereotypes, creating identities.* New York: New York University Press.

LeCroy, C. W. (2004). Evaluation of an empowerment program for early adolescent girls. *Adolescence, 39,* 427–441.

Leff, S. S., Power, T. J., Manz, P. H., Costigan, T. E., & Nabors, L. A. (2001). School-based aggression prevention programs for young children: Current status and implications for violence prevention. *School Psychology Review, 30,* 344–353.

Maxwell, K. (2002). Friends: The role of peer influence across adolescent risk behaviors. *Journal of Youth and Adolescence, 31*(4), 267–277.

Miller, J. B. (1991). The development of women's sense of self. In J. Jordan, A. Kaplan, J. B. Miller, I. P. Stiver, J. L. Surrey. (Eds.), *Women's growth in connection: Writings from the Stone Center* (pp. 11–26). New York: Guilford Press.

Nash, B. (2005). *The numbers: Box office data, movie stars, idle speculation.* Retrieved July 25, 2005, from www.the-numbers.com/index.php.

National Youth Violence Prevention Resource Center. (2005, July). *Bullying statistics.* Retrieved July 11, 2005, from www.safeyouth.org/scripts/teens /bullying.asp.

O'Dea, J. A., & Abraham, S. (2000). Improving the body image, eating attitudes, and behaviors of young male and female adolescents: A new educational approach that focuses on self-esteem. *International Journal of Eating Disorders, 28,* 43–57.

Odgers, C. L., & Moretti, M. M. (2002). Aggressive and antisocial girls: Research update and challenges. *International Journal of Forensic Mental Health, 1*(2), 103–119.

Office of Juvenile Justice and Delinquency Prevention. (1998, October). *Guiding principles for promising female programming: An inventory of best practices.* Washington, DC: Author.

Olweus, D. (1993). *Bullying at school: What we know and what we can do.* Cambridge, MA: Blackwell.

Patrick, H., Ryan, A. M., Alfeld-Liro, C., Fredericks, J. A., Hruda, L. Z., & Eccles, J. S. (1999). Adolescents' commitment to developing talent: The role of peers in continuing motivation for sports and the arts. *Journal of Youth and Adolescence, 28,* 741–763.

Patton, P., & Morgan, M. (2001). *How to implement Oregon's guidelines for effective gender-responsive programming for girls.* Oregon Criminal Justice Commission, Juvenile Crime Prevention Program and the Oregon Commission on Children and Families.

Phillips, L. (1998). *The girls report: What we know and need to know about growing up female.* New York: National Council on Research for Women.

Pipher, M. (1994). *Reviving Ophelia: Saving the selves of adolescent girls.* New York: Ballantine Books.

Pleydon, A., & Schner, J. (2001). Female adolescent friendship and delinquent behavior. *Adolescence, 36,* 189.

Roa, J., Irvine, A., & Cervantez, K., (2007). *Girls Circle national research project: Evaluation results year one.* Santa Cruz, CA: Ceres Policy Research.

Rolland, K., Farnhill, D., & Griffiths, R. A. (1997). Body figure perceptions and eating attitudes among Australian school children aged 8 to 12 years. *International Journal of Eating Disorders, 21,* 273–278.

Rotheram, M. J., Dopkins, S., Sabate, N., & Lightfoot, M. (1996). Personal and ethnic identity, values, and self-esteem among Black and Latino adolescent girls. In B. J. Leadbeater, & N. Way (Eds.), *Urban girls: Resisting stereotypes, creating identities* (pp. 35–52). New York: New York University Press.

Rough, J., & Matthews, G. (2005). *Understanding the intervention of girls circle on friendship quality and self-efficacy: A replication and extension.* Unpublished manuscript, Dominican University of California, San Rafael.

Royse, D. (1998). Scouting and Girl Scouts curriculum as interventions: Effects on adolescents' self-esteem. *Adolescence, 33,* 159–168.

Schoenberg, J., Riggins, T., & Salmond, K. (2003). *Feeling safe: What girls say* [Executive summary]. New York: Girl Scouts of the United States of America, Girl Scouts Research Institute.

Schwarzer, R., & Scholz, U. (2000, August). *Cross-cultural assessment of coping resources: The general perceived self-efficacy scale.* Paper presented at the First Asian Congress of Health Psychology: Health Psychology and Culture, Tokyo, Japan.

Simmons, R. (2002). *Odd girl out: The hidden culture of aggression in girls.* Orlando, FL: Harcourt.

Steese, S., Dollete, M., Phillips, W., Matthews, G., Hossfeld, E., & Taormina, G. (Spring 2006). Understanding Girls Circle as an intervention on perceived social support, body image, self-efficacy, locus of control, and self-esteem. *Adolescence, 41,* 55–74.

Storch, E. A., Masia-Warner, C. L., & Brassard, M. R. (2003). The relationship of peer victimization to social anxiety and loneliness in adolescence. *Child Study Journal, 33*(1), 1–18.

United Way of the Bay Area. (2003). *Girls on the edge: A report on girls in the juvenile justice system.* San Francisco: Author.

Vaux, A. (1988). *Social support: Theory, research, and intervention.* New York: England Praeger.

Van Schoiack-Edstrom, L., Frey, K. S., & Beland, K. (2002). Changing adolescents' attitudes about relational and physical aggression: An early evaluation of a school-based intervention. *School Psychology Review, 31,* 201–216.

Waggoner, I. R. (1999). Cognitive-behavior therapy and cognitive therapy for body image awareness in sixth grade females (Doctoral dissertation, Auburn University, 1999). *Dissertation Abstracts International, 59,* 11-A.

Ward, J. V. (2000). *The skin we're in: Teaching our children to be emotionally strong, socially smart, and spiritually connected.* New York: Free Press.

Wentzel, K. R. (1998). Social relationships and motivation in middle school: The role of parents, teachers, and peers. *Journal of Educational Psychology, 90*(2), 202–209.

Wentzel, K. R., Barry, C. M., & Caldwell, K. A. (2004). Friendships in middle school: Influences on motivation and school adjustment. *Journal of Educational Psychology, 96*(2), 159–203.

Wiseman, R. (2003). *Queen bees and wannabees: Helping your daughter survive cliques, gossip, boyfriends, and other realities of adolescence.* New York: Crown.

Wiseman, R. (Book Author), Fey, T. (Screenwriter), & Waters, M. (Director). (2004). *Mean girls* [Motion Picture]. United States: Paramount Pictures. Retrieved July 27, 2005, from www.the-numbers.com/movies.

Zimet, G. D., Dahlem, N. W., Zimet, S. G., & Farley, G. K. (1998). The multidimensional scale of perceived social support. *Journal of Personality Assessment, 52,* 30–41.

Chapter 3 ——————————————————————————

A DISSONANCE-BASED INTERVENTION FOR THE PREVENTION OF EATING DISORDERS AND OBESITY

HEATHER SHAW AND ERIC STICE

One in ten adolescent females experiences threshold or subthreshold bulimia nervosa (Lewinsohn, Streigel-Moore, & Seeley, 2000; Stice, Killen, Hayward, & Taylor, 1998). Characterized by a chronic course, medical complications, and functional impairment, this disorder increases the risk for future onset of obesity, depression, suicide attempts, anxiety disorders, substance abuse, and health problems (Johnson, Cohen, Kasen, & Brook, 2002; Stice, Cameron, Killen, Hayward, & Taylor, 1999; Wilson, Becker, & Heffernan, 2003). Unfortunately, less than 25% of individuals with this disorder receive treatment (Johnson et al., 2002) and only 30% of patients assigned to the treatment of choice show symptom remission that persists for at least 4 weeks (Agras, Walsh, Fairburn, Wilson, & Kraemer, 2000).

Obesity is associated with an increased risk for subsequent death from all causes, coronary heart disease, atherosclerotic cerebrovascular disease, and colorectal cancer, as well as serious medical problems, including hyperlipidemia, hypertension, gallbladder disease, and diabetes mellitus (Calle, Thun, Petrelli, Rodriguez, & Heath, 1999; Pietrobelli et al., 1998). Obesity is credited with almost 400,000 deaths annually in the United States (Mokdad, Marks, Stroup, & Gerberding, 2004). Moreover, obesity is associated with lower educational attainment, poverty, and lower marriage rates (Dietz, 1998). It is estimated that the economic burden of obesity is as high as $100 billion per year (Wolf & Colditz, 1998). The prevalence of obesity has increased sharply over the last several decades; approximately 65% of adults are currently overweight or obese (Hedley et al., 2004). The prevalence of obesity has risen even more sharply among adolescents and young adults (Hedley et al., 2004; Ogden, Flegal, Carroll, & Johnson, 2002), which is alarming because approximately 70% of obese adolescents will be obese adults (Magarey, Daniels, Boulton, & Cockington, 2003).

Accordingly, the need to develop prevention programs for eating disorders and obesity has been recognized as imperative. However, although numerous prevention programs have been evaluated in controlled trials, only a few have produced intervention effects for eating disorder symptoms. A meta-analysis found that only 6 of the 38 eating disorder prevention programs that have been evaluated produced reductions in current or future symptoms that persisted over follow-up, which ranged from 1 to 24 months (Stice & Shaw, 2004). Similarly, of the numerous obesity prevention programs that have been evaluated in controlled trials over the last several decades, very few have produced weight-gain prevention effects. A meta-analytic review of obesity prevention trials (and cardiovascular disease prevention programs promoting weight control) involving children, adolescents, or young adult college students (Stice, Shaw, & Marti, 2006) found that of 38 published prevention trials, only 7 produced significantly lower rates of weight gain in the intervention condition relative to the control condition (Eliakim, Makowski, Brasel, & Cooper, 2000; Killen et al., 1988; Lionis et al., 1991; Manios, Kafatos, & Mamalakis, 1998; Robinson, 1999; Stice & Ragan, 2002; Tamir et al., 1990).

One intervention that appears to be promising in preventing both eating disorders and obesity onset is a cognitive dissonance-based intervention developed by our research group. This program has received empirical support in controlled trials conducted by our lab and has been replicated by other labs. First, three controlled trials found that participants in the dissonance intervention showed significantly greater reductions in thin-ideal internalization, body dissatisfaction, negative affect, and bulimic symptoms than waitlist controls, with most effects persisting through 6-month follow-up (Stice, Mazotti, Weibel, & Agras, 2000; Stice, Shaw, Burton, & Wade, 2006; Stice, Trost, & Chase, 2003). Another controlled trial found that compared to a healthy weight intervention, the dissonance intervention resulted in significantly greater reductions in thin-ideal internalization and body dissatisfaction (Stice, Chase, Stormer, & Appel, 2001). Second, this intervention is one of only two programs that produced a prophylactic effect—it actually prevented significant increases in bulimic symptoms (Stice et al., 2000, 2006). The intervention has also been found to impact two ecologically valid outcomes: mental health service utilization and risk for obesity onset (Stice et al., 2006). The evidence that this intervention resulted in a threefold decrease in risk for obesity onset may be the most important finding, as most obesity prevention programs have not reduced obesity onset (Story, 1999). This is important from a public health standpoint, as it suggests that a single, brief intervention may produce positive effects for both eating pathology and obesity.

Three independent labs have also replicated the positive effects produced by the dissonance intervention in controlled trials (Becker, Smith, & Ciao, 2006 ; Green, Scott, Diyankova, Gasser, & Pederson, 2005; Matusek, Wendt, & Wiseman, 2004). This is noteworthy for two reasons. First, we only shared the script for the dissonance intervention with these research groups—we did not provide direct training in the delivery of the intervention or supervise facilitators. The fact that these researchers were able to deliver the intervention in a manner that produced significant intervention effects suggests that this intervention can be effectively delivered by a range of facilitators with minimal training—a criterion for effectiveness research. Second, two of these studies found that the dissonance intervention produced superior effects to alternative prevention programs, which is the most rigorous test of an intervention trial.

According to the American Psychological Association (1995), to be considered efficacious an intervention has to have produced significantly stronger effects than a waitlist or measurement-only control condition in at least two trials conducted by independent labs, and significantly stronger effects than a placebo or alternative treatment. The dissonance intervention has now received enough empirical support to be termed *efficacious,* setting it apart from virtually all other eating disorder prevention programs.

In sum, the dissonance program has produced intervention effects for eating pathology in four controlled trials in our lab and three trials conducted by independent labs, was superior to four alternative interventions (and assessment-only control conditions), produced effects that persisted through 1-year follow-up, and resulted in a threefold decrease in the risk for future onset of obesity. In the next section, we describe the theoretical development behind the dissonance intervention, as well as specific instructions on how to deliver the intervention.

THE DISSONANCE INTERVENTION

Development

To date, the majority of eating disorder prevention programs have been psycho educational, and have met with limited success (Stice & Shaw, 2004). Therefore, we attempted to develop an alternative approach to producing attitudinal and behavioral change that could result in the prevention of eating disorders. Clinical experience suggested that a dissonance-based approach was a promising technique. Developed by social psychologists, dissonance theory states that holding inconsistent cognitions creates psychological discomfort that motivates people to alter their cognitions to produce greater consistency (Festinger, 1957). In standard induced-compliance experiments, participants are induced to act contrary to a current attitude, which generates cognitive dissonance that leads to an attitudinal shift to reduce the inconsistency (Leippe, 1994). That is, when participants take a counterattitudinal stance, they show attitudinal shift toward the new perspective. Participants must feel that they voluntarily assumed the counterattitudinal position; otherwise, their inconsistent behavior is attributed to the demands of the situation and no attitudinal change results. As dissonance has been found to be an effective route to producing attitudinal change in lab experiments, we thought it might be useful to adapt this technique for use in eating disorder prevention programs.

The dual pathway model (Stice, 1994) provided the theoretical framework within which the dissonance approach could be applied to eating disorder prevention. This etiologic model posits that thin-ideal internalization and perceived pressure to be thin leads to body dissatisfaction, also affected by elevated body mass, and mediated by dieting and negative affect, which then predicts bulimic pathology. This model and constituent risk factors have received considerable empirical support (e.g., Stice & Agras, 1998; Stice, Presnell, & Bearman, 2001; Vogeltanz-Holm et al., 2000; Wertheim, Koerner, & Paxton, 2001).

We reasoned that if we could induce at-risk females who had internalized the thin-ideal to voluntarily argue against it, the extent to which they endorsed this ideal would be reduced. Such a dissonance-based intervention resembles strategic self-presentation interventions, which also use role-plays to produce attitude and behavior change. These interventions have been shown to impact an array of behaviors, ranging from smoking onset to coping with chronic illnesses (Killen, 1985; Leake, Friend, & Wadhwa, 1999). In the dissonance intervention, adolescent girls and young women who subscribe to the thin-ideal are encouraged to voluntarily critique it through a series of verbal, written, and behavioral exercises. These activities are theorized to produce cognitive dissonance, which reduces the extent to which they subscribe to the thin-ideal, resulting in consequent improvements in body dissatisfaction, negative affect, dieting, and eating disorder symptoms.

Thus, the overarching goal of this intervention is to stimulate the participants to speak, write, or act in a way that is contrary to the thin-ideal. To induce cognitive dissonance, it is vital for participants, rather than group leaders, to generate the costs of the thin-ideal. In addition, from a theoretical perspective, participants should never focus on any benefits of the thin-ideal, because this will only undermine the dissonance induced by the intervention. It is also important that group leaders not embellish this intervention in any way (e.g., discuss a past history of an eating disorder), as research indicates that this could also compromise the goals of the intervention.

Several general principles guided the development of the dissonance intervention. First, we minimized didactic presentation because psychoeducational interventions appear to be less effective than interventions that actively engage participants (Stice & Shaw, 2004). Second, we included in-session exercises that require participants to apply the skills taught in the intervention to facilitate skill acquisition. Third, we relied on between-session homework to reinforce the skills taught in the sessions and help participants learn how to apply these skills. Fourth, we used motivational enhancement exercises (Miller, 1983) to maximize motivation to use the new skills (e.g., we reviewed costs of body image concerns as a group). Finally, we included group activities to foster social support and group cohesion.

We have taken an iterative approach to our program development, wherein information is gleaned from randomized trials regarding how the program can be improved and used to refine the program for the next evaluation (Coie et al., 1993). Thus, we have collected qualitative input from participants and facilitators regarding our program throughout the research process, and then use this information to guide revisions of the intervention in each successive trial. This has helped ensure that the program is positively received and has likely contributed to its success.

Description

In this section, we describe the dissonance intervention. It should be noted that the version of the program that has been evaluated thus far includes three 1-hour sessions, but a fourth session was developed for the effectiveness trial that is currently underway. The three-session version of the intervention is virtually identical to the four-session version. The description provided here is adapted from a training manual that was developed for practitioners (e.g., school nurses and counselors) interested in delivering the intervention.

Structure of Intervention

Intervention groups consist of a female group leader, who can be a school counselor, psychologist, nurse, or teacher. It is often useful to include a coleader, who can be a participant from a previous group, to help facilitate the sessions (e.g., pass out material and write participant responses on a whiteboard). Experience suggests that the optimal group size is approximately 6 to 8 participants, as this ensures that all group members will be able to participate verbally. The group meets for four consecutive weeks in 1-hour sessions.

Common Problems

Attaining participant compliance in completing homework assignments can be difficult, especially assignments that seem "school-like." Participants' adherence to between-session assignments depends on whether leaders empha-size the importance of completing these exercises and how well leaders track the assignments in subsequent sessions. Contacting participants via email or phone a day before the scheduled session can help prompt participants to com-plete their assignments and bring them to their next session. Additionally, all home exercise forms should be placed in folders, which should be distributed to each participant at the first session.

Participants often are extremely invested in the thin-ideal and have difficulty letting go of this pursuit. However, it is important not to allow participants to argue for the thin-ideal, as this will only solidify their position further. Always keep in mind that the primary goal of the intervention is to get the participants to criticize and challenge the thin-ideal. Group leaders should encourage other group members to speak out against the thin-ideal or pose counterarguments to pro thin-ideal statements voiced by participants. Experience indicates that the program does not work if leaders, rather than participants critique the thin-ideal. It is also important for group leaders to keep self-disclosure to a minimum, to make sure that participants can maximize the time spent critiquing the thin-ideal.

It is necessary to distinguish between the thin-ideal and the healthy-ideal. The thin-ideal is about appearing ultraslender. People may be willing to engage in very unhealthy behaviors to attain this slenderness, including laxative abuse, and go to extreme ends, such as cosmetic surgery, to attain this ultra-slender look. In contrast, the healthy-ideal is about striving for a healthy body, which is typically nowhere near as slender as the thin-ideal, in part because muscle tissue is heavier than fat tissue. Further, individuals legitimately pur-suing the healthy-ideal do not engage in unhealthy weight control behaviors, such as fasting and laxative abuse.

It is also important to engage all participants during the group sessions. Al-though it is crucial to follow the manual closely, participants often get bored if group leaders consistently read directly from the script. Thus, we recommend becoming familiar with the main points to minimize the extent to which it is necessary to read from the script. Maintaining eye contact with participants during the sessions helps encourage discussion as well. Be sure to look at each participant and try to draw her in to the discussions, paying special attention to those who are less talkative or reluctant to speak up. If one or two participants tend to dominate the discussion, call on other participants to share their opin-ions. We recommend going around the entire group so that each group member participates in each main activity (change the order so the same person does not always have to go first). Try to use humor when possible, be relaxed, smile and laugh when appropriate, and listen carefully to what participants are saying.

When a participant shares personal information or discusses her difficulties with body image, make empathetic statements (e.g., "Wow, it sounds like you're really struggling with this," "That must have been hurtful when your father made that comment to you about your weight"). While it is extremely important to stay on track and cover the necessary information for each session, participants want to feel heard and understood.

Therapist Training

It is vital for group leaders to carefully read the guidelines for this program and to practice each activity (i.e., role-play) before attempting to lead a group. Experience indicates that participants quickly lose interest if the group leaders are not familiar with the activities and the flow of the sessions.

Guidelines

This curriculum has been demonstrated in several randomized clinical studies to be an effective prevention program for individuals at risk for eating disorders. Adherence to the study protocol is critical in obtaining positive outcome results.

It is particularly crucial for group leaders to manage the sessions effectively and make sure that *all listed exercises* are completed. It is sometimes necessary to tactfully interrupt particularly talkative individuals so that the group leader can move the group onto the next exercise in the manual.

If a participant misses a session, try to schedule a brief 15-minute minisession that covers the important points and exercises with them. We often do this right before the next session begins. Although this represents extra work for the facilitators, it helps to minimize missed sessions and communicates that each participant is important.

Session Descriptions

In the following sections, each of the four one-hour intervention sessions is described. For each session, information is provided on:

- Materials used for the session
- Topic areas to be covered
- Main procedural elements for group leaders to follow
- Assigned home exercises for the participants to complete between sessions

Throughout these sections, all handout names are enclosed in quotation marks (e.g., "Letter to Adolescent Girl Form"). Instructions to group leaders are presented in regular typeface. Verbal instructions that group leaders should say, or paraphrase, to participants are presented as extracts. Homework assignments can be found in Appendix A.

SESSION 1

Materials

Handout: "Letter to Adolescent Girl Form" (Exercise 1)

Handout: "Self-Affirmation Form" (Exercise 2)

Pictures of different body shapes from magazines

Flipchart and markers

Place all handouts in participants' folders.

Topic Areas

    I. Introduction (5 Minutes)

   II. Voluntary Commitment and Overview (2 Minutes)

 III. Definition and Origin of the Thin-Ideal (15 Minutes)

 IV. Costs Associated with Pursuing the Thin-Ideal (20 Minutes)

    V. Home Exercises (3 Minutes)

Session Overview

The focus of session 1 is to provide an overview and introduce participants to the rules and expectations of the group. This initial session is largely interactive, with discussions of the definition and origins of the thin-ideal, and costs associated with pursuing the thin-ideal. The importance of attendance and completing the home exercises is also stressed.

I. Introduction (5 Minutes)

Thanks for joining us. All of you decided to take part in these groups because of your body image concerns—an issue very common among girls/women.

This class is based on a study indicating that when women discussed the thin-ideal and how individuals can resist pressures to be thin, it improved how they felt about their bodies. This is probably because understanding the cultural pressures that contribute to body image and learning how to respond to them can help improve our body image.

The group leader begins by introducing herself to the group. Introductions include name, professional status, and personal information (e.g., something interesting or unique about themselves). The group leader asks the coleader (if available) and group members to introduce themselves.

> Let's get to know each other better. Can each of you tell us your name, where you're from (or grade level), and something unique or interesting about you?

Group leaders should spend a few moments with *each participant* to elicit specific information and show interest (e.g., How long have you been horseback riding? What kind of paintings do you do?).

II. Voluntary Commitment and Overview (2 Minutes)

Solicit voluntary commitment to participating in the class.

> The main idea in this class is that discussing the social pressures behind body dissatisfaction and how to respond to them will improve your body image. Experience suggests that people get the most out of these groups if they attend all four meetings, participate verbally, and complete all of the between meeting exercises. Are you willing to do this?

Go around the room and have *each participant* say she is willing to actively participate.

> During the four sessions we will:
>
> 1. *Define* the thin-ideal and explore its origin.
> 2. Examine the *costs* of pursuing this ideal.
> 3. Explore ways in which we can *resist* pressures to be thin.
> 4. Discuss how to *challenge* our personal body-related concerns.
> 5. Learn new ways to *talk more positively* about our bodies.
> 6. Talk about how we can *best respond to future pressures* to be thin.

Confidentiality

> In this class we will be talking about personal details of our lives. It is often difficult to trust others. We would like to ask that everything said in these groups remains confidential. Can everyone agree to this?

Attendance

It is important that you attend all four sessions of this group. If for some reason you need to miss a session, please let me know so a make-up session can be scheduled before the next session.

Group leaders should call or email participants the day before each session to remind them of the session and to bring any assignments they should have completed. If a participant must miss a session for any reason, please schedule a brief (15-minute) individual make-up session to discuss key points from the session and get the participant caught up before the next session. Ask her to complete the home exercises before the next session, too.

III. Definition and Origin of the Thin-Ideal (15 Minutes)

The group leader displays pictures from magazines, showing a variety of women of different shapes and sizes, on the table (there should be at least enough pictures for each participant to select one).

First, I would like each of you to choose one of these pictures that appeals to you.

Do not tell participants the purpose of this exercise—just ask them to pick one that is appealing to them.

Now that each of you has selected a picture, I want you to comment on what you notice about the picture and what it says about our society's view of women.

Seek a response from *each participant.*
Pose questions to the group and promote participation and collaboration on their responses. Promoting discussion is key—let participants talk, not group leaders.

Q: What are we told that the "perfect woman" looks like?

(Thin and attractive, a perfect body, toned, large-chested, tall, like a supermodel)
Focus the discussion on the thin part of the thin-ideal, though it is fine to note other aspects, such as clear complexion and white teeth. Note seemingly incompatible features, such as ultraslenderness and large breasts. Write down each of the qualities on a flipchart or whiteboard.

We call this look—this thin, toned, busty woman—"the thin-ideal."

Q: Has this thin-ideal always been the gold standard for feminine attractiveness?

(No, it has differed in other periods in history.)

Solicit examples of different beauty standards over time (e.g., Marilyn Monroe, figures in the Renaissance period, Twiggy, supermodels of today).

Q: Where did this ideal come from? What are the origins of the thin-ideal?

(For example, media, fashion industry, diet/weight-loss industry)

Q: How is the thin-ideal perpetuated?

(For example, media: television shows, magazines; diet/weight-loss industry)

Q: How do thin-ideal messages from your family, peers, and dating partners affect how you feel?

Discuss participant's' personal experiences in these areas and the impact on their feelings and self-worth.

Q: How do thin-ideal messages from the media impact the way you feel about your body? What are your thoughts and feelings about your own body when you look at the magazine picture of the thin-ideal?

(Feel inadequate because they do not look like a model; dislike their own bodies; have negative moods)

Q: What does our culture tell us will happen if we look like the thin-ideal?

(We will be accepted, loved, happy, successful, and wealthy.)

Differentiate the thin-ideal from the healthy-ideal if they say you are healthier if you conform to the thin-ideal.

Q: Are the expected benefits of achieving the thin-ideal realistic?

(No; they will likely have little impact.)

Be careful not to convey that trying to be healthy is bad; briefly make a distinction between the healthy-ideal and the thin-ideal (avoiding obesity and resulting health consequences versus striving for an unrealistic appearance by whatever means necessary). However, do not describe (or allow participants to discuss) the benefits of thinness in general or give the impression that the thin-ideal is close to the healthy ideal (i.e., it is possible to be well within the healthy weight range, but not meet the cultural standards for the ultra thin-ideal).

IV. Costs Associated with Pursuing the Thin-Ideal (20 Minutes)

We've discussed the thin-ideal and where it comes from; now let's think about the costs involved with this ideal.

Solicit participation from group.

Q: What are the costs of pursing the thin-ideal for the individual?

(For example, decreased self-worth; expensive; physically and mentally exhaustion; danger to themselves)

Q: How does the thin-ideal negatively influence people's health?

(Often negatively, as it encourages unhealthy weight management techniques, depression, and anxiety)

Q: What are the costs for society?

(Increased mental health care costs, and promotes culture of discontent)

Q: Who benefits from the thin ideal?

(The diet industry, media, and fashion industry)

Q: Are you one of the individuals who benefit from the thin-ideal?

(For example, are you a media executive, a supermodel, the founder of a diet program?)

Q: Given these costs, does it make sense to pursue the thin-ideal?

(No.)

Make sure that *each participant* makes a public statement against the thin-ideal at this stage (and anywhere else possible).

V. Home Exercises (3 Minutes)

Remind group participants of the home-based assignment for the next session.

Now that we have begun discussing costs of the thin-ideal, would you be willing to write a letter to an adolescent girl who is struggling with body image concerns about the costs associated with pursuing the thin ideal? Think of as many costs as you can. Feel free to work with a friend or family member in generating ideas or use any of the ones we have discussed today. Please bring this letter to our next meeting so we can discuss your responses and feelings about this assignment.

Hand out "Letter to Adolescent Girl Form" (Exercise 1).
Hand out "Self-Affirmation Form" (Exercise 2).

SESSION 2

Prep

Email/call each participant before this class to remind her to complete each homework exercise.

Materials

Handout: "Verbal Challenge Form" (Exercise 3)

Handout: "Top-10 List Form" (Exercise 4)

Place all handouts in participants' folders.

Topic Areas

    I. Letter to an Adolescent Girl Debriefing (15 Minutes)

    II. Self-Affirmation Exercise Debriefing (10 Minutes)

    III. Role-Plays to Discourage Pursuit of the Thin-Ideal (20 Minutes)

    IV. Home Exercises (3 Minutes)

Session Overview

The focus of session 2 is to review the materials addressed in the previous session and discuss reactions to the two home assignments. Additionally, this session involves role-plays to elicit verbal statements that counter the thin-ideal.

In this session, we will further discuss the costs of pursuing the thin-ideal and explore ways we can resist pressures to be thin.

I. Letter to an Adolescent Girl Debriefing (15 Minutes)

Last week we asked if you would be willing to write a letter to an adolescent girl about the costs of pursuing the thin ideal. Let's start with your thoughts about this exercise:

    Q: Did you find this exercise difficult?

    Q: What were your feelings as you wrote the letter?

Q: Who is willing to read a portion of the letter she wrote?

Have *each participant* read several costs out loud to the group. Encourage group discussion.

Q: Were there any additional costs to pursuing the thin-ideal you thought of that have not been mentioned?

Collect letters. Record participant's initials on each letter.

II. Self-Affirmation Exercise Debriefing (10 Minutes)

The other exercise we asked you to do was to look in a mirror and list some of your positive qualities.

Q: How did you feel when you did this exercise?

Q: Was it challenging? How so?

Q: Why do we have this culture of shame/humbleness about ourselves?

(For example, media and industry perpetuates the thin-ideal)

Q: What are two aspects of yourself that you are satisfied with, including one physical feature?

Have *each participant* share two of the qualities she listed. Discourage "qualified" statements, such as "I guess my stomach is not too horrible." If you get qualified statements, accept them and ask the participant for an additional statement that is completely positive (e.g., "Okay, can you give me one more statement that is completely positive?").

Q: In the end, did you feel the exercise was useful?

Hopefully, you recognize the positive things about yourselves and will remember them, particularly as the pressure of the thin-ideal surrounds you. Given that these are potent pressures, let's discuss ways to resist them.

III. Role-Plays to Discourage Pursuit of the Thin-Ideal (20 Minutes)

Leaders take the role of either a severe dieter or eating-disordered individual for *each participant.*

Let each participant spend approximately 3 minutes attempting to dissuade the character from pursuing the thin-ideal. Parrot, or echo back, any pro thin-ideal comments previously made by participants while you are playing a thin-ideal role. Focus on the unrealistic benefits of the thin-ideal ("I'll be happy all of the time if I'm thin," "Everyone will like me," "I'll have the perfect partner," "All my problems will be solved.") Make sure each participant tries to talk you out of pursuing the thin-ideal.

> Now I would like to do some role-plays. I will play a person who is obsessed with the thin-ideal, and your job will be to convince me that I should not pursue the thin-ideal. Feel free to use any of the information brought up in our earlier discussions.

Select group members to participate, making sure *each participant* has a turn. Here are sample statements for leaders:

> Swimsuit season is just around the corner so I think I will start skipping breakfast to take off the some extra weight.
>
> An anorexic says, I am sure that people will accept me and love me if I only lose a little more weight.
>
> I just saw an ad for this new weight-loss pill and I'm going to order it right away. I can finally be as thin as I want.
>
> An anorexic says to her friend, I can't meet you for dinner tonight because I have to go spend a few hours at the gym. I only went for two hours yesterday.
>
> I feel a little dizzy lately, which may be from these diet pills I'm on, but I don't care because I have already lost 10 pounds.
>
> Most people have weak willpower and give in to hunger. I will show people how much self-control I have by not eating anything but grapefruit.
>
> To be the best runner, I have to be down to my lightest weight. I am only doing this for my health—this will help me avoid injuries.
>
> I have to be thin, or my life will be ruined.
>
> Anyone could have the body of a supermodel if they really wanted it.
>
> No guy is ever going to ask me to the prom unless I drop some of this weight.

Leaders should generate additional statements as needed, and may tailor the statements to be appropriate for their group members.

Role-Play Debriefing

> How did it feel to do these role-plays?

Let participants reflect on how it felt to argue against someone who is fixated on pursuing the thin-ideal.

Do you think it might be beneficial for you to challenge people when they make thin-ideal statements?

Promote discussion on why it is helpful to speak out against pressure to conform to the thin-ideal. Let participants generate the arguments.

IV. Home Exercises (3 Minutes)

Remind participants about the home-based assignment for next session.

We would like you to again complete a couple of exercises at home before the next session. The first exercise is to provide examples from your real life concerning pressures to be thin that you have encountered and then come up with verbal challenges, as we just did in the role-plays.
  Here are some examples of thin-ideal statements:

- A boyfriend might say that he thinks the ideal dress size is a 2.
- Your mom might comment on how another mom has really let herself go because she gained some weight.
- A friend might say that she wished she looked like a particular supermodel when looking through a fashion magazine.

How could you respond to these comments to indicate that you do not agree with the thin-ideal and think these sorts of comment are unhealthy?
  Please come up with at least three such examples from your life. These examples probably won't be how you actually responded to the pressure. Instead, they should be how you might respond *now* based on what you know about the thin-ideal.

Hand out the "Verbal Challenge Form" (Exercise 3).

The second exercise is to generate a top-10 list of things girls/women can do to resist the thin-ideal. What can you avoid, say, do, or learn to battle this beauty ideal? Please write your top-10 list down and bring it to the next group.

Hand out "Top-10 List Form" (Exercise 4).

Elicit one or two examples, such as:

- Write a letter to a fashion magazine editor saying he or she should include a variety of body sizes in the magazine.
- Write a letter to a company indicating that you are boycotting its product because it promotes the thin-ideal in its ads.
- Stop subscribing to a fashion magazine.

At the next meeting, we will further discuss resisting the thin-ideal and how to challenge our personal body-related concerns. Does anyone have any questions before we leave today?

Thanks again for coming. We are looking forward to seeing you next week.

SESSION 3

Prep

Email/call each participant before this class to remind them to complete each homework exercise.

Materials

Handout: "Behavioral Exercise Form" (Exercise 5)

Handout: "Body Activism Form" (Exercise 6)

Place all handouts in participants' folders.

Topic Areas

    I. Verbal Challenge Exercise Debriefing (10 Minutes)

   II. Role-Play Making Counter Thin-Ideal Statements (10 Minutes)

 III. Reasons for Signing Up for This Class (10 Minutes)

 IV. Behavioral Challenge (10 Minutes)

  V. Top-10 List Debriefing (10 Minutes)

 VI. Home Exercises (3 minutes)

Session Overview

The focus of session 3 is to further discuss how to resist the thin-ideal, how to challenge personal body-related concerns, and how to respond to future pressures to be thin. Role-plays are also used so participants can practice making statements that counter the thin-ideal.

I. Verbal Challenge Exercise Debriefing (10 Minutes)

The first exercise asked you to provide examples from your life concerning pressure to be thin and to come up with examples of how you might verbally challenge these pressures.

Can you each share one example with the group?

Solicit examples from *each participant.* If anyone cannot come up with any examples, have her think of a time when she felt pressure from *herself* to be thin (e.g., after looking in the mirror or comparing themselves to a thin friend, thinking, "I really should lose weight"). Help her understand that pressure can often be subtle, and can come in different forms.

II. Role-Play Making Counter Thin-Ideal Statements (10 Minutes)

Now we will do another role-play exercise. I want you to challenge my thin-ideal statements with just a sentence or two.

Role-play using counter thin-ideal statements to resist pressure from peers. Ask *each participant* to generate two counter thin-ideal statements in response to statements that leaders generate. Sample statements:

Wow, summer is right around the corner, I am going to have to start skipping lunch to lose my winter fat.

Look at that fatso over there!

Lindsay really gained weight over the holidays.

I am thinking of going on a diet; do you want to also?

Don't you think that girl is a cow?

I would never be friends with someone that heavy.

My brother says I look too fat; what do you think?

Don't you think Jennifer Lopez is a little too heavy?

If I don't lose some weight, I may be dropped from the diving team.

I hate my body so much. I wish I could just wake up in a different one.

You know if you just stopped eating cheese, you would lose enough weight to look attractive.

Only skinny girls get asked out by boys.

She really doesn't have the body to be wearing that outfit.

Role-Play Debriefing

How did it feel to do these role-plays?

What are some of the difficulties in resisting the thin-ideal, and how can we deal with them?

Encourage discussion.

III. Reasons for Signing Up for This Class (10 Minutes)

At this point in the class, we find it is helpful for participants to share the reasons they were interested in this group so that they can get some feedback from the group. Is anyone willing to share why she signed up for this group?

Have participants share as much as they are comfortable. The purpose is to allow them to share specific body image concerns and have the group challenge those thoughts and feelings.

As we talk about what led you to join this group, it sounds as if some of you could benefit from challenging yourself regarding some of your body-related fears and concerns.

IV. Behavioral Challenge (10 Minutes)

What are the particular body-related issues that make you uncomfortable?

(For example, wearing certain clothes, going specific places)

Would you be willing to do a behavioral experiment to help you feel better about your bodies?
   We would like to challenge each of you to do something that you currently do not do because of body image concerns to increase your confidence—for example, wearing shorts to school, going to the pool in a swimsuit, exercising in public. Can you commit to do this at least once in the next week? We would like each of you to take this behavioral challenge and then let us know during the next session how it turned out. Please take a moment to think of something you would like to do but haven't done yet. I'd like to ask each of you what your plan is before we leave.

Note that the purpose of this exercise is not to have participants do something they would not normally do (e.g., wear a tight shirt because it isn't their style preference); rather, it should be something they would do *if they did not have body image concerns* (e.g., would like to wear a tight shirt, but do not because they think it makes their stomach look too fat).
   Instruct *each participant* to come up with a behavioral challenge and agree upon what that will be. Group leaders should help participants select challenges that are appropriate and that they will be able to do in the next week (e.g., do not select wearing a bathing suit to the pool if it is winter).
   Hand out the "Behavioral Exercise Form" (Exercise 5).

How do you think doing this exercise might help you feel better about your body?

(It provides evidence that the fears we have about our bodies are unfounded— people do not stare at our "huge thighs" or "flabby stomach," as we sometimes expect.)

V. Top-10 List Debriefing (10 Minutes)

The second exercise from last session asked you to list 10 things that girls/women could do to resist the thin-ideal—what you can avoid, say, do, or learn to combat this social pressure. This might be referred to as "body activism."

Can each of you share a few of the items on your list?

Are there specific barriers to engaging in this activism?

How can we overcome these barriers?

Would you be willing to do at least one of the activism behaviors and then let us know how it went?

Have *each participant* choose one behavior from her list to do during the next week.

Hand out the "Body Activism Form" (Exercise 6).

VI. Home Exercises (3 Minutes)

Remind group participants of the home-based assignment for next session:

Again, we would like each of you to: (a) do the behavioral experiment relating to your personal body image concerns, and (b) engage in one act of body activism. We will discuss how each of these exercises went during the next session.

Once again, thanks for participating in this group. See you next week for the final session!

SESSION 4

Prep

Email/call each participant before this class to remind them to complete each homework exercise.

Materials

Handout: "Fat Talk List"

Handout: "Self-Affirmation Exercise Form" (Exercise 7)

Handout: "Letter to Adolescent Girl Form" (Exercise 8)

Place all handouts in participants' folders.

Topic Areas

   I. Behavioral Challenge Debriefing (10 Minutes)

  II. Body Activism Debriefing (10 Minutes)

 III. Challenging Fat Talk (10 Minutes)

 IV. Future Pressures to Be Thin (10 Minutes)

  V. Self-Affirmation Exercise (5 Minutes)

 VI. Home Exercises (3 Minutes)

Session Overview

The focus of session 4 is to discuss participants' experiences with the behavioral challenge and body activism exercises, and to address how the ways we talk about our bodies may promote the thin-ideal. This final session focuses on asking participants to come up with more positive alternative ways of talking about their bodies, and encouraging them to continue to challenge their body image issues in the future.

I. Behavioral Challenge Debriefing (10 Minutes)

    Q: How did the behavioral challenge go?

    Q: What did you notice? How did others react to you? Was it what you expected?

    Q: What were your thoughts and feelings as you did this?

    Q: Did you find this exercise useful? What did you learn?

Have *each participant* discuss her experiences. If anyone did not do the exercise, ask her about the barriers to doing it. How might she overcome them? Is there something she can do that might be easier to try out first? Encourage participants to continue to challenge their body-related concerns.

    Hopefully, you will continue to challenge yourselves and your body image concerns in the future in a similar way.

Praise participants for having the courage to try something new.

II. Body Activism Debriefing (10 Minutes)

    Q: How did the body activism go?

    Q: Did you find this exercise difficult?

Q: What were your thoughts and feelings as you did this?

Q: How do you think this type of exercise could make a difference?

Try to let participants talk themselves into doing more of these types of body activism.

Have *each participant* discuss her experiences.

III. Challenging Fat Talk (10 Minutes)

We've spent a lot of time discussing obvious pressures to be thin and that we encounter on a regular basis from the media, friends, and family members. However, we often do not recognize some of the more subtle ways the thin-ideal is perpetuated.

Can you think of some ways you (or others) might be promoting the thin-ideal without even realizing it?

(For example, complimenting others on weight loss, joining in when friends complain about their bodies)
Hand out the "Fat Talk List."

Here are some common things we often say or might hear others say.

Q: How does each of these statements keep the thin-ideal going?

Q: What can you do differently?

Q: How do you think changing the way you talk about your body might impact how you feel about your body and how others respond to you?

Try to help participants become more aware of the ways they can begin to promote more healthy attitudes about their bodies.

IV. Future Pressures to Be Thin (10 Minutes)

What are some future pressures to be thin that each of you is likely to face?

(For example, fitting into a prom dress, "Freshman Fifteen," pregnancy, getting older/slower metabolism)

How do you plan to respond to them? It may seem strange to be talking about this now, but it is often easier to generate responses ahead of time so you are prepared to deal with these pressures when they arise.

Have *each participant* provide an example and discuss how she will respond to that pressure.

V. Self-Affirmation Exercise (5 Minutes)

As we come to the end of our sessions, we would like to encourage you to continue to challenge some of your body-related concerns. Part of doing this is talking about your bodies in a positive, rather than a negative, way. Here are some ideas to get you started:

• Choose one friend or family member and discuss one thing you like about yourself.

• Keep a journal of all the good things your body allows you to do (e.g., sleep well and wake up rested, play tennis).

• Pick one friend to make a pact with to avoid negative body talk. When you catch your friend talking negatively about his or her body, remind your friend of the pact.

• Make a pledge to end complaints about your body, such as "I'm so flat-chested" or "I hate my legs." When you catch yourself doing this, make a correction by saying something positive about that body part, such as, "I'm so glad my legs got me through soccer practice today."

The next time someone gives you a compliment, rather than objecting ("No, I'm so fat"), practice taking a deep breath then saying "Thank you."

Does anyone have any other ideas of ways to talk more positively about your body?

We would like to ask you to choose one of these and do it sometime during the next week and let us know, via email, how it goes. Consider this an "exit exercise." It may sound false at first, but practicing it will make it more likely that you will talk about yourself in a more positive way. Think of which specific self-affirmation exercise you can do. I'd like to go around the room and ask each of you to share.

Hand out the "Self-Affirmation Exercise Form" (Exercise 7).

Have *each participant* state which affirmation exercise she is willing to do during the next week.

We would also like to ask you to complete one more exit exercise.

Would you be willing to write another letter to an adolescent girl telling her how to avoid developing body image concerns? Use any of the information you have learned in these sessions and any additional ways you may think of on your own. The goal is to help her understand the different things she can do, say, avoid, or learn that will help her develop or maintain a positive body image.

Hand out the "Letter to Adolescent Girl Form" (Exercise 8).

VI. Home Exercise (3 Minutes)

Remind group participants of the home-based assignment.

> We would like each of you to engage in one of the positive body talk exercises during the next week then email us to tell us how it went. In addition, we ask that you write an email letter to an adolescent girl telling her how to avoid developing body image concerns—and send it to us as well.
>
> Once again, thanks again for deciding to participate in this group. I have been very impressed with your thoughtful comments and participation—they are much appreciated!

STUDIES EVALUATING THE DISSONANCE INTERVENTION

To demonstrate that a prevention program works, it is necessary to conduct both efficacy and effectiveness trials. *Efficacy* trials exercise considerable control over the implementation of the intervention with highly selective samples, whereas *effectiveness* trials examine the effects of interventions that are delivered by endogenous providers to heterogeneous samples in natural settings (e.g., schools).

Efficacy Trial 1

In the first preliminary trial, 30 high-risk adolescent females (M age = 18) with elevated body image concerns were assigned to a three-session dissonance intervention or a waitlist control condition (Stice et al., 2000). Compared with controls, dissonance participants showed significantly greater decreases in thin-ideal internalization, body dissatisfaction, negative affect, and bulimic symptoms from pretest to posttest. All effects, except for negative affect, persisted through the 1-month follow-up. It was noteworthy that this intervention appeared to prevent the significant increases in bulimic symptoms that were observed in the waitlist controls over the 2-month study because only one other prevention program has produced prophylactic effects (Neumark-Sztainer, Butler, & Palti, 1995).

Efficacy Trial 2

Although these findings were encouraging, this trial had limitations. We sought to improve on the first trial by using a larger sample, random assignment, and a placebo control condition (Stice et al., 2001). We wanted to compare our intervention to a placebo control group to rule out the possibility that expectancies or demand characteristics explained our intervention effects. We selected a healthy weight management intervention as our placebo control group, because past trials of this type of psychoeducational program did not produced intervention effects (e.g., Killen et al., 1993; Smolak, Levine, & Schermer, 1998). In the healthy weight intervention, participants were told that body image concerns are based on incomplete information about effective weight control behaviors. The intervention provided information about nutrition and exercise, and used behavioral techniques to help participants design an individualized healthy diet and exercise program. We randomly assigned 87 high-risk adolescent females (M age = 19) with body image concerns to the dissonance or the healthy weight intervention. Participants in the dissonance intervention again showed significant decreases in thin-ideal internalization, body dissatisfaction, dieting, negative affect, and bulimic symptoms from pretest to posttest and pretest to 1-month follow-up. Unexpectedly, participants in the healthy weight control group also showed significant decreases in three of the outcomes. It was reassuring that the reductions in two of the outcomes (thin-ideal internalization and body dissatisfaction) were significantly stronger in the dissonance condition than in the healthy weight condition because this provided some evidence that the dissonance intervention was superior to an alternative intervention.

Efficacy Trial 3

Because the positive intervention effects for the healthy weight management program were challenging to interpret, we conducted a third efficacy trial that compared the dissonance intervention to a healthy weight intervention and a waitlist control group (Stice et al., 2003). We improved upon our prior trial by using a longer follow-up period (6 months), a larger sample, younger participants, new facilitators (to assess the generalizability of the effects), and a waitlist comparison group, to permit a less ambiguous interpretation of the findings. In this trial, 148 high-risk adolescent girls (M age = 17) with body image concerns were randomly assigned to the three conditions. Participants in both interventions reported significantly greater decreased thin-ideal internalization, negative affect, and bulimic symptoms at posttest and follow-ups relative to controls, although no significant effects were observed for body dissatisfaction or dieting. There were no significant differences in the effects for the two interventions, which may suggest that training of new group facilitators needed to be improved (the dissonance intervention produced smaller effects relative to those observed in our past trials). Thus, findings from the third trial provided additional evidence for the efficacy of the dissonance intervention.

Large-Scale Efficacy Trial

Because the findings from these efficacy trials were promising relative to the effects observed for most eating disorder prevention trials, we revised both interventions to make them more effective, enhanced the facilitator training protocol, and initiated a large-scale efficacy trial of these two interventions relative to a new alternative intervention and an assessment-only control condition. We improved upon past trials from our lab by using blinded diagnostic interviews, a larger sample, and a longer 3-year follow-up. In this trial, 481 body-dissatisfied adolescent girls were randomized to a dissonance intervention, healthy weight management intervention, expressive writing control, and assessment only control conditions. Dissonance participants showed significantly greater reductions in eating disorder risk factors and bulimic symptoms than healthy weight, expressive writing, and assessment-only participants; and healthy weight participants showed greater reductions in risk factors and symptoms than expressive writing and assessment-only participants from pretest to posttest. Although effects faded over the 3-year follow-up, dissonance participants showed lower risk for obesity onset through 1-year follow-up; and healthy weight participants showed lower risk for onset of bulimic symptoms through 1-year follow-up and lower risk for obesity onset through 3-year follow-up.

Large-Scale Effectiveness Trial

We recently initiated a large-scale effectiveness trial of the dissonance intervention that is currently underway. We have randomized 298 at-risk girls (aged 14 to 18) recruited from three school districts to the dissonance program or a psychoeducational control condition, and will follow them for 2 years. School counselors are recruiting and screening participants, and delivering both interventions in high schools. Analyses of available data indicate that dissonance participants have shown significantly greater reductions in thin-ideal internalization, body dissatisfaction, dieting, and eating disorder symptoms than controls from pre- to posttest. The effects for thin-ideal internalization, body dissatisfaction, dieting, and eating disorder symptoms remained significant at 1-year follow-up and the effects at 2-year follow-up are similar in magnitude and may be significant when data collection is complete. Results suggest that the dissonance intervention produces effects for eating disorder symptoms when real-world providers recruit participants and deliver the intervention under real-world conditions.

INDEPENDENT EVALUATIONS OF THE DISSONANCE INTERVENTION

To our knowledge, the dissonance program has received empirical support in controlled trials conducted by six independent labs (Becker, Smith, & Ciao, 2005; Becker, Smith, & Ciao, 2006; Green, Scott, Diyankova, Gasser, & Pederson, 2005; Matusek, Wendt, & Wiseman, 2004; Mitchell, Mazzeo, Rausch, & Cooke, 2007; Pineda, 2006; Roehrig, Thompson, Brannick, & van den Berg, 2006). For example, Becker and associates (2006) evaluated the effectiveness of both the dissonance intervention and a media advocacy intervention when administered on a semi-mandatory basis to sorority members and delivered by trained peer-leaders. Ninety new sorority members to the six campus sororities were randomized to one of these two interventions. Peer leaders consisted of active sorority members who had participated in the intervention previously and completed 9 hours of experiential training. Although both interventions reduced bulimic pathology at 8-month follow-up, dissonance resulted in significantly greater improvement in thin-ideal internalization, body dissatisfaction, and dieting compared to media advocacy.

Green et al. (2005) examined whether manipulating levels of cognitive dissonance affected outcomes in asymptomatic compared to symptomatic participants. They randomly assigned participants to high-level dissonance, low-level dissonance, or no treatment control conditions. Their results suggested that participants in the high-level dissonance condition showed fewer eating disorder attitudes and behaviors compared to those in the low-level dissonance condition at posttest.

Matusek et al. (2004) examined whether dissonance and healthy behavior interventions could lead to improved body image, less thin-ideal internalization, and other outcomes. College women with body image concerns were randomly assigned to dissonance-based, psychoeducational healthy weight, or waitlist conditions. Results indicated that both the dissonance and healthy weight conditions resulted in improvements in body image, thin-ideal internalization, and eating behaviors.

Discussion

The dissonance intervention has been supported by five trials conducted by our lab and seven trials conducted by independent labs. Data from exit interviews suggest that the intervention is enjoyable and intuitively appealing to both participants and facilitators. Further, the underlying tenets and features of the intervention are supported by a recent meta-analysis of eating disorder prevention programs (Stice & Shaw, 2004).

- The meta-analysis found that intervention effects were significantly greater for targeted versus universal prevention programs. Presumably, high-risk individuals, such as girls struggling with body image concerns, are more motivated to engage in the programs and to attempt to change factors that contribute to their distress. It is also likely that low-risk girls have less room for improvement (a floor effect).

- The meta-analysis indicated that intervention effects were significantly stronger for interactive versus didactic interventions. An interactive format might be necessary to ensure that participants engage in the program material, which likely facilitates acquisition of concepts and skills and promotes attitudinal and behavioral change.

- The meta-analysis revealed that interventions were more effective for adolescents over the age of 14 relative to younger adolescents. We suspect that because older adolescents have struggled with body image and eating disturbances longer, they are more motivated to engage in the intervention. It may be best to intervene immediately before or during the period of greatest risk for onset of eating pathology because this might maximize motivation. Prospective research suggests that binge eating and bulimic pathology primarily emerge between the ages of 16 and 18 (Stice et al., 1998). It is also possible that younger adolescents possess limited insight, based on the fact that their abstract reasoning skills are still developing, which may constrain their ability to effectively argue against the thin-ideal. Younger girls might also have such low levels of eating disturbances that the statistical power to detect effects is attenuated.

- The meta-analysis indicated that prevention programs were more effective when offered solely to females versus mixed-sex populations. Intervention effects may be stronger for female samples because the elevated body image and eating disturbances that occur in girls could motivate them to engage in the intervention and because there might be floor effects for males. That the underlying tenets of the dissonance intervention are directly supported by this meta-analysis further bolsters the confidence that can be placed in its efficacy.

IMPLICATIONS FOR PREVENTION AND FUTURE RESEARCH

This chapter has reviewed the dissonance intervention and explained why we think it is a promising prevention program. As research is an iterative process, more research is needed to inform future program refinements and evaluations.

- It is important that future researchers examine factors that putatively mediate the effects for the dissonance intervention. For instance, it would be useful to directly test whether this program produces intervention effects because it induces cognitive dissonance regarding subscription to the thin-ideal. Although this will be challenging because dissonance is typically inferred rather than directly measured, it would provide an important test of the conceptual basis of this intervention. Similarly, in the same vein as Green et al. (2005), developing a greater understanding of how different levels of cognitive dissonance potentially affect eating pathology and obesity is also important.

- It would be useful to investigate factors that may moderate the intervention effects, such as initial levels of thin-ideal internalization for the dissonance intervention.

- It will be vital to determine ways to enhance the magnitude and duration of the intervention effects. Strategies such as integrating promising programs, drawing further upon persuasion principles from social psychology, or using adjunctive interventions that target parents may enhance intervention effects.

- Additional efforts should be devoted to designing interventions that affect multiple health and mental health outcomes because this would greatly improve the yield of prevention efforts.

- It will be important to initiate effectiveness trials to determine whether these interventions will produce effects in the real world (e.g., all high schools in a district) when delivered by natural providers (e.g., school counselors). Finally, dissemination studies need to be conducted to determine how best to implement these prevention programs on a large-scale basis.

CONCLUSIONS

The dissonance intervention is one of the most promising eating disorder and obesity prevention interventions currently available to clinical practitioners. It has been supported in numerous controlled trials, and is one of only two prevention programs that meets the American Psychological Association's definition of efficacious. The theoretical background, session scripts, and therapist guidelines provided in this chapter should enable clinicians to appropriately implement the intervention. We hope to see the intervention used more widely and adapted according to feedback received by future facilitators and participants, to continue the iterative process that has defined this research. Most important, we hope that we can continue to see positive effects of the intervention in the form of reduced levels of eating pathology and obesity.

REFERENCES

Agras, W. S., Walsh, B. T., Fairburn, C. G., Wilson, G. T., & Kraemer, H. C. (2000). A multicenter comparison of cognitive-behavioral therapy and interpersonal therapy for bulimia nervosa. *Archives of General Psychiatry, 57,* 459–466.

American Psychological Association Task Force on Psychological Intervention Guidelines. (1995). *Template for developing guidelines: Interventions for mental disorders and psychological aspects of physical disorders.* Washington, DC: American Psychological Association.

Becker, C. B., Smith, L. M., & Ciao, A. C. (2005). Reducing eating disorder risk factors in sorority members: A randomized trial. *Behavior Therapy, 36,* 245–254.

Becker, C. B., Smith, L. M., & Ciao, A. C. (2006). Peer facilitated eating disorders prevention: A randomized effectiveness trial of cognitive dissonance and media advocacy. *Journal of Counseling Psychology, 53,* 550–555.

Calle, E. F., Thun, M. J., Petrelli, J. M., Rodriguez, C., & Heath, C. W. (1999). Body mass index and mortality in a prospective cohort of U.S. adults. *New England Journal of Medicine, 341,* 1097–1105.

Coie, J., Watt, N., West, S., Hawkins, D., Asarnow, J., Markman, H., et al. (1993). The science of prevention: A conceptual framework and some directions for a national research program. *American Psychologists, 48,* 1013–1022.

Dietz, W. H. (1998). Childhood weight affects adult morbidity and mortality. *Journal of Nutrition, 128,* 411S–414S.

Eliakim, A., Makowski, G. S., Brasel, J. A., & Cooper, D. M. (2000). Adiposity, lipid levels, and brief endurance training in nonobese adolescent males. *International Journal of Sports Medicine, 21,* 332–337.

Festinger, L. (1957). *A theory of cognitive dissonance.* Stanford, CA: Stanford University Press.

Green, M., Scott, N., Diyankova, I., Gasser, C., & Pederson, E. (2005). Eating disorder prevention: An experimental comparison of high-level dissonance, low-level dissonance, and no-treatment control. *Eating Disorders, 13,* 157–170.

Hedley, A. A., Odgen, C. L., Johnson, C. L., Carroll, M. D., Curtin, L. R., & Flegal, K. M. (2004). Prevalence of overweight and obesity among U.S. children, adolescents, and adults, 1999–2000. *Journal of the American Medical Association, 291,* 2847–2850.

Johnson, J. G., Cohen, P., Kasen, S., & Brook, J. S. (2002). Eating disorders during adolescence and the risk for physical and mental disorders during early adulthood. *Archives of General Psychiatry, 59,* 545–552.

Killen, J. D. (1985). Prevention of adolescent tobacco smoking: The social pressure resistance training approach. *Journal of Child Psychology and Psychiatry and Allied Disciplines, 26,* 7–15.

Killen, J. D., Taylor, C. B., Hammer, L., Litt, I., Wilson, D. M., Rich, T., et al. (1993). An attempt to modify unhealthful eating attitudes and weight regulation practices of young adolescent girls. *International Journal of Eating Disorders, 13,* 369–384.

Killen, J. D., Telch, M. J., Robinson, T. N., Maccoby, N., Taylor, C. B., & Farquar, J. W. (1988). Cardiovascular disease risk reduction for tenth graders: A multiple-factor school-based approach. *Journal of the American Medical Association, 260,* 1728–1733.

Leake, R., Friend, R., & Wadhwa, N. (1999). Improving adjustment of chronic illness through strategic self-presentation: An experimental study on a renal dialysis unit. *Health Psychology, 18,* 54–62.

Leippe, M. R. (1994). Generalization of dissonance reduction: Decreasing prejudice through induced compliance. *Journal of Personality and Social Psychology, 67,* 395–413.

Lewinsohn, P. M., Striegel-Moore, R. H., & Seeley, J. R. (2000). Epidemiology and natural course of eating disorders in young women from adolescence to young adulthood. *Journal of the American Academy of Child and Adolescent Psychiatry, 39,* 1284–1292.

Lionis, C., Kafatos, A., Vlachonikolis, J., Vakaki, M., Tzortzi, M., & Petraki, A. (1991). The effects of a health education intervention program among Cretan adolescents. *Preventive Medicine, 20,* 685–699.

Magarey, A. M., Daniels, L. A., Boulton, T. J., & Cockington, R. A. (2003). Predicting obesity in early adulthood from childhood and parental obesity. *International Journal of Obesity and Related Metabolic Disorders, 27,* 505–513.

Manios, Y., Kafatos, A., & Mamalakis, G. (1998). The effects of a health education intervention initiated at first grade over a 3-year period: Physical activity and fitness indices. *Health Education Research, 13,* 593–606.

Matusek, J. A., Wendt, S. J., & Wiseman, C. V. (2004). Dissonance thin-ideal and didactic healthy behavior eating disorder prevention programs: Results from a controlled trial. *International Journal of Eating Disorders, 36,* 376–388.

Miller, W. R. (1983). Motivational interviewing with problem drinkers. *Behavioral Psychotherapy, 11,* 147–172.

Mitchell, K. S., Mazzeo, S. E., Rausch, S. M., & Cooke, K. L. (2007). Innovative interventions for disordered eating: Evaluating dissonance-based and yoga interventions. *International Journal of Eating Disorders, 40,* 120–128.

Mokdad, A. H., Marks, J. S., Stroup, D. F., & Gerberding, J. L. (2004). Actual causes of death in the United States, 2000. *Journal of the American Medical Association, 291,* 1238–1245.

Neumark-Sztainer, D., Butler, R., & Palti, H. (1995). Eating disturbances among adolescent girls: Evaluation of a school-based primary prevention program. *Journal of Nutritional Education, 27,* 24–31.

Ogden, C. L., Flegal, K. M., Carroll, M. D., & Johnson, C. L. (2002). Prevalence and trends in overweight among U.S. children and adolescents, 1999–2000. *Journal of the American Medical Association, 288,* 1728–1732.

Pietrobelli, A., Faith, M. S., Allison, D. B., Gallagher, D., Chiumello, G., & Heymsfield, S. (1998). Body mass index as a measure of adiposity among children and adolescents: A validation study. *Journal of Pediatrics, 132,* 204–210.

Pineda, G. G. (2006). Estrategias preventivas de factores de riesgo en trastornos de la conducta alimentaria. Tesis doctoral inédita. Facultad de Psicología. Universidad Nacional Autónoma de México, México.

Robinson, T. N. (1999). Reducing children's television viewing to prevent obesity: A randomized controlled trial. *Journal of the American Medical Association, 282,* 1561–1567.

Roehrig, M., Thompson, J. K., Brannick, M., & van den Berg, P. (2006). Dissonance-based eating disorder prevention program: A preliminary dismantling investigation. *International Journal of Eating Disorders, 39,* 1–10.

Smolak, L., Levine, M., & Schermer, F. (1998). A controlled evaluation of an elementary school primary prevention program for eating problems. *Journal of Psychosomatic Research, 44,* 339–353.

Stice, E. (1994). A review of the evidence for a sociocultural model of bulimia nervosa and an exploration of the mechanisms of action. *Clinical Psychology Review, 14,* 633–661.

Stice, E., & Agras, W. S. (1998). Predicting onset and cessation of bulimic behaviors during adolescence: A longitudinal grouping analysis. *Behavior Therapy, 29,* 257–276.

Stice, E., Cameron, R., Killen, J. D., Hayward, C., & Taylor, C. B. (1999). Naturalistic weight reduction efforts prospectively predict growth in relative weight and onset of obesity among female adolescents. *Journal of Consulting and Clinical Psychology, 67,* 967–974.

Stice, E., Chase, A., Stormer, S., & Appel, A. (2001). A randomized trial of a dissonance-based eating disorder prevention program. *International Journal of Eating Disorders, 29,* 247–262.

Stice, E., Killen, J. D., Hayward, C., & Taylor, C. B. (1998). Age of onset for binge eating and purging during adolescence: A four-year survival analysis. *Journal of Abnormal Psychology, 107,* 671–675.

Stice, E., Mazotti, L., Weibel, D., & Agras, W. S. (2000). Dissonance prevention program decreases thin-ideal internalization, body dissatisfaction, dieting, negative affect, and bulimic symptoms: A preliminary experiment. *International Journal of Eating Disorders, 27,* 206–217.

Stice, E., Presnell, K., & Bearman, S. K. (2001). Relation of early menarche to depression, eating disorders, substance abuse, and comorbid psychopathology among adolescent girls. *Developmental Psychology, 37,* 608–619.

Stice, E., & Ragan, J. (2002). A preliminary controlled evaluation of an eating disturbance psychoeducational intervention for college students. *International Journal of Eating Disorders, 31,* 159–171.

Stice, E., & Shaw, H. (2004). Eating disorder prevention programs: A meta-analytic review. *Psychological Bulletin, 130,* 206–227.

Stice, E., Shaw, H., Burton, E., & Wade, E. (2006). Dissonance and healthy weight eating disorder prevention programs: A randomized efficacy trial. *Journal of Consulting and Clinical Psychology, 74,* 263–275.

Stice, E., Shaw, H., & Marti, C. N. (2006). A meta-analytic review of obesity prevention programs for children and adolescents: The skinny on interventions that work. *Psychological Bulletin, 132,* 667–691.

Stice, E., Trost, A., & Chase, A. (2003). Healthy weight control and dissonance-based eating disorder prevention programs: Results from a controlled trial. *International Journal of Eating Disorders, 33,* 10–21.

Story, M. (1999). School-based approaches for preventing and treating obesity. *International Journal of Obesity and Related Metabolic Disorders, 23,* S43–S51.

Tamir, D., Feurstein, A., Brunner, S., Halfon, S., Reshef, A., & Palti, H. (1990). Primary prevention of cardiovascular diseases in childhood: Changes in serum total cholesterol, high-density lipoprotein, and body mass index after 2 years of intervention in Jerusalem schoolchildren age 7–9 years. *Preventive Medicine, 19,* 22–30.

Vogeltanz-Holm, N. D., Wonderlich, S. A., Lewis, B. A., Wilsnack, S. C., Harris, T. R., Wilsnack, R. W., et al. (2000). Longitudinal predictors of binge eating, intense dieting, and weight concerns in a national sample of women. *Behavior Therapy, 31,* 221–235.

Wertheim, E. H., Koerner, J., & Paxton, S. J. (2001). Longitudinal predictors of restrictive eating and bulimic tendencies in three different age groups of adolescent girls. *Journal of Youth and Adolescence, 31,* 69–81.

Wilson, G. T., Becker, C. B., & Heffernan, K. (2003). Eating disorders. In E. J. Mash & R. A. Barkley (Eds.), *Child psychopathology* (2nd ed., pp. 687–715). New York: Guilford Press.

Wolf, A. M., & Colditz, G. A. (1998). Current estimates of the economic cost of obesity in the United States. *Obesity Research, 6,* 97–106.

APPENDIX A: HANDOUTS

Exercise 1: Letter to Adolescent Girl

Please write a letter to an adolescent girl who is struggling with body image concerns about the costs associated with pursuing the thin-ideal. Think of as many costs as you can. Feel free to work with a friend or family member in generating ideas, or use any of the ones we discussed in the group. Please bring this letter to our next meeting so we can discuss your responses and feelings about this assignment.

_____

_____

_____

_____

_____

_____

_____

_____

Exercise 2: Self-Affirmation Form

Please stand in front of a mirror and look at yourself, then write down all your positive qualities. This includes physical, emotional, intellectual, and social qualities. For instance, you may like the shape of your arms, the strength of your legs, your long dark hair, the sound of your laugh, or the fact that you are a good friend. Please make sure to include at least some physical attributes on your list.

_____

_____

_____

_____

_____

_____

_____

Exercise 3: Verbal Challenge Form

Please provide examples from your real life concerning pressures to be thin that you have encountered, and then come up with verbal challenges, as we did in the role-plays.

Here are some examples of thin-ideal statements:

- A boyfriend says he thinks the ideal dress size is a 2.
- Your mom comments that another mom has really let herself go because she gained some weight.
- A friend says that she wished she looked like a particular supermodel when looking through a fashion magazine.

How might you respond to these comments to indicate that you do not agree with the thin-ideal and that these sorts of comments are unhealthy?

Please come up with at least three such examples from your life. These examples probably won't be how you actually responded to such pressure in the past. Instead, they should be how you might respond *now* based on what you learned about the thin-ideal.

1. *Situation:*

_____

_____

_____

_____

Verbal response:

_____

_____

_____

_____

2. *Situation:*

_____

_____

_____

_____

Verbal response:

_____

_____

_____

_____

3. *Situation:*

_____

_____

_____

Verbal response:

_____

_____

_____

_____

Exercise 4: Top-10 List Form

Please generate a top-10 list of things girls/women can do to resist the thin-ideal. What can you avoid, say, do, or learn to battle this beauty ideal? Please write down your top-10 list and bring it to the next group meeting.

_____

_____

_____

_____

_____

_____

_____

_____

_____

_____

Exercise 5: Behavioral Exercise Form

We would like to challenge each of you to do something to increase your confidence that you currently do not do because of body image concerns. For example: wearing shorts to school, going to the pool in a swimsuit, exercising in public. Please do this at least once in the next week. We would like each of you to take this behavioral challenge and then let us know during the next session how it turned out. Please take a moment to think of something you would like to do but haven't done yet. You may wish to write your behavioral goal down on this page to remind yourself of it.

_____

_____

_____

_____

_____

_____

Exercise 6: Body Activism Form

The second exercise from last session asked you to list 10 things that girls/women could do to resist the thin-ideal—what you can avoid, say, do, or learn to combat this social pressure. This might be referred to as "body activism."

Please choose one behavior from your list to do during the next week. You may want to write your body activism goal on this sheet to remind yourself of it.

_____

_____

_____

_____

_____

Handout: Fat Talk List

We've spent a lot of time discussing obvious pressures to be thin that we encounter on a regular basis from the media, friends, and family members. However, the thin-ideal is also perpetuated by our everyday conversations.

Below is a list of common things we often say or might hear others say. How does each of these statements keep the thin-ideal going? What can you say that's different? How do you think changing the way you talk about your body might impact how you feel about your body and how others respond to you?

- I'm so fat.
- I need to lose 10 pounds.
- Do I look fat in this?
- You think you're fat? Look at me!
- Gee, you look great. Have you lost weight?
- I can't eat that; it will make me fat.
- I'm way too fat to be eating this.
- I'm too fat to get into a bathing suit.
- She's too fat to be wearing those pants.
- She's a little bit too heavy to be dating that guy.
- You're so thin; how do you do it?
- Can you believe how much she's let herself go?
- I've really been doing well on this diet; you should try it.
- You'd be so pretty if you lost weight.
- Wow, look at the big butt on that girl!

Exercise 7: Self-Affirmation Exercise Form

Part of challenging body-related concerns involves talking about our bodies in a positive, rather than negative, way. We discussed some examples of this in the group; for instance, making a pledge to end complaints about your body or accepting compliments rather than objecting to them. Please choose an idea that we talked about, or one of your own, to practice over the next week, and let us know how it goes, via email.

Exercise 8: Letter to Adolescent Girl

Please write another letter to an adolescent girl telling her how to avoid developing body image concerns. Use any of the information you have learned in these sessions, and any additional ways you may think of on your own. The goal is to help her understand the different things she can do, say, avoid, or learn that will help her develop or maintain a positive body image.

_____

_____

_____

_____

_____

_____

Qualitative Interview Questions

Which aspects of the group did you find most valuable?

- Which aspects of the group did you find less valuable?
- What motivated you to attend group?
- How could we have motivated you better to do the homework assignments?
- How helpful were the group facilitators?
- Were there any unique or particular aspects of the group that made it work either better of worse for you personally?
- How could we make the groups more interesting and enjoyable for future participants?

Exit Exercises

We would like to challenge you to do something that you currently do not do because of body image concerns. For example, wearing shorts to school or going to a pool in a swimsuit. Please try this behavioral experiment in the next week.

Engage in one act of body activism (e.g., something you avoid, say, do, or learn to combat social pressure to be ultrathin).

Good luck.

Chapter 4

PREVENTING DEPRESSION IN EARLY ADOLESCENT GIRLS

The Penn Resiliency and Girls in Transition Programs

JANE E. GILLHAM, TARA M. CHAPLIN,
KAREN REIVICH, AND JOHN HAMILTON

Depression is one of the most common psychological disorders affecting children and adolescents today. In the United States, at any given time, approximately 2% to 3% of children and 6% to 9% of adolescents suffer from a major depressive disorder (Cohen et al., 1993; Costello et al., 2002; Lewinsohn, Hops, Roberts, & Seeley, 1993). Rates of depression increase dramatically during the transition from childhood to adolescence, indicating that this is a particularly vulnerable developmental period (Hankin, Abramson, Moffit, Silva, & McGee, 1998). As many as 9% of youth may experience an episode of unipolar depression by the end of middle school (Garrison, Schluchter, Schoenbach, & Kaplan, 1989), and as many as 20% may experience an episode by the time they graduate from high school (Lewinsohn et al., 1993). Many more youth struggle with high levels of depressive symptoms (Petersen et al., 1993) that can lead to the same kinds of difficulties in interpersonal relationships and academic achievement as depressive disorders (Gotlib, Lewinsohn, & Seeley, 1995). Despite these statistics, depression is underdiagnosed and undertreated in youth. Only about 20% to 25% of adolescents with depression receive treatment (Hirschfeld et al., 1997).

Over the past 2 decades, the understanding of the phenomenology of depression, particularly child and adolescent depression, has changed. Once viewed as an acute disorder that typically resolved within several months to a year, depression has come to be seen a recurrent disorder. Individuals who suffer from one episode are at high risk for future episodes, and some individuals may suffer from chronic elevated symptoms. Adolescents who suffer from depression are more likely than their peers to experience depression again during adulthood (Garber, Kriss, Koch, & Lindholm, 1988; Harrington, Fudge, Rutter, Pickles, & Hill, 1990). This recurrence suggests that some risk factors for depression are fairly stable. In addition, the experience of depression may change (or scar)

The authors are grateful to the children and parents who have participated in research on the Penn Resiliency Program (PRP); to the teachers, counselors, graduate students, and clinicians who have led PRP groups; to the school and clinic administrators and personnel who have assisted us in carrying out our research over the years, and to the National Institutes of Mental Health and the Kaiser Foundation Research Institute for funding our previous research on PRP.

youth in ways that increase vulnerability (e.g., Gotlib, Lewinsohn, Seeley, Rohde, & Redner, 1993; Nolen-Hoeksema, Girgus, & Seligman, 1992).

In the United States and most industrialized countries, women are twice as likely as men to develop depression throughout most of their lives. Recent research suggests that this sex difference begins to emerge around the age of 13 when depression rates start to rise in girls (Angold, Costello, & Worthman, 1998; Hankin & Abramson, 2001). By mid to late adolescence, depression rates in girls are similar to those in women. Despite their greater vulnerability to depression, few interventions have been evaluated that focus specifically on reducing or preventing depression in females.

In part, the lack of focus on women is understandable. Depression is quite common in boys and men: 10% to 15% of males in this country will suffer from clinical depression during their lifetimes (Kessler et al., 1994). In addition, many risk factors that have been identified appear to be related to depression in both males and females (Hankin & Abela, 2005; Nolen-Hoeksema & Girgus, 1994). These risk factors include biological factors (e.g., genetic factors), intrapsychic factors (e.g., pessimistic cognitive styles, coping styles), interpersonal and family risk factors (e.g., a lack or loss of social support, parental depression, family conflict, abuse), and community or societal risk factors (e.g., poverty). In general, depression treatments that are found to be efficacious, such as pharmacotherapy, interpersonal therapy, and cognitive-behavioral therapy (CBT), appear to be efficacious for both men and women (but see Thase, Frank, Kornstein, & Yonkers, 2000).

The Penn Resiliency Program (PRP; Gillham, Jaycox, Reivich, Seligman, & Silver, 1990, 2003), the intervention described in this chapter, is based largely on CBT for depression (Beck, 1976; Beck, Rush, Shaw, & Emery, 1979; Ellis, 1962).* CBT teaches a variety of skills for effective problem solving and for counteracting the pessimistic cognitive styles and information processing biases that are linked to depression. A major goal of CBT is to impart a set of skills that clients can use when they encounter stressors and negative emotional reactions outside of therapy, and long after therapy has ended.

PRP aims to prevent depression by teaching children and adolescents these cognitive-behavioral techniques before depression develops. It has been investigated in several controlled studies, and, overall, results suggest that it reduces

---

*The Penn Resiliency Program for Children and Adolescents is owned by the University of Pennsylvania. The University of Pennsylvania has licensed this program to Adaptiv Learning Systems. Dr. Reivich owns stock in Adaptiv and could profit from the sale of this program. The other authors of this chapter do not have a financial interest in Adaptiv.

and prevents depressive symptoms during the transition to adolescence (Cardemil, Reivich, & Seligman, 2002; Chaplin et al., 2006; Gillham, Reivich, Jaycox, & Seligman, 1995; Jaycox, Reivich, Gillham, & Seligman, 1994; Yu & Seligman, 2002). There is growing evidence that PRP prevents symptoms of anxiety as well (Gillham, Reivich, et al., 2006; Roberts, Kane, Bishop, & Matthews, 2004; Roberts, Kane, Thomson, Bishop, & Hart, 2003). Although some inconsistent findings exist, in general, PRP appears to be effective for girls and boys.

Several risk factors for depression appear to be more relevant to females, however, and these often are not targeted well by existing interventions. For example, girls are more likely to have concerns about body image during the transition to puberty, and these concerns appear to be closely connected to depression (Ge, Conger, & Elder, 2001; Petersen, Sarigiani, & Kennedy, 1991). Interventions that target these additional risk factors may be particularly powerful in treating and preventing depression in girls and women.

We are writing this chapter at a turning point in our work on depression prevention. Over the past decade, research on PRP (and depression prevention in general) paid relatively little attention to gender. But we have become increasingly concerned about the high rate of depression in girls and women, and about the possibility that PRP and other interventions may not adequately address the risk factors that are especially important for girls. Therefore, we and our colleagues are in the process of developing and evaluating a new intervention, the Girls in Transition (GT) program, designed to prevent depression in girls as they make the transition into adolescence. GT includes many of the cognitive-behavioral skills covered in PRP but also helps girls to address concerns about body image and interpersonal relationships, counteract societal pressures they may experience, and explore their competencies and goals. Components of this intervention are also described within this chapter.

LITERATURE REVIEW

Cognitive-Behavioral Models of the Development of Depression

Cognitive-behavioral models have been proposed to explain depression in adulthood, and have recently been applied to the development of depression in childhood and adolescence (Garber, Quiggle, & Shanley, 1990). Some of the most well-researched cognitive models are Beck's (1976) model and the various forms of the Learned Helplessness Model (Seligman, 1972), including the Reformulated Learned Helplessness (Abramson, Seligman, & Teasdale, 1978), and Hopelessness Models (Abramson, Metalsky, & Alloy, 1989). Beck (1976) proposes that a tendency to view one's self, the world, and the future in overly negative ways, combined with a lack of behavioral coping skills, puts one at risk for depression and anxiety. Some research with children and adolescents supports this model. For example, children who hold negative views of the self and the future tend to show elevated levels of depression (Cole, Martin, Peeke, Seroczynski, & Fier, 1999; Kazdin, Rodgers, & Colbus, 1986).

The Learned Helplessness Model proposes that after repeatedly experiencing uncontrollable negative events, some individuals may begin to feel helpless about their ability to control future events. This helplessness may lead to symptoms of depression, including apathy, decreased appetite, and despair (Seligman, 1972, 1991). The Learned Helplessness Model was revised to better understand the mechanisms by which people develop helplessness. The reformulated Learned Helplessness Model posits that, over time, people develop cognitive styles for explaining the events in their lives, which account for whether or not they experience helplessness and depression (Abramson et al., 1978). Some individuals develop a pessimistic explanatory style, by which they tend to attribute negative events to internal, stable, and global factors, and positive events to external, unstable, and specific factors. For example, an adolescent with a pessimistic explanatory style who fails a science test might think to herself, "I'm stupid" or "I have no ability in math or science." If she gets an A on a science test, she might think, "That test was easy." This explanatory style would lead to expectations of future helplessness as the student expects failure to continue and believes that there is nothing she can do to improve her performance. When this kind of pessimistic interpretive style is used to explain multiple events over time, it can lead to a more generalized sense of helplessness, which, in turn, leads to passivity, hopelessness, and despair. The Hopelessness Theory (Abramson et al., 1989), another revision of the Learned Helplessness Model, proposes that a pessimistic explanatory style (particularly global and stable explanations for negative events) interacts with negative life events to lead to hopelessness, which is a proximal cause of depression. Numerous studies document a link between pessimistic explanatory style and depression in adults and in children (Buchanan & Seligman, 1995; Gladstone & Kaslow, 1995; Hankin & Abela, 2005).

In addition to interpreting events in a negative way, depressed children also may lack behavioral skills for coping effectively with social situations (Kaslow, Brown, & Mee, 1994). For example, Altmann and Gotlib (1988) found that depressed fourth- and fifth-grade children had more negative interactions with peers than nondepressed children. Depression is also linked to greater reliance on passive, unassertive, and ruminative styles, and less engagement in problem solving (Abela, Vanderbilt, & Rochon, 2004; Chaplin & Cole, 2005; Nolen-Hoeksema, 1991; Spence, Sheffield, & Donovan, 2002).

Developmentally, cognitive-behavioral factors associated with depression appear to become more important as children mature. In adolescence, there are increases in abstract thinking, self-consciousness, and thinking about future possibilities. These developments may intensify pessimistic explanatory styles, helpless and hopeless expectancies, and, in turn, depressive symptoms. In addition, adolescence brings biological and social changes. For girls, these changes may be particularly difficult because pubertal changes often occur in early adolescence, at the same time as the transition to middle school, which involves changes in academics and peer relationships (Eccles et al., 1993; Simmons & Blythe, 1987). Thus, children who enter adolescence without ways to challenge unrealistic negative thoughts or with limited problem-solving skills may be at increased risk for depression.

Cognitive-Behavioral Interventions for Depression in
Children and Adolescents

CBT targets many of these risk factors. In CBT, clients typically learn cognitive-restructuring and behavioral techniques (e.g., assertiveness, relaxation) that may help them think more accurately about events in their lives and respond more effectively to the problems they encounter. Numerous studies have demonstrated that CBT is an efficacious treatment for depression in adults (for recent reviews see Hollon & DeRubeis, 2004; Strunk & DeRubeis, 2001). In general, CBT appears to be as effective as medication treatment, although there is some debate about its effectiveness among clients with very severe depression (Hollon et al., 2002). Although less research exists on CBT for depression during childhood and adolescence, findings are promising (Compton et al., 2004). For example, the Adolescent Coping with Depression Course has been found to alleviate depression in several studies (Rohde, Lewinsohn, Clarke, Hops, & Seeley, 2005). This is particularly encouraging given recent concerns about the safety and effectiveness of selective serotonin reuptake inhibitors as a treatment for depression in children and adolescents. Moreover, recent research suggests that the combination of CBT and pharmacotherapy reduces suicidal ideation compared with medication alone (The Tads Team, 2007).

In addition to alleviating depression, there is growing evidence that CBT skills prevent the occurrence of future depression. Depressed adults who are treated with CBT are less likely than those treated with medication to relapse following the end of treatment (Hollon et al., 2005). Continuation of CBT following initial treatment has also been found to prevent relapse (Jarrett et al., 2001). Such findings suggest that CBT skills may be able to prevent depression from occurring in the first place.

In the past few years, several depression prevention programs have been developed based on CBT (for recent reviews, see Dozois & Dobson, 2004; Gillham, Shatté, & Freres, 2000; Horowitz & Garber, 2006; Merry, McDowell, Hetrick, Bir, & Muller, 2004; Sutton, 2007). Much of this work has focused on children and adolescents, perhaps with the hope that by delivering interventions early, depression may be prevented across the lifespan. If one episode of depression increases vulnerability to future episodes, prevention of the first episode of depression, which is often during adolescence (Kim-Cohen et al., 2003), may be particularly important. Although we still know very little about the long-term effects of such interventions, short-term findings are promising. The Coping with Stress Course, developed by Clarke and colleagues, cuts the rate of depressive disorders by more than half across a 12- to 15-month follow-up period (Clarke et al., 1995, 2001). Other cognitive-behavioral prevention programs that have shown positive effects in youth include the prevention programs for college students evaluated by Bearman, Peden, Seligman, and their colleagues (Bearman, Stice, & Chase, 2003; Gillham et al., 1991; Peden, Rayens, Hall, & Beebe, 2001; Seligman, Schulman, DeRubeis, & Hollon, 1999); the Resourceful Adolescent Program (Shochet et al., 2001), and the LISA-T Program (Pössel, Horn, Groen, & Hautzinger, 2004) for children in late middle school and high school years; and the PRP (Gillham et al., 1990), an intervention for children in late elementary and middle school years, which has been the focus of much of our own research.

Like most of the depression prevention programs that have been empirically evaluated, PRP is a group intervention based largely on CBT for depression (Beck, 1976; Beck et al., 1979; Ellis, 1962). PRP differs from many depression prevention programs in that it includes more discussion of cognitive styles, particularly pessimistic explanatory styles (Abramson et al., 1978; Seligman, 1998) and targets children in late childhood and early adolescence. Most other depression prevention programs have focused on mid to late adolescence and adulthood, when depression is more common.

Importance and Challenges of Early Adolescence

The period from ages 10 to 14 is a time of enormous change, unrivaled by any developmental period except the first years of life. On a physical level, tremendous growth and maturation occurs. Most girls go through puberty during this time. On a cognitive level, children's thinking becomes more sophisticated. They are better able than younger children to engage in hypothesis testing and to consider alternative theories, perspectives, and possibilities (Bemporad, 1994; Inhelder & Piaget, 1958). Their self-perceptions become more complex and more stable, and are increasingly based on social comparison (Damon & Hart, 1988). Cognitive styles may also become more stable (Gillham, Reivich, & Shatté, 2001; McCauley, Mitchell, Burke, & Moss, 1988). On an interpersonal level, relationships with friends deepen, and interactions with friends and peers assume increasing importance (Berndt, 1987; Csikszentmihalyi & Larson, 1984). At the same time, relationships with parents and other family members remain important, but go through changes as adolescents and parents negotiate the adolescent's growing need for autonomy (Paikoff & Brooks-Gunn, 1991; Smetana, 1995). Several other social transitions occur as well. Most children experience one or more school transitions (into middle school or junior high, and then into high school) during this time. With these transitions come changes in school structure that usually result in larger class sizes, interactions with more teachers and more students during the school day, and less opportunity to interact with close friends or teachers who know students very well. At the same time, there is an increase in academic pressures including greater workloads, increased competition and a focus on social comparison as the basis of evaluating performance (Eccles & Midgely, 1990). These changes and challenges may make early adolescence a vital time for intervention.

The period from 10 to 14 also may be an ideal window for intervention. Children may be more receptive to adult advice than in later adolescence, when it is more common for adolescents to express cynicism and resist advice from parents, teachers, and other adults. If children learn effective coping and problem-solving skills in childhood or early adolescence, they may be better prepared to deal with the stressors, challenges, and setbacks that most children face as they enter their high school years, a time of increased vulnerability for depression.

DEVELOPING AND EVALUATING THE PENN RESILIENCY PROGRAM

At the time PRP was developed, little work existed on CBT for depression in children and adolescents. CBT was originally an adult intervention that has at its core cognitive-restructuring skills and techniques that rely on abstract reasoning and metacognitive abilities. Cognitive therapy teaches clients to identify thoughts, to suspend judgment, to systematically examine evidence, and to consider other possibilities. Such skills are at the heart of the stage that Piaget called formal operations. Although these skills are developing in middle school-age children, Piaget and other developmental psychologists have suggested that proficiency is not usually achieved until later in adolescence or adulthood (e.g., Inhelder & Piaget, 1958).

PRP uses a variety of means to make the abstract concepts and techniques of CBT more accessible to children. Concepts and skills are introduced through characters, hypothetical examples, cartoons, skits, and role-plays in an effort to make them more concrete and understandable. "Say It Straight Samantha," for example, illustrates self-assertiveness, and a drawing of her acts as a visual mnemonic for that skill. Structured activities allow children to practice the skills in and out of group sessions. In the initial sessions, activities help children identify and label their emotional experiences, prerequisites for applying the cognitive model.

The first draft of the PRP intervention was piloted with approximately 30 fifth- and sixth-grade children. Children were divided into three groups, with each group led by two of the program developers. The main purpose of the pilot was to see how children would respond to the curriculum, so no control group was included. PRP participants' depressive symptoms declined significantly from baseline to postintervention. However, it also became apparent that some activities fell flat and some of the concepts (e.g., the global or pervasive dimension of explanatory style) were difficult for students to understand. Extensive revisions were made following this pilot, and a study was launched to compare the effects of the revised PRP to a no-intervention control (Gillham et al., 1995; Gillham & Reivich, 1999; Jaycox et al., 1994).

During the past 10 years, we have continued to revise the program. Although key concepts and skills have changed little since the initial controlled study, new activities, examples, and wording have been included to make these concepts and skills more accessible to children and adolescents. As noted, initially an intervention for fifth- and sixth-grade (10- to 12-year-old) children, the PRP materials have been adapted to be appropriate for children between fifth and eighth grades (approximately 10 to 14 years old). The PRP curriculum also has been adapted for use with inner-city children of Latino and African American descent (Cardemil et al., 2002), children in Australia (e.g., Roberts et al., 2003), and children in Beijing, China (Yu & Seligman, 2002). In addition, a resiliency program for college students was developed that, in part, is based on the PRP curriculum (Gillham et al., 1991).

Over time, we have come to view PRP as broader than a depression prevention program. We believe that the cognitive-behavioral skills covered in PRP can be beneficial to most children and adults. This shift is reflected in the changes to the intervention's name over the years—from Penn Depression Prevention Program to Coping Skills Program to Penn Optimism Program to Penn Resiliency Program.

PENN RESILIENCY PROGRAM

The PRP (Gillham et al., 1990; Gillham et al., 2003; see also Seligman, Reivich, Jaycox, & Gillham, 1995) is a cognitive-behavioral intervention designed for groups of 6 to 15 participants. Group leaders in our current research projects typically participate in a 4- to 5-day training workshop, where they first apply PRP skills in their own lives and then learn to deliver the curriculum to groups of late-elementary and middle school students. A leader's manual includes a detailed summary of the concepts, skills, and activities to cover in each session. A participant notebook includes lists of main points, copies of handouts, and assignments and activities to complete between sessions. From the second session on, each session opens with a discussion of the homework activities and students' experiences during the preceding week. Although originally designed for delivery in twelve 90- to 120-minute sessions, the program can be divided into twenty-four 45- to 60-minute sessions. In addition, eight-session versions of the program have been used in at least two studies (Gillham, Reivich, et al., 2006; Quayle, Dziurawiec, Roberts, Kane, & Ebsworthy, 2001). The following is a brief summary of the PRP sessions and some of the activities included in the program.

Session 1: Introduction and the Link between Thoughts and Feelings

Goals and Overview

The major goals of this session are to:

- Introduce the group members and group goals.
- Build rapport and socialize participants to talking about their experiences in the group setting.
- Teach students to identify their self-talk.
- Introduce the cognitive (ABC) model.

Approximately 30 to 40 minutes of the session are devoted to introductions, rapport-building activities, a discussion of the purpose and goals of the group, and a discussion of logistical issues such as the group schedule, ground rules, and confidentiality. Although a relatively short part of the intervention, the program introduction is critical because it helps to set the tone and expectations for the remainder of the program. Group leaders also use this time to "normalize" students' participation in the group and to clear up any misconceptions students may have about the program or why they have been selected to participate. The remainder of the session is devoted to several activities (e.g., the M&M's activity, self-talk skits and discussion, and ABC cartoons) that encourage children to discuss common problems for their age group, help students identify and label their own emotions and self-talk, and introduce the cognitive (ABC) model.

M&M's Activity

This activity uses M&M's (other colorful candies or objects can be substituted) to launch a discussion of different emotions. The group leader passes out M&M's to participants and suggests that each color represents a different emotion. For example, red might represent angry; blue, sad; and yellow, happy. The leader asks for volunteers with a given color candy to describe times when they experienced that emotion. Participants are also encouraged to think about the intensity of emotions by rating their emotions on a 0 (none) to 10 (extreme) scale. With younger students, leaders can use the "feel-o-meter," which charts a variety of emotions of different intensities. The M&M's activity helps children to label emotions and to become comfortable talking about their feelings and experiences with other members of the group.

Self-Talk Skits and Discussion

The concept of self-talk, or internal dialogue, is introduced through brief skits. In each skit, a character encounters a problem (e.g., receiving a bad haircut, being picked last for a team in gym class) and then thinks aloud about the causes, implications, and/or consequences of the event. Following the skits, participants are encouraged to reflect on their own experiences and to describe situations in which they have noticed their self-talk. The group leader points out that identifying self-talk can be especially important when they encounter a problem or have a very strong emotional reaction (such as intense anger, sadness, or anxiety). Participants are encouraged to attend to their self-talk over the next several days.

ABC Cartoons

Ellis's (1962) ABC model is introduced with three panel cartoons:

1. The first panel illustrates the activating event (A), for example, two parents yelling at each other in front of the child.
2. The second panel includes a thought bubble with the child's beliefs (B), for example, "It's my fault. They wouldn't fight so much if I were a better kid and didn't cause so much trouble."
3. The third panel illustrates the consequences (C) of the belief, for example, sadness or crying.

The leader describes the cognitive model: When events (A) occur, our beliefs or self-talk (B) have a strong effect on our feelings or emotions and behaviors (C).

The leader encourages students to think about B-C connections by asking them first to imagine other beliefs a child could have in the situation and then consider the consequences of those beliefs. Similarly, children are asked which beliefs would lead to specific emotions. For homework, participants fill in missing Bs and Cs in three-panel cartoons, and create cartoons depicting events in their own lives.

Session 2: Thinking Styles

Goals and Overview

The major goals of this session are to:

- Provide participants with more practice identifying the link between thoughts and feelings.
- Teach participants about thinking styles, particularly pessimistic interpretive styles.
- Help participants generate alternative thoughts that are more realistic and more optimistic.

After reviewing the homework assignment, leaders cover several activities (e.g., thinking styles skits and discussion) that introduce the concept of thinking styles and illustrate the effects of different thinking styles on emotions and behaviors. The leader points out that thinking styles can often apply to a domain (e.g., for achievement situations). In addition, activities are included that help children identify their own negative beliefs and then practice generating alternative beliefs, first in hypothetical situations and then for events in their own lives.

Thinking Styles Skits and Discussion

The concept of thinking styles is introduced through pairs of skits that depict characters with different thinking styles as they encounter similar setbacks. For example, Gloomy Greg and Hopeful Holly both attend the school dance. Each asks another child to dance and is turned down. Greg displays a pessimistic thinking style. His self-talk includes statements like "I'm a loser" and "No one will ever dance with me." Holly's self-talk is more positive and optimistic. The leader uses these skits to launch the discussion of thinking styles. Participants explore the qualities of pessimistic beliefs (e.g., they typically imply that the cause of a problem is permanent and unchangeable; they usually aren't accurate). Participants also explore the consequences of pessimistic beliefs, and the leader makes the point that they can lead to self-fulfilling prophecies in which the belief ("No one likes me") leads to a behavior (withdrawing from others) that produces an outcome ("No one dances with me") that seems to confirm the initial belief.

Session 3: Alternatives and Evidence

Goals and Overview

The major goals of this session are to:

- Give participants more practice generating alternative thoughts.
- Teach participants to evaluate thoughts by examining evidence.

After reviewing the homework, the leader encourages the students to participate in several activities and discussions (e.g., the detective story, the file game) that emphasize the importance of accurate thinking, illustrate the process of evaluating thoughts, and provide participants with practice engaging in these skills.

The Detective Story

The detective story illustrates the process and benefits of generating alternatives and evaluating evidence. In this story, two detectives attempt to solve a crime. The first detective (Merlock Worms) thinks of one possible suspect and is certain that this person committed the crime because "his was the first name that popped into my head." The second detective (Sherlock Holmes) makes a list of suspects (analogous to generating alternatives) and then carefully examines the evidence for and against each one.

The File Game

In the file game, students are presented with a large file that contains information about a fictional middle school student. The file includes a cover page describing a few negative events in the child's life (e.g., receiving a low grade, getting in a fight with a friend) and the child's beliefs following these events. The remainder of the file is filled with a variety of materials (transcripts, journal entries, invitations, notes from friends). Participants are asked to evaluate the student's beliefs by examining these materials. At the end of this activity, the leader reviews the activity with the group and encourages participants to discuss the evidence they found. Students are encouraged to use the skill of examining evidence in their own lives.

Session 4: Evaluating Thoughts and Putting a Negative Event in Perspective

Goals and Overview

The major goals of this session are to:

- Introduce the concept of catastrophizing.
- Teach students how to challenge catastrophic thoughts by applying the putting-it-in perspective technique.
- Teach participants to evaluate their negative thoughts the moment they occur.

After reviewing the homework, the leader encourages students to participate in several activities and discussions (e.g., putting it in perspective, the "hot seat") that emphasize the importance of thinking accurately about the future and quickly evaluating negative thoughts. Then the leader gives students practice engaging in these skills through hypothetical examples and examples from their own lives.

Putting a Negative Event in Perspective

When a negative event happens, children may catastrophize about the event, imagining that the worst-case outcome will occur. Often this happens in a causal chain. For example, if a child's mother is late coming home from work, the child may think, "She is not usually this late. → Something must have happened to her. → Maybe she got in an accident. → She must have been hurt. → She must be lying dead in the road somewhere!" This cascade of (usually inaccurate) thoughts can lead the child to feel anxious and upset. In the putting-it-in perspective activity, students are asked to identify this cascade, which we label the "worst-case scenario." Next, they list the best-case scenario, a positive cascade of events (e.g., my mother won the lottery and that's why she's late), which is also unlikely. Considering the best-case scenario encourages participants to think flexibly. Often, this best case seems humorous, which helps to illustrate that both the worst- and best-case scenarios are unlikely. This paves the way for the next step, in which the leader encourages participants to think about the most likely outcomes. When likely outcomes are negative, students are encouraged to think about what they can do to problem solve or cope effectively.

Rapid Fire Disputation: The Hot Seat

At this point in the PRP curriculum, students have been taught to evaluate and challenge their unrealistic negative beliefs about the causes and consequences of events. However, often students will need to access these cognitive skills at the moment adversity strikes. To accomplish this, we teach students the technique of *rapid fire disputation*—or, for middle school students in PRP, the *hot seat*. In this activity, the leader presents hypothetical negative events (e.g., "I failed a math test") and lists possible pessimistic beliefs about them (e.g., "I must be stupid"). Next, the student on the hot seat fights back against those negative thoughts using the skills of generating evidence against the thought (e.g., "That's not true because I did well on my English test"), providing an alternative interpretation (e.g., "Another way of seeing it is that the test was a hard one and many students failed"), or putting it in perspective (e.g., "The most likely outcome is that my grade for the semester will be lowered but I won't fail the class and I can ask the teacher if I can do extra credit to help with that").

After mastering the hot seat skill in session 4, students are encouraged in future sessions to use it with negative events and thoughts from their own lives. The hot seat is practiced several times throughout the PRP course. Throughout this process, the leader carefully guides students to apply the skills correctly and to avoid common pitfalls, such as dismissing the grain of truth in the situation (e.g., "It's fine. I'll get an A in math for the semester anyway!"). For homework, students try out the hot seat skill when they find themselves thinking pessimistically about an event.

Session 5: Discussion of Conflict and Review

Goals and Overview

The goals of this session are to:

- Apply the cognitive restructuring skills to the common stressors of interparental and family conflict.
- Review material from sessions 1 to 4.

After reviewing the homework, the leader shows a brief video of two parents arguing. The leader encourages students to discuss the video clip, including their thoughts about possible causes and consequences of the argument. Some students catastrophize about the outcomes of parental conflict, for example, thinking that the parents will divorce and that, as a consequence, they will never see one parent again. The leader guides students through the putting-it-in perspective activity in order to generate the most likely outcomes of the fight and to discuss ways to cope with those outcomes. After this section, leaders guide students through a review of the material from the first four sessions by playing *PRP Jeopardy*.

Session 6: Assertiveness and Negotiation

Goals and Overview

The major goals of this session are to:

- Discuss the consequences of passive, aggressive, and assertive interpersonal styles.
- Teach students assertiveness and negotiation skills.

After reviewing the homework, the leader introduces the concept of assertiveness (using three styles of interacting skits), teaches four steps to assertiveness, encourages students to practice assertiveness through hypothetical role-plays and through writing assertive responses to real-life situations in their student notebooks, and teaches a four-step model of negotiation (Say what you want. Listen to what they say. Be wise—compromise. Make a fair deal.).

Styles of Interacting: Skits

Three skits are presented in which characters use an aggressive style (Bully Brenda), a passive style (Pushover Pete), and an assertive style (Say-It-Straight Samantha). Students discuss the outcomes of each skit and discover the benefits of an assertive style: that the Say-It-Straight Samantha character got what she wanted in the situation without angering the other person.

Four Steps to Assertiveness

Students are taught a four-step model of assertiveness (Bower & Bower, 1977), which is referred to as the DEAL (for describe-express-ask-list) model. Students are taught to:

1. Describe the problem.
2. Express how they feel (using "I" statements).
3. Ask for a change (a small, reasonable change).
4. List the improvements the change would make.

Students practice the DEAL model by role-playing being assertive in hypothetical situations. For example:

Whenever you are on the phone and your older brother wants to make a call, he makes you get off, insisting, "I'm older. My phone calls are more important." Your calls are just as important as his; tell him how you feel.

Next, students apply the assertiveness skill to their own lives by completing a worksheet on which they go through the DEAL model using a situation in their lives. Students are encouraged to role-play these situations and to practice their assertive responses. For homework, students are asked to try acting assertively. At the beginning of the next session, students discuss their experiences practicing assertiveness, with the leader providing guidance and coaching. Assertiveness is reviewed and practiced several times in subsequent lessons.

Session 7: Coping Strategies

Goals and Overview

The goals of this session are to:

- Teach students skills for coping with situations that are out of their control, such as when they witness their parents fighting.
- Teach students coping skills to help reduce negative emotions that may interfere with effective problem solving.

After reviewing the homework, the leader teaches the students several coping strategies to include: thinking of something good (positive imagery); leaving the room and coming back later (temporary distraction); and talking to someone (elicit help from adults). The leader also guides students through three kinds of relaxation techniques: deep breathing, progressive muscle relaxation, and visualization techniques. Next, through the use of skits and hypothetical dilemmas, leaders guide students in applying coping techniques to control excessive anger and sadness in social situations. For homework, students are asked to practice the coping strategies in their own lives.

Session 8: Overcoming Procrastination, and Social Skills Training

Goals and Overview

The major goals of this session are to:

- Teach participants skills they can use to combat procrastination.
- Teach participants social skills techniques.

Children who are depressed often have difficulties with procrastination and social skills. Therefore, this lesson targets these difficulties. After reviewing the homework, students complete an activity in which they break up a large task (e.g., a big science project) into multiple smaller steps (e.g., choose a topic, collect library books on that topic, read first book, summarize the book) and then identify rewards proportional to each step completed (e.g., take a break to listen to music or watch TV for 10 minutes). To help make this activity engaging and more concrete, we give students a drawing of a ladder with 10 rungs and ask them to write each step of their task on a rung of the ladder. This technique can be especially helpful for students who are facing large projects and are feeling overwhelmed by the increasing workload and complexity of assignments in middle school.

Following the procrastination activity, students are taught several techniques for meeting others, interacting with peers (including catching the attention of a group, listening, asking questions, etc.). Students then practice these techniques through role-plays. These kinds of techniques are designed to address some of the social skills difficulties that have been linked to depression in children and adolescents.

Session 9: Decision Making and Review

Goals and Overview

The major goals of this lesson are to:

- Teach a model for decision making.
- Review previous skills, including assertiveness and relaxation.

After reviewing the homework, the leader teaches students a technique for decision making that can be applied to a variety of life domains, including achievement and social situations. This skill is then incorporated into the problem-solving approach that is presented in lesson 10.

Decision Making

Students are presented with a situation that involves making a difficult decision. For example: What would they do if they saw a classmate cheating on an exam? What if they really wanted to get an A and the teacher said that only the top five scores would be given an A? The leader uses this example to introduce a decision-making technique that involves listing possible solutions, including the pros and cons (pluses and minuses) of each decision, and considering which pros and which cons are most important (hence, should be given the most weight).

Students discuss this process for several hypothetical examples before applying the skill to make decisions in their own lives.

Session 10: Problem Solving

Goals and Overview

The major goals of this lesson are to:

- Teach a model for problem-solving skills, specifically in the context of difficult interpersonal problems.
- Help students apply this model to day-to-day problems that are common during middle school.

The leader presents a five-step model for problem solving, based, in part, on Dodge and Crick's model of social information processing (Dodge & Crick, 1990). The model encourages students to:

1. Stop and think, and make sure they are evaluating the situation accurately.
2. Choose a goal.
3. Make a list of possible solutions.
4. Decide what to do.
5. Go for the goal.

Students are also taught to evaluate the outcome of this process, and continue to use the process when one solution doesn't seem to work. The leader helps students apply this model through a group discussion of scenarios depicting interpersonal problems and then to situations in their own lives.

Session 11: Problem Solving (Continued) and Review

Goals and Overview

The major goals of this lesson are to:

- Reinforce learning of the five-step problem-solving model.
- Review concepts from the entire program.

Students are encouraged to apply the five-step model to hypothetical and real-life situations as a group. Then, students practice skills and play games designed to review the content of previous sessions.

Session 12: Review and Party

Goals and Overview

The major goals of this lesson are to:

- Review content of the program.
- Encourage students to use the skills in the future.
- Celebrate students' completion of the program and say goodbye.

As in Session 11, students play games that review program content. Students also act out skits illustrating the program skills and discuss future uses of the skills.

Discussion: Using Skills in the Future

Leaders encourage students to summarize what they will take away from the program and how they think they might apply the skills in the future. First, students discuss difficult situations that they anticipate in the next few months or the next academic year (e.g., making the transition to high school). Then, they consider which skill(s) they could use in each situation.

Clinical Examples

Although PRP is usually delivered as a manualized intervention to a school-based (and, therefore, normative) population, PRP skills and activities may also be useful to child psychotherapists. A therapist can match a specific clinical dilemma with a skill taught in PRP and thereby "import" into the therapy an established intervention. For example, skills of self-assertiveness, represented by the graphic icon Say-It-Straight Samantha, might be useful with a 10-year-old girl who reveals to her therapist how scared she is to tell her divorced father she doesn't like his constant criticism.

An interesting parallel exists here with the observation that therapists need creativity and imagination to breathe life into a structured, manualized therapy (Kendall, Chu, Gifford, Hayes, & Nauta, 1998): therapists who match "imported" snippets of manualized, proven therapies to clinical dilemmas may in effect breathe efficacy into a therapy. The PRP visual icons are helpful representations of coping skills a therapist may want to introduce to a child. For example, cartoons with thought bubbles depict the capacity for understanding self-talk in common

(continued)

situations, and other cartoonlike figures summarize important psychological functions or dilemmas:

- Sherlock Holmes is the detective who checks his ideas against the facts and comes up with a plan and thereby represents realistic thinking.
- Chicken Little, the ultimate in negative cognition, catastrophizes a tiny acorn into a cosmic calamity.
- Hopeful Holly sees setbacks as temporary and surmountable.
- A chart of pluses and minuses aids in decision making.
- A sliced-up pie helps sort out the contribution from each of many factors that contribute to a single setback.

The child therapist imports that skill which is the best fit for the dilemma confronted by the child. This is a dilemma-specific approach to importing curative elements from manualized therapies. It has the advantage that it may bypass therapists' well-known resistance to manuals, yet nevertheless allow importing the specific and proven skill needed just when the child is seeking such resolution to his or her dilemma. This approach of encouraging therapists to import elements of PRP into their psychotherapies is consistent with calls for increased efforts to implement effective therapies (Kazdin & Weisz, 2003).

The following are some illustrations of PRP skills from our work leading and supervising PRP groups, and conducting and supervising therapy with children and adolescents. Identifying information has been altered to protect confidentiality.

Looking for Evidence to Test Ideas: The Child as Sherlock

Roberta, a 12-year-old girl, often blamed herself and felt guilty about problems in her single-parent family. She felt she was the cause of fights between her mother and her brother whenever she told her brother he was not welcome in her room. Her brother would then plead with their mother, leading to a fight. In response to Roberta's blaming herself, the therapist introduced the basic idea: "Don't believe the first thought that pops into your head. Be like Sherlock. Look for evidence!" The therapist mimed Sherlock by pretending to hold up a magnifying glass to look for clues, and then pointed to the cutout on her desk of Sherlock holding such a tool.

To structure the resulting list of what precipitated fighting in their home, Roberta was taught to: "Make a pie of all the things that cause fights between your mother and your brother. Make it a big slice if we count a lot of fights that started that way, and a little slice if it isn't a big deal." Roberta labeled one slice, "George gets scared at night and acts like a baby," another "George won't take no for an answer," a third "Mom blows up," and a final small piece, "I like to be alone in my room." Roberta had taken inventory of actual precipitants the way Sherlock might have, and used the results to "make a pie" to parcel out causes in a more realistic way than her first thought, "It's my fault when George and Mom fight."

Easing Pain in the Midst of Loss: Examining Evidence

Dawn's 17-year-old sister Tanya was killed in a car accident a month before her PRP group began. Understandably, Dawn was devastated. She missed her sister terribly, and her family life had been shattered. Dawn reported intense feelings of sadness and loss. During the fourth session, she described additional feelings of guilt and remorse, which made the group leader even more concerned about her. When asked about those feelings, Dawn reported that she and her sister had been fighting the day Tanya was killed. She hated herself for this and was convinced that Tanya's spirit was angry with her and would never forgive her. The leader and other group members listened to Dawn's concerns and provided empathy and support.

After some time, the leader also gently asked Dawn questions that encouraged her to examine her beliefs more closely and consider the evidence for these beliefs. For example, did she and Tanya usually stay angry at each other for long, or did they typically make up after arguments? (Dawn reported that they always made up.) How quickly did they usually make up? How long did she think Tanya would stay angry with her this time? Did she think Tanya would stay angry with her forever, or would she forgive her? This last question had a powerful effect on Dawn. Her relief was palpable, as she said, "Tanya never stayed angry with me for very long. We definitely would have been friends again if she were alive. I guess her spirit can't be that angry with me anymore either."

The leader encouraged Dawn to attend to her self-talk and to challenge negative thoughts about herself by examining evidence and considering alternatives. Although Dawn's sadness continued for some time, important changes began to occur over the next few weeks. Her feelings of guilt and remorse subsided and her energy level increased.

Putting an Event in Perspective

Twelve-year-old Brittany was discouraged after losing her best friend Amanda when her family moved. Brittany often catastrophized with thoughts such as, "I'll never find anyone to stay over at my house now," and "I'll never find another best friend again." The therapist encouraged her to think about the worst, best, and most likely outcome of her efforts to find an equally good friend now. She was already imagining a range of worst-case scenarios, like "No one at my new school will ever sit with me at lunch," and, even, "I'll be alone forever." With some coaching, she and her therapist created an equally unlikely best outcome: "All the

(continued)

girls will decide it's so cool I moved here, they'll all want to be friends. The phone will be ringing all night!" Then they discussed the middle ground. The most likely outcome was, "I'll probably have another best friend, eventually."

By pushing thinking toward an unrealistic best outcome, this technique offers children a sometimes amusing look at how wide a range of thoughts can be created about a single situation. By encouraging them to create a most likely outcome, the technique encourages them to "be like Sherlock" and look for evidence in evaluating alternative interpretations.

Healthy Self-Assertion: Saying It Straight

Thirteen-year-old Brett came into therapy because she became irritable and depressed around her grandfather, who was often grumpy and overly critical of her. Brett was coached in four basic steps of assertiveness:

1. Telling her grandfather what he was doing that bothered her.
2. Expressing how she felt as a result.
3. Suggesting to her grandfather how he might change his behavior.
4. Describing how she would feel as a result.

   Brett also learned how to prepare for the difficult days when she might have more exposure to her grandfather, by doing relaxation through deep breathing and negotiating time out of the house.

Using Pluses and Minuses in Decision Making: A Lesson from Ben Franklin

Eleven-year-old Jessie and her mother were trying to decide which private school would be best for her, but were having difficulty structuring their discussion. To help, Jessie, her mother, and the therapist constructed a pluses and minuses rating sheet for the four schools, with columns for the factors that seemed most important to Jessie and her mother: how convenient the school location was, whether it offered art, whether she knew kids there, the size of the classes, the price, and the school's academic reputation. The therapist mentioned afterward that Ben Franklin's pluses and minuses system is a useful way to think about decisions.

EVIDENCE OF EFFECTIVENESS

The first controlled study of PRP evaluated the intervention with fifth- and sixth-grade children who reported elevated depressive symptoms or high levels of family conflict. PRP participants were compared with a matched control group. Findings suggested that PRP's effects were significant and long-lasting. Following the intervention, and through 3 years of follow-up, children in the

PRP condition scored less pessimistically than controls on a measure of cognitive style (Gillham et al., 1995; Gillham & Reivich, 1999; Jaycox et al., 1994). Children in PRP reported fewer symptoms of depression for 2 years after the intervention ended, and were only about half as likely as controls to report moderate to severe levels of symptoms at the 2-year follow-up (Gillham et al., 1995).

More than 10 controlled studies of PRP have followed, most with positive results (e.g., Cardemil et al., 2002; Chaplin et al., 2006; Gillham, Reivich, et al., 2006; Yu & Seligman, 2002). For example, in an evaluation of a Chinese version of PRP with children in Beijing, PRP prevented depressive symptoms through the 6-month follow-up period (Yu & Seligman, 2002). A recent study of PRP in a primary care setting found that PRP significantly prevented psychological disorders related to depression and anxiety in participants with high levels of initial symptoms (Gillham, Hamilton, et al., 2006). However, a few studies have failed to replicate PRP's effects on depressive symptoms (e.g., Pattison & Lynd-Stevenson, 2001; Roberts et al., 2003, 2004) and some studies have found significant effects among some subgroups of participants but not others (e.g., Cardemil et al., 2002; Gillham, Hamilton, et al., 2006).

There is increasing evidence that PRP may affect a variety of outcomes in addition to depression. For example, PRP appears to prevent symptoms of anxiety (Gillham, Reivich, et al., 2006; Roberts et al., 2003, 2004), and may reduce behavioral problems as well (Cutuli, 2004; Jaycox et al., 1994). These findings support our impression that the PRP skills may be useful for many children and adolescents, not just those at risk for depression.

Current work on PRP is focusing on how to make PRP's effects stronger and more consistent. Booster sessions have been designed to remind children of the PRP skills and help them apply them to new situations as they make the transition into adolescence. A parent component (Reivich, Gillham, & Shatté, 2002) to the intervention teaches parents to use the core PRP skills in their own lives, with the hope that this will enable them to model and encourage their children's use of the skills. In a recent pilot study, the combination of the student and parent PRP programs prevented symptoms of depression and anxiety, and substantially prevented clinical levels of anxiety through the 12-month follow-up (Gillham, Reivich, et al., 2006). A larger-scale evaluation of this program has been funded by the National Institute of Mental Health and is currently underway.

PREVENTING DEPRESSION IN GIRLS

Penn Resiliency Program's Effectiveness with Girls

In general, PRP appears to be effective for both girls and boys. At least two studies have found PRP's effects differed by gender, however. A reanalysis of data from the first PRP study revealed a significant preventive effect in boys, but not girls (Reivich, 1996). Boys in the control group reported the highest level of depressive symptoms across the follow-up, with relatively low levels of symptoms in PRP boys, PRP girls, and control girls. Because this was the first controlled study of PRP, it was unclear whether the pattern of findings resulted from limited effects of PRP with girls or limited room for an effect on depressive symptoms in the girls in this study (because their mean levels of symptoms were already quite low). Subsequent studies have not consistently found stronger effects for boys. In a recently completed study, PRP significantly prevented depressive symptoms among girls, but not boys (Gillham, Hamilton, et al., 2006).

Following the 1996 finding, we were concerned that co-ed PRP groups might have limited effectiveness with girls because girls may experience different challenges than boys during the transition to adolescence, and they may be reluctant to discuss some of these challenges (e.g., concerns about body image) in a co-ed environment. In addition, boys often receive more attention than girls in co-ed group settings (Bailey, 1993; Jones, 1989; Krupnick, 1985). There are several likely reasons for this. Boys may be more comfortable expressing their opinions in groups, and they are more likely than girls to call out demandingly in class (Altermatt, Jovanovic, & Perry, 1998). It is well documented that boys are more likely than girls to exhibit aggressive and disruptive behaviors (Achenbach, 1991). Our PRP group leaders reported that they often managed such behavioral difficulties by working hard to engage boys in the group activities and discussions, perhaps at the expense of girls who were usually more cooperative.

These concerns led us to wonder whether PRP might be more effective for girls when delivered in an all-girls format. We recently completed a study that tested this hypothesis (Chaplin et al., 2006). In this study, girls were randomly assigned to three conditions: co-ed PRP, all-girls PRP, or no-intervention control. Leaders covered the same material in the co-ed and all-girls PRP conditions. The only difference was in whether the group was composed of both girls and boys, or just girls. Findings from this study suggested that girls benefited more from the all-girls than co-ed group format. Following the intervention, girls in both PRP conditions reported significantly lower levels of depressive symptoms than girls in the control condition; however, girls in the all-girls PRP attended more sessions than girls in the co-ed PRP, and experienced greater reductions in hopelessness than girls in the co-ed PRP and girls in the control condition (Chaplin et al., 2006). Moving to an all-girls format was a relatively small change. The all-girls format may increase girls' comfort with discussing body image and other concerns that are particularly relevant to girls as they enter adolescence; but an all-girls intervention that explicitly targets gender-related risk factors could have even stronger effects on depression.

Building Stronger Prevention Programs for Girls

Like most depression prevention programs, PRP focuses on cognitive risk factors and problem-solving strategies that appear to be related to depression in boys and girls. Several risk factors may be more relevant to depression in girls, however. Women are more likely than men to respond to stressors with passive coping and rumination, which may amplify negative emotion and depression (Keenan & Hipwell, 2005; Nolen-Hoeksema, 1991). Girls and women are often socialized to restrict anger expression, and this restriction may also be linked to depression, particularly for girls (Chaplin & Cole, 2005). Body image concerns are more common in females than males and are closely tied to depressive symptoms (Stice & Bearman, 2001). In addition, girls view the physical changes of puberty more negatively than do boys, which appears to be one reason that transition to puberty is more closely linked to depression in girls than boys (Ge et al., 2001; Petersen et al., 1991).

On a societal level, girls may receive different messages from boys about their value, their capabilities, and their potential roles in society. Although opportunities for girls and women have increased dramatically in this country in the past century, even today girls are bombarded with images and information that convey the importance of attractiveness, along with unrealistic standards for beauty. These images also portray traditional roles for women. In addition, there are still limited numbers of women in many careers and in positions of power (Becker, Burwell, Gilman, Herzog, & Hamburg, 2002; LeCroy & Daley, 2001; Malkin, Wornian, & Chrisler, 1999; Smith, 1994). The internalization of these negative cultural messages may increase girls' vulnerability to depression and other problems (Stice, Spangler, & Agras, 2001). Importantly, sex differences in depression may be attenuated in countries that don't have a thin-ideal for women's attractiveness (McCarthy, 1990).

Recently, depression prevention researchers have called for interventions that target women and girls (e.g., Le, Muñoz, Ippen, & Stoddard, 2003). Few depression prevention programs target body image, rumination, or social-contextual risk factors that are particularly relevant for girls. One notable exception is the cognitive-behavioral intervention for college women evaluated by Bearman and colleagues (Bearman et al., 2003). This intervention targeted body image concerns and reduced body dissatisfaction and symptoms of bulimia and depression through a 3-month follow-up period (Bearman et al., 2003). Although not specifically designed to prevent depression, the Go Grrrls program developed by

LeCroy and Daley (2001) strives to enhance well-being in early adolescent girls by helping them reflect on societal messages, develop positive self-images, set goals, and establish and maintain friendships. A recent study evaluated the immediate effects of the intervention and found that the Go Grrrls curriculum improved girls' scores on measures of body image satisfaction, assertiveness, self-efficacy, and self-liking and competence, relative to a no-intervention control condition. The intervention also tended to improve levels of hopelessness (LeCroy, 2004).

One New Direction: The Girls in Transition Program

We are currently working on an intervention, the GT program, that focuses on several gender-related risk factors. GT includes many of the skills covered in PRP and other cognitive-behavioral depression prevention programs, but expands the discussion of these skills to highlight issues that may be particularly important for girls in early adolescence. For example, the assertiveness section includes a discussion of societal messages and pressures that may make it difficult for many girls and women to be assertive. Girls are encouraged to reflect on these pressures, to identify messages they may have internalized, and to evaluate these messages by examining evidence and alternatives and by examining the pros and cons of engaging in assertive behavior.

GT covers many additional concepts and skills. For example, one session focuses on response styles, such as rumination, that appear to be more common in girls and women. Girls are encouraged to identify times when they ruminate or dwell on negative emotions and events, to discuss the pros and cons of ruminating, and to break the cycle of rumination by trying out other coping strategies. Other sessions encourage girls to examine media messages about body image and to reflect on how these messages may affect them and other girls their age. Girls are encouraged to think critically about unrealistic physical standards for attractiveness. The intervention also strives to reduce focus on body image by helping girls to identify positive role models, consider their goals, and identify the qualities they possess that are important in their close relationships.

GT also hopes to create an environment that will nurture girls as they make the transition into early adolescence. The parent sessions and teacher workshops present information about girls' development, cognitive and problem-solving skills that may increase resilience and prevent depression (in boys and girls), and ways they can promote girls' well-being during the transition to adolescence.

CONCLUSIONS

Depression is a common problem among youth, especially girls, when they reach adolescence. Fortunately, several interventions have shown promise in treating and prevention depression. Among these are cognitive-behavioral interventions, such as the PRP, which was described in this chapter. Like most cognitive-behavioral interventions, PRP teaches a variety of skills designed to help youth think more accurately about the problems they encounter and to develop effective problem-solving and coping strategies. PRP has been evaluated in several studies over the past 15 years. Findings from most of these studies suggest that PRP reduces and prevents symptoms of depression in late childhood and early adolescence.

Because interventions like PRP are manualized programs, they can be delivered in school, clinics, and other community settings by a variety of providers including teachers, counselors, and clinicians. The specific cognitive-behavioral concepts and techniques also can be added to ongoing therapies on an as-needed basis, for example, when they are relevant to the specific problems and dilemmas that confront children and adolescents. Our research suggests that the PRP skills prevent depressive symptoms in children with high levels of symptoms, as well as in children with few or no current symptoms. Based on this research and our clinical work with children and adolescents, we believe that the resilience skills covered in PRP are helpful to most children and adolescents.

Given the sex difference in depression that emerges in adolescence, it is important to develop interventions that successfully treat and prevent depression in girls. Most of the existing depression prevention programs for youth, including PRP, are designed for boys and girls. Although these programs are usually beneficial to both boys and girls, they usually do not target risk factors such as body image concerns, rumination, or social-contextual factors that may be particularly relevant to depression in girls. Depression may be more powerfully prevented in adolescent girls by cognitive-behavioral interventions that are designed specifically for them. We hope that future work on depression prevention will explore this possibility.

For information on obtaining the PRP curriculum, please contact info@pennproject.org, or contact Dr. Gillham directly. For information on the GT program, please contact Dr. Gillham or Dr. Chaplin.

REFERENCES

Abela, J. R. Z., Vanderbilt, E., & Rochon, A. (2004). A test of the integration of response styles and social support theories of depression in third- and seventh-grade children. *Journal of Social and Clinical Psychology, 23,* 653–674.

Abramson, L. Y., Metalsky, G. I., & Alloy, L. B. (1989). Hopelessness depression: A theory-based subtype of depression. *Psychological Review, 96,* 358–372.

Abramson, L. Y., Seligman, M. E. P., & Teasdale, J. E. (1978). Learned helplessness in humans: Critique and reformulation. *Journal of Abnormal Psychology, 87,* 49–74.

Achenbach, T. M. (1991). *Manual for the child behavior checklist.* Burlington: University of Vermont.

Altermatt, E. R., Jovanovic, J., & Perry, M. (1998). Bias or responsivity? Sex and achievement level effects on teachers' classroom questioning practices. *Journal of Educational Psychology, 90,* 516–527.

Altmann, E. O., & Gotlib, I. H. (1988). The social behavior of depressed children: An observational study. *Journal of Abnormal Child Psychology, 16,* 29–44.

Angold, A., Costello, E. J., & Worthman, C. M. (1998). Puberty and depression: The roles of age, pubertal status, and pubertal timing. *Psychological Medicine, 28,* 51–61.

Bailey, S. M. (1993). The current status of gender equity research in American schools. *Educational Psychologist, 28,* 321–339.

Bearman, S. K., Stice, E., & Chase, A. (2003). Evaluation of an intervention targeting both depressive and bulimic pathology: A randomized prevention trial. *Behavior Therapy, 34,* 277–293.

Beck, A. T. (1976). *Cognitive therapy and the emotional disorders.* New York: International Universities Press.

Beck, A. T., Rush, A. J., Shaw, B. F., & Emery, G. (1979). *Cognitive therapy of depression: A treatment manual.* New York: Guilford Press.

Becker, A. E., Burwell, R. A., Gilman, S. E., Herzog, D. B., & Hamburg, P. (2002). Eating behaviours and attitudes following prolonged exposure to television among ethnic Fijian adolescent girls. *British Journal of Psychiatry, 180,* 509–514.

Bemporad, J. (1994). Dynamic and interpersonal theories of depression. In W. M. Reynolds & H. F. Johnston (Eds.), *Handbook of depression in children and adolescents: Issues in clinical child psychology* (pp. 81–95). New York: Plenum Press.

Berndt, T. J. (1987). The distinctive features of conversations between friends: Theories, research, and implications for sociomoral development. In W. M. Kurtines & J. L. Gewirtz (Eds.), *Moral development through social interaction* (pp. 281–300). Chichester, West Sussex, England: Wiley.

Bower, S. A., & Bower, G. H. (1977). *Asserting yourself: A practical guide for positive change.* Cambridge, MA: Addison-Wesley.

Buchanan, G. M., & Seligman, M. E. P. (Eds.). (1995). *Explanatory style.* Hillsdale, NJ: Erlbaum.

Cardemil, E. V., Reivich, K. J., & Seligman, M. E. P. (2002, May). The prevention of depressive symptoms in low-income minority middle school students. *Prevention and Treatment, 5.*

Chaplin, T. M., & Cole, P. M. (2005). The role of emotion regulation in the development of psychopathology. In B. L. Hankin & J. R. Z. Abela (Eds.), *Development of psychopathology: A vulnerability-stress perspective* (pp. 49–74). Thousand Oaks, CA: Sage.

Chaplin, T. M., Gillham, J. E., Reivich, K., Elkon, A. G. L., Samuels, B., Freres, D. R., et al. (2006). Depression prevention for early adolescent girls: A pilot study of all-girls versus co-ed groups. *Journal of Early Adolescence, 26,* 110–126.

Clarke, G. N., Hawkins, W., Murphy, M., Sheeber, L. B., Lewinsohn, P. M., & Seeley, J. R. (1995). Targeted prevention of unipolar depressive disorder in an at-risk sample of high school adolescents: A randomized trial of a group cognitive intervention. *Journal of the American Academy of Child and Adolescent Psychiatry, 34,* 312–321.

Clarke, G. N., Hornbrook, M., Lynch, F., Polen, M., Gale, J., Beardslee, W., et al. (2001). A randomized trial of a group cognitive intervention for preventing depression in adolescent offspring of depressed parents. *Archives of General Psychiatry, 58,* 1127–1134.

Cohen, P., Cohen, J., Kasen, S., Velez, C. N., Hartmark, C., Johnson, J., et al. (1993). An epidemiological study of disorders in late childhood and adolescence: I. Age and gender-specific prevalence. *Journal of Child Psychology and Psychiatry, 34,* 851–867.

Cole, D. A., Martin, J. M., Peeke, L. A., Seroczynski, A. D., & Fier, J. (1999). Children's over- and underestimation of academic competence: A longitudinal study of gender differences, depression, and anxiety. *Child Development, 70,* 459–473.

Compton, S. N., March, J. S., Brent, D., Albano, A. M., Weersing, V. R., & Curry, J. (2004). Cognitive-behavioral psychotherapy for anxiety and depressive disorders in children and adolescents: An evidence-based medicine review. *Journal of the American Academy of Child and Adolescent Psychiatry, 43,* 930–959.

Costello, E. J., Pine, D. S., Hammen, C., March, J. S., Plotsky, P. M., Weissman, M. M., et al. (2002). Development and natural history of mood disorders. *Biological Psychiatry, 52*(6), 529–542.

Csikszentmihalyi, M., & Larson, R. (1984). *Being adolescent.* New York: Basic Books.

Cutuli, J. J. (2004). *Preventing externalizing symptoms and related features in adolescence.* Unpublished honors thesis, University of Pennsylvania, Philadelphia.

Damon, W., & Hart, D. (1988). *Self-understanding in childhood and adolescence.* New York: Cambridge University Press.

Dodge, K. A., & Crick, N. R. (1990). Social information-processing bases of aggressive behavior in children. *Personality and Social Psychology Bulletin, 16,* 8–22.

Dozois, D. J. A., & Dobson, K. S. (Eds.). (2004). *The prevention of anxiety and depression: Theory, research, and practice* (pp. 185–204). Washington, DC: American Psychological Association.

Eccles, J. S., & Midgley, C. (1990). Changes in academic motivation and self-perception during adolescence. In R. Montemayor, G. R. Adams, & T. P. Gullotta (Eds.), *From childhood to adolescence: A transitional period? Advances in adolescent development: An annual book series* (Vol. 2, pp. 134–155). Thousand Oaks, CA: Sage.

Eccles, J. S., Midgley, C., Wigfield, A., Buchanan, C. M., Reuman, D., Flanagan, C., et al. (1993). Development during adolescence: The impact of stage-environment fit on young adolescents' experiences in schools and in families. *American Psychologist, 48,* 90–101.

Ellis, A. (1962). *Reason and emotion in psychotherapy.* New York: Lyle Stuart.

Garber, J., Kriss, M. R., Koch, M., & Lindholm, L. (1988). Recurrent depression in adolescents: A follow-up study. *Journal of the American Academy of Child and Adolescent Psychiatry, 27,* 49–54.

Garber, J., Quiggle, N., & Shanley, N. (1990). Cognition and depression in children and adolescents. In R. E. Ingram (Ed.), *Contemporary psychological approaches to depression: Theory, research, and treatment* (pp. 87–115). New York: Plenum Press.

Garrison, C. Z., Schluchter, M. D., Schoenbach, V. J., & Kaplan, B. K. (1989). Epidemiology of depressive symptoms in young adolescents. *Journal of the American Academy of Child and Adolescent Psychiatry, 28,* 343–351.

Ge, X., Conger, R. D., & Elder, G. H. (2001). Pubertal transition, stressful life events, and the emergence of gender differences in adolescent depressive symptoms. *Developmental Psychology, 37,* 404–417.

Gillham, J., Hamilton, J., Freres, D. R., Patton, K., & Gallop, R. (2006). Preventing depression among early adolescents in the primary care setting: A randomized controlled study of the Penn Resiliency Program. *Journal of Abnormal Child Psychology, 34,* 203–219.

Gillham, J., Jaycox, L., Reivich, K., Hollon, S. D., Freeman, A., DeRubeis, R. J., et al. (1991). *The APEX Project manual for group leaders.* Unpublished manual, University of Pennsylvania.

Gillham, J., Jaycox, L., Reivich, K., Seligman, M. E. P., & Silver, T. (1990). *The Penn Optimism Program.* Unpublished manual, University of Pennsylvania.

Gillham, J., Jaycox, L., Reivich, K., Seligman, M. E. P., & Silver, T. (2003). *The Penn Resiliency Program.* Unpublished manual, University of Pennsylvania and Adaptiv Learning Systems.

Gillham, J., & Reivich, K. J. (1999). Prevention of depressive symptoms in school children: A research update. *Psychological Science, 10,* 461–462.

Gillham, J., Reivich, K., Freres, D. R., Lascher, M., Litzinger, S., Shatté, A., et al. (2006). School-based prevention of depression and anxiety symptoms in early adolescence: A pilot of a parent intervention component. *School Psychology Quarterly, 21,* 323–348.

Gillham, J., Reivich, K., Jaycox, L., & Seligman, M. E. P. (1995). Preventing depressive symptoms in schoolchildren: Two year follow-up. *Psychological Science, 6,* 343–351.

Gillham, J., Reivich, K., & Shatté, A. J. (2001). Building optimism and preventing depressive symptoms in children. In E. C. Chang (Ed.), *Optimism and pessimism* (pp. 301–320). Washington, DC: American Psychological Association.

Gillham, J., Shatté, A. J., & Freres, D. R. (2000). Depression prevention: A review of cognitive-behavioral and family interventions. *Applied and Preventive Psychology, 9,* 63–88.

Gladstone, T. R. G., & Kaslow, N. J. (1995). Depression and attributions in children and adolescents: A meta-analytic review. *Journal of Abnormal Child Psychology, 23,* 597–606.

Gotlib, I. H., Lewinsohn, P. M., & Seeley, J. R. (1995). Symptoms versus a diagnosis of depression: Differences in psychosocial functioning. *Journal of Consulting and Clinical Psychology, 63,* 90–100.

Gotlib, I. H., Lewinsohn, P. M., Seeley, J. R., Rohde, P., & Redner, J. E. (1993). Negative cognitions and attributional style in depressed adolescents: An examination of stability and specificity. *Journal of Abnormal Psychology, 102,* 607–615.

Hankin, B. L., & Abela, J. R. Z. (2005). Depression from childhood through adolescence and adulthood: A developmental vulnerability and stress perspective. In B. L. Hankin & J. R. Z. Abela (Eds.), *Development of psychopathology: A vulnerability-stress perspective* (pp. 245–288). Thousand Oaks, CA: Sage.

Hankin, B. L., & Abramson, L. Y. (2001). Development of gender differences in depression: An elaborated cognitive vulnerability-transactional stress theory. *Psychological Bulletin, 127,* 773–796.

Hankin, B. L., Abramson, L. Y., Moffitt, T. E., Silva, P. A., & McGee, R. (1998). Development of depression from preadolescence to young adulthood: Emerging gender differences in a 10-year longitudinal study. *Journal of Abnormal Psychology, 107,* 128–140.

Harrington, R., Fudge, H., Rutter, M., Pickles, A., & Hill, J. (1990). Adult outcomes of childhood and adolescent depression. *Archives of General Psychiatry, 47,* 465–473.

Hirschfeld, R., Keller, M., Panico, S., Arons, B., Barlow, D., Davidoff, F., et al. (1997). The National Depressive and Manic-Depressive Association consensus statement on the undertreatment of depression. *Journal of the American Medical Association, 277,* 333–340.

Hollon, S. D., & DeRubeis, R. J. (2004). Effectiveness of treatment for depression. In R. L. Leahy (Ed.), *Contemporary cognitive therapy: Theory, research, and practice* (pp. 45–61). New York: Guilford Press.

Hollon, S. D., DeRubeis, R. J., Shelton, R. C., Amsterdam, J. D., Salomon, R. M., O'Reardon, J. P., et al. (2005). Prevention of relapse following cognitive therapy vs. medications in moderate to severe depression. *Archives of General Psychiatry, 62,* 417–422.

Hollon, S. D., Muñoz, R. F., Barlow, D. H., Beardslee, W. R., Bell, C. C., Bernal, G., et al. (2002). Psychosocial intervention development for the prevention and treatment of depression: Promoting innovation and increasing access. *Biological Psychiatry, 52,* 610–630.

Horowitz, J. L., & Garber, J. (2006). The prevention of depressive symptoms in children and adolescents: A meta-analytic review. *Journal of Consulting and Clinical Psychology, 74,* 401–415.

Inhelder, B., & Piaget, J. (1958). *The growth of logical thinking from childhood to adolescence.* New York: Basic Books.

Jarrett, R. B., Kraft, D., Doyle, J., Foster, B. M., Eaves, G. G., & Silver, P. C. (2001). Preventing recurrent depression using cognitive therapy with and without a continuation phase. *Archives of General Psychiatry, 58,* 381–388.

Jaycox, L. H., Reivich, K. J., Gillham, J., & Seligman, M. E. P. (1994). Prevention of depressive symptoms in school children. *Behaviour Research and Therapy, 32*(8), 801–816.

Jones, G. (1989). Gender bias in classroom interactions. *Contemporary Education, 60,* 216–222.

Kaslow, N. J., Brown, R. T., & Mee, L. L. (1994). Cognitive and behavioral correlates of childhood depression: A developmental perspective. In W. M.

Reynolds & H. F. Johnston (Eds.), *Handbook of depression in children and adolescents* (pp. 97–121). New York: Plenum Press.

Kazdin, A. E., Rodgers, A., & Colbus, D. (1986). The Hopelessness Scale for Children: Psychometric characteristics and concurrent validity. *Journal of Consulting and Clinical Psychology, 54*(2), 241–245.

Kazdin, A. E., & Weisz, J. R. (2003). Introduction: Context and background of evidence-based psychotherapies for children and adolescents. In A. E. Kazdin & J. R. Weisz (Eds.), *Evidence-based psychotherapists for children and adolescents* (pp. 3–20). New York: Guilford Press.

Keenan, K., & Hipwell, A. E. (2005). Preadolescent clues to understanding depression in girls. *Clinical Child and Family Psychology Review, 8,* 89–105.

Kendall, P. C., Chu, B., Gifford, A., Hayes, C., & Nauta, M. (1998). Breathing life into a manual: Flexibility and creativity with manual-based treatments. *Cognitive and Behavioral Practice, 5,* 177–198.

Kessler, R. C., McGonagle, K. A., Zhao, S., Nelson, C. B., Hughes, M., Eshelman, S., et al. (1994). Lifetime and 12-month prevalence of DSM-III-R psychiatric disorders in the United States: Results from the National Comorbidity Survey. *Archives of General Psychiatry, 51,* 8–19.

Kim-Cohen, J., Caspi, A., Moffitt, T. E., Harrington, H., Milne, B. J., & Poulton, R. (2003). Prior juvenile diagnoses in adults with mental disorder: Developmental follow-back of a prospective-longitudinal cohort. *Archives of General Psychiatry, 60,* 709–717.

Krupnick, C. (1985). Women and men in the classroom. *On Teaching and Learning, 12,* 18–25.

Le, H., Muñoz, R. F., Ippen, C. G., & Stoddard, J. L. (2003, September). Treatment is not enough: We must prevent major depression in women. *Prevention and Treatment, 6,* np.

LeCroy, C. W. (2004). Experimental evaluation of "Go Grrrls" preventive intervention for early adolescent girls. *Journal of Primary Prevention, 25,* 457–473.

LeCroy, C. W., & Daley, J. (2001). *Empowering adolescent girls: Examining the present and building skills for the future with the Go Grrrls Program.* New York: Norton.

Lewinsohn, P. M., Hops, H., Roberts, R. E., & Seeley, J. R. (1993). Adolescent psychopathology: I. Prevalence and incidence of depression and other

DSM-III-R disorders in high school students. *Abnormal Psychology, 102,* 133–144.

Malkin, A. R., Wornian, K., & Chrisler, J. C. (1999). Women and weight: Gendered messages on magazine covers. *Sex Roles, 40,* 647–656.

McCarthy, M. (1990). The thin ideal, depression, and eating disorders in women. *Behavioural Research and Therapy, 28,* 205–218.

McCauley, E., Mitchell, J. R., Burke, P., & Moss, S. (1988). Cognitive attributes of depression in children and adolescents. *Journal of Consulting and Clinical Psychology, 56,* 903–908.

Merry, S., McDowell, H., Hetrick, S., Bir, J., & Muller, N. (2004). Psychological and/or educational interventions for the prevention of depression in children and adolescents. *The Cochrane Library, 2.*

Nolen-Hoeksema, S. (1991). Responses to depression and their effects on the duration of depressive episodes. *Journal of Abnormal Psychology, 100,* 569–582.

Nolen-Hoeksema, S., & Girgus, J. S. (1994). The emergence of gender differences in depression during adolescence. *Psychological Bulletin, 115,* 424–443.

Nolen-Hoeksema, S., Girgus, J. S., & Seligman, M. E. P. (1992). Predictors and consequences of childhood depressive symptoms: A five-year longitudinal study. *Journal of Abnormal Psychology, 101,* 405–422.

Paikoff, R. L., & Brooks-Gunn, J. (1991). Do parent-child relationships change during puberty? *Psychological Bulletin, 110,* 47–66.

Pattison, C., & Lynd-Stevenson, R. M. (2001). The prevention of depressive symptoms in children: The immediate and long-term outcomes of a school-based program. *Behaviour Change, 18,* 92–102.

Peden, A. R., Rayens, M. K., Hall, L. A., & Beebe, L. H. (2001). Preventing depression in high-risk college women: A report of an 18-month follow-up. *Journal of American College Health, 49,* 299–306.

Petersen, A. C., Compas, B. E., Brooks-Gunn, J., Stemmler, M., Ey, S., & Grant, K. E. (1993). Depression in adolescence. *American Psychologist, 48,* 155–168.

Petersen, A. C., Sarigiani, P. A., & Kennedy, R. E. (1991). Adolescent depression: Why more girls? *Journal of Youth and Adolescence, 20,* 247–271.

Pössel, P., Horn, A. B., Groen, G., & Hautzinger, M. (2004). School-based prevention of depressive symptoms in adolescents: A 6-month follow-up. *Journal of the American Academy of Child and Adolescent Psychiatry, 43,* 1003–1010.

Quayle, D., Dziurawiec, S., Roberts, C., Kane, R., & Ebsworthy, G. (2001). The effect of an optimism and lifeskills program on depressive symptoms in preadolescence. *Behaviour Change, 18,* 194–203.

Reivich, K. J. (1996). *The prevention of depressive symptoms in adolescents.* Unpublished doctoral dissertation, University of Pennsylvania, Philadelphia.

Reivich, K. J., Gillham, J. E., & Shatté, A. J. (2002). *The Penn Resiliency Program for Parents.* Unpublished intervention manual, University of Pennsylvania.

Roberts, C., Kane, R., Bishop, B., & Matthews, H. (2004). The prevention of depressive symptoms in rural children: A follow-up study. *International Journal of Mental Health Promotion, 6,* 4–16.

Roberts, C., Kane, R., Thomson, H., Bishop, B., & Hart, B. (2003). The prevention of depressive symptoms in rural school children: A randomized controlled trial. *Journal of Consulting and Clinical Psychology, 71,* 622–628.

Rohde, P., Lewinsohn, P. M., Clarke, G. N., Hops, H., & Seeley, J. R. (2005). The adolescent coping with depression course: A cognitive-behavioral approach to the treatment of adolescent depression. In E. D. Hibbs & P. S. Jensen (Eds.), *Psychosocial treatments for child and adolescent disorders: Empirically based strategies for clinical practice* (2nd ed., pp. 218–237). Washington, DC: American Psychological Association.

Seligman, M. E. P. (1972). Learned helplessness. *Annual Review of Medicine, 23,* 407–412.

Seligman, M. E. P. (1991). *Helplessness: On depression, development, and death* (2nd ed.). New York: Freeman.

Seligman, M. E. P. (1998). *Learned optimism* (2nd ed.). New York: Knopf.

Seligman, M. E. P., Reivich, K. J., Jaycox, L. H., & Gillham, J. E. (1995). *The optimistic child.* New York: Houghton Mifflin.

Seligman, M. E. P., Schulman, P., DeRubeis, R. J., & Hollon, S. D. (1999). The prevention of depression and anxiety. *Prevention and Treatment, 2.*

Shochet, I. M., Dadds, M. R., Holland, D., Whitefield, K., Harnett, P. H., & Osgarby, S. M. (2001). The efficacy of a universal school-based program to prevent adolescent depression. *Journal of Clinical Child Psychology, 30,* 303–315.

Simmons, R. G., & Blythe, D. A. (1987). *Moving into adolescence: The impact of pubertal change and school context.* Hawthorne, NY: Aldine de Gruyter.

Smetana, J. G. (1995). Parenting styles and conceptions of parental authority during adolescence. *Child Development, 66,* 299–316.

Smith, L. J. (1994, Spring). A content analysis of gender differences in children's advertising. *Journal of Broadcasting and Electronic Media,* 323–337.

Spence, S. H., Sheffield, J., & Donovan, C. (2002). Problem-solving orientation and attributional style: Moderators of the impact of negative life events on the development of depressive symptoms in adolescence? *Journal of Clinical Child and Adolescent Psychology, 31,* 219–222.

Stice, E., & Bearman, S. K. (2001). Body-image and eating disturbances prospectively predict increases in depressive symptoms in adolescent girls: A growth-curve analysis. *Developmental Psychology, 37,* 597–607.

Stice, E., Spangler, D., & Agras, W. S. (2001). Exposure to media-portrayed thin-ideal messages adversely affects vulnerable girls: A longitudinal experiment. *Journal of Social and Clinical Psychology, 20,* 270–288.

Strunk, D. R., & DeRubeis, R. J. (2001). Cognitive therapy for depression: A review of its efficacy. *Journal of Cognitive Psychotherapy: Special Review of Cognitive Behavioral Therapy, 15,* 289–297.

Sutton, J. (2007). Prevention of depression in youth: A qualitative review and future suggestions. *Clinical Psychology Review, 27,* 552–571.

TADS Team (2007). The treatment for adolescents with depression study (TADS): Long-term effectiveness and safety outcomes. *Archives of General Psychiatry, 64,* 1132–1144.

Thase, M. E., Frank, E., Kornstein, S. G., & Yonkers, K. A. (2000). Gender differences in response to treatments of depression. In E. Frank (Ed.), *Gender and its effects on psychopathology.* American Psychopathological Association series (pp. 103–129). Washington, DC: American Psychiatric Press.

Yu, D. L., & Seligman, M. E. P. (2002). Preventing depressive symptoms in Chinese children. *Prevention and Treatment, 5.*

Chapter 5

PREVENTING HIV AMONG AFRICAN AMERICAN FEMALE ADOLESCENTS

Development and Evaluation of a Gender and Culturally Congruent Prevention Intervention

GINA WINGOOD, JESSICA SALES, NIKIA BRAXTON, AND RALPH DiCLEMENTE

The risk of acquiring a sexually transmitted disease (STD), including human immunodeficiency virus (HIV), is one of the most significant and immediate risks to the health and well-being of adolescents. While there has been marked progress in the development of HIV prevention interventions for adolescents, programs designed specifically for females, and more specifically for African American females, have lagged behind those of other at-risk adolescent populations. Thus, the goal of this chapter is to provide a detailed description of an HIV prevention intervention specially tailored for African American adolescent females that has been demonstrated to be efficacious for this understudied and underserved at-risk population.

ADOLESCENTS AND STDS: THE RISK IS REAL

Despite recently reported declines in the percentage of school-age adolescents who are sexually active, the proportion of adolescents initiating sexual intercourse at younger ages has increased (Kann et al., 2000; Meschke, Bartholomae, & Zentall, 2000), and the prevalence of sexual risk-taking among adolescents in the United States remains high (Centers for Disease Control [CDC], 2002c). Specifically, a recent study found that while 47% of adolescents attending high school had never had sexual intercourse, 14% reported four or more lifetime sexual partners (Grunbaum et al., 2004). Moreover, approximately one third of all adolescent males and one half of adolescent females attending high school reported not using a condom at last sexual intercourse (CDC, 2002c). Perhaps as a consequence, the incidence and prevalence of STDs among adolescents is exceptionally high (Cates, Herndon, Schultz, & Darroch, 2004).

In the United States, the risk of acquiring an STD is higher among teenagers than among adults (CDC, 2000). Only 10 years ago, 3 million adolescents in the country were infected with sexually transmitted infections (STIs; Donovan, 1993). More recent investigations have reported that approximately one quarter of new STD cases, almost 4 million, are diagnosed in teenagers (CDC, 2000; National Institute of Allergy and Infectious Diseases, 1997). Even more alarming, recent estimates suggest that about one half of all new HIV infections occur in adolescents/young adults under the age of 25, and one quarter of new HIV infections occur among adolescents 21 or younger (CDC, 2002d, 2002a). The primary mode of HIV transmission among adolescents is sexual contact, as opposed to other methods of acquisition (e.g., injection drug use with shared needles and syringes; CDC, 2003).

The risk of adverse consequences associated with high-risk sexual behavior, such as STD/HIV infection, is not equally distributed among adolescents. Females are at particularly high risk for contracting STIs because they are physiologically more vulnerable to both viral and nonviral STIs, including HIV, and the effects of such STD infections are notably more problematic and costly (Aral, Hawkes, Biddlecom, & Padian, 2004; Bauer et al., 1991; Burk et al., 1996; W. Cates, 1999; CDC, 2004; Walsh & Irwin, 2002).

In addition to gender differences in STD prevalence rates, the risk of contracting STDs is substantially greater for African American adolescents (DiClemente & Crosby, 2003), as is the risk for HIV infection (DiClemente, 1990; Eng & Butler, 1997; National Institutes of Allergy & Infectious Diseases, 1997; Office of National AIDS Policy, 1996). For instance, African American adolescent females have higher infection rates of chlamydia and gonorrhea, as compared to Caucasian adolescent females (CDC, 2001; Ellen, Aral, & Madger, 1998), with studies reporting that among females aged 15 to 19, African Americans have almost 7 times the rate of chlamydia when compared to Caucasian females (CDC, 2002b). African American adolescent females are also more likely than their similar-age Caucasian females to have AIDS (DiClemente, 1996). A large-scale seroepidemiologic study conducted among Job Corps applicants indicated that African American adolescent females had an HIV prevalence significantly higher relative to same-age Caucasian or Hispanic adolescent females (4.9 versus 0.7, and 0.6/1,000; Valleroy, MacKellar, Karon, Janssen, & Hayman, 1998). Among this population, those residing in urban areas in the southern United States experience an even greater risk of HIV acquisition (CDC, 2001).

STD/HIV RISK-REDUCTION INTERVENTIONS FOR ADOLESCENTS: THE NEED IS REAL

Not surprising given these statistics, the CDC and Institute of Medicine have recommended that adolescents be targeted as a high-priority population for HIV prevention (Eng & Butler, 1997; Valleroy et al., 1998). In response to this call, multisession, small group interventions have been developed and their efficacy demonstrated in altering theoretically important mediators associated with sexual risk behavior, such as partner communication and attitudes toward condom use (Boyer, Schafer, & Tschann, 1997; Coyle et al., 1999; Jemmott & Jemmott, 2000; Main et al., 1994) and on measurable behavioral outcomes, such as condom use (Jemmott, Jemmott, & Fong, 1998; Shain et al., 1999; Shrier et al., 2001; Stanton et al., 1996; St. Lawrence et al., 1995).

In spite of their demonstrated efficacy, the impact of the interventions is not always uniform across genders. In at least two of the aforementioned effective trials targeting African American adolescents, the interventions were not tailored to be gender-appropriate for young females, and the programs were less effective for female participants in comparison to males (Stanton et al., 1996; St. Lawrence et al., 1995). One possible reason for these results is that males have direct control over condom use, whereas females have to negotiate with males to use condoms. Negotiating condom use is often a difficult skill to learn, especially in light of gender roles, cultural norms, power imbalances, and age differences, often resulting in younger females having to negotiate safer sex behaviors with older male sexual partners.

Just as important as tailoring interventions to be gender-appropriate, they also benefit from tailoring to the unique cultural background of the population being served. Mounting evidence indicates that a critical component for effective HIV intervention programs for adolescent females is that they thoroughly address the sexual and relational culture surrounding adolescent females' sexual decision making (Jemmott & Jemmott, 2000; Shain et al., 1999). In spite of this evidence, coupled with the fact that African American adolescent females are disproportionately affected by the HIV/STD epidemic, no intervention designed specifically for this population has demonstrated efficacy in reducing HIV-associated risk behaviors (Ellen, 2003; Mullen, Ramirez, Strouse, Hedges, & Sogolow, 2002).

THE CURRENT STUDY: THE SISTAS INFORMING, HEALING, LIVING, AND EMPOWERING INTERVENTION

In attempt to address this health disparity, as well as to attend to some of the limitations of previous intervention studies, our research team recently developed and evaluated a theory-guided, culturally appropriate, and gender-tailored sexual risk reduction program for African American female adolescents, ages 14 to 18 years, called Sistas Informing, Healing, Living, and Empowering (SiHLE). SiHLE was conceptualized by Drs. DiClemente and Wingood and is a modified version of an established and efficacious HIV intervention specifically for African American women (18 to 29 years of age) that has been adopted by the CDC in its *Compendium of HIV Prevention Programs with Demonstrated Evidence of Effectiveness* (DiClemente & Wingood, 1995). Additionally, the Centers for Disease Control and Prevention (CDC) has identified the current HIV intervention for African American female adolescents (SiHLE) as a "best practice" HIV intervention and will be packaging and disseminating this intervention nationally (Lyles et al., 2007).

Participants

The study was conducted from September 1995 to August 2002. From December 1996 through April 1999, recruiters screened 1,130 African American adolescent females seeking services at four community health agencies. Of these, 609 (53.9%) met eligibility criteria, which included:

- Being an African American female
- Being 14 to 18 years of age
- Reporting vaginal intercourse in the preceding 6 months
- Providing written informed consent (parental consent was waived)

Of those not eligible, nearly 93% were not sexually experienced. Thus, 522 adolescents agreed to participate in the study, completed baseline assessments, and were randomized to study conditions. Participants were compensated $25 for travel and child care to attend intervention sessions and complete assessments. The University of Alabama at Birmingham Institutional Review Board approved the study protocol prior to implementation.

Study Procedures

The study design was a randomized controlled trial. Participants were randomly assigned, using a computer-generated algorithm, to either the HIV intervention (SiHLE) or a general health promotion condition. The HIV intervention consisted of four, 4-hour interactive group sessions, implemented over consecutive Saturdays. Each session averaged 10 to 12 participants, and was implemented by a trained African American female health educator; two African American female peer educators cofacilitated each condition. Peer educators were instrumental in modeling skills and creating group norms supportive of HIV prevention.

To reduce the likelihood that the effects of the HIV prevention could be attributed to group interaction or Hawthorne effects, participants randomized to the general health promotion condition also received four 4-hour interactive group sessions, two sessions emphasizing nutrition and two sessions emphasizing exercise, administered on consecutive Saturdays. Given the focus of this chapter, the content and activities of the general health promotion condition will not be discussed further.

HIV Intervention Condition—Sistas, Informing, Healing, Living, and Empowering

Sistas, Informing, Healing, Living, and Empowering (SiHLE) aims to reduce the risk of HIV and STDs among sexually active African American adolescent females (DiClemente et al., 2004). Social Cognitive Theory (SCT; Bandura, 1994) and the Theory of Gender and Power (Wingood & DiClemente, 2000) were complementary theoretical frameworks guiding the design and implementation of the SIHLE intervention. SCT addresses both the psychosocial dynamics facilitating health behavior and the methods of promoting behavior change. Applying the gender-relevant theoretical framework of the Theory of Gender and Power was critical, as it highlights HIV-related social processes prevalent in the lives of African American female adolescents, such as: having older male sex partners, having violent dating partners, being stereotyped by the media, perceiving society as having a limited regard of African American teens, engaging in serial monogamy, experiencing peer pressure, and communicating nonassertively about safer sex. Ultimately, by creating an intervention for adolescent females grounded in both SCT and the Theory of Gender and Power we hoped to more fully address the processes that specifically impede young women's adoption of risk-promoting behaviors while teaching them multidimensional strategies to protect themselves from acquiring STDs and HIV (see Table 5.1 for details on how the theories were applied to the intervention).

By using theory mapping, intervention activities associated with constructs articulated in SCT and the Theory of Gender and Power were designed to address the social realities that are more prevalent among African American adolescents. To be effective, HIV prevention programs must be behavior-specific and teach adolescents about safe versus risky sexual practices, as well as the outcomes associated with each practice. Effective programs must also teach adolescents critical skills, such as setting goals, recognizing stimuli that trigger unsafe behaviors, reinforcing positive behaviors, and practicing effective communication skills, which are vital for relationship formation and negotiating safer sex (Bandura, 1992). Thus, in an effort to be deemed effective intervention activities, all sessions were designed to be engaging, with liberal use of

Table 5.1   Mapping of Theory to the SiHLE Intervention Sessions

	Social Cognitive Theory	Theory of Gender and Power
Session 1	Provide an opportunity for goal setting. Reinforce health-promoting thoughts and actions in the group.	Address and challenge the societal norms that dictate appropriate emotional and sexual behavior for females. Address factors that place women at an economic disadvantage
Session 2	Provide knowledge on condom use, and correct misconceptions of risk-reduction practices. Discuss positive outcomes of reducing risky sexual behavior. Reinforce previous session's message through discussion, problem solving, and decision making. Promote norms supportive of reducing risky sexual behavior.	Reaffirm personal self-worth and pride as it relates to gender and ethnicity.
Session 3	Enhance emotional coping responses by practicing communication skills in arousing situations. Enhance self-efficacy through role-plays. Promote mastery through skills-learning activities. Provide opportunities for decision making and problem solving.	Create an atmosphere of normality surrounding women taking control of sexual health.
Session 4	Enhance coping during emotion-arousing situations. Consider multiple avenues to reduce risky sexual behavior.	Break down societal and institutional structures that create a power imbalance in relationships.

interactive games, music, role-plays, and open discussions. Additionally, the thematic focus of the intervention, "Stay Safe for Yourself, Your Family, and Your Community," was designed to promote a sense of solidarity and ethnic pride among participants, and may have inspired them to modify risk behaviors for altruistic motives—by enhancing their health they were also enhancing the health of their family and the broader African American community. Unlike many HIV/STD prevention interventions that focus only on cognitive decision making and social and technical competency skills, SiHLE also focused on developing relational skills, amplifying intrinsic motivation (altruism, pride, self-esteem, perceived value, and importance in the community), and mobilizing extrinsic motivators (peer-normative influences from the group, modeling by the peer educator) to create an environment that enhanced the likelihood that adolescents would adopt and, as important, sustain preventive behaviors after participation in the intervention. The following subsections describe, albeit briefly, each of the four sessions of SiHLE.

Session 1

The first session, titled "My Sistas . . . My Girls," began with an icebreaker activity, which consisted of a game, to help the group members become acquainted with one another. This activity was followed by providing vital information about the program, introducing the young women to the SiHLE motto, and establishing group ground rules.

The goal of the first session was to foster sisterhood among young women through activities that promote discussion about topics relevant to African American adolescents. Throughout the session, the young women were encouraged to begin developing positive relationships within the group. It was important for the young women to gain a sense of camaraderie with each other, as well as with the health educator and peer educator, to help make the program a success.

Working from the gender-relevant theoretical framework of the Theory of Gender and Power, the activities in this session were created to highlight HIV-related social processes prevalent in the lives of African American female adolescents. Through the examination of poetry written by African American women, discussion of challenges and joys of being an African American female, exposure to artwork from African American women, identification of African American role models, and prioritization of personal values, participants were empowered to raise their expectations of what it is to be a woman who is cognizant of her sexuality, regardless of how society may view them.

Also following from the Theory of Gender and Power, other activities in the first session were designed to be economically empowering, including: stressing the importance of completing educational requirements, developing career goals, and writing effective professional resumes.

Table 5.2 provides a detailed overview of the specific activities employed in session 1. One activity that demonstrates how the message of sisterhood and self-pride was articulated and promoted in session 1 is activity F, "A Room Full of Sisters," exemplified by this excerpt of a poem by Mona Lake Jones and the discussion that followed:

> A room full of sisters, like jewels in a crown
> Vanilla, cinnamon, and dark chocolate brown . . .
> Now picture yourself in the midst of this glory
> As I describe the sisters who are part of this story.
> They were wearing purples, royal blues, and all shades of reds

Table 5.2 Themes and Activities in Session 1: My Sistas . . . My Girls

	Theme	Description
Activity A	Greeting and Icebreaker	Helps the group members to introduce themselves to all others in the group by participating in a fun activity.
Activity B	SiHLE Program Introduction	Discusses the name of the program and the objectives of the program.
Activity C	Who Are SiHLE Sistas?	Introduces the SiHLE concept and fosters a sense of sisterhood.
Activity D	The SiHLE Pact	Discusses the importance of young women participating in the workshops as an important step in learning how to be a SiHLE Sista. Also covers the SiHLE motto.
Activity E	Young, Black, and Female	Encourages the SiHLE Sistas to think of positive characteristics that describe young black women by giving them the opportunity to assert their self-worth and pride.
Activity F	A Room Full of Sisters	Encourages the SiHLE Sistas to further discuss pride among young black women by describing the many shades of beauty that are so common among black women.
Activity G	Strong Black Women	Encourages the SiHLE Sistas to recognize the importance of African American women as role models, by identifying important women in their life and learning about African American women important in shaping their history.
Activity H	A Taste of Culture	Teaches the SiHLE Sistas about African American culture as they make their own pictures using African American prints.
Activity I	Values—What Matters Most?	Encourages the SiHLE Sistas to recognize their personal values, and assists them in understanding why it is important to consider their personal values before they make a decision.
Activity J	Thought Works	Promotes the participants' identification of their goals and dreams.

> Some had elegant hats on their heads
> With sparkling eyes and shiny lips
> They moved through the room swaying their hips
> Speaking with smiles on their African faces
> Their joy and laughter filled all the spaces.

Peer Educator: Did Mona Lake Jones reveal her pride in being a black woman in this poem? If so, how?

Participant: "Mona Lake Jones described black women's outer beauty."

Peer Educator: What were some descriptive phrases she used to describe black women's outer beauty?

Participant: ". . . like jewels in a crown."

Participant: ". . . wearing purples, royal blues, and all shades of reds."

Participant: ". . . with sparkling eyes and shiny lips."

Peer Educator: How did she describe black women's inner beauty?

Participant: ". . . Their beauty was in the values they revered."

Participant: ". . . loving and caring."

Session 2

The goal of the second session, titled "It's My Body," was to introduce the young women to the risks related to STDs, especially HIV, and what this can mean to them. This workshop began with a review of the young women's values, goals, and dreams. Additionally, the girls were provided information about STDs and HIV, including a discussion of behaviors that put them at risk for the diseases, and how the diseases can impact their goals and dreams. Subsequently, correct condom skills were introduced as a means of lowering STD risk. The workshop ended with a review of STD/HIV information.

The majority of activities in this session focused on itemizing facts revolving around AIDS, STDs, and HIV, defining prevention strategies, and describing situations and behaviors that may increase women's HIV risk (douching, having older partners, gang involvement, and sexually degrading media exposures). Dispensing this information is imperative to provide, so that adolescents have the knowledge to prevent infection.

Table 5.3 provides a detailed overview of the specific activities employed in session 2. One activity that exemplifies how the message of protecting oneself from STDs and HIV is activity L, "Introducing OPRaH."

Peer Educator: OPRaH consists of four simple steps: open, pinch, roll, and hold!

O = Open the package and remove rolled condom without twisting, biting, or using your fingernails. This could damage the condom and allow fluid to leak out.

P = Pinch the tip of the condom to squeeze the air out, leaving one-fourth to one-half inch extra space at the top.

R = Roll condom down on penis as soon as the penis is hard, *before* you start to make love.

a = and after sex is over . . .

H = Hold the condom at the rim or base while your partner pulls out after ejaculation but before the penis goes soft. You could lose protection if the condom comes off inside you.

Table 5.3   Themes and Activities in Session 2: It's My Body

	Theme	Description
Activity A	Greetings and Icebreaker	Participants greet one another; group bonds are reinforced.
Activity B	Motto	SiHLE motto is recited and reinforced.
Activity C	Call Me Black Woman	Reinforces the concept that SiHLE Sistas are beautiful women with a strong rich heritage by reading and discussing poetry written by an African American.
Activity D	Share Your Thought Works	Reviews the SiHLE Sistas personal values and future goals, and reinforces their importance in decision making.
Activity E	SiHLE Sistas Are Special!	Reinforces and reexamines concepts taught in session 1.
Activity F	Speaking of STDs . . .	Teaches SiHLE Sistas about STDs and explains how having an STD affects pregnancy.
Activity G	Card Swap Game	Illustrates to the SiHLE Sistas how HIV is spread by heterosexual contact and injection drug use.
Activity H	HIV/AIDS: What Every SiHLE Woman Should Know	Educates the SiHLE Sistas about what AIDS is, debunks myths about AIDS, and explains how to protect oneself from AIDS.
Activity I	R U at Risk?	Informs the SiHLE Sistas about sexual behaviors that reduce their chance of getting STDs, including HIV.
Activity J	Consider This: The Penetrating Question	Evaluates how getting an STD, including HIV, could change the SiHLE Sistas values and goals.
Activity K	Takin' Care of You!	Introduces the concept of responsibility, by having women state how they care for themselves.
Activity L	Introducing OPRaH	Refines participants' knowledge of HIV/STD prevention.
Activity M	SiHLE Jeopardy	Refines participants' knowledge about HIV/STD transmission and prevention.

Session 3

The third session, titled "SiHLE Skills," addressed resisting partner pressure to engage in unsafe sex. Often, it is difficult for young women to make healthy choices about sex when they are not assertive during sexual encounters—especially if their partner plays the dominant role in those encounters. If they are to make choices for a healthier lifestyle, young women must be able to convey their sexual intentions assertively, as well as possess the skills to negotiate safer sex. While both males and females are responsible for safe sex, the responsibility often falls on the female partner because young women typically bear the burden of adverse health outcomes, thus males are less motivated to practice safe sex.

Sessions 1 and 2 focused on the fact that females can protect themselves from engaging in unsafe sex. In this session, young women were taught the skills to properly use condoms and refuse risky sex. Through role-plays women learned how to eroticize condom use, for two reasons: to help develop a positive attitude themselves about using condoms, and to enhance their male partner's acceptance of condom use. The involvement of the group facilitators was especially crucial in this session, for it was up to them to create a norm as it relates to females putting condoms on their male partners. Furthermore, this activity led into a group discussion about how a woman's ability to apply a condom tends to reduce the perceived barrier to utilizing this contraceptive for the prevention of HIV/STDs.

Role-plays were also used to model assertive communication. They were designed as a hierarchical gradient, first in nonsexual scenarios, then in progressively more sexual situations. As the women actively participated in role-plays focusing on assertive communication, they were able to increase their communicative self-efficacy, as well as develop new strategies for coping with emotions that often accompany difficult conversations with romantic partners. Facilitators provided positive, reinforcing feedback for the young women who used assertive communication, and corrective feedback for those who did not. They also provided positive, reinforcing feedback for demonstrations of correct condom use.

Table 5.4 provides a detailed overview of the specific activities employed in session 3. One activity that is highly representative of the focus on skill development emphasized in session 3 is activity I, "Talking the Talk."

Scenario: Andre and Tijuana

Peer Educator: Tijuana has been attending a woman's group called SiHLE. She has learned a lot about being a strong black woman who has a right to realize her dreams and goals. She has learned an important way to stay healthy, a simple way to prevent STDs, HIV, and unplanned pregnancy. She has made the decision to use condoms *every* time they have sex.

Instructions: Role-play Tijuana's talk with Andre. Make sure that you use an assertive style of communication. Pay particular attention to both your body language and your verbal language. Make sure they are clear, consistent, and unambiguous.

Session 4

The fourth session, titled "Relationship and Power," was designed to encourage women to take ownership of their bodies by informing them that their partner's decisions and choices regarding their bodies should be second to their own

Table 5.4   Themes and Activities in Session 3: SiHLE Skills

	Theme	Description
Activity A	Greeting and Icebreaker	Participants greet one another; message of time-liness is reinforced; group bonds are enhanced.
Activity B	Motto	SiHLE motto is read and reinforced.
Activity C	Phenomenal Woman	Refines the SiHLE Sistas sense of beauty, self-worth, and pride.
Activity D	Luv and Kisses	Enhances the SiHLE Sistas knowledge about which sexual behaviors put women at risk for HIV/STD infection.
Activity E	What's in It for You?	Increases the SiHLE Sistas knowledge about HIV/STD prevention.
Activity F	Why Don't People Use Condoms?	Introduces the SiHLE Sistas to common reasons young women don't use condoms, and reiterates the concept of sexual responsibility for using condoms.
Activity G	KISS—Keep it Simple Sista!	Gives the SiHLE Sistas a model to assist them in asking their sex partner(s) to use condoms.
Activity H	Three Ways to Say It	Teaches the SiHLE Sistas to distinguish between passive, assertive, and aggressive communication styles.
Activity I	Talking the Talk	Teaches the SiHLE Sistas the difference between passive, aggressive, and assertive communication styles, by having them role-play these communication styles in sexual scenarios, both through verbal and body language.
Activity J	OPRaH Rehearsal	Teaches the SiHLE Sistas the steps for proper condom use.
Activity K	Alcohol and Sex—Not a Good Mix	Teaches the SiHLE Sistas the importance of avoiding alcohol prior to and during sex.
Activity L	Condom Consumer Report	Teaches the SiHLE Sistas the importance of examining condoms for safety, personal appeal, and ease of application.
Activity M	Thought Works Assignment	Reviews the concepts taught in this session.

decision and choice. The session commenced by distinguishing healthy from un-healthy relationships and defining the words "abuse" and "respect." Adolescent women were taught that the lack of recognition by other people is disrespectful and abusive. Subsequently, these adolescents were taught coping skills to more effectively handle a verbally or physically abusive partner. Participants were also taught coping skills to more effectively handle abuse that may occur as a consequence of introducing HIV/STD prevention practices (i.e., condom use) into the relationship.

The majority of activities in the fourth session were designed to address and break down the power imbalance that is often present in sexual-heterosexual dyadic relationships. Defining healthy and unhealthy relationships; discussing local community resources for participants who are in unhealthy relationships; and explaining the relationship between having an unhealthy partner, HIV/STD risk-taking, and HIV/STD acquisition were all activities in this session that enabled the participants to act on or to change their relationships.

Table 5.5 provides a detailed overview of the specific activities employed in session 4. One that exemplifies the emphasis on relationships and power in is activity E, "What Do Healthy and Unhealthy Relationships Look Like?"

Table 5.5   Themes and Activities in Session 4: Relationship and Power

	Theme	Description
Activity A	Greeting	Participants greet one another; Assertive communication skills are reinforced and practiced.
Activity B	Motto	SiHLE motto is read and reinforced.
Activity C	Poem: Still I Rise	Enhances self-confidence and pride among the SiHLE Sistas, by reciting poetry written by African American women.
Activity D	What Have We Learned?	Refines the participants' knowledge about HIV/STD transmission and prevention.
Activity E	What Do Healthy and Unhealthy Relationships Look Like?	Discusses the influence of power, communication, respect, and trust on relationships.
Activity F	Pieces and Parts	Raises participants' awareness about the differences between healthy and unhealthy relationships.
Activity G	What Does Abuse Look Like?	Increases women's knowledge about verbal, emotional, physical, and sexual abuse.
Activity H	The Power Pie	Discusses how imbalances of power within a relationship can make it difficult to practice safe sex.
Activity I	Your Options	Discusses a woman's options for seeking safety and counseling if she is concerned about her relationship.
Activity J	Your Time to Shine	Refines and enhances the participants' knowledge of safe sex and healthy relationships skills, by conducting role-reversal activities.
Activity K	Graduation	Acknowledges the SiHLE Sistas for participating in the SiHLE program, by the presentation of certificates of empowerment during a graduation exercise.

Peer Educator: When you are in a healthy relationship, it is easier to negotiate with your male partner to use a condom *every* time you have sex. Let's look at why this is true. First, let's talk about what a healthy relationship is. A group of SiHLE women like you were asked to describe a healthy relationship. The characteristics and attributes listed below are what they identified as important in a healthy relationship.

- *Power is balanced.* No one has an unfair advantage over the other.
- *Communication is good.* Both partners talk and listen.
- *Respect is real.* For oneself and one another.
- *Trust is strong.* Feeling safe, both physically and emotionally with one another.

When you are in an unhealthy relationship, it is more difficult to negotiate with your male partner to use a condom *every* time you have sex. Let's look at why this is true. First, let's talk about and describe an unhealthy relationship.

- *Power is not balanced.* One partner has an unfair advantage over the other.
- *Communication is not good.* Partners don't talk or listen to each other.
- *Respect is not real.* Not for oneself and not for others.
- *Trust is not strong.* Not feeling safe, either physically and emotionally, with one another.

Assessing the Efficacy of the SiHLE Intervention

To assess the effectiveness of the SiHLE HIV intervention on reducing risk-associated behaviors, data collection occurred at baseline (i.e., before the participants were randomly assigned to either the SiHLE intervention or a time-equivalent general health promotion comparison condition), as well as at 6 and 12 months after participating in either the SiHLE or general health promotion intervention. At each assessment, data were obtained from four sources. First, participants completed a self-administered questionnaire assessing sociodemographics and psychosocial mediators of HIV-preventive behaviors. Subsequently, a trained African American female interviewer conducted an interview assessing sexual behaviors. Next, the interviewer assessed participants' ability to correctly apply condoms using a direct observation of skills assessment protocol. Finally, participants provided two self-collected vaginal swab specimens that were analyzed for the presence of three STDs: chlamydia, trichomonasis, and gonorrhea.

EFFECTS OF THE HIV INTERVENTION

Relative to participants in the general health promotion condition, participants in the SiHLE intervention condition were more likely to report using condoms consistently in the 30 days preceding the 6-month assessment (intervention = 75.3% versus comparison = 58.2%), and at the 12-month assessment (intervention = 73.3% versus. comparison = 56.5%). Likewise, participants in the SiHLE intervention were more likely to report using condoms consistently during the 6 months prior to the 6-month assessment (intervention = 61.3% vs. comparison = 42.6%), and the 12-month assessment (intervention = 58.1% versus comparison = 45.3%). Additionally, participants in the SiHLE intervention were more likely to report using a condom at last vaginal sexual intercourse, less likely to self-report a pregnancy, and less likely to report having a new male sex partner in the 30 days prior to the follow-up assessments. Importantly, this was the first intervention to demonstrate effectiveness in reducing new chlamydia infections in the SiHLE intervention group participants over the entire 12-month follow-up period (see DiClemente et al., 2004 for a detailed description of the findings).

The SiHLE intervention also had strong effects on empirically and theoretically derived psychosocial mediators of HIV-preventive behaviors. In general, participants in the SiHLE intervention reported fewer perceived partner-related barriers to condom use, more favorable attitudes toward using condoms, more frequent discussions with male sex partners about HIV prevention, higher condom use self-efficacy scores, higher HIV prevention knowledge scores, and demonstrated greater proficiency in using condoms at the 6- and the 12-month assessments and over the entire 12-month period.

While other studies have shown that self-reported sexual risk behaviors can be reduced in adolescents, this is the first trial demonstrating that an HIV intervention can result in substantial reductions in sexual risk behaviors, including the acquisition of a new male sex partner, and markedly enhance theoretically important mediators and skills associated with HIV preventive behaviors among sexually experienced African American adolescent females. Given that STDs, particularly chlamydia, are prevalent among adolescents (Weinstock, Berman, & Cates, 2004), and facilitate HIV transmission (Fleming & Wasserheit, 1999; Wasserheit, 1992), even small reductions in incidence could result in considerable reductions in treatment costs, as well as sizeable reductions in HIV morbidity (Bozzette et al., 2001) and their associated treatment costs (Chesson, Blandford, Gift, Tao, & Irwin, 2000). This is particularly important in light of findings from mathematical modeling studies suggesting that reductions in incident chlamydia infections may be one of the most promising surrogate markers for HIV incidence in prevention trials (Pinkerton & Layde, 2002).

CONCLUSIONS

This chapter has highlighted the public health problem created by increased rates of STDs and HIV in adolescents, especially in African American adolescent females. This disproportionate burden necessitates the urgent design and implementation of gender- and culturally tailored STD/HIV risk-reduction interventions specifically targeting this particularly vulnerable subpopulation of adolescents. Thus, the main focus of the chapter was to provide a detailed description of what is, to our knowledge, the only demonstrated effective HIV intervention specifically designed for sexually active African American adolescent females.

Several characteristics of the SiHLE program may have contributed to the efficacy of the intervention in reducing risk-associated behaviors in African American adolescent females. First, the utilization of SCT, which provided a theoretical framework for developing the skills training components of the SiHLE intervention, in addition to the theory of gender in power, which was employed to address the role of contextual and sociocultural variables such as gender, class, and ethnicity, and their influence on adolescent females sexual behavior, was a successful combination that broadened the scope of the intervention beyond the individual.

Related to this, the efficacy of the SiHLE intervention may be attributable partly to the gender-tailored and culturally appropriate framework that highlighted the underlying social processes, such as the dyadic nature of sexual interactions, and relationship power and emotional commitment that may promote and reinforce risk behaviors. Conceptualizing HIV prevention within the broader context of a healthy relationship also marshaled new intervention strategies and offered new options for motivating STD/HIV preventive behavior change. Additionally, the thematic focus of the intervention, "Stay Safe for Yourself, Your Family, and Your Community" was designed to promote a sense of solidarity and ethnic pride among participants, and may have inspired them to modify risk behaviors for altruistic motives—by enhancing their health they were also enhancing the health of their family and the broader African American community.

Finally, the role of the facilitator was vital to the overall success of the program and, ultimately, to the young ladies making healthy changes in their lives. Therefore, having the SiHLE intervention implemented by a trained and experienced African American female health educator, in conjunction with African American female peer educators as cofacilitators, likely was a contributing factor to the efficacy of the intervention. Employing health educators and peer educators matched to the participants' gender and race was instrumental in modeling social and technical competency skills and creating a group norm supportive of HIV/STD prevention.

In the current era of HIV prevention, there is a need to prioritize the design of adolescent STD/HIV prevention programs that are developmentally, culturally, and gender appropriate. As the SiHLE intervention illustrates, it is possible to develop programs that address contextual factors or conditions that confer significant vulnerability for young women's risk of HIV/STD (i.e., age, ethnicity, and risk behaviors). Encouragingly, empirical data suggests that the greater the specificity between the HIV prevention intervention and the contextual factors prevalent among a target population, the greater the likelihood the program will be effective in reducing HIV risk (Wingood & DiClemente, 2006). Combining the three aforementioned features (theoretical frameworks that expand the scope of the intervention to include broader contextual and social variables; specificity of content tailored to the gender and culture of the participants, and employing trained, matched-to-sample health educators to implement the intervention) in the SiHLE intervention optimally enhanced the specificity between the HIV interventions and directly addressed, through diverse learning strategies, contextual factors that enhanced participants' risk for STDs and HIV. Undoubtedly, this targeted and tailored approach significantly contributed to the overall success of the SiHLE intervention.

In conclusion, as the need for effective STD/HIV risk-reduction interventions for adolescents remains high, we as clinicians, practitioners, and prevention researchers working with America's youth must continue to strive to meet the requirements of the population we serve. As suggested by this chapter, acknowledging that adolescents are not a homogeneous group, but rather a heterogeneous population, is a critical first step in designing effective risk-reduction interventions tailored for diverse at-risk adolescent subgroups.

REFERENCES

Aral, S. O., Hawkes, S., Biddlecom, A., & Padian, N. (2004, November). Disproportionate impact of sexually transmitted diseases on women [Conference summary]. *Emerging Infectious Diseases.* Retrieved January 10, 2005, from www.cdc.gov/ncidod/EID/vol10no11/04-0623_02.htm.

Bandura, A. (1992). A social cognitive approach to the exercise of control over AIDS infection. In R. J. DiClemente (Ed.), *Adolescents and AIDS: A generation in jeopardy* (pp. 89–116). Newbury Park, CA: Sage.

Bandura, A. (1994). Social cognitive theory and exercise of control over HIV infections. In R. J. DiClemente & J. Petersons (Eds.), *Preventing AIDS: Theories and methods of behavioral interventions* (pp. 25–29). New York: Plenum Publishing.

Bauer, H. M., Ting, Y., Greer, C. E., Chambers, J. C., Tashiro, C. J., Chimera, J., et al. (1991). Genital human papillomavirus infection in female university students as determined by a PCR-based method. *Journal of the American Medical Association, 265*(4), 472–477.

Boyer, C. B., Shafer, M., & Tschann, J. M. (1997). Evaluation of a knowledge-and-cognitive-behavioral skills-building intervention to prevent STDs and HIV infection in high school students. *Adolescence, 32*(125), 25–42.

Bozzette, S. A., Joyce, G., McCaffrey, D. F., Leibowitz, A. A., Morton, S. C., Berry, S. H., et al. (2001). Expenditures for the care of HIV-infected patients in the era of highly active antiretroviral therapy. *New England Journal of Medicine, 344(11),* 817–823.

Burk, R., Ho, G., Beardsley, L., Lempa, M., Peters, M., & Bierman, R. (1996). Sexual behavior and partner characteristics are the predominant factors for genital human papillomavirus infection in young women. *Journal of Infectious Diseases, 174*(4), 679–689.

Cates, J. R., Herndon, N. L., Schultz, S. L., & Darroch, J. E. (2004). *Our voice, our lives, our futures: Youth and sexually transmitted diseases.* Chapel Hill,

NC: School of Journalism and Mass Communication, University of North Carolina at Chapel Hill.

Cates, W. (1999). Estimates of the incidence and prevalence of sexually transmitted diseases in the United States. *Sexually Transmitted Diseases, 26*(4), S2–S7.

Centers for Disease Control and Prevention. (2000). *Tracking the hidden epidemics: Trends in STDs in the United States.* Atlanta, GA: United States Department of Health and Human Services, Public Health Service.

Centers for Disease Control and Prevention. (2001). *Sexually transmitted disease surveillance, 2000.* Atlanta, GA: U.S. Department of Health and Human Services, Centers for Disease Control and Prevention.

Centers for Disease Control and Prevention. (2002a). *HIV/AIDS Surveillance Report: Cases of HIV infection and AIDS in the United States, 2002.* Atlanta, GA: U.S. Department of Health and Human Services, Centers for Disease Control and Prevention.

Centers for Disease Control and Prevention. (2002b). *Sexually transmitted disease surveillance, 2001.* Atlanta, GA: U.S. Department of Health and Human Services, Centers for Disease Control and Prevention.

Centers for Disease Control and Prevention. (2002c). Trends in sexual risk behaviors among high school students—United States, 1991–2001. *Morbidity and Mortality Weekly Report, 51,* 856–862.

Centers for Disease Control and Prevention. (2002d). *Young people at risk: HIV/AIDS among America's youth.* Retrieved November 16, 2004, from www.cdc.gov/hiv/pubs/facts/youth.htm.

Centers for Disease Control and Prevention. (2003, July 8). *Young people at Risk: HIV/AIDS among America's Youth* [Fact sheet]. CDC-NCHSTP–Divisions of HIV/AIDS Prevention.

Centers for Disease Control and Prevention. (2004). Chlamydia screening among sexually active young female enrollees of health plans—United States, 1999–2001. *Morbidity and Mortality Weekly Report, 53,* 983–985.

Chesson, H. W., Blandford, J. M., Gift, T. L., Tao, G., & Irwin, K. L. (2000). The estimated direct medical cost of sexually transmitted diseases among American youth, 2000. *Perspectives on Sexual and Reproductive Health, 36,* 11–19.

Coyle, K., Basen-Engquist, K., Kirby, D., Parcel, G., Banspach, S., Harrist, R., et al. (1999). Short-term impact of safer choices: A multicomponent, school-based HIV, other STD, and pregnancy prevention program. *Journal of School Health, 69*(5), 181–188.

DiClemente, R. J. (1990). The emergence of adolescents as a risk group for human immunodeficiency virus infection. *Journal of Adolescent Research, 5,* 7–17.

DiClemente, R. J. (1996). Adolescents at risk for acquired immune deficiency syndrome: Epidemiology of AIDS, HIV prevalence, and HIV incidence. In S. Oskamp & S. Thompson (Eds.), *Understanding and preventing HIV risk behavior* (pp. 13–30). Newbury Park, CA: Sage.

DiClemente, R. J., & Crosby, R. A. (2003). Sexually transmitted diseases among adolescents: Risk factors, antecedents, and prevention strategies. In G. R. Adams & M. Berzonsky (Eds.), *The Blackwell handbook of adolescence* (pp. 573–605). Oxford, England: Blackwell.

DiClemente, R. J., & Wingood, G. M. (1995). *Journal of the American Medical Association, 274(16),* 1271–1276.

DiClemente, R. J., Wingood, G. M., Harrington, K. F., Lang, D. F., Davies, S. L., Hook, E. W., et al. (2004). Efficacy of an HIV prevention intervention for African American adolescent girls: A randomized controlled trial. *Journal of the American Medical Association, 292*(2), 171–179.

Donovan, P. (1993). *Testing positive: Sexually transmitted disease and the public health response.* New York: Alan Guttmacher Institute.

Ellen, J. M. (2003). The next generation of HIV prevention for adolescent females in the United States: Linking behavioral and epidemiological sciences to reduce incidence of HIV. *Journal of Urban Health, 80,* 40–49.

Ellen, J., Aral, S., & Madger, L. (1998). Do differences in sexual behaviors account for the racial/ethnic differences in adolescents' self-reported history of a sexually transmitted disease? *Sexually Transmitted Diseases, 25,* 125–129.

Eng, T., & Butler, W. (Eds.). (1997). *The hidden epidemic: Confronting sexually transmitted diseases.* Washington, DC: National Academy Press.

Fleming, D. T., & Wasserheit, J. N. (1999). From epidemiological synergy to public health policy and practice: The contribution of other sexually transmitted diseases to sexual transmission of HIV infection. *Sexually Transmitted Infections, 75,* 3–17.

Grunbaum, J., Kann, L., Kinchen, S., Ross, J., Hawkins, J., Lowry, R., et al. (2004). Youth risk behavior surveillance—United States (2003). *Morbidity and Mortality Weekly Report, 53,* 1–95.

Jemmott, J. B., & Jemmott, L. S. (2000). HIV behavioral interventions for adolescents in community settings. In J. L. Peterson & R. J. DiClemente (Eds.), *Handbook of HIV prevention* (pp. 103–128). New York: Plenum Press.

Jemmott, J. B., III, Jemmott, L. S., & Fong, G. T. (1998). Abstinence and safer sex HIV risk-reduction interventions for African American adolescents: A randomized controlled trial. *Journal of the American Medical Association, 279,* 1529–1536.

Kann, L., Kinchen, S. A., Williams, B. I., Ross, J. G., Lowry, R., Grunbaum, J., et al. (2000). Youth risk behavior surveillance—United States. *Morbidity and Mortality Weekly Report, 49(SS-05),* 1–96.

Lyles, C. M., Kay, L. S., Crepaz, N., Herbst, J. H., Passin, W. F., Kim, A. S., et al. (2007). Best evidence interventions: Findings from a systematic review of HIV behavioral interventions for U.S. populations at high risk, 2000–2004. *American Journal of Public Health, 97,* 133–143.

Main, D. S., Iverson, D. C., McGloin, J., Banspach, S. W., Collins, J. L., Rugg, D. L., et al. (1994). Preventing HIV infection among adolescents: Evaluation of a school-based education program. *Preventive Medicine, 23,* 409–417.

Meschke, L. L., Bartholomae, S., & Zentall, S. R. (2000). Adolescent sexuality and parent-adolescent processes: Promoting healthy teen choices. *Family Relations, 49,* 143–154.

Mullen, P. D., Ramirez, G., Strouse, D., Hedges, L. V., & Sogolow, E. (2002). Meta-analysis of the effects of behavioral HIV prevention interventions on the sexual risk behavior of sexually experienced adolescents in controlled studies in the United States. *Journal of Acquired Immune Deficiency Syndromes, 30,* S94–S105.

National Institute of Allergy and Infectious Diseases. (1997). *Sexually transmitted diseases statistics.* Washington, DC: U.S. Department of Health and Human Services.

Office of National AIDS Policy. (1996). *Youth and HIV/AIDS: An American agenda.* Washington, DC: Office of National AIDS Policy.

Pinkerton, S. D., & Layde, P. M. (2002). Using sexually transmitted disease incidence as a surrogate marker for HIV incidence in prevention trial. *Sexually Transmitted Diseases, 29,* 298–307.

Shain, R. N., Piper, J. M., Newton, E. R., Perdue, S. T., Ramos, R., Chapion, J. D., et al. (1999). A randomized, controlled trial of a behavioral intervention to prevent sexually transmitted disease among minority women. *New England Journal of Medicine, 320*(2), 93–100.

Shrier, L. A., Ancheta, R., Goodman, E., Chiou, V. M., Lyden, M. R., & Emans, S. J. (2001). Randomized controlled trial of a safer sex intervention for high-risk adolescent girls. *Archives of Pediatrics and Adolescent Medicine, 155*(1), 73–79.

St. Lawrence, J. S., Brasfield, T. L., Jefferson, K. W., Alleyne, E., O'Bannon, R. E. I., & Shirley, A. (1995). Cognitive-behavioral intervention to reduce African American adolescents' risk for HIV infection. *Journal of Consulting and Clinical Psychology, 63*(2), 221–237.

Stanton, B. F., Li, X., Ricardo, I., Galbraith, J., Feigelman, S., & Kaljee, L. (1996). A randomized, controlled effectiveness trial of an AIDS prevention program for low-income African American youths. *Archives of Pediatrics and Adolescent Medicine, 150,* 363–372.

Valleroy, L., MacKellar, D., Karon, J., Janssen, R., & Hayman, C. (1998). HIV infection in disadvantaged out-of-school youth: Prevalence for, U.S. Job Corps entrants, 1990 through 1996. *Journal of Acquired Immune Deficiency Syndromes and Human Retrovirology, 19,* 67–73.

Walsh, C., & Irwin, K. (2002). Combating the silent chlamydia epidemic. *Contemporary OB/GYN, 47*(4), 90–98.

Wasserheit, J. N. (1992). Epidemiological synergy: Interrelationship between human immunodeficiency virus infection and other sexually transmitted diseases. *Sexually Transmitted Diseases, 19,* 61–77.

Weinstock, H., Berman, S., & Cates, W. (2004). Sexually transmitted diseases in American youth: Incidence and prevalence estimates. *Perspectives on Sexual and Reproductive Health, 36,* 6–10.

Wingood, G. M., & DiClemente, R. J. (2000). Application of the theory of gender and power to examine HIV related exposures, risk factors, and effective interventions for women. *Health Education and Behavior, 27,* 313–347.

Wingood, G. M., & DiClemente, R. J. (2006). Enhancing adoption of evidence-based HIV interventions: Promotion of a suite of HIV prevention interventions for African American women. *AIDS Education and Prevention, 18*(Suppl. A), 161–170.

Chapter 6

MANIFESTING THE STRENGTHS OF RURAL LATINA GIRLS

VELIA G. LEYBAS

This chapter describes key elements in the development of the Latina Institute, a program for 11- to 13-year-old Latina girls in two rural Arizona communities. The concept arose during a debriefing meeting regarding an annual conference for Latina girls and their mentors/mothers. Josefina Ahumada, a long-time steering committee member, challenged the group to expand the vision of the 1-day conference to include a leadership institute that would extend over several days. Although the women agreed, one could almost picture the images floating in their minds of the resources needed to operationalize such a vision. Nevertheless, most of the committee members volunteered their already-overcommitted time, and the seed was planted firmly in one committee member's mind. She nurtured it until the leadership institute (Latina Institute) became a reality, in June 2004, approximately 5 years after it had been introduced.

EXPLANATION OF THE PROBLEM AND ITS CONTEXT

The Latino population continues it exponential growth in the United States, with reports indicating 1 in 8 persons in the country are Latino (Ramirez & U.S. Census Bureau, 2002)—of which the largest group is Mexican (67%). Latinos tend to be a young ethnic group, with approximately 34%, compared to 23% non-Latino whites, under the age of 18 (Ramirez & U.S. Census Bureau, 2002).

Patterns of immigration emphasize the growing number of Spanish speakers in the nation. Of those native-born Latinos, more are likely to speak English as their primary language than are their foreign-born counterparts—61% versus 4% (Pew Hispanic Center & Kaiser Family Foundation, 2002). Of foreign-born Latinos, more are likely than native-born Latinos to speak Spanish primarily—72% versus 4% (Pew Hispanic Center & Kaiser Family Foundation, 2002).

Duration in the United States and language proficiency both have an influence on adaptation to the American way of life. Typically, children adapt to U.S. practices more quickly than their parents, and the stress associated with the varying levels of adaptation creates a separation between children and their parents, according to the National Alliance for Hispanic Health (NAHH; 2000). Furthermore, girls sometimes act on behalf of the family to link the U.S. culture with that of their home country. The added responsibility increases stress during this already-complicated phase of the girls' life (NAHH, 2000). Not surprisingly, girls report being negatively affected by family conflict (National Research Council, Institute of Medicine, 1998).

Social concerns faced by American girls also are exacerbated among Hispanic adolescent girls (NAHH, 2000). Of particular concern is the epidemic of depression and suicide attempts among Hispanic girls, who carry the greatest burden compared to other ethnicities (NAHH, 2000 and Substance Abuse and Mental Health Services Administration [SAMHSA], 2003). The NAHH reports Latina girls rank first in attempted suicides, and 1 of every 3 Latina girls considers suicide as a serious option.

Acculturation is cited as an indicator of the increasing number of Latino youth and young adults experiencing depression or who commit suicide. Specifically, native-born Latinos tend to disengage from cultural traditions such as religious beliefs and practices that serve as protective factors. A study of California health care services found Mexican immigrants experienced less depression and posttraumatic stress disorder compared to Latinos born in the United States (Escobar, 1998). More recent studies show acculturation has a positive effect in terms of being bicultural. The study described youth's ability to learn social skills applicable in both cultural communities: foreign and American. Of youth with these bicultural skills, fewer were likely to engage in substance use or delinquency, and they experienced fewer family problems associated with acculturation (NAHH, 2000).

As Latina girls become more acculturated, they are more likely to be sexually active (NAHH, 2000). Beginning in the mid-1990s, Latinas ranked as the ethnic group with the highest teen birth rates in the United States (National Campaign to Prevent Teen Pregnancy, 2004). In Arizona, Hispanic girls have 2 times as many births during their teenage years, compared to white girls, and 6 times as many as Native American girls (U.S. Census Bureau, 2000). Interestingly, one study found several factors help Latina girls postpone sexual activity, among them, "being immigrant, Spanish as a first language, and regular church attendance at the age of fourteen" (Ku, Sonenstein, & Pleck, 1993, p. 23).

The Arizona Coalition on Adolescent Pregnancy and Parenting (2003) identified school and behavioral problems during early adolescence, along with family conflicts and poverty, as the antecedents associated with adolescent pregnancy. As antecedents increase, risk of pregnancy increases: from 11% with 0 antecedents up to 50% with 3 or 4.

As far as education is concerned, 15% of Latino students do not graduate from high school, which is two times higher than white students (Pew Hispanic Center, 2003). In the past, the percent of Latino students leaving school prior to high school graduation was 30%; however, this number included immigrant students who left their home-country school (Pew Hispanic Center, 2003). The dropout rates, then, can be considered more a measure of immigration than leaving school prior to high school graduation. Immigrant youth are more likely to seek employment than education. This choice, however, appears to be one based on need (for livelihood) as opposed to a disregard for education.

Low high school completion rates contribute to fewer Latinas entering college. This is quantified when considering that Latinas are also the least likely of any group of women to complete a bachelor's degree (Ginorio & Huston, 2001), and even fewer a degree with a mathematics or science emphasis (Clune, M. S., Nuñez, A. M., & Choy, 2001).

Higher educational achievement has been associated with higher income. The Pew Hispanic Center (2003) reports Latino youth who leave school prior to high school graduation, or never enroll in school, are more likely to hold lower-paying jobs and, thus, low-income rates. Poverty has been associated with shorter life expectancy, too. Regardless of race or gender, people who make at least $25,000 a year on average live 3 to 7 years longer than people who make less than $10,000 annually (Ramirez & U.S. Census Bureau, 2002). These disparities in income and education are associated with the incidence of health conditions such as heart disease, diabetes, obesity, and low birth weight. Greater wealth, obviously, enables access to a greater variety of improved living standards, such as better health care and housing in safer neighborhoods, at the same time it offers more opportunities to engage in health-promoting behaviors (Ramirez & U.S. Census Bureau, 2002).

Vasquez and del las Fuentes (1999) describe the need for research on girls of color from various social classes, highlighting the often-unaccounted influence of social environment. Social threads such as poverty, ethnic background, and gender weave part of the social context in which Hispanic adolescent girls live and influence the course of their lives.

THE LATINA INSTITUTE PILOT INTERVENTION

The goal of the Latina Institute is to implement an early outreach educational intervention for 11- to 13-year-old girls in two rural communities in Arizona. The specific aim is to reduce barriers to academic achievement and prepare girls for college enrollment, thereby increasing their likelihood of completing college and finding gainful employment.

Formation of Community Advisory Board and Stakeholder Meetings

The program began with only a concept; no funding supported the program initially. Thus, it became imperative to begin with human resources and build on the strengths of the expertise within the community.

To that end, a community advisory board was formed in order to add a sense of community-based ownership and to serve as the initial infrastructure for the program. The author organized meetings with key stakeholders: parents, school administrators, and health educators. Each stakeholder meeting was treated with a high degree of professionalism to ensure they came away with the recognition that this was a program with a strong mission and with the capacity to move forward. Each stakeholder was given a packet containing a clear outline of the goals and objectives and the program design.

Reactions from stakeholders were consistently positive. Commitment was strong, too; if one stakeholder could not participate, she or he would identify someone within the organization who could. Often, because the purpose of the program matched the mission of the stakeholder organization, board members were allowed work time to participate in Latina Institute activities.

After several stakeholder meetings, the advisory board was formed. Figure 6.1 illustrates the board structure, along with responsibilities for each subcommittee.

Participants and Communities

Participants were sixth-grade Latina students from two participating schools serving rural communities (Community A and Community B). Baseline surveys were collected for 22 girls with a mean age of 11.8 ($n = 22$); however, 20 girls completed the program. Virtually all girls reported being Mexican American, which is congruent with the 91% of girls who said they lived in the United States their entire lives.

The U.S. Census (2000) defines "rural" as those places not in the urban category. "Urban," in contrast, is defined as "all territory, population, and housing units in urbanized areas and in places of 2,500 or more persons outside urbanized areas." Geographically rural communities, compared to urban areas, have low population density, fewer living and employment options, and fewer re-

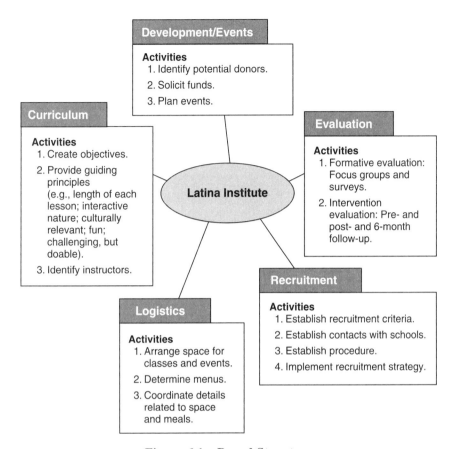

Figure 6.1   Board Structure

sources such as supermarkets, health care facilities, and places of entertainment (Castro & Gutierres, 1997). Schools are smaller, which enables administrators to get to know each student and her family, and, conversely, for the students to know the names of the administrators and staff. If, for example, students are sent to the principal, they are told to go see Mrs. So and So versus "the principal" (personal communication, Principal, Community A School, January 11, 2006). In short, rural communities tend to function as an extended family.

Community A is a copper-mining area, approximately 40 miles outside the nearest city, with a population of fewer than 2,000. Community B is approximately 30 miles from the nearest city and less than an hour from the United States-Mexico border, with approximately 5,500 residents. Although Community B did not meet the U.S. Census Bureau definition of rural, its neighboring towns did. Girls in these towns were bused to Community B schools, thereby enabling the program to reach rural girls.

Recruitment

The importance of the relationships with intervention communities cannot be overemphasized. A basis of trust and commitment are fundamental to performing work in the best interests of the community and promoting a positive relationship. To this end, recruitment strategies involved community liaisons to provide personal contact and engender familiarity, often referred to in the literature as *personalismo*. Personalismo combines a personal touch while completing formal procedures (Kanel, 2002). Flyers and in-class presentations were also employed. Table 6.1 delineates the recruitment eligibility requirements and goals.

In Community A, the liaison was a bilingual Mexican American woman who had previous volunteer experience at the local elementary school. Her long history in the community was vital in establishing a sense of trust and familiarity among the participant girls and their parents. She contacted Spanish-speaking parents to provide information and invite them to the parent night (informed-consent session). The Community A school personnel contacted English-speaking parents and reminded girls of activities.

In Community B, a Mexican American community advisory board member volunteered at the intermediate school. Her bilingual skills and her professional reputation made it possible to introduce the project intervention easily. She knew the parents and was able to converse with them on a personal level.

Information Sessions

Parents/guardians were invited to an information session, which included dinner at their daughters' school. This was deemed the most effective approach, as

Table 6.1   Recruitment Eligibility and Goals

Source School	Sixth Graders N (Girls)	Latinos (Entire School %)	Eligible Girls (n)	Enrollment Goal (Girls)
Community A	35 (16)	81	~12	10
Community B	237 (119)	50	~59	15
Total				25

opposed to a lecture format, which engaged parents less and created a distance. A facilitator sat at each table and presented the program to each family, again employing personalismo. Because some parents spoke English and others Spanish, all documents were printed in both languages, and the presenters were bilingual/bicultural.

Role Models

Various role models were involved, from recruitment through intervention implementation. The participant girls were regularly exposed to role models of the same ethnicity as well as from other ethnic groups. For instance, at the welcome lunch, a Latino physician and two Latina professors spoke to the girls.

During the program, each girl was assigned a group leader, a Latina college student, at a ratio of 1:6. Further interaction with college Latinas occurred during a barbeque hosted by a Latina sorority. Girls also interacted with non-Latino role models through their mathematics instruction and the campus scavenger hunt.

On the final day, friends and family participated in the graduation ceremony. All presenters were Latinos of various ages, from elders and parents to early college-age women.

Curriculum

The goal of the Latina Institute is to increase health knowledge and college preparedness through an early-outreach program for rural early-adolescent Latinas.

In June 2005, the first cohort of 20 girls completed the pilot intervention held at the University of Arizona. Girls were bused from their schools to the university for a 3-day, 2-night stay.

The ritual of opening and closing the event was incorporated into the program by hosting an opening ceremony and a graduation. Throughout the 3 days, participants were exposed to university life, while increasing their health knowledge and college preparedness in a cultural context. Key components of each day are presented in the following sections.

Day 1

One aim of the program was to set a tone of excitement upon the girls' arrival. To this end, girls were greeted warmly and were given gift bags filled with health and college information, along with school supplies (e.g., a

Spanish-English dictionary and university writing utensils). Each girl also received a binder containing program handouts and related materials. And, the Hispanic Alumni organization offered university memorabilia to welcome the girls.

Because the participants came from two different schools, an icebreaker adapted for Latinos was held, which included a scavenger hunt that involved various Latino practices. Then girls listened to a few Latino professors speak about opportunities for advancing one's education and professionally.

Later, girls checked into their residence hall, where the sense of independence became apparent—they were given a key to their own dorm, which seemed significant to them.

Next, a cultural consultant led the participants in a talking circle, to discuss gossip and developing trust in friendships. Each girl took a turn speaking while the rest of the group listened. This exercise reinforced the importance of respect, by giving each girl time to speak if she chose to do so.

Afterward, the girls made the approximately quarter mile walk to the recreation center to attend hip-hop dance instruction. Regardless of skill level, all the girls seemed to enjoy dancing.

The day ended with a barbeque, hosted by a Latina sorority, and a movie.

Day 2

The American Association of University Women (1992) recommends programs that help students familiarize themselves with college environments, terminology, and prerequisites. To this end, the participants were divided into teams that competed against one another in a campus scavenger hunt. Girls visited multiple centers collecting the information on their assignment sheets.

Later, the girls rode the university shuttle to the health sciences center where they were greeted by a nurse at the Women's Health and Resource Center. The nurse led the girls through the facility and showed them the equipment used for annual gynecological exams. She also gave a presentation on the menstrual cycle and how to prevent sexually transmitted diseases. Notably, the girls' questions indicated they had many misperceptions.

From the health class, participants went to a biostatistics lesson, where the instructor engaged the girls in a game, which they seemed to move through with ease—in contrast to the adults in the room, who seemed to have a more difficult time being attentive.

Then, to address both the advantages and challenges of being bicultural, a graduate student facilitated a workshop on biculturalism. (*Note:* In the 6-month follow-up, a couple of girls reported feeling more in touch with their ethnic background. One reported she plans to major in Mexican American studies, and now subscribes to a Latina magazine to help her learn more about her culture.)

By late afternoon of day 2, the girls were ready for another dance. (*Note:* In the 6-month follow-up one girl reported being able to transfer the "attitude" she learned in dance class to cheerleading.)

In the evening, girls visited the science museum, featuring interactive stations.

Day 3

The final day began by preparing the girls for program closure. They completed the first follow-up surveys, then participated in a final talking circle, during which they discussed their experiences in the program. As a gift, girls received journals, which they quickly began passing around for signatures from their newfound friends.

The program culminated with a formal graduation ceremony, followed by a dinner in the Chicano/Hispano Center. There was standing-room only in the hall set up for 85 guests, who watched as 20 girls graduated in front of their friends and families. Each girl was publicly acknowledged by her group leader when she received the certificate of completion (suitable for including with a college application). Group leaders also wrote a sentence or two to describe the uniqueness of each girl. One girl was so overcome with emotion she walked to the front of the hall crying the entire way.

It is important to note that parents had to travel from rural communities to attend this ceremony, and for some it was their first time on the university campus. One parent arrived one hour early, dressed up and carrying a rose to give to her daughter. Families also viewed a slide show of the program activities, with each slide tied to a specific goal of the program, to enable them to better understand the objectives of the institute. Family members enjoyed picking out their daughters in the photos.

And to further encourage parents and support their efforts to raise their daughters and send them to college, a father spoke about his experience of returning to college as an adult, and described how he supports his 12-year-old daughter. A mother detailed her and her husband's experience raising three college graduates with limited financial resources.

After, the cultural consultant closed the graduation ceremony with a blessing, and families and program staff shared a traditional Mexican meal in the Cesar Chavez Building. The pride and gratitude visible on the faces of parents was indescribable.

EVALUATION

The University of Arizona Human Subjects Committee approved the pilot intervention instruments and consent forms. Parents/guardians and the girls signed consent forms.

Self-report surveys were collected at baseline, on the last day of the program, and 6 months after the program. Survey domains included demographics (e.g., age, ethnicity, language), leisure-time activities (e.g., hours watching television, hours spent on the phone, hours spent doing homework), risk behaviors (e.g., smoking, drinking, fighting), culture (e.g., ethnic identity, experiences of discrimination), and education (e.g., grades, intent to quit school).

RESULTS

Thus far, *baseline* descriptive statistics are available for 22 girls. The majority of girls identified themselves as Mexican American, as shown in Figure 6.2.

Girls reported having language skills in both English and Spanish, but mainly English. Although most said they spoke with their friends in English, many also said they watched television in English or Spanish and listened to music and the radio in either language (see Table 6.2).

Academically, 82% of girls reported earning As or Bs in school; 5 of 22 reported ever thinking about quitting school. Regarding health, participants gave themselves grades of good or better on their overall health. Significantly, many

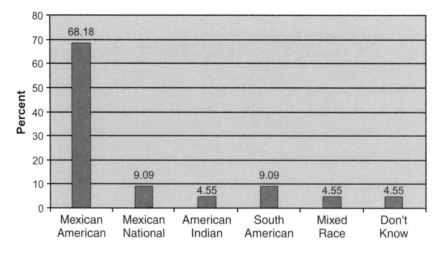

Figure 6.2   Ethnicity

Table 6.2   **Participant Language Skills**

	English % (n)	Spanish % (n)
Always speak . . .	63.64 (22)	16.67 (18)
Always speak with friends in . . .	85.71 (21)	10.53 (19)
Always watch television programs in . . .	80.95 (21)	4.76 (21)
Always listen to music or the radio in . . .	71.43 (21)	9.52 (21)

said they had concerns about body image: 13 described their weight as just right or slightly underweight, compared to 9 who reported being slightly or very overweight; half the girls said they were trying to lose weight, with 68% doing so by exercising and 50% by eating less food.

FUTURE WORK

In order to address feelings of homesickness (two girls reported feeling homesick—one left the first night, after reporting a stomachache; the second cried for a short time on the first evening, but recovered by the following day), the next intervention will add an after-school series to build rapport with the girls and their families. The program will also ask at least one community member to be a constant presence during the university component, to provide reassurance and a sense of familiarity. Near the end of the series and prior to the 3-day university component, girls will be taken on a 1-day field trip as a short interval away from familiar surroundings.

Three days is not enough time to reinforce messages. In subsequent interventions, we will add the after-school series based on the Go Grrrls program (LeCroy & Daley, 2001). In addition to helping the girls to establish relationships with the facilitators, it will enable the program to address areas of concern identified in the results, such as body image.

To address the many questions of parents, the program needs a parental component. It is, however, at the time of this writing, unclear how to incorporate mothers and fathers (or guardians) in a manner that is respectful to the culture, given the limited resources currently available.

A number of studies make recommendations for facilitating opportunities and health for Latinas. Kazdin (1993, p. 136) discusses the need for broad-based programming in school settings for adolescents to reduce peer pressure and increase social skills. The Pew Hispanic Center (2003) makes a similar recommendation, stating a need for a range of programs to respond to the needs of adolescents. Specific to academic achievement, the U.S. Department of Education (2003) recommends setting new, and higher, expectations and creating a pathway to college graduation. Tolan, Guerra, and Kendall (1995, p. 579) note that interventions based on prevention theory emphasize developmental stage, importance timing, and predicting the potential for future risk behaviors.

CONCLUSIONS

The Latina Institute is an ethnically responsive intervention designed to address a primary issue faced by many Latina girls: low college enrollment. With success, better career pathways can be formed for this fast-growing segment of the U.S. population.

REFERENCES

American Association of University Women. (1992). *How schools shortchange girls: Study of major findings on girls and education.* Washington, DC: American Associate of University Women Educational Foundation.

Arizona Coalition on Adolescent Pregnancy and Parenting. (2003). *The school connection to teen pregnancy: No child left behind?* Retrieved November 2005, from www.azteenpregnancy.org.

Castro, F. G., & Gutierres, S. (1997). Drug and alcohol use among rural Mexican Americans. In E. B. Robertson, Z. Slobodia, G. M. Boyd, L. Beatty, & N. J. Kozel (Eds.), *Rural substance abuse: State knowledge and issues.* (NIDA research monograph, pp. 498–530). Rockville, MD: National Institute on Drug Abuse.

Clune, M. S., Nuñez, A. M., & Choy, S. P. (2001). *Competing choices: Men's and women's paths after earning a bachelor's degree* (NCES 2001-154). Washington, DC: Department of Education, National Center for Education Statistics.

Escobar, J. I. (1998). Immigration and mental health: Why are immigrants better off? *Archives of General Psychiatry, 55*(9), 781–782.

Ginorio, A., Huston, M., & American Association of University Women Educational Foundation. (2001). *Si, se puede! Yes, we can: Latinas in school.* Washington, DC: Library of Congress.

Kanel, K. (2002). Mental health needs of Spanish-speaking Latinos in southern California. *Hispanic Journal of Behavioral Sciences, 24*(1), 74–91.

Kazdin, A. E. (1993). Adolescent mental health: Prevention and treatment programs. *American Psychologist, 48,* 127–141.

Ku, L., Sonenstein, F. L., & Pleck, J. H. (1993). Factors influencing first intercourse for teenage men. *Public Health Reports, 108*(6), 680–694.

LeCroy, C. W., & Daley, J. (2001). *Empowering adolescent girls: Examining the
present and building skills for the future with the Go GRRRLS Program.* New
York and London: Norton.

National Alliance for Hispanic Health. (2000). *The state of Hispanic girls.*
Washington, DC: Estrella Press.

National Campaign to Prevent Teen Pregnancy. (2004). *Teen sexual activity,
pregnancy, and childbearing among Latinos in the United States* [Fact sheet].
Washington, DC: Author.

National Research Council, Institute of Medicine. (1998). *From generation to
generation: The health and well-being of children of immigrant families.*
Washington, DC: National Academy Press.

Pew Hispanic Center. (2003). *Hispanic youth dropping out of U.S. schools: Mea-
suring the challenge* [Press release].

Pew Hispanic Center & Kaiser Family Foundation. (2002). *National survey of
Latinos.* Menlo Park, CA, and Washington, DC: Authors.

Ramirez, R. R., & U.S. Census Bureau. (2002). *The Hispanic population in the
United States: March 2002.* Washington, DC: U.S. Government Printing
Office.

Substance Abuse and Mental Health Services Administration (SAMHSA).
(2003). *Risk of suicide among Hispanic females aged 12–17: The National
Health Survey on Drug Abuse Report.* Washington, DC: Office of Applied
Studies.

Tolan, P. H., Guerra, N. G., & Kendall, P. C. (1995). A developmental-ecological
perspective on anti-social behavior in children and adolescents: Toward a
unified risk and intervention framework. *Journal of Consulting and Clinical
Psychology, 63*, 579–584.

U.S. Census Bureau. (2000). *Economics and statistics administration.* Washington, DC: U.S. Department of Commerce.

U.S. Department of Education. (2003). *President's Advisory Commission on Education Excellence for Hispanic Americans Releases: Final report.* Washington,
DC: Author.

Vasquez, M. T., & del las Fuentes, C. (1999). American-born Asian, African, Latina, and American Indian adolescent girls. In N. G. Johnson, M. C. Roberts, & J. Worell (Eds.), *Beyond appearance: A new look at adolescent girls* (pp. 151–173). Washington, DC: American Psychological Association.

Chapter 7

ATHLETES TARGETING HEALTHY EXERCISE AND NUTRITION ALTERNATIVES

Harm Reduction/Health Promotion Program for Female High School Athletes

DIANE L. ELLIOT AND LINN GOLDBERG

More than 7 million students participate in high school athletics. The involvement of young women in sports has expanded since 1972, when the Title IX provision of the Education Amendments was enacted. The result is that almost half of high school athletes are now female (National Federation of State High School Associations, 2004). Although participating in sports has many benefits, contrary to public perceptions, neither young male nor female athletes are protected from drug use and other unhealthy behaviors (DuRant, Escobedo, & Heath, 1995; Kulig, Brener, & McManus, 2003; Naylor, Gardner, & Zaichkowsky, 2001; Pate, Trost, Levin, & Dowda, 2000). Rather, young women athletes may be at greater risk for disordered eating and use of body-shaping agents (e.g., diuretics, laxatives, tobacco, diet pills, amphetamines, or cocaine). These problems are present among all sports; and despite the usual stereotypes, they are not confined to activities that encourage pursuit of a slender, immature body type (e.g., gymnastics, dance, and cross-country running; Taub & Blinde, 1992).

In this chapter, we present information on the Athletes Targeting Healthy Exercise and Nutrition Alternatives (ATHENA) program, which is a school-based, sports-team-centered harm reduction and health promotion program for young female high school athletes. ATHENA has been shown to prevent body-shaping drug use, disordered eating, and other health-harming behaviors (Elliot et al., 2004), and in the longer term to promote healthy nutrition and reduce the use of cigarettes, alcohol, and marijuana (Elliot et al., 2006).

The development and assessment of the ATHENA curriculum was funded by a grant from the National Institute on Drug Abuse 5R01 DA07356, with assistance from PHS Grant 5 M01 RR000334.

We are grateful to the many coaches and athletes who have participated in ATHENA, and to our research team, including: Carol DeFrancesco, MA, RD; Kristen Dulacki, MPH; Melissa Durham, MPH; Lisa Kelleher; Sean Kolmer, MPH; Kerry Kuehl, MD, DrPH; Gina Markel; Wendy McGinnis, MS; Esther Moe, PhD, MPH; Sandy Sadowitz, MA; Dalice Vulkasin; and Leslie Zoref, PhD.

Oregon Health & Science University (OHSU) and Drs. Elliot and Goldberg have a significant financial interest in the commercial sale of technologies used in this research. This potential conflict of interest has been reviewed and managed by the OHSU Conflict of Interest in Research Committee.

ATHENA was developed following the proven efficacy of Athletes Training and Learning to Avoid Steroids (ATLAS), a parallel sports-team-centered program for young male high school athletes (Goldberg et al., 1996, 2000; MacKinnon et al., 2001). As ATHENA's predecessor, and because gender equity often requires that schools implement both programs, this chapter also describes ATLAS and its outcomes. Both are evidence-based curricula with documented efficacy in reducing drug use and other unhealthy behaviors, and enhancing the health of adolescent sports participants.

DRUG USE AND ITS PREVENTION

In general, the prevalence of drug use has increased in the past 30 years, reaching its highest levels in the mid-1990s. Since that peak period, for many substances, use has shown a leveling off or slight decline. Of particular relevance for ATHENA, which targets female high school students, is that the decline in drug use primarily is among younger teens, with use among older adolescents remaining fairly stable at high levels during recent years (Johnston, O'Malley, Bachman, & Schulenberg, 2004). Currently, more than half of high school seniors have tried illicit drugs, usually marijuana, and 20% have tried other illicit drugs. Alcohol consumption has been relatively constant since the mid-1990s. Among 12th-grade students in the last month, half had been drinking; one third had ridden with a drinking driver, and one quarter had been drunk. More than one third have had intercourse, and most did not use condoms or any other birth control method (Grunbaum et al., 2004).

Research, primarily funded by the National Institute on Drug Abuse, has identified the content and process components that characterize effective school-based drug prevention programs (Botvin & Griffin, 2003; Brook, Brook, Richter, & Whiteman, 2003; Faggiano et al., 2005). These aspects are listed in Table 7.1, and are outlined in the National Institute of Drug Abuse publication, *Preventing Drug Use among Children and Adolescents* (Robertson, David, & Rao, 2003) and on the web site of the U.S. Department of Health and Human Services Center for Substance Abuse Prevention (Center for Substance Abuse Prevention, 2006). In addition, both the NIDA publication and web site list the primary drug use prevention programs with proven efficacy. Although programs are available for elementary and middle school students, only one other classroom-based curriculum (other than those described here) is available for high school students.

As adolescents mature, males and females differ in their risk and protective factors for drug use, and are more influenced by their friends than they are by

Table 7.1   Principles of Effective School-Based Drug Prevention

Enhance protective factors and reduce risk factors specific to the group, based on age, gender, ethnicity, and culture.

Correct misperception that many students are using drugs; reinforce antidrug attitudes and strengthen personal commitments to avoid drug abuse.

Increase social competence by enhancing communication and coping abilities and drug resistance skills.

Use interactive educational techniques, such as peer teaching, that allow active involvement.

If possible, provide alternatives to harmful behaviors.

Use booster programs to reinforce the original prevention goals.

teachers and fellow students sitting next to them in health class (National Center on Addiction and Substance Abuse, 2003; National Institute on Drug Abuse, 1996; Rohrbach & Milam, 2003). As a result, the common wisdom has been that, by high school, primary prevention efforts are less effective. However, high school is an important life stage for health promotion. Overall rates of drug use approximately double during these years, and habits established in late adolescence can have lifetime effects (National Center on Addiction and Substance Abuse, 1997).

PREVENTION OF DISORDERED EATING BEHAVIOR AND BODY-SHAPING DRUG USE

Unhealthy eating habits are prevalent among female adolescents. Almost half of all U.S. women are trying to lose weight, and teens often are obsessed with their weight (Camp, Klesges, & Relyea, 1993). A spectrum of eating problems occur, which progresses from poor food choices and inconsistent nutrition that typifies most young teens (Lytle & Kubik, 2003) to a more intense focus on dieting and disrupted eating habits. *Disordered eating* occurs when there is ongoing use of pathologic means to modify nutrient balance, such as self-induced vomiting, fasting, binging, purging, food restriction, and/or use of body-shaping drugs, such as anabolic steroids, laxatives, diuretics, tobacco, diet pills, amphetamines, and cocaine (Sigman, 2003).

Those individuals who progress further meet diagnostic criteria for an eating disorder, with a prevalence of anorexia nervosa and bulimia nervosa of approximately 1% and 8%, respectively (Yager, 2005). However, disordered eating is much more common than those end-stage disorders (Whitaker et al., 1989). And the morbidity of these behaviors is not confined to those with advanced problems. Even in their earlier stages, these behaviors have adverse consequences, including metabolic abnormalities, reduced immunity, hypokalemia, muscle weakness, cardiac arrhythmias, renal dysfunction, and cardiac abnormalities (Roberts & Elliot, 1991). In extreme forms, eating disorders have higher mortality rates than any other psychiatric diagnoses (Fisher, 2003):

> ATHENA does not have a parent component, as we found that our ability to enlist their involvement was variable. However, students are encouraged to share information with their families. When surveyed, more than three-quarters of parents knew about ATHENA, and one-third reported seeing definite changes in their daughter's eating habits. Typical parent comments included: "Thanks for educating my daughter," "My daughter is eating better breakfasts and drinking more milk," "The information that my daughter received helped her understand her choices and the consequences of unhealthy eating."

The prevalence of eating disorders may be increased among athletes (Brunet, 2005; Currie, 2005). To address this concern, in 1997 the American College of Sports Medicine published a position stand on the *female athletic triad* (American College of Sports Medicine, 1997). The triad refers to a combination of: (a) disordered eating and use of body-shaping drugs (amphetamines, tobacco, diet pills, laxatives, diuretics, and anabolic steroids), which can result in (b) amenorrhea. Athletic amenorrhea is associated with reduced estrogen levels and a predisposition to (c) osteoporosis. In turn, osteoporosis can lead to an increase in musculoskeletal injuries (Lloyd et al., 1986), scoliosis, and skeletal fractures (Drinkwater, Bruemner, & Chesnut, 1990).

Anabolic steroids are all similar to the male hormone testosterone. The properties of these "imitation testosterone" molecules vary slightly, depending on their structure. A normal female's body makes a small amount of testosterone, and her cells can respond to the hormone, just as can a male's. But because a woman's testosterone level is normally 2% that of an adult male's, lower doses of anabolic steroids can result in marked effects among females, including a loss in body fat and an increase in muscle (Elliot & Goldberg, 2000). Those effects are the reason steroids were administered to young female competitors in former Eastern bloc countries, who ultimately won many gold medals (Franke & Berendonk, 1997). Steroid use also can have marked side effects on females, as shown in Table 7.2.

During the 1990s, three major national studies found a doubling of female adolescents' steroid abuse (Yesalis, Barsukiewicz, Kopstein, & Bahrke, 1997).

Table 7.2   Side Effects of Anabolic Steroid Use in Females

Reduced body fat and breast size
Increased muscle mass
Deepened voice[a]
Increased clitoral length
Acne
Increased body hair
Reduced scalp hair[b]
Increased libido and aggressiveness
Bone fusion and halt of linear growth

[a] Occurs within a few weeks and is irreversible.

[b] Occurs in approximately 50% of women and can result in diffuse scalp hair loss, rather than male-patterned loss.

The most recent national data from the Centers for Disease Control and Prevention indicate that more than 7% of ninth-grade girls report prior anabolic steroid use (Grunbaum et al., 2004).

A common misconception is that young women who exhibit disordered eating behavior and use body-shaping drugs are "good girls," who obey all the rules. In general, disordered eating habits cluster with other health-harming actions, including drug use (French, Story, Downes, Resnick, & Blum, 1995; Neumark-Sztainer, Story, & French, 1996). The sequence may be that girls with lower self-esteem are more prone to feel depressed, and so engage in disordered eating and body-shaping drug use, followed by use of alcohol and other drugs.

Consistent with the clustering of health-harming behaviors, young women who use steroids have higher rates of using all drugs. They use more alcohol, tobacco, marijuana, and other illicit substances; they also have more sexual partners (Elliot, Moe, Duncan, & Goldberg, 1999). However, because anabolic steroids take time before their effects manifest, unlike other body-shaping drugs, most young women who use them appear to experiment only briefly with them before turning to body-shaping drugs with more immediate effects, such as diet pills, laxatives, and amphetamines.

Developing effective programs to prevent disordered eating has proved to be a challenge. Several reviews have compiled the many published studies of programs to prevent disordered eating (Levine & Smolak, 2006; Stice & Shaw, 2004), the majority of which have not achieved positive behavioral effects; some have even had adverse outcomes (Carter, Stewart, Dunn, & Fairburn, 1997).

Information from drug prevention efforts may shed light on the reasons that preventing disordered eating has proven so difficult. When adolescents who are already experimenting with drug use were assembled with other same-age peers for a more targeted program to prevent drug use, paradoxically, the consequences were a worsening of drug use. The explicit focus on drug use may be stigmatizing; furthermore, bonding between deviant and nondeviant teenagers appeared to cause some of the latter to adopt the harmful behaviors (Robertson, David, & Rao, 2003). Although unintended, the unhealthy activities may become the norms, and thus perceived as not that harmful. By analogy, a focus on disordered eating may actually increase those behaviors; accordingly, ATHENA limits explicit teaching about disordered eating, body weight, and specific recommendations about caloric intake.

SPORTS TEAMS AS VEHICLES FOR HEALTH PROMOTION

High school is a critical time for establishing healthy life styles. Teens who avoid harmful habits have a much reduced risk of subsequently developing those problems (National Center on Addiction and Substance Abuse, 1997). However, traditional classroom-based curricula to prevent health-harming behaviors, such as drug use and disordered eating habits (Levine & Smolak, 2006; Robertson et al., 2003), are limited in their positive effects among older adolescents.

Athletic teams have the potential to change behavior, as they are natural gender-specific settings where bonded teammates meet repeatedly with influential adults to work together toward common goals. Since the early 1990s, we have studied sports team-based programs as means to deter drug use and promote healthy behaviors (Goldberg & Elliot, 2000). As shown in Table 7.3, sports-team-centered curricula can address many of the features that typify effective school-based prevention programs.

Athletes Training and Learning to Avoid Steroids Program

ATLAS is a student-led, sports-team-centered drug-use prevention curriculum for male high school athletes. Young male athletes typically are not protected from drug use; moreover, they are more likely to drink alcohol, engage in binge drinking, and develop other deviant behaviors (Aaron et al., 1995; Carr, Kennedy, & Dimick, 1990). Although the word "steroids" is part of the ATLAS title, the program is designed not only to deter steroid use, as well as the use of

Table 7.3   Team Sports and Effective Drug Prevention

Prevention Principles	ATHENA's Sports-Team-Centered Format
Enhance protective factors and reduce risk factors tailored to the group.	Settings are natural, gender- and age-specific (e.g., varsity versus freshman teams). ATHENA was developed based on cross-sectional studies to define the appropriate content.
Correct misperception about drugs use and other unhealthy behaviors; reinforce antidrug attitudes and strengthen personal commitments to avoid drug abuse.	Curriculum includes accurate norms for drug use and avoids normalizing disordered eating habits. Coaches can state and reinforce antidrug attitudes and expectations for healthy behaviors. Public service campaigns reinforce health team attitudes and behaviors.
Increase social competence by enhancing communication and coping abilities and drug resistance skills.	All female, peer-led format increases participation and social skills. Curriculum includes rehearsing resistance skills, and depression prevention component increases coping abilities.
Interactive curriculum	A sport team is a natural setting for student-led activities, where returning older athletes work with younger teammates. ATHENA activities are fast-paced and involve problem solving and immediate application of new learning.
Alternatives	Focusing on sport performance leads to healthy alternatives (nutrition and strength training) replacing unhealthy behaviors.
Booster curriculum	Booster curriculum is available. In a natural setting older students return and can serve as squad leaders for new participants.

other drugs, but also to encourage appropriate and effective decision-making and communication skills and healthy nutrition behaviors.

The outcomes of ATLAS were determined in a randomized control trial involving three consecutive cohorts of high school football teams from 16 control and 15 intervention high schools (Goldberg et al., 1996, 2000). Measures were collected prior to the program, at the season's end, and approximately 1 year after the intervention. The results indicated that compared to control student athletes, the ATLAS-trained group reported half the use of "athletic enhancing" supplements, half the use of illicit drugs (marijuana, narcotics, amphetamines), and one fourth the incidence of drinking and driving.

Athletes Targeting Healthy Exercise and Nutrition Alternatives

A logical extension of the success of the ATLAS program was to use the team-centered format with young female sports participants, but with a different focus. For although anabolic steroid use is of increasing concern among young women (Yesalis et al., 1997), the greater problems among this group are disordered eating and body-shaping drug use (Golden, 2002; Ireland & Ott, 2004). Furthermore, unlike their male counterparts, young women athletes often want to be leaner and lighter (Stice, 2002), rather than bigger and stronger. Thus, creating an effective prevention program for female student athletes required determining and prioritizing the risk factors that relate to future disordered eating and body-shaping drug use.

Many factors have been linked to drug use and disordered eating among young females. For example, female adolescents at higher risk have lower self-esteem and higher rates of depression than peers less likely to have these problems (Emery, McDermott, Holcomb, Marty, 1993; French et al., 1995; Stice, 2002). In addition, the cultural bias toward extreme thinness affects drug use and weight-loss practices among young women (Rodin, 1993). Media images promote women with extremely thin physiques as a standard of both beauty and sports performance (Holmlund, 1989), and the resulting pressure to lower their body weight may promote disordered eating behaviors and body-shaping drug use among this population (Garner, Garfinkel, Schwartz, & Thompson, 1980).

However, much of the previous research on risk factors for eating disorders has been conducted with individuals who already have those conditions. For them, associations with disordered eating may be a consequence of, rather than a risk factor leading to, the problem. Prior to developing the ATHENA curriculum, we used findings from surveys of more than 1,000 female middle and high school students to identify and prioritize elements for a sports-team-centered program to deter disordered eating and body-shaping drug use (Elliot et al., 2006).

Working with a general cross section of students made it possible to use their self-reported intentions toward future disordered eating practices to define a higher-risk subgroup. The resulting potential risk and protective factors were then prioritized based on their relative impact on that higher future risk. Those factors with the greatest impact were mood/self-esteem and societal pressures to be thin; consequently, we designed the ATHENA curriculum to emphasize those aspects. Because disordered eating behaviors share risk and protective factors with the abuse of drugs in general and other unhealthy behaviors (French et al., 1995; Killen et al., 1987; Neumark-Sztainer et al., 1996; Striegel-Moore & Huydic, 1993), we predicted the curriculum also would be reduce these other harmful behaviors.

ATHENA is delivered as eight 45-minute sessions during a team's playing season. The sessions are scheduled at the coaches' discretion and integrated into the usual practice activities. The athletes met as a team for the sessions, with participants divided into stable learning groups of approximately six members, with one student per group functioning as the assigned squad (peer) leader. Squad leaders and coaches used manuals that contained scripted lesson plans; other teammates used matching workbooks. All received a pocket-sized nutrition and exercise guide, as well.

The scripted format assists fidelity, meaning that coaches and squad leaders require minimal training, which greatly reduces preparation time prior to each session.

Program Adoption

Although the Department of Health and Human Services has made major efforts to encourage and support school use of evidence-based drug prevention programs, such as ATLAS and ATHENA, in general, it has been difficult to get schools to adopt programs with proven effectiveness (Hogan et al., 2003; Ringwalt et al., 2002; Zarella, 2002). (Both the ATHENA and ATLAS curricula are commercially available as self-contained exportable programs, at a cost of approximately $11 per student athlete. Information about ATHENA and its purchase is available from the web site, www.athenaprogram.com.)

In addition to the usual barriers that accompany the adoption of any new curriculum, ATHENA and ATLAS comprise a new paradigm for drug use prevention and health promotion. Unlike the traditional health class, ATHENA and ATLAS are facilitated by coaches and held outside of the usual curricular hours. Still, the programs have been implemented in more than half the states; and, in general, at each site a forward-minded individual has advocated for the programs. These innovators, or change agents have overcome reluctance to use the programs, as well as the resistance of some coaches, who may see the programs as another burden. Once implemented, however, the eventual enthusiasm of the coaches, apparent positive changes among participants, and the ability to include the curricula without additional classroom hours often sustain the programs' use.

As noted, the ATLAS and ATHENA materials are designed so that they can be used without additional training. The *Coach Manual* contains background information, instructions on implementing the program, and the explicitly scripted lesson plans. Nevertheless, because it is a new format, school districts often request training for coaches, sometimes with their squad leaders. Therefore, information on local training is made available at the ATLAS and ATHENA web sites, and the format has varied depending on the needs at each locale (Table 7.4). The training

Table 7.4   Program Training Formats

Trainees	Duration	Content
Coaches and other school personnel wanting to learn more about the programs	3 hours	Review of drug use among athletes; description of the program(s) and their outcomes
Coaches planning on implementing ATLAS, ATHENA, or both	3 to 5 hours	Review of drug use among athletes; background on program(s); experience with the activities; implementation specifics
Coaches and their squad leaders	5 to 7 hours	Review of drug use among athletes; background on program(s); experience with the activities; implementation specifics

sessions usually are individualized according to the needs and resources of the site. In addition to teaching the program mechanics, on-site training generates enthusiasm, helps coaches and squad leaders become a team, and forms mutual commitments to implement the programs.

It is important to point out that because ATLAS is regarded as a model and exemplary program, both it and ATHENA qualify for funding resources through the U.S. Department of Education and the Substance Abuse and Mental Health Services Administration. The Center for Substance Abuse web site provides information on how to access these and other resources to acquire and implement the programs (http://www.samhsa.gov /grants/index.aspx).

IMPLEMENTING ATHLETES TARGETING HEALTHY EXERCISE AND NUTRITION ALTERNATIVES

During the initial efficacy trial of ATHENA, 20 sports teams at nine high schools implemented the program. That process began with our meeting with a participant school's athletic director and coaches of the women's sports, cheerleading, and dance-and-drill teams. At this meeting, we explained the program and invited all coaches and teams to participate. Ultimately, male and female coaches from the soccer, volleyball, dance, cheerleading, golf, basketball, crosscountry, track, swimming, softball, and tennis teams participated.

In the following sections, we review the steps participant coaches followed, to provide a realistic guide to ATHENA implementation.

Preseason Activities

Prior to the playing season, a team implementing ATHENA must obtain the curriculum materials, which can be ordered from the ATHENA web site (www .athenaprogram.com). But before ordering, an estimate of the number of team members is required. There are three types of ATHENA participants—coaches, squad leaders, and team members—and each requires different materials.

During the ATHENA sessions, the team meets are assembled into stable groups of approximately six students (the squads), one of whom is identified as the student athlete squad leader. The coach must have a *Coach Manual*; squad leaders must have the *Squad Leader Manual*; all other team members receive workbooks. In addition, both squad leaders and other team members receive an *Athlete's Guide,* a pocket-sized booklet that contains background information on nutrition, strength training, normal maturation, and drug use. These booklets also include pages the athletes use to monitor their protein and calcium intake and to record their moods and activities.

The *Coach Manual* and *Squad Leader Manual* contain the scripted lesson plans. Explicitly scripting the curriculum ensures that all the teams received the same content. It also makes the program easy to implement, a critical feature for busy coaches. In addition, the playbook-like structure of the manuals makes them familiar and user-friendly. Furthermore, studies of classroom prevention curricula reveal that few teachers use programs with fidelity to their original content, and those modifications, although well-intended, reduce program effectiveness (Silvia & Thorne, 1997); therefore, ATHENA's reliance on peer teaching and scripted lesson plans for both coaches and squad leaders helps maintain adherence to its intended content. Figure 7.1 shows a page from the curriculum, with its key features.

Between ATHENA sessions, the manuals and workbooks are stored in a team box in the coach's office or equipment room (Figure 7.2). Storing materials in the team box prevents players from losing them and makes them readily accessible for the next session. The factual information and any activities tracked by the athletes themselves, such as protein intake, are kept in the *Athlete's Guide,* which the students are advised to keep in their gym bags or backpacks.

The Role of Coaches

Coaches have been called the missing link in promoting adolescent health (Brown & Butterfield, 1992). During a playing season, a coach may have more than 100 contact hours with her or his athletes—more than most classroom

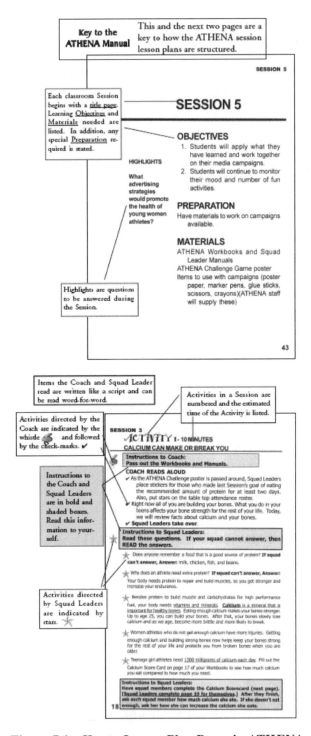

Figure 7.1 Key to Lesson Plan Pages in ATHENA
Coach Manual and *Squad Leader Manual*

Figure 7.2   ATHENA Team Box and Curriculum Components

teachers. And that contact may be repeated annually during a student athlete's career. Thus, coaches are positioned to have far greater influence than most other educators. Accordingly, it is critical that team members believe that their coach supports the program, and reinforces its principles during their workouts and games. That said, the coach does not have to be the person facilitating the ATHENA classroom sessions; a trainer or an assistant coach may fill that role:

> Coaches told us that ATHENA helped them reinforce what they were already teaching their athletes about nutrition, strength training, and mental toughness. Their athletes were changing what they ate before and after training. One coach began taking her athletes to a grocery store to purchase pre- and postgame meals, rather than stopping at fast-food restaurants.

Coaches and others facilitating the ATHENA program have varying backgrounds. Surveys of coaches have shown that although they recognize the potential of health-harming practices among young athletes, they generally underestimate their prevalence (Elliot, Goldberg, Wolf, & Moe, 1998). As with parents, coaches also tend to think that such problems are more common on other teams than among their athletes.

As noted, the lesson plans are scripted; nevertheless, there is ample opportunity for the coaches and other facilitators to personalize the material using their own examples. And because the educational backgrounds of coaches differ, the *Coach Manual* includes an introductory section that contains information on the nutrition and strength-training principles and other aspects of the curriculum:

> The assistant coach for one of the ATHENA soccer teams was a former player and recent graduate, now attending a local community college. Her taking on the role of coach during the ATHENA sessions seemed to work to everyone's benefit. Peer teaching and near-peer teaching by one only slightly older than participants, may be especially successful. Studies show that peers may be more effective than experienced instructors, by enhancing information relevance and increasing a team's sense of ownership and personal investment in activities (Buller et al., 1999).

Selection and Training of Squads and Squad Leaders

As noted, during ATHENA sessions, a team is divided into groups of approximately six students. Students remain in those same groups throughout ATHENA. Specifically, we recommend that the coach assign students to these squads, rather than allow the players to form groups themselves. The point is to encourage more diverse interactions, as opposed to reinforcing existing cliques. To simplify this step, initially, the coach can assign groups alphabetically, then do some rearranging, as necessary, to ensure that each squad has members of different ages.

> We have worked with hundreds of coaches, and all cared about their players. However, all were not as sensitive as others about the potential harmful effect of a stray remark. One coach related that he had no idea that calling a team member "porky" could be damaging. We and others (Carson, Bridges, & Canadian Academy of Sport Medicine, 2001) recommend that coaches not weigh their athletes or record their weights.

The coach then selects a squad leader for each student group. We recommend that the coach *offer* (rather than require) the selected student the opportunity to be a squad leader, explaining that by accepting the position, she will be helping her teammates to become better athletes and avoid health-harming behaviors, such as drug use and disordered eating behaviors. Giving a selected student the chance to decline, ideally, prevents the possibility that an individual experiencing such problems will not undermine the program by exhibiting the very behaviors the program seeks to avoid. That said, some coaches have selected girls with suspected problems to be squad leaders and have reported that giving them the responsibility seemed to help the individual change her behaviors.

The next step is to train the squad leaders, which must take place before the first session. Included in the *Coach Manual* is a scripted lesson plan for the 90-minute squad leader training session. Its main objectives are to:

- Review the *Squad Leader Manuals* with the students and orient them to the format of the sessions.
- Build their enthusiasm.
- Underscore their important role in the sessions.

In addition, it's important at this time to reassure them that being a squad leader will not require additional time because squad leaders often are students involved in other activities.

During the training session, squad leaders also are told that many young athletes like themselves have successfully served as squad leaders, and they and their teams will enjoy the ATHENA program.

(Note: The ATHENA program materials include templates for letters and certificates of recognition to commend the squad leaders for their role in the program, similar to those that might be used for a team captain. In subsequent years of the program, squad leaders often may be returning team members, who already are familiar with the curriculum and its format.)

SCHEDULING THE ATHLETES TARGETING HEALTHY EXERCISE AND NUTRITION ALTERNATIVES SESSIONS

ATHENA is delivered during eight meetings, of 45 minutes, which are integrated into the usual team practice activities. This number was chosen to coincide with the typical number of weeks in a playing season. Optimally, sessions are scheduled approximately once a week, to reinforce the activities between meetings; however, sessions may be held daily, or with only a day or two between meetings. Because game and training schedules differ for each school, season, and sport, the coach will decide how best to schedule the sessions into the existing team activities.

A classroom is not required to hold the sessions; in fact, teams often meet in the gym, the weight room, or, in nice weather, on the field. But regardless where they're held, we recommend that coaches specify dates and times for all eight meetings, otherwise the normal disruptions caused by the busy playing season (e.g., rescheduling games due to bad weather or other circumstances) may cause cancellation of sessions. As a curriculum, with activities building on those prior, it is important that students participate in all eight sessions.

> During the first depression prevention component, the coach introduces the concept by having students rate their mood; and then half the class plays a fun game while the other half circles the Ys in a long list of random letters. Then everyone rerates their mood. The scripted curriculum points out that people can like different things, which acknowledges the one or two student athletes who like circling the Ys.

Session Content

Each 45-minute ATHENA session is composed of three to five activities, designed to foster active learning and application of new abilities. The scope and sequence of the ATHENA sessions is shown in Table 7.5. In general, the majority of activities are led by the squad leaders, with the coach (or other individual filling that role) facilitating the sessions, beginning and wrapping up each meeting. During the session, the coach can circulate among groups, keep student athletes focused on the activity at hand, and assist when needed.

Sports Nutrition

The sports nutrition component emphasizes a few basic principles relevant to young female athletes. In order to not reinforce an already heightened awareness of calorie intake and body weight, unlike the male ATLAS curriculum, in

Table 7.5 ATHENA Scope and Sequence

	1	2	3	4	5	6	7	8
Healthy sports nutrition	■	■	■		■	■		■
Strength training								
Adverse effects of drugs and disordered eating on athletes	■	■	■	■	■		■	■
Media deconstruction				■				
Depression prevention			■	■	■	■	■	
Public service announcement						■	■	
Refusal skills							■	
Goal setting	■	■	■	■	■	■	■	

ATHENA, specific advice about calorie consumption is not included. Rather, the nutrition component is sequenced, first, to help students identify which common foods are primarily carbohydrates, proteins, and high in fat; and, second, to learn the relationship of those nutrients to athletic performance.

> Before beginning to use their mood diaries, students write down 4 or 5 fun things that they could do most days. Certain items appeared on everyone's list, such as taking a nap and talking on the phone. Other items were more school-specific—for example, "brushing my pony," was an entry from a rural participant.

In both ATLAS and ATHENA, we make an analogy between cars and nutrition. Carbohydrates are referred to the "high-octane" fuel needed for intense exercise. Athletes are told they can perform best when their "fuel tanks" are full, and that they need to "fill up their tanks" after training. Proteins are called the building blocks of the car's engine (their muscles), and participants are told that without enough protein to repair their "engines" after a vigorous workout or game, they cannot benefit from training. Specific advice is also provided concerning calcium requirements: it is pointed out that just as calcium strengthens bones it also strengths tendons and ligaments, which may reduce their risk of injury.

> During session 6, as part of the depression prevention sequence, squad members pair up and write down two positive things about themselves and two about their partner. Because the squads are assigned, rather than self-selecting, sometimes girls who otherwise might not interact, do so. It was remarkable to see the look on a senior's face when a sophomore told her how important it had been that she had talked to her when she first joined the varsity team. An act of kindness was rewarded and reinforced.

Strength Training

Strength training has been reported to increase women's self-esteem (Williams & Cash, 2001). ATHENA's female-only, peer-led format also may increase participants' self-esteem, assertiveness, and social skills (American Association of University Women Education Foundation, 1995; Sadker & Sadker, 1994). But a common misconception is that increasing strength necessitates bigger muscles. To dispel that myth, one of the ATHENA activities asks participants clap, to demonstrate how muscle fibers contracting in unison can lead to an increase in strength without bigger muscles. Students also review the benefits of lower-intensity, higher-repetition versus higher-weight and lower-repetition training.

Because most strength training occurs during the off-season, the ATHENA *Athlete's Guide* provides training regimes for different sports, with pictures and descriptions of different lifts.

Affects of Drug Use and Other Unhealthy Behaviors on Sport Performance

Using games and drawings, students receive a balanced presentation of the risks and benefits for athletes of disordered eating and drug use. In the Puzzling Differences activity, students learn about how drug use affects males and females differ: they assemble a puzzle using the criterion of whether a fact is true for males or females. Scare tactics are avoided, because they can backfire (Goldberg, Bents, Bosworth, Trevison, & Elliot, 1991).

To avoid unintentionally normalizing disordered eating behavior, this topic is only a minor aspect of the curriculum. The effects of behaviors are related to immediate consequences relevant to young female athletes, rather than distant outcomes, such as lung cancer and heart disease.

Alternatives

In a review of drug prevention programs, the alternatives component reported the largest effect size and most robust positive outcomes (Tobler, 1992). Rather than an Outward Bound experience, which may not be feasible, in the ATHENA program, nutrition and exercise training are given as alternatives to health-harming actions, to address the immediate performance goals of the participant athletes.

Media Deconstruction

The widespread depiction in all forms of media of idealized, extremely thin, unhealthy women may encourage harmful weight-loss practices (Andrist, 2003; Garner et al., 1980; Guillen & Barr, 1994; Holmlund, 1989; Rodin, 1993). Although other health promotion programs have targeted the media in addressing unhealthy behavior patterns in young females (National Eating Disorders Association, 1999; U.S. Department of Health and Human Services, 1998; Women's Sports Foundation, 2004), they were designed for younger teenagers; none were school-based, and the outcome of the interventions has not been confirmed with prospective randomized trials.

The ATHENA curriculum counters media influences by directing student athletes to discuss, deconstruct, and remake magazine advertisements for cigarettes, alcohol, and nutritional supplements.

Depression Prevention

Depression is more common among females, and a low mood is a risk implicated in disordered eating and drug use behaviors (Stice, Presnell, & Spangler, 2002). To address this, ATHENA incorporated a depression prevention program with established efficacy (Clarke, Rohde, Lewinsohn, Hops, & Seeley, 1999), using sequenced cognitive restructuring tasks adapted for the sports team setting. Figure 7.3 shows a

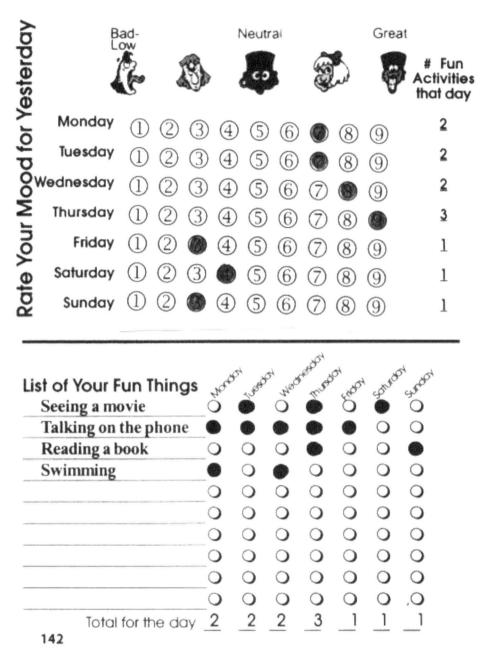

142

Figure 7.3 *Athlete's Guide* Pages for Recording Mood and Fun Activities

page from the *Athlete's Guide* where participants are asked to record their mood and number of fun activities they engage in. Beginning in the third session, and continuing through each of the next four, participants practice establishing the relationship between what they do and how they. The activity is designed to improve their "mental game," as individuals and as a team.

Goal Setting and Team Accountability

Sports, cheerleading, and dance-and-drill teams are natural settings in which cohesion and mutual accountability can occur to enhance the motivation and ability to change attitudes and behaviors (Carron & Spink, 1993; Estabrooks, 2000). We distinguish a "team" from a "group," as the latter requires only member contact and common goals or tasks. Team members, in contrast, are interdependent; they have complementary abilities, share a common commitment, are mutually accountable, and form a shared identity; thus, the power of a team is greater than the sum of its members (Katzenbach & Smith, 2005). The actions of each team member are prompted, modeled, and valued by others on the team, so the social persuasion for change may be more durable (Ryan & Deci, 2000).

To introduce the goal-setting component of the ATHENA program, the coach uses a sports analogy—explaining that a team first has small goals, such as having a good practice or winning a single game, and that over time, succeeding at those smaller goals will help them achieve the larger objective of having a winning season.

The ATHENA squads serve as teams within the team, and during each session students are assigned a goal. At the next session, they report to their squad whether they achieved their goal. The sequence of goals is listed in Table 7.6. Squad leaders track their members' goals by placing a check on a goal card that

Table 7.6 Between-Session Goals for ATHENA Participants

Session	Goal
1	Eat a high-carbohydrate snack before two workouts or training session.
2	Eat daily protein requirement for at least two days.
3	Eat recommended amount of calcium for at least two days.
4	Fill in mood diary each day.
5	Coach selects this session's goal.
6	Eat breakfast every day.
7	Place positive thoughts page in locker or other place where it can be seen each day.

they keep in their manual. Squad leaders and members are encouraged to help one another achieve each of the goals.

For certain of the goal-setting activities, students are asked to complete a game plan section to specify how they will achieve the goal.

Public Service Campaign, Refusal Skills, and the Last Session

By the fifth session, participants are becoming experts, so each squad is asked to develop a brief public service announcement (PSA) to promote the health of young athletes. For example, squads may make posters, perform skits, or sing funny songs. The PSAs designed during the fifth meeting are presented during session 6.

This activity reinforces healthy norms as students rehearse and perform their PSAs:

> The PSAs are one of the session highlights, as students have amazing creativity. In our first pilot study of ATLAS, one of the skits featured a big lineman holding a frying pan containing two grapefruit, while saying, "These are your testicles." In the next scene, he has two peanuts in the pan, and says, "These are your testicles on steroids. Any questions?"

A memorable ATHENA skit was a puppet show, with song lyrics that included, "Eat your peas; it will help your knees," and "Don't do drugs; it will shrink your jugs."

Some schools videotape the PSAs to show to younger students on the freshman and middle school teams.

During the final session, squads play the ATHENA game. The coach asks a set of questions of the squads. When each one is answered correctly, a squad member throws a ball at a target—drug-using ATHENA (Figure 7.4), and receives extra points for hitting her stated target. In general, the questions address the main aspects of the ATHENA knowledge component. The objective is to end on a fun activity and increase athletes' self-efficacy by reviewing what they have learned and accomplished.

> During the final session squads compete by answering questions from the coach. One question was, "How long should a person rest between sets, if she is trying to build strength?" However, the students heard it as, "How long should a person rest between sex." The squad was silent, until they all burst out laughing when the coach reread the question. One of the advantages of a single-gender format is that students report increased comfort discussing certain personal issues (Buddeberg-Fischer & Reel, 2001).

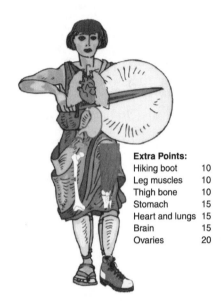

Extra Points:

Hiking boot	10
Leg muscles	10
Thigh bone	10
Stomach	15
Heart and lungs	15
Brain	15
Ovaries	20

Figure 7.4   Drug-Using ATHENA for Final Session's ATHENA Game

As a concluding activity, the coach recognizes the contribution of the squad leaders and asks team members sign a pledge to be healthy athletes.

Booster Curriculum

Among younger adolescents, the effects of middle school drug prevention programs diminish as students age; therefore, effective programs often include booster sessions in subsequent years (Botvin, Baker, Dusenbury, Bovtin, & Diaz, 1995; Resnicow & Botvin, 1993). ATHENA, too, includes a five-session booster curriculum for teams implementing the program 2 years in a row.

Because the teams that used ATHENA in its initial efficacy study varied widely, it is not possible to define the best time to implement ATHENA. However, the longer-term data suggest that the program may be particularly useful for girls in their final years of high school. An optimal strategy, then, may be to use ATHENA 2 years in a row, then wait a year before reintroducing the curriculum. Sophomores who participated in ATHENA would become the squad leaders when ATHENA is reintroduced their senior year.

Students pay attention to advice from their peers much more than from their parents. One of the girls in my family (DLE) asked why her legs felt like rubber when running the day after a soccer match. Although she had heard about the relationship between carbohydrates and muscle glycogen stores for years, it did not "stick" until she read it in the ATHENA *Athlete's Guide.*

ATHLETES TARGETING HEALTHY EXERCISE AND NUTRITION ALTERNATIVES OUTCOMES

Details of ATHENA's development and its immediate outcomes have been reported (Elliot et al., 2004, 2006). Sports, cheerleading, and dance-and-drill teams from 18 public high schools from northwest Oregon and southwest Washington participated in a prospective trial of the ATHENA intervention. Schools underwent a balanced randomization to study condition, and enrollment was offered to all athletes from participating teams. For the 20 intervention and 20 control teams participating, athletes completed questionnaires at baseline (immediately before the playing season) and within 2 weeks of the season's conclusion. For intervention teams, research assistants observed the sessions and used lesson plan checklists to monitor implementation and fidelity to the curriculum.

The outcome analysis used a generalized estimating equations random effects model framework, which takes into account the nesting of students within schools and on teams; and because the intervention was designed to prevent harmful behaviors, onset of disordered eating and body-shaping drug use also was an important outcome.

Table 7.7 lists the characteristics of the participating female high school athletes. All enrolled teams assigned to the intervention and control conditions were retained in the study. All intervention coaches found it feasible to incorporate the

Table 7.7   Efficacy Study of ATHENA Participants

	Study Participants (%)
Parent with college degree	63
Average age in years	15.4
Percent Caucasian	92
Self-reported prior alcohol use	50
Self-reported prior tobacco use	30
Self-reported prior marijuana use	19
Self-reported prior diet pill use	13
Self-reported prior fasting to lose weight	27
Self-reported prior anabolic steroid use	0.2

eight ATHENA sessions and deliver the program with high fidelity; on average, teams covered more than 80% of the content items each session.

Following completion of the ATHENA program, participating athletes reported significantly less new and ongoing diet pill use ($p < .05$), with a relative risk of beginning to use those agents of approximately one third that of control participants. They also were significantly less likely to begin use of performance-enhancing substances (amphetamines, anabolic steroids, and sports supplements; $p < .05$), with a risk of about half that of control athletes. ATHENA athletes had concurrent positive changes in strength training self-efficacy ($p < .005$) and healthy eating behaviors ($p < .001$). The components addressed in the curriculum were significantly altered in the appropriate direction (better able to control one's mood: $p < .005$; enhanced refusal skills: $p = .05$; less belief in the media: $p < .005$; more appropriate perceptions of closest friends' body-shaping drug use: $p < .001$; and greater perceived personal vulnerability: $p < .005$).

Several significant changes occurred in areas not specifically targeted in the curriculum. Following the program, intervention students were less likely to ride in a car with an alcohol-drinking driver ($p = .05$) and more likely to use seatbelts ($p < .05$). In addition, fewer intervention students became sexually active ($p < .05$). Finally, injuries were reduced among curriculum participants ($p < .05$).

In 2004, 1 year after the program's final intervention, we mailed a one-page anonymous survey, along with self-addressed, stamped envelopes to all intervention and control participants who had completed high school and were 18 years of age and older. During the 1 to 3 years following graduation, ATHENA participants reported significantly less use of cigarettes, alcohol, and marijuana ($p < .05$ for each). The overall use of diet pills, diuretics, laxatives, as well as self-induced vomiting (which were behaviors immediately impacted by the curriculum) became less prevalent among all subjects over time, with less than 10% of respondents indicating those activities in the last 3 months. Along with that general reduction, a trend toward continued reductions ($p = .14$) was seen among intervention graduates. Intervention graduates also reported sustained differences in knowledge of calcium and reported greater calcium intake ($p < .005$ for both).

We recognize that our long-term findings have limitations. Our data are based on self-report, which can be biased by situational and cognitive factors (Brener, Billy, & Grady, 2003). However, when assured of confidentiality, findings are considered valid, and biochemical measures usually confirm self-reports (Forman & Linney, 1991). For both nonresponders and underreporters, the biases might be expected to have attenuated, rather than augmented, intervention effects. Last, ethnic minorities were underrepresented among our study subjects, reflecting both local demographics and the relatively lower participation of female minority students in school sports (Lopiano, 2006); thus, our findings may not be applicable to those groups.

> ATLAS was evaluated among football teams, and although it was not a study objective, the teams participating in the program won more games than the control teams.
> ATHENA teams were too varied to keep those statistics. However, hearing a volleyball team shout "ATHENA" after they huddled up between points made us believe that our participants were all winners.

Despite those limitations, ATHENA's longer-term findings are opposite to those among younger adolescents. For drug prevention programs delivered to middle school students, the reductions in drug use diminish over time. For ATHENA, the shorter-term benefits persisted, and new, positive behavioral effects emerged 1 to 3 years following high school graduation. School-based programs are embedded in a developmental and social context that may constrain their outcomes and limit their apparent efficacy. However, life transitions, such as leaving high school, may help abilities developed in those programs to emerge.

CONCLUSIONS

During the past 2 decades, participation by young women in sports has increased, and while this participation may have many benefits, still today, school sports cannot be said to either prevent harmful behaviors or ensure life-long physical activity (Tammelin, Nayha, Hills, & Jarvelin, 2003). Moreover, the overriding focus on winning may diminish the fun aspect of sports and the health-enhancing potential of athletics (McCloskey & Bailes, 2005; Miracle & Rees, 1994).

In high school, factors limiting efficacy of classroom programs may contribute to the utility of a sports team format. Because both harmful and health-promoting behaviors cluster and share mediating factors, programs such as ATHENA and its male analogue ATLAS, which are designed to target those antecedents and increase psychological well-being and social competence, may have benefits across a range of behavioral outcomes. Establishing and reinforcing those abilities while in high school may be especially potent as graduates enter new environments and transition to adulthood. The positive findings of the ATLAS and ATHENA programs support strengthening the health-enhancing mission of sports by incorporating harm reduction and health promotion curricula into the athletic team setting.

REFERENCES

Aaron, D. J., Dearwater, S. R., Anderson, R., Olsen, T., Kriska, A. M., & La-Porte, R. E. (1995). Physical activity and the initiation of high-risk health behaviors in adolescents. *Medical Science Sports and Exercise, 27,* 1639–1642.

American Association of University Women Education Foundation. (1995). *Growing smart: What's working for girls in school?* Washington, DC: American Association of University Women Education Foundation.

American College of Sports Medicine. (1997). Position stand on the female athlete triad. *Medical Science Sports and Exercise, 29,* i–ix.

Andrist, L. C. (2003). Media images, body dissatisfaction, and disordered eating in adolescent women. *American Journal of Maternal Child Nursing, 28,* 119–123.

Botvin, G. J., Baker, E., Dusenbury, L., Botvin, E. M., & Diaz, T. (1995). Long-term follow-up results of a randomized drug abuse prevention trial in a White middle-class population. *Journal of the American Medical Association, 273*(14), 1106–1112.

Botvin, G. J., & Griffin, K. W. (2003). Drug use prevention curricula in schools. In Z. Sloboda & W. J. Bukoski (Eds.), *Handbook of drug abuse prevention: Theory, science, and practice* (pp. 45–47). New York: Kluwer Academic/Plenum Press.

Brener, N. D., Billy, J. O., & Grady, W. R. (2003). Assessment of factors affecting the validity of self-reported health-risk behavior among adolescents: Evidence from the scientific literature. *Journal of Adolescent Health, 33,* 436–457.

Brook, J. S., Brook, D. W., Richter, L., & Whiteman, M. (2003). Risk and protective factors of adolescent drug use: Implications for prevention programs. In Z. Sloboda & W. J. Bukoski (Eds.), *Handbook of drug abuse prevention: Theory, science, and practice* (pp. 265–287). New York: Kluwer Academic/Plenum Press.

Brown, B. R., Jr., & Butterfield, S. A. (1992). Coaches: A missing link in the health care system. *American Journal of the Disabled Child, 146,* 211–217.

Brunet, M. (2005). Female athlete triad. *Clinical Sports Medicine, 24,* 623–636.

Buddeberg-Fischer, B., & Reel, V. (2001). Preventing disturbed eating behaviors: An intervention program in Swiss high school classes. *Journal of Eating Disorders,* 109–124.

Buller, D. B., Morrill, C., Taren, D., Aickin, M., Sennott-Miller, L., Buller, M. K., et al. (1999). Randomized trial testing the effect of peer education at increasing fruit and vegetable intake. *Journal of the National Cancer Institute, 91,* 1491–1500.

Camp, D. E., Klesges, R. C., & Relyea, G. (1993). The relationship between body weight concerns and adolescent smoking. *Health Psychology, 12,* 24–32.

Carr, C. N., Kennedy, S. R., & Dimick, K. M. (1990). Alcohol use among high school athletes: A comparison of alcohol use and intoxication in male and female high school athletes and non-athletes. *Journal Alcohol Drug Education, 36,* 39–43.

Carron, A. V., & Spink, K. S. (1993). Team building in an exercise setting. *Sports Psychology, 7,* 8–18.

Carson, J. D., & Bridges, E., & Canadian Academy of Sport Medicine. (2001). Abandoning routine body composition assessment: A strategy to reduce disordered eating among female athletes and dancers. *Clinical Journal of Sport Medicine, 11,* 280.

Carter, J. C., Stewart, D. A., Dunn, V. J., & Fairburn, C. G. (1997). Primary prevention of eating disorders: Might it do more harm than good? *International Journal of Eating Disorders, 22,* 167–172.

Center for Substance Abuse Prevention. (2006). *SAMHSA model programs.* Retrieved January 2006, from http://modelprograms.samhsa.gov/template .cfm?CFID=663995&CFTOKEN=94643044.

Clarke, G. N., Rohde, P., Lewinsohn, P. M., Hops, H., & Seeley, J. R. (1999). Cognitive-behavioral treatment of adolescent depression: Efficacy of acute group treatment and booster sessions. *Journal of American Academy of Child Adolescent Psychology, 38,* 272–279.

Currie, A. (2005). Eating disorders in athletes: Managing the risks. *Clinical Sports Medicine, 24,* 871–883.

Drinkwater, B. L., Bruemner, B., & Chesnut, C. G. H., III. (1990). Menstrual history as a determinant of current bone density in young athletes. *Journal of American Medical Association, 263,* 545–548.

DuRant, R. H., Escobedo, L. G., & Heath, G. W. (1995). Anabolic-steroid use, strength training, and multiple drug use among adolescents in the United States. *Pediatrics, 96,* 23–28.

Elliot, D. L., & Goldberg, L. (2000). Women and anabolic steroids. In C. E. Yesalis (Ed.), *Anabolic steroids in sports and exercise* (2nd ed., pp. 225–246). Champaign, IL: Human Kinetics.

Elliot, D. L., Goldberg, L., Moe, E. L., DeFrancesco, C. A., Durham, M. B., & Hix-Small, H. (2004). Preventing substance use and disordered eating: Initial outcomes of the ATHENA (Athletes Targeting Healthy Exercise and Nutrition Alternatives) program. *Archives of Pediatric Medicine, 158,* 1043–1051.

Elliot, D. L., Goldberg, L., Moe, E. L., DeFrancesco, C. A., Durham, M. D., & McGinnis, W. (2006). *The ATHENA program for high school female athletes: Effects following graduation.* Unpublished manuscript.

Elliot, D. L., Goldberg, L., Wolf, S. L., & Moe, E. L. (1998). Coaches' estimates of drug use and disordered eating: A potential blind spot? *Strength and Conditioning, 20,* 31–34.

Elliot, D. L., Moe, E. L., Duncan, T., & Goldberg, L. (1999). Who are the young women at risk for anabolic steroid use? *Medical Science and Sports Exercise, 31,* 122.

Elliot, D. L., Moe, E. L., Goldberg, L., DeFrancesco, C. A., Durham, M. B., & Hix-Small, H. (2006). Definition and outcome of a curriculum to prevent disordered eating and body-shaping drug use. *Journal School Health, 76*(2), 67–73.

Emery, E. M., McDermott, R. J., Holcomb, D. R., & Marty, D. S. (1993). The relationship between youth substance use and area-specific self-esteem. *Journal of School Health, 63*(5), 224–228.

Estabrooks, P. A. (2000). Sustaining exercise participation through group cohesion. *Exercise and Sport Science Review, 28,* 63–67.

Faggiano, F., Vigna-Taglianti, F. D., Versino, E., Zambon, A., Borraccino, A., & Lemma, P. (2005). School-based prevention for illicit drugs use. *Cochrane Database Systematic Review, 18,* CD003020.

Fisher, M. (2003). The course and outcome of eating disorders in adults and in adolescents: A review. *Adolescent Medicine, 14,* 149–158.

Forman, S. G., & Linney, J. A. (1991). Increasing the validity of self-report data in effectiveness trials. *National Institute of Drug Abuse Research Monograph, 107,* 235–247.

Franke, W. W., & Berendonk, B. (1997). Hormonal doping and androgenization of athletes: A secret program of the German Democratic Republic government. *Clinical Chemistry, 43,* 1262–1279.

French, S. A., Story, M., Downes, B., Resnick, M. D., & Blum, R. W. (1995). Frequent dieting among adolescents: Psychosocial and health behavior correlates. *American Journal of Public Health, 85,* 695–701.

Garner, D. M., Garfinkel, P. E., Schwartz, D., & Thompson, M. (1980). Cultural expectations of thinness in women. *Psychological Reports, 47,* 483–491.

Goldberg, L., Bents, R., Bosworth, E., Trevisan, L., & Elliot, D. L. (1991). Anabolic steroid education and adolescents: Do scare tactics work? *Pediatrics, 87,* 283–286.

Goldberg, L., & Elliot, D. L. (2000). Prevention of anabolic steroid use. In C. E. Yesalis (Ed.), *Anabolic steroids in sports and exercise* (2nd ed., pp. 117–136). Champaign, IL: Human Kinetics.

Goldberg, L., Elliot, D. L., Clarke, G., MacKinnon, D. P., Moe, E., et al. (1996). Effects of a multi-dimensional anabolic steroid prevention intervention: The ATLAS (Adolescents Training and Learning to Avoid Steroids) Program. *Journal of the American Medical Association, 276,* 1555–1562.

Goldberg, L., MacKinnon, D., Elliot, D. L., Moe, E. L., et al. (2000). The Adolescents Training and Learning to Avoid Steroids Program: Preventing drug use and promoting health behaviors. *Archives of Pediatric Medicine, 154,* 332–338.

Golden, N. H. (2002). A review of the female athlete triad (amenorrhea, osteoporosis, and disordered eating). *International Journal of Adolescent Medical Health, 14,* 9–17.

Grunbaum, J. A., Kann, L., Kinchen, S., Ross, J., Hawkins, J., Lowry, R., et al. (2004). Youth risk behavior surveillance—United States. *Morbidity and Mortality Weekly Report Surveill Summ., 53*(2), 1–96.

Guillen, E. O., & Barr, S. I. (1994). Nutrition, dieting, and fitness messages in a magazine for adolescent women, 1970–1990. *Journal of Adolescent Health, 15,* 464–472.

Hogan, J. A., Baca, I., Daley, C., Garcia, T., Jaker, J., Lowther, M., et al. (2003). Disseminating science-based prevention: Lessons learned from CSAP's CAPTs. *Journal of Drug Education, 33,* 233–243.

Holmlund, C. A. (1989). The body, sex, sexuality, and race. *Cinema Journal, 28,* 38–51.

Ireland, M. L., & Ott, S. M. (2004). Special concerns of the female athlete. *Clinics Sports Medicine, 23,* 281–298.

Johnston, L. D., O'Malley, P. M., Bachman, J. G., & Schulenberg, J. E. (2004). *Monitoring the future national results on adolescent drug use: Overview of key findings* (NIH Publication No. 05-5726). Bethesda, MD: National Institute on Drug Abuse.

Katzenbach, J. R., & Smith, D. K. (2005). The discipline of teams. *Harvard Business Review, 83,* 162–171.

Killen, J. D., Taylor, C. B., Telch, M. J., Robinson, T. N., Maron, D. J., Saylor, K. E., et al. (1987). Depressive symptoms and substance use among adolescent binge eaters and purgers: A defined population study. *American Journal of Public Health, 77,* 1539–1541.

Kulig, K., Brener, N. D., & McManus, T. (2003). Sexual activity and substance use among adolescents by category of physical activity plus team sports participation. *Archives of Pediatric Adolescent Medicine, 157,* 905–912.

Levine, M. P., & Smolak, L. (2006). *The prevention of eating problems and eating disorders: Theory, research and practice.* Mahwah, NJ: Erlbaum.

Lloyd, T., Triantafyllou, S. J., Baker, E. R., Houts, P. S., Whiteside, J. A., Kalenak, A., et al. (1986). Women athletes with menstrual irregularity have increased musculoskeletal injuries. *Medical Science Sports and Exercise, 18*(4), 374–379. Erratum in *19*(4), 421.

Lopiano, D. (2006). *Gender equity and the black female in sport.* Retrieved January 5, 2006, from www.womenssportsfoundation.org/cgi-bin/iowa/issues /disc/article.html?record=869.

Lytle, L. A., & Kubik, M. Y. (2003). Nutritional issues for adolescents. *Best Practices in Research and Clinical Endocrinology Metabolism, 17,* 177–189.

MacKinnon, D. P., Goldberg, L., Clarke, G. N., Elliot, D. L., Cheong, J., Lapin, A., et al. (2001). Mediating mechanisms in a program to reduce intentions to use anabolic steroids and improve exercise self-efficacy and dietary behavior. *Prevention Science, 2,* 15–28.

McCloskey, J., & Bailes, J. (2005). *When winning costs too much: Steroids, supplements, and scandal in today's sports.* Lanham, MD: Taylor.

Miracle, A. W., & Rees, C. R. (1994). *Lessons of the locker room: The myth of school sports.* Amherst, NY: Prometheus Books.

National Center on Addiction and Substance Abuse. (1997). *Back to School 1997—CASA national survey of American attitudes on substance abuse III: Teens and their parents, teachers, and principals.* New York: National Center on Addiction and Substance Abuse. Retrieved January 2, 2006, from www .casacolumbia.org/pdshopprov/files/1997_Teen_Survey_9_1_97.pdf.

National Center on Addiction and Substance Abuse. (2003). *The formative years: Pathways to substance abuse among girls and young women ages 8–22.* New York: National Center on Addiction and Substance Abuse. Retrieved August 2004, from www.casacolumbia.org/pdshopprov/files/151006.pdf.

National Eating Disorders Association. (1999). *GO GIRLS! (Giving our girls inspiration and resources for lasting self-esteem).* Retrieved August 2003, from www.nationaleatingdisorders.org/p.asp?WebPage_ID=296.

National Federation of State High School Associations. (2004). *2003–04 participation summary.* Retrieved September 2004, from www.nfhs.org/scriptcontent/ VA_Custom/SurveyResources/2003_04_Participation_Summary.pdf.

National Institute on Drug Abuse. (1996). *Women and gender differences research: Director's report to council.* Retrieved January 2006, from www .nida.nih.gov/WHGD/WHGDDirRep5.html.

Naylor, A. H., Gardner, D., & Zaichkowsky, L. (2001). Drug use patterns among high school athletes and nonathletes. *Adolescence, 144,* 627–639.

Neumark-Sztainer, D., Story, M., & French, S. A. (1996). Covariations of unhealthy weight loss behaviors and other high-risk behaviors among adolescents. *Archives of Pediatric Adolescent Medicine, 150,* 304–308.

Pate, R. R., Trost, S. G., Levin S., & Dowda, M. (2000). Sports participation and health-related behaviors among U.S. youth. *Archives of Pediatric Adolescent Medicine, 154,* 904–911.

Resnicow, K., & Botvin, G. (1993). School-based substance abuse prevention programs: Why do effects decay? *Preventive Medicine, 22,* 484–490.

Ringwalt, C. L., Ennett, S., & Vincus, A., Thorne, J., Rohrbach, L. A., Simons-Rudolph, A. (2002). Prevalence of effective substance use prevention curricula in U.S. middle schools. *Prevention Science, 3,* 257–265.

Roberts, W. O., & Elliot, D. L. (1991). Malnutrition in a compulsive runner. *Medicine Science Sports and Exercise, 23,* 513–516.

Robertson, E. B., David, S. L., & Rao, S. A. (2003). *Preventing drug abuse among children and adolescents* (NIH Publication No. 04-4212, 2nd ed.). Retrieved January 2, 2006, from www.drugabuse.gov/pdf/prevention/RedBook.pdf.

Rodin, J. (1993). Cultural and psychosocial determinants of weight concerns. *Annals of Internal Medicine, 119,* 643–645.

Rohrbach, L. A., & Milam, J. (2003). Gender issues in substance abuse prevention. In Z. Sloboda & W. J. Bukoski (Eds.), *Handbook of drug abuse prevention: Theory, science, and practice* (pp. 351–363). New York: Kluwer Academic/Plenum Press.

Ryan, R. M., & Deci, E. L. (2000). Self-determination theory and the facilitation of intrinsic motivation, social development, and well-being. *American Psychologist, 55,* 68–78.

Sadker, M., & Sadker, D. (1994). *Failing at fairness: How America's schools cheat girls.* New York: Charles Scribner's Sons.

Sigman, G. S. (2003). Eating disorders in children and adolescents. *Pediatric Clinics of North America, 50*(5), 1139–1177, vii.

Silvia, E. S., & Thorne, J. (1997). *School-based drug prevention programs: A longitudinal study in selected school districts.* Research Triangle Park, NC: Research Triangle Institute.

Stice, E. (2002). Risk and maintenance factors for eating pathology: A meta-analytic review. *Psychological Bulletin, 128,* 825–848.

Stice, E., Presnell, K., & Spangler, D. (2002). Risk factors for binge eating onset in adolescent girls: A 2-year prospective investigation. *Health Psychology, 21,* 131–138.

Stice, E., & Shaw, H. (2004). Eating disorder prevention programs: A meta-analytic review. *Psychological Bulletin, 130,* 206–227.

Striegel-Moore, R. H., & Huydic, E. S. (1993). Problem drinking and symptoms of disordered eating in female high school students. *International Journal of Eating Disorders, 14,* 417–425.

Tammelin, T., Nayha, S., Hills, A. P., & Jarvelin, M. R. (2003). Adolescent participation in sports and adult physical activity. *American Journal of Preventive Medicine, 24,* 22–28.

Taub, D. E., & Blinde, E. M. (1992). Eating disorders among adolescent female athletes: Influence of athletic participation and sport team membership. *Adolescence, 27,* 833–848.

Tobler, N. S. (1992). Drug prevention programs can work: Research findings. *Journal of Addictive Disease, 11,* 1–28.

U.S. Department of Health and Human Services. (1998). *Girl power.* Retrieved January 2006, from www.girlpower.gov/default.aspx.

Whitaker, A., Davies, M., Shaffer, D., Johnson, J., Abrams, S., Walsh, B. T., et al. (1989). The struggle to be thin: A survey of anorexic and bulimic symptoms in a non-referred adolescent population. *Psychological Medicine, 19,* 143–163.

Williams, P. A., & Cash, T. (2001). Effects of a circuit weight training program on the body images of college students. *International Journal of Eating Disorders, 30,* 75–82.

Women's Sport Foundation. (2004). *GoGirlGo!* Retrieved January 2006, from www.kintera.org/faf/home/default.asp?ievent=50274.

Yager, J. (2005). Clinical practice: Anorexia nervosa. *New England Journal of Medicine, 353,* 1481–1488.

Yesalis, C. E., Barsukiewicz, C. K., Kopstein, A. N., & Bahrke, M. S. (1997). Trends in anabolic-androgenic steroid use among adolescents. *Archives of Pediatric Adolescent Medicine, 151,* 1197–1206.

Zarella, K. J. (2002). Developing effective school-based drug abuse prevention programs. *American Journal of Health Behavior, 26,* 252–265.

Chapter 8

TEENS WITH ANOREXIA NERVOSA

A Family-Based Approach to Treatment

DANIEL Le GRANGE AND JAMES LOCK

Anorexia nervosa (AN) is a serious disorder that has a profound impact on the lives of many young individuals. Outcomes are generally not optimistic: 44% of patients followed for at least 4 years after the onset of their illness fully recovered, 25% remained seriously ill, and 5% succumbed to the illness (American Psychiatric Association, 1993; Steinhausen, 2002). While there is general consensus about the severe morbidity and mortality of AN, only modest effort has been devoted to the exploration of psychosocial treatments of this disorder. For teens with AN, 8 uncontrolled and 6 controlled studies have been published, involving a broad range of psychotherapies. Of these, a particular type of family-based treatment (FBT) for adolescents with AN has received the strongest support.

FBT was developed at the Maudsley Hospital in London by Christopher Dare, Ivan Eisler, and members of their team, and has been refined in a series of controlled treatment studies since 1987 (Eisler et al., 2000; Le Grange, Eisler, Dare, & Russell, 1992; Lock, Agras, Bryson, & Kraemer, 2005; Russell, Szmukler, Dare, & Eisler, 1987). This approach has consistently demonstrated efficacy in approximately two thirds of AN patients treated, and although individual therapy has been promoted to address adolescent problems of individuation and control, no randomized controlled trial has yet demonstrated that it is superior to FBT. Moreover, follow-up studies suggest that treatment effects are maintained long term (Eisler et al., 1997; Eisler, Le Grange, & Asen, 2003; Eisler, Simic, Russell & Dare, 2007; Lock, Couturier, & Agras, 2006).

Preceding the work at the Maudsley Hospital, Salvador Minuchin and Mara Selvini Palazzoli can be credited for pioneering family therapy for AN in the 1970s (Minuchin, Rosman, & Baker, 1978; Palazzoli, 1974). Working with a structural and strategic therapy philosophy, respectively, these clinicians and their adherents proposed that the family's structure or style of management of problems needed to be corrected for recovery of AN to occur. This view was in keeping with many earlier family therapy approaches that conceptualized the problem or symptom as belonging to the entire family. Consequently, the therapeutic approach was aimed at the entire family system. In contrast, in the Maudsley approach as advocated by Dare and Eisler, families are viewed as essential in the treatment of AN, rather than seen as pathological or to blame for the development of AN (Dare, 1983; Dare & Eisler, 1997). This group proposed an "agnostic" view of the cause of AN consistent with the theoretical work of Jay Haley and Milton Erickson, and suggested that the family is an important resource at the therapist's disposal in order to ensure recovery. The Maudsley approach incorporates elements of a variety of treatment methods developed by clinicians with different theoretical perspectives—for example, the use of family meals, specific techniques for family empowerment, a nonauthoritarian therapeutic stance, and externalizing the illness from the patient and family.

FBT for adolescent AN is modeled on the Maudsley approach and detailed in a clinician manual (Lock, Le Grange, Agras, & Dare, 2001). While many clinicians are skeptical about treatment manuals, which are often viewed as "recipes" rather than treatment, manuals can help provide a focus for this process, set appropriate goals, time interventions, codify effective treatments and experience, and establish an overall structure. Manualized FBT for adolescent AN proceeds through three clearly defined phases. In Phase I, the therapist focuses on the dangers of severe malnutrition associated with AN and emphasizes the need for parents to take immediate action to reverse this. The patient's surrender to the demands of the parents to increase her food intake (as evidenced by steady weight gain), as well as a change in the mood of the family (i.e., relief after having taken charge of the eating disorder), signal the start of Phase II of treatment. The therapist advises the parents that the main task is the return of their child to physical health, and to hand control over eating back to the adolescent. Symptoms remain central in the discussions, while weight gain with minimum tension is encouraged. In addition, all other issues that the family has had to postpone can now be brought forward for review. Phase III is initiated when the patient achieves a stable weight, and the self-starvation has abated. The central theme here is the establishment of a healthy adolescent or young adult relationship with the parents in which the distorted eating does not constitute the basis of interaction.

Published reports on short- and long-term follow-up of FBT for AN using the Maudsley approach suggest that it holds great promise for short-duration illness among adolescents (Le Grange & Lock, 2005). As a specific therapy, it has roots in the rich tradition of family therapy and incorporates much from these approaches in a new synthesis designed to address the developing adolescent in the context of the debilitating and life-threatening behaviors associated with AN. The manualized version helps properly prepared clinicians stay focused on the role of eating-disordered behaviors in inhibiting, complicating, and disturbing the usual developmental processes of adolescence. Therapists thus have a tool at their disposal to add to their strategies in combating AN. In addition, researchers who have received training in the use of the manual can systematically examine the treatment more closely, to better understand the predictors and moderators of response to treatment.

In the remainder of this chapter, we first provide a brief review of the treatment literature for adolescent AN. This is followed by a detailed discussion of manualized FBT, which has now been used in three recent studies: at Stanford University, where two levels of intensity and duration of this treatment have been studied for adolescents with AN (Lock et al., 2005); at the University of Chicago, where manualized FBT was studied in a case series (Le Grange, Binford, & Loeb, 2005); and at Columbia University, which conducted an open trial of FBT (Loeb, Walsh, Lock, Le Grange, Jones, Marcus, et al., 2007). Some clinical examples of this approach are then presented. Finally, a brief summary with future clinical directions is given.

REVIEW OF THE LITERATURE

Early Accounts of Family Therapy for Adolescent Anorexia Nervosa

The first effort to include families in the treatment of AN in adolescents was conducted by Minuchin and his colleagues at the Child Guidance Clinic in Philadelphia (Minuchin et al., 1975, 1978). These clinicians treated a series of 53 patients and provided outcome data in a follow-up of this cohort. Most patients were adolescents who had been ill for a relatively brief period of time (less than 3 years). Treatment was quite mixed, with most patients initially receiving inpatient treatment and some individual therapy. However, the primary intervention was family therapy, and the authors reported successful outcome in about 86% of patients. It is due to this success rate, as well as the theoretical model of the "psychosomatic family," upon which much of Minuchin's work was based, that he and his colleagues ultimately exerted considerable influence on ensuing treatment efforts for adolescents with AN (Minuchin et al., 1975, 1978).

Optimism for Minuchin's findings is tempered, however, by methodological weaknesses that underlie this study. That is, members of the treatment team conducted patient evaluations; there were no comparison treatment groups; and follow-up varied greatly (range: 18 months to 7 years). Because this study did not claim to be a controlled clinical trial, it should be recognized as having played a significant part in preparing the foundation for the effective involvement of families in the ensuing controlled trials of family therapy for AN.

First Controlled Trials of Family Therapy for Adolescent Anorexia Nervosa

Maudsley Studies

The first controlled study to build on Minuchin's work was conducted at the Maudsley Hospital in London (Dare, Eisler, & Russell, 1990; Russell et al., 1987). It was a comparison of outpatient FBT and individual supportive therapy following inpatient weight restoration. This study included 80 consecutive admissions of all ages to the Maudsley Hospital. One of four subgroups ($n = 21$) consisted of young patients (age of onset < 18; mean = 16.6 years) with a short duration of illness (< 3 years). All study patients were initially admitted to the inpatient unit (average stay = 10 weeks) for weight restoration before being randomized to one of the two outpatient follow-up treatments. After 1 year of outpatient treatment, this subgroup of adolescents had a significantly better outcome with FBT than the individual supportive treatment. At 5-year follow-up, 90% of those who were assigned to FBT had a good outcome, while only 36% of those who were in the individual therapy had a good outcome (Eisler et al., 1997). Progress in treatment was defined using the Morgan-Russell Outcome Assessment Schedule (Morgan & Russell, 1975), with good outcome indicating a return to normal weight and menses.

The FBT employed in this Maudsley study contained several aspects of Minuchin's approach, but also differed in significant ways. Most important of these was that Russell and his colleagues, unlike Minuchin, encouraged parents to persist in their efforts to restore their adolescent's weight *until* normal body weight had been achieved. In other words, the Maudsley approach deferred general adolescent and family issues *until* the eating disorder behavior was under control.

Since this seminal work, two studies from the Maudsley group have compared different forms of FBT in adolescent AN (Eisler et al., 2000; Le Grange et al., 1992). Both these studies compared the family treatment that was employed in the original Maudsley study in its conjoint format (CFT), versus separated family therapy (SFT). In the latter, the same therapist would meet with the parents and the adolescent, but in separate sessions. The therapeutic goals for both CFT and SFT were identical and were provided on an outpatient basis. Most notable was that none of the patients in the Le Grange et al. (1992) study, and only 10% of those in the Eisler et al. (2000) study, required inpatient treatment during the course of the study. Admission was usually instigated when weight was not responding to the family's efforts, and/or the study physician considered the patient to be at medical risk for continuing outpatient management. Overall results for these two studies were similar, and, regardless of type of FBT, approximately 70% of patients were considered to have made a good or intermediate outcome (weight restored or menses returned) at the end of treatment. In a description of the Maudsley FBT (Eisler et al., 2003), it is noted that preliminary results from a 5-year follow-up of Eisler et al.'s (2000) cohort show that, irrespective of the type of FBT, 75% of patients had a good outcome, 15% an intermediate outcome, and 10% a poor outcome (weight not restored and no menses).

Continuing the Maudsley Approach Outside the United Kingdom

An important development since the original Maudsley work has been the manualization of FBT, which was developed to accurately reflect the content and procedures of this specific treatment (Lock et al., 2001). The first controlled study outside the United Kingdom, and the first to use the FBT treatment manual, was completed by a group at Stanford in California (Lock et al., 2005). In this study, 86 adolescents between the ages 12 and 18 were randomly allocated to either a short-term (10 sessions over 6 months) or long-term (20 sessions over 12 months) FBT. An intent-to-treat analysis found no differences in outcome between these two groups. Post hoc analysis, however, suggested that patients who presented with severe obsessive-compulsive behaviors around their eating disorders, or who came from nonintact families, needed the longer-term version of FBT. Overall outcomes of the subjects in the study were similar to those achieved in other controlled trials, with more than 80% being considerable improved or recovered (Couturier & Lock, 2006; Lock et al., 2005).

In addition to this controlled study, three case series also employed manualized FBT. In the first of these, Lock and Le Grange (2001) describe the process of manualizing the Maudsley approach and report on the results of 19 adolescents with AN who were part of the randomized trial mentioned earlier (Lock et al., 2005). These authors report favorable outcomes for the majority of cases. Moreover, these results suggest that, through the use of this manual, a valuable treatment approach can now be tested more broadly in controlled as well as uncontrolled settings. In the second case series, Le Grange and his colleagues (2005) report pre- and posttreatment data for 45 adolescents with AN who have received a course of manualized FBT. Overall, their findings are favorable, in that 89% of cases were recovered or made significant improvements in outpatient treatment over a relatively short period of time (mean = 10 months; and mean number of treatment sessions = 17). They conclude that their series further provides preliminary support for the feasibility of outpatient FBT, which underscores the beneficial impact of active parental involvement in the treatment of adolescents with AN. In the most recent of these series utilizing manualized FBT, an open trial of 20 adolescents with AN (Loeb et al., 2007), demonstrates high retention rates and significant improvement in the specific and associated psychopathology of their patients.

Treatment Modeled on the Maudsley Approach

In the United States, Robin and his colleagues (Robin, Siegel, Koepke, Moye, & Tice, 1994; Robin et al., 1999), based their behavioral systems family therapy (BSFT) on the Maudsley treatment, and compared this treatment to ego-orientated individual treatment (EOIT). These researchers reported significant improvement in AN symptomatology at the end of treatment. More than two thirds (67%) of patients reached target weight, and 80% regained menstruation. Patients continued to improve; at 1-year follow-up, approximately 75% had reached their target weight, and 85% had started or resumed menses.

However, there were noticeable differences between the two treatments. Patients in BSFT achieved significantly greater weight gain than those in EOIT, both at the end of treatment and at follow-up. Similarly, patients who received BSFT were significantly more likely to have returned to normal menstrual functioning at the end of treatment compared to those in EOIT. Both treatments were similar in terms of improvements in eating attitudes, depression, and self-reported eating-related family conflict. Neither group reported much family-related conflict regarding eating, either before or after treatment. Taken together, Robin and colleagues concluded that BSFT produced greater weight gain and higher rates of resumption of menstruation compared to EOIT. Both treatments produced comparable improvements in eating attitudes and depression, but BSFT produced a more rapid treatment response.

While BSFT was modeled after the Maudsley approach, it differed in some important, albeit subtle, ways. First, Robin et al. (1999) defined the adolescents in their study as "out of control" and not able to take care of themselves, while the parents were coached to implement a behavioral weight gain program. This differs somewhat from the Maudsley approach, in that parents were to explore and, with the help of the therapist, find the optimal way to restore healthy weight in their adolescent with AN. Second, Robin et al. (1999) broadened the focus of treatment to include cognitions and problems in "family structure" while the parents were still in charge of the refeeding process. The Maudsley approach typically would refrain from distractions of this type until weight had been restored. Both BFST and the Maudsley approach would return control over eating to the adolescent when the target weight was achieved; and in the final stage of treatment focus discussions on adolescent issues such as individuation, sexuality, and career.

Family Treatment in an Inpatient Setting

Only one study employed family therapy in an inpatient setting. Geist and her colleagues (Geist, Heineman, Stephens, Davis, & Katzman, 2000) compared this mode of treatment with family group psychoeducation in a cohort of hospitalized adolescents. The effects of these interventions are difficult to evaluate, because it was not possible to disentangle these treatment effects from those of the typical inpatient interventions. For instance, most of the recorded weight gain (76%) was achieved prior to discharge from the hospital, with equivalent treatment effects observed with both family interventions. Nevertheless, the authors argue that family group psychoeducation is an effective and economical method of involving the family in treatment.

Current Family Treatment Studies

Since pioneering the family-based approach to the treatment of adolescents with AN, the Maudsley group has also embarked on a more intensive form of this treatment. This intensive form of FBT is aimed at supporting those patients and their families who do not respond to the typical outpatient FBT alone (Eisler, personal communication 2006; Lim, 2000). In conjunction with colleagues in Germany (Scholz & Asen, 2001), the London group has taken preliminary steps to develop an intensive program for adolescents with AN and their families, called multiple-family day treatment (MFDT). This treatment shares some similarities with outpatient FBT used in the Maudsley studies and aims to enable families to uncover their own resources in order to restore their starving adolescent's weight. Families are encouraged to explore how the eating disorder and the interactional patterns in the family have become entangled, and how this entanglement has made it problematic for the family to get back on track with its normal developmental course. This program is quite different from outpatient FBT in that the sharing of experiences among families and the intensity of the treatment program (meeting together for several consecutive days) makes it a unique experience for families. Architects of MFDT argue that an emphasis on helping families find their own solution is even more apparent in this treatment format than is typically the case in FBT.

This work with adolescent AN is still in a developmental stage, so only preliminary findings can be offered at this stage. Both research groups have reported notable symptomatic improvements in several cases, including weight gain, return of menses, reduction of binge eating and vomiting, and decreased laxative abuse. All parents, and a majority of the adolescent patients (80%), regarded working together with other families in a day hospital setting as "helpful" and "desirable," thus drop-out rates were low. In particular, parents who participated in MFDT reported that this treatment was helpful because of its collaborative nature—sharing ideas with other families about how to cope with their common predicament (Lim, 2000; Scholz & Asen, 2001).

Also in progress, at Chicago and Stanford, is a multisite controlled trial of FBT and EOIT (an individually based treatment wherein the adolescent is in charge of refeeding herself and the focus of therapy is on promoting self-esteem, self-efficacy, and developmentally appropriate behaviors generally). Researchers at these two treatment centers are optimistic that they will be able to randomize 120 adolescents with AN to one of these two treatment modalities. When completed, this study will be one of the largest treatment trials for AN, and hopes to demonstrate the relative efficacy of FBT when compared to EOIT.

With an overview of the research support for FBT concluded, the next section of this chapter outlines the implementation of this treatment in more detail.

FAMILY-BASED TREATMENT FOR ADOLESCENTS WITH ANOREXIA NERVOSA

Introduction to This Treatment Approach

The theoretical understanding and overall philosophy of FBT is that the adolescent is embedded in the family, and that the parents' involvement in treatment is vitally important to secure a favorable outcome. In this model, normal adolescent development is seen as having been arrested by the presence of the eating disorder, varying, of course, in degree from patient to patient. Therefore, parents should be involved in their offspring's treatment, while showing respect and regard for the adolescent's point of view and experience. This treatment pays close attention to adolescent development and aims to guide the parents to assist their child with developmental tasks once weight has been restored. To do so, fundamental work on other family conflicts or disagreements has to be deferred until the eating-disorder behaviors are out of the way. The parents temporarily take the lead in helping their daughter find ways to reduce the hold this disorder has over her life. Once successful in this task, the parents will return control over eating to their daughter and assist her in negotiating predictable adolescent development tasks.

Differences between Family-Based and Other Adolescent Treatments

FBT differs from other treatments for adolescents with AN in several key ways. First, as pointed out previously, the adolescent is not viewed as being in control of her behavior; instead, the eating disorder controls her. Thus, and in this way only, provided there is no comorbid psychiatric condition, the adolescent is seen as not functioning in the way that she normally could, and stands to benefit considerably if her parents were to provide some help. Second, the treatment aims to correct this set of circumstances by "giving the parents permission" to involve themselves more actively in their daughter's eating. This involvement has often been lost because parents might feel that it is inappropriate to "control" their daughter's life in this way, that they are to blame for the eating disorder, or the symptoms have frightened them to the extent that they are reluctant to act decisively. Third, FBT strongly advocates that the therapist should primarily focus his or her his attention on the task of addressing the eating-disorder symptoms, especially in the early part of treatment. FBT, as opposed to Minuchin's structural family therapy, tends to "stay with the eating disorder" for longer—that is, the therapist remains alert so as not to become distracted from the central therapeutic task, which is to keep the parents focused on restoring their daughter's weight to normal levels and freeing her from the control of the eating disorder. The presence of comorbid psychiatric issues can, of course, derail the therapist as well as the family, as prioritizing the eating disorder in the presence of a severe mood disorder could be problematic. However, it is perhaps only acute suicidality that could cause the therapist to temporarily take his or her focus from the weight restoration task at hand.

Fundamental Assumptions of Family-Based Treatment

The intervention style that typifies this treatment approach can be briefly summarized by the following five tenets:

1. Agnostic view of cause of illness (parents and patient are not to blame),
2. Initial focus on symptoms (behavioral change),
3. Parents are responsible for weight restoration (empowerment),
4. Nonauthoritarian therapeutic stance (joining), and
5. Separation of child and illness (respect for adolescent).

Agnostic View of Cause of Illness

No one is blamed for this illness; in fact, the therapist works particularly hard to absolve the parents from feeling blamed for their child's illness. However, absolving the parents of blame does not mean that they should not be responsible for her recovery. In working toward absolving the parents from feeling guilty, the therapist also aims to raise the parents' anxiety so that they can take effective charge of the weight restoration process. In keeping with this agnostic view of the illness, the therapist does not pathologize the adolescent or her family, either directly or indirectly. In other words, the therapist does not look for the cause of illness because the etiology is not the focus of treatment in this approach.

Initial Focus on Symptoms

At the start of treatment, the emphasis is on behavioral change in the adolescent, that is, for the parents to help their daughter eat normally and gain weight to a healthy level. At this time in the treatment, the history taking focuses on symptom development, and the therapist delays addressing other issues until the patient is less behaviorally and psychologically involved with AN.

Empowering the Parents

The parents are charged with the task of restoring their child's weight and are seen as the primary resource for helping the adolescent patient. While every family presents with a different skill set, the general principle of this treatment approach is that most families *can* help the patient. The challenge for the therapist is to leverage parental skills and relationships to bring about change in the adolescent—that is, to identify and strengthen the parents' efficiency in helping their child recover from AN.

Nonauthoritarian Therapeutic Stance

The therapist "joins" the family, in that he or she takes a nonauthoritarian stance in the treatment process and serves as an expert consultant to the family. As a result, the therapist does not control the parents or patient but instead assists the parents in finding their own ways to restore their child to health, while also being sympathetic toward the adolescent, given the dilemma she finds herself in. The therapist takes an active stance in this treatment, but still leaves the decision making to the parents. The goal is to foster the parents' confidence in their judgment and increase independence from the therapist throughout this treatment, as they work out for themselves how to put their daughter back on track with her adolescent development.

Externalize the Illness

One of the therapist's main tasks is to demonstrate respect for the adolescent. One way to achieve this goal is to externalize the illness by not pathologizing the patient. The adolescent is not to blame for the eating disorder, and is not regressed or immature, but ill. This stance shows respect for the adolescent's status without negotiating with the AN. The therapist will support increased autonomy for the adolescent as she approaches recovery from the eating disorder.

The effect of these tenets results in FBT being a highly focused, staged treatment with an emphasis on behavioral recovery, rather than insight and understanding. This is an approach that appears to indirectly improve family functioning, and ultimately supports the gradual increased independence of the adolescent and her family from therapy (Krautter & Lock, 2004).

FBT in Practice: The Three Phases of Treatment

FBT for AN typically proceeds through three defined phases over a period of 12 months. Phase I usually lasts between 3 and 5 months, with sessions scheduled at weekly intervals. While this spacing of sessions is prescribed for all cases, the schedule should ultimately be based on the patient's clinical progress. Toward Phase II, the therapist may schedule sessions every second to third week, while monthly sessions are advisable toward the conclusion of treatment in Phase III. All sessions are 50 to 60 minutes in duration. A brief narrative description of the treatment phases is summarized next, and Table 8.1 provides a synopsis of the three phases and the specific goals and treatment strategies that are typical for each.

Phase I: Parental Control of Weight Restoration (Sessions 1 to 10)

The therapist focuses on the dangers of severe malnutrition associated with AN and emphasizes the need for parents to take immediate action to reverse this process. This can be achieved by a careful review of the development of the eating disorder, while highlighting the devastating effects that AN has had on the adolescent's medical and psychological well-being. The therapist stresses these concerns in order to support the development of a parental alliance around refeeding. The parents' task in this phase of treatment is to work out, as a team, how they will convince their daughter to eat a sufficient amount and variety of calories to reverse starvation. This is best achieved by encouraging the parents to temporarily take charge of all food-related decisions and be available to serve and supervise every meal. The parents are also encouraged to think of ways in which they might have to limit their child's activities to conserve as much energy as possible; for example, ballet or cross-country might have to be postponed. While the parents are working at helping their daughter gain necessary weight, the therapist will also make an effort to align the patient with the sibling subsystem; that is, the parents are charged with the refeeding, and the patient's

Table 8.1   Family-Based Treatment: Phases and Interventions

Treatment Phase	Aims	Main Interventions	End Point
I: Restore adolescent's weight	Help parents to take charge of restoring adolescent's weight.	Modulate parental anxieties to encourage taking action; support and educate parents in their activities; assist siblings in supporting their ill sibling; support patient to tolerate refeeding.	Weight near 90% IBW, and eating without undo conflict or distress under parental supervision.
II: Hand control over eating back to adolescent.	To transition the control of eating and weight to the adolescent under parental guidance.	Assist family to identify patient's readiness to begin to take control of eating and weight behaviors appropriate for age; manage parental anxiety about this transition; problem solve around issues specifically related to food and weight in the adolescent's life.	The adolescent controls her own eating and weight-related behaviors and is gaining or maintaining weight at level appropriate for height. Adolescent is able to manage eating in social settings outside the family, as is age-appropriate.
III: Address adolescent issues and treatment termination.	Promote understanding of adolescence, and support family in identifying issues that may require attention. Little or no focus on eating-disorder symptoms.	Conduct a psychoeducational review of adolescent development, and examination of implications for the patient and family, given patient's age. Identify any other emotional or developmental issues that were postponed, and in need of assistance.	Assure adolescent and family that patient is back on track with development. Identify other psychological issues not specific to AN that need treatment (e.g., OCD, depression) and recommend treatment.

siblings are to be engaged in age-appropriate sibling activities, such as watching television or making crafts together.

During this phase, a family meal is typically conducted at the second treatment session. The parents are instructed to bring along a meal for all family members, which includes food for their daughter with AN that will begin to reverse the starvation. This session usually allows the therapist to observe familial interaction patterns around eating, and help the parents find ways to succeed in getting their child to eat more than she had intended. It also allows the therapist to show the adolescent his or her support, given the unenviable position she must be in. Throughout this phase, the therapist will continue to carefully review with the parents their weekly efforts around helping their child gain weight, while showing the patient support and understanding for her struggle around this issue.

Phase II: Returning Control Over Eating to the Adolescent
(Sessions 11 to 16)

Phase II begins once the patient accepts the demands of the parents, steady weight gain is evident, and weight is approaching near-normal levels (e.g., ~90% IBW). The parents are encouraged to help their child take more control over her own eating once it is evident that there is less anxiety, both for the patient and parents, around mealtimes and weight gain. The therapist cautiously guides the parents to begin taking a step back from their present level of involvement with the refeeding process. For instance, whereas until now the parents made food decisions, dished up portions, and supervised all meals and snacks, the adolescent is given the opportunity to make some food choices for herself while parents are still present to make necessary corrections. Or, the adolescent is allowed for the first time to have lunch at school with her friends, instead of a parent or school counselor being present to make sure lunch is taken as intended by the parents. It is also at this stage of treatment during which the parents begin to experiment in giving their daughter freedom around other adolescent activities, such as going out with friends. Any such decisions, however, should only be taken if the parents feel reassured that these would not provide opportunities for excessive exercising or skipping a meal.

Phase III: Adolescent Development and Treatment Termination
(Sessions 17 to 20)

When the patient is maintaining a stable normal weight on her own, treatment focus shifts away from the eating disorder per se, and instead examines the impact AN has had on establishing a healthy adolescent identity. The therapist provides a detailed review of the stages of adolescent development (e.g., concerns associated with puberty, worries about peer relationships, and struggles regarding independence from the family and establishing significant relationships outside the family). For example, in the case of an older adolescent (18 years of age), these discussions will focus on supporting increased personal autonomy and the development of appropriate parental boundaries.

PUTTING TOGETHER A TREATMENT TEAM

Treating AN is a complex endeavor and almost always requires a treatment team. The degree to which one can assemble a treatment team, as well as technical support (e.g., video recording of sessions, or one-way mirror observation facilities), depends on the therapist's experience with families in general and eating-disorder patients in particular. This support, of course, will also depend on the setting in which the clinician operates. Few therapists, however, should aim to work entirely without any support structures, as this treatment is a complex therapeutic task and it is relatively easy for the therapist to become overwhelmed by the illness or get caught up in family dynamics. Unlike individual psychotherapy, the clinician has to keep track of the dynamics of the entire family, which may be a daunting task for even experienced therapists. Many therapists, when first learning the treatment, can benefit from working with an observing clinician who is familiar with the physiology, psychology, and family processes related to eating disorders in adolescents.

AN almost always presents with psychological, psychiatric, and medical dilemmas. Therefore, the primary clinician or team leader (e.g., a child and adolescent psychiatrist, psychologist, or social worker) is best supported by a consulting team, which could consist of a pediatrician, nurse, and nutritionist. An ideal treatment setup is one in which all team members are concentrated within the same facility. "Partitioning" the treatment to various clinicians not in direct contact with the primary clinician is cause for concern. For instance, the patient may suggest to her pediatrician that an important aspect of treatment, usually her weight, be deemphasized and best be relegated to the sideline of discussions. An inexperienced pediatrician, who may not be intimately familiar with the primary clinician's treatment philosophy, may inadvertently provide the patient with conflicting information, which will more than likely negatively impact the treatment process. However, the degree to which a treatment team can be assembled in the same locale without having to partition certain examinations or measurements to others will, of course, depend on the nature of the setting in which the primary clinician operates.

The lead therapist is often someone who cannot do a physical examination or does not have expert nutrition knowledge. Therefore, a secondary line of clinicians, who are not directly involved in psychological treatment, may have to act as consultants to inform the lead therapist. The lead therapist has to orchestrate a system wherein he or she has immediate access to the information gathered by the consultants—for example, the pediatrician or the nutritionist. In other words, all team members have to be "on the same page." The lead therapist should also coordinate regular contact with the consulting team members. This may be in the form of weekly face-to-face team meetings, weekly teleconferences, or weekly contact through electronic mail or faxing media. It is of the utmost importance that the lead clinician be clear in terms of directing the treatment philosophy while taking into consideration the available clinical data.

Likewise, the team members should be familiar with the family therapist's philosophy and allow this philosophy to guide their contact with the patient.

In general, the role of the treatment team is to support the empowerment of the family and, specifically, the parents early in treatment. The pediatrician, therefore, provides relevant medical information to the parents (e.g., weight progress, vital sign information, bone study results) and does not exclude parents from the results of medical visits. This does not preclude there being confidential topics between the pediatrician and the adolescent, but these would not concern eating or weight. Similarly, if a nutritionist is involved, dietary advice is given in a manner that supports the parents' role in refeeding. Hence, specific meal plans and recommendations of calorie amounts or portion pyramids are not part of nutritional advice. Rather, consultative suggestions based on parental concerns are the basis of the limited nutritional guidance appropriate for out patient FBT.

If the team members are not part of the same facility, one way to stay on the same page is for the lead therapist to develop a checklist that should be completed at the end of each session and then distributed to all other team members. Such a checklist might include questions such as:

- What was the patient's most recent weight?
- What is the status regarding any bulimic symptoms (if present)?
- What new problems were noted?
- What are your recommendations?

SETTING UP TREATMENT

Before the therapist's first meeting with the family, arrangements should already have been made for a visit to the pediatrician's office for a physical examination of the patient. This information, along with a weight chart, must be available to the therapist prior to meeting with the family. Then, the therapist will weigh the patient during subsequent meetings, and measure height if growth is predicted. Facilities to monitor weight, height, blood chemistry, and cardiac and endocrine status should be available, or arrangements should be set up for routine medical examination and relevant laboratory tests. There are a variety of ways this can be accomplished, and depend on the patient's medical status (e.g., regular orthostatic checks are advisable, as well as electrolyte screening, in patients who purge frequently). Essential components of a typical physical examination for an adolescent with AN are summarized in Table 8.2.

Table 8.2   Essential Components of a Medical Evaluation for Anorexia Nervosa

Complete physical exam. Check for evidence of the following:

Weight and height

Orthostasis

Bradycardia

Dehydration

Hypothermia

Physical signs of malnutrition (dry skin, lanugo, etc.)

If bulimic symptoms are suspected, check for tooth erosion and esophageal tears

Examination to include the following laboratory tests:

Complete blood count

Electrocardiogram

Electrolytes

Blood urea nitrogen

Creatinine

Thyroid studies

Urine-specific gravity

Identifying Appropriate Candidates for Family-Based Treatment

Patients most appropriate for FBT are those 18 years of age and younger who have been diagnosed with AN and are living at home with their families. This is due in part to the fact that FBT assumes that the family eats together and has routine access to one another by living in the same household, or that the treatment process can encourage families to spend more time together around eating. Furthermore, FBT expects that parental figures will assume leadership in reestablishing healthy eating in their daughter. Therefore, it is necessary that meals be routinely eaten together, especially during the early part of treatment.

Because the makeup of families in the twenty-first century can vary considerably, for practical purposes, we define "family" as those persons who live in the same household as the identified patient. This may mean that a family session could include nonbiologically related household members, or grandparents if they live in the home; conversely, it may exclude parental figures who are not involved in the day-to-day care of the child with AN. Therefore, FBT as described here involves all family members who reside with the adolescent. This requires a substantial commitment on the part of parents and siblings to attend therapy sessions, and may, for instance, require that siblings miss school or other activities to assure their attendance. In particular, therapy requires serious dedication on the part of parental figures to do what is necessary to help their child with AN. This may include taking time away from work, setting aside other pressing issues, and forgoing expected activities for a period. To engage in FBT with any chance of success requires that families be prepared to make these sacrifices.

It is important to point out that although the description of the treatment offered here more easily applies to intact families, FBT for AN can be modified for nonintact families, depending on their status—that is, reconstituted families, the specifics of custodial arrangements, single-parent families, and so on. For instance, single parents may have to take on the task of addressing the eating disorder in their child by themselves, or they may wish to co-opt the assistance of a friend or other relative.

Summary of Treatment Guidelines

Thanks to the existence of a detailed manual describing FBT for AN, this treatment is available to a great number of practitioners. We recognize that no treatment works for every patient or family under all conditions. Also, the judgment of individual clinicians will apply in each case, especially those outside research studies where strict protocols are needed. Although we have endeavored to be as detailed as possible given the space allowed for the foregoing discussion, we recognize and fully expect clinicians to modify certain aspects of treatment to fit their practice circumstances.

Despite individual variability, however, adherence to the key tenets of FBT is likely important to optimize eventual treatment success. Also, the pacing of the therapy should, in general, follow the overall guideline of the phases of treatment. That is to say, the focus of the initial period of treatment must be to restore the adolescent's weight. This process is under the control of the parents, and not until these issues have been resolved is it advisable to proceed to discuss more general family dynamics or adolescent issues.

We also recommend that therapists remind themselves of the outline of the therapeutic interventions for each phase (refer back to Table 8.1). The purpose of this brief outline, and the details contained in the treatment manual (Lock et al., 2001), is to help the therapist keep track of where they are in the treatment process and to follow the appropriate treatment steps.

Clinical Example*

AN with Continuing Interruption in Psychosocial Development Due to Frequent Hospitalizations

Chris, now 16, has been ill with AN since she was 12 years old. She has spent most of the past 4 years in and out of the hospital, which has made it very hard for her to spend significant periods of time at home with her parents and siblings; it has also kept her from making friends at school and prevented her from having the opportunity to build and learn from meaningful relationships outside her family. In addition, she has fallen seriously behind with her schoolwork even though the hospital unit to which she usually is admitted provides schooling for the adolescents in their program.

At every admission, Chris would present as severely emaciated, the result being that she would be put on strict bed rest—with tube feeding on some occasions. Every time her weight would begin to approach healthy levels, she would maintain her weight under hospital supervision, and then would be discharged into her parents' care. At every discharge, her parents were always told not to "interfere," and that Chris should now take care of her own eating. She would try to eat properly on her own but would never consume sufficient amounts to promote further weight gain. In fact, she would very quickly begin to restrict and lose weight, while her parents stood on the sidelines, frustrated because they weren't supposed to help Chris, and saddened, knowing that, soon, they would probably have to return her to the hospital.

When at home, Chris would check in with her pediatrician, who was extremely concerned by the speed at which Chris always managed to lose weight once she was discharged. Chris's pediatrician was also becoming very worried because Chris would start to vomit after almost every meal, regardless of the fact that her meals were small, both in terms of content and caloric value. An added component of Chris's weight loss was that her electrolyte levels had started to drop to dangerous levels. Every couple of weeks, Chris would be admitted to a medical ward to replace her electrolytes to normal levels. While this was a life-saving necessity, it again took Chris away from her home environment, her friends, and school.

This cycle—going to eating-disorder inpatient units, back home, and then in and out of the medical unit—along with the multitude of different medications, had, for many years, become a sad routine for Chris and her family.

---

*Not an actual case, but a combination of treatment dilemmas to highlight how FBT operates from a premise different from more traditional inpatient treatment with individual psychotherapy follow-up.

Chris's treatment history, which shows a reliance on inpatient refeeding programs, followed by individual psychotherapy, where the onus is on the adolescent to manage her eating disorder, is a common path for many young patients; and it works for some of them (e.g., Robin et al., 1999). Would FBT have approached Chris's case any differently? FBT recognizes that some adolescents require and will benefit from hospitalization for weight restoration. But for Chris, the treatment course took a different route once FBT was considered.

First, instead of repeated hospitalizations to accomplish weight restoration, at the time of discharge following Chris's last inpatient stay, FBT recommended that the nursing team hand over control of eating to the adolescent's parents. Typically, weight management would have been handed to Chris. Instead, upon discharge, her parents were consulted as to how *they* would go about making sure that Chris continued to eat what *they* thought was an adequate diet, to ensure that their daughter continued to gain weight, as appropriate, and to start her menses.

Second, Chris's parents were encouraged to continue to manage her illness in this way until they determined, in consultation with the therapist, that it was appropriate to carefully and gradually allow Chris to take small steps at regaining some of this control. For instance, although at least one of her parents continued to supervise all meals and snacks, a first step was to let Chris eat lunch at school on her own. Once that was seen to be going well, Chris was allowed to serve herself meals at home; next she was allowed to prepare her own breakfast under parental supervision, and eventually to take care of all her meals, as is age-appropriate, and in keeping with the habits and practices of her family.

Third, once everyone was reassured that Chris could continue to take care of herself, her parents were advised to step back, yet continue to monitor her progress to ensure the eating disorder did not regain a foothold over her life; then the focus turned to helping Chris get on track with other adolescent developmental tasks and challenges that had been halted or postponed during the years spent struggling with AN.

When Chris had been outside of an inpatient setting for an uninterrupted period of 6 months, she began to take some tentative steps toward greater independence from her family: she became more integrated at school and with her friends, and even began dating. All this time, her parents kept a watchful eye on her ongoing efforts to distance herself from her eating disorder. If they noted any backsliding on Chris's part, they were quick to step in to support her in regaining her control over AN.

(continued)

For many cases like that of Chris, parental help, as constituted through FBT, appears to be critical for changing the trajectory from chronicity to recovery. Chris's parents were typical, in terms of their skill set, in helping their daughter restore her weight and become reengaged with normal adolescent development, which is so often interrupted by an eating disorder. It has been more than 2 years now, and Chris has maintained a healthy weight; she is well integrated at high school, has been dating for some months, and is making plans to go to college in the next year or so.

Future Directions

In addition to FBT's promise for treating adolescents with a relatively short duration of AN, pilot work from the Maudsley group (Dodge, Hodes, Eisler, & Dare, 1995), as well as in Chicago (Le Grange, Lock, & Dymek, 2003), suggests that this treatment may also be helpful in the treatment of adolescents with bulimia nervosa (BN). In fact, two large randomized controlled trials, one in London (Schmidt, Lee, Beecham, Perkins, Treasure, Yi, et al., 2007) and one in Chicago (Le Grange, Crosby, Rathouz, & Leventhal, 2007), have been completed, and both demonstrate support for FBT for this patient population. As a specific therapy, FBT-BN is a direct adaptation of the FBT manual for AN (Le Grange & Lock, 2007). FBT-BN, modified somewhat to address the specific developmental, behavioral, and medical differences between adolescents with AN and BN, may well be a helpful treatment for addressing the debilitating and life-threatening behaviors associated with binge eating and purging. As is the case for AN, a manualized strategy for BN helps properly prepared clinicians to stay focused on the role of eating-disordered behaviors in inhibiting, complicating, and disturbing the usual developmental processes.

Clinical Implications

As outlined in this chapter, it is evident that manualized FBT is an effective treatment approach for adolescent AN. Indeed, use of a manual might focus and structure the treatment process by setting appropriate treatment goals in the context of a time-limited intervention. In terms of future research, it is imperative that treatment studies employ manual-based treatments to allow for consistent application of interventions across participants. Moreover, with manualized treatments, interventions would be less dependent on the individual characteristics of therapists for efficacy, amplifying deliverability, and would provide a clearer description of the components and course of treatment. The lack of a manual detailing the treatment originally employed in the Maudsley studies has, until now, curtailed any chances of an accurate replication of this treatment in new sites and settings.

In summary, FBT for AN holds great promise for most adolescents 18 years of age and younger who have been ill for a relatively short period of time (i.e., less than 3 years). FBT can prevent hospitalization and assist the adolescent in recovery, provided that parents are treated as a resource, and are allowed to play an active role in treatment. In addition to the guidelines outlined in this chapter, a detailed clinician's manual that spells out how parents should be involved in this treatment approach is also available (Lock et al., 2001). While results from available studies provide preliminary support for the feasibility of FBT for adolescent AN, controlled studies with adequate cogency are necessary to answer this question more definitively. Such a multisite study is currently underway at Stanford and Chicago.

CONCLUSIONS

In the majority of adolescents with AN, manualized FBT can bring about significant weight gain and the onset or return of menses, as well as psychological recovery. These goals can reliably be achieved on an outpatient basis, with patients requiring, on average, fewer than 20 visits. Taken together, the outcomes of the various studies demonstrate that the majority of adolescents with AN, even severe cases, respond positively to treatment, provided that the family plays an active role in this process.

Until recently, published reports of the Maudsley approach have been limited to the United Kingdom; however, since the manualization of this approach, FBT is now formally implemented in at least five centers in the United States (the University of Chicago, Columbia University, Mt. Sinai School of Medicine, Duke University, and Stanford University), as well as in locations in Canada and Australia. Our own studies using manualized FBT have also demonstrated that clinicians from a variety of professional backgrounds and with varying expertise can implement this treatment with great efficiency. It has been heartening to note that patients at both the Chicago and Stanford sites fare equally well, regardless of the training level or experience of the therapist. That is, adherence to the treatment manual appears to have enhanced therapists' ability to meet therapeutic targets (i.e., weight gain to medically stable levels), irrespective of extensive therapist training or experience.

AN often follows a prolonged course, and treatment is usually considered to be intensive and longer term (American Psychiatric Association, 1993;

Steinhausen, 2002). In contrast, FBT treatment for the majority of patients is relatively brief, requiring on average fewer than 20 sessions to achieve treatment goals (Le Grange et al., 2005; Lock et al., 2005). Moreover, findings from our programs challenge the notion that FBT effectiveness is limited to very young adolescents. We have found no difference in outcome between younger and older adolescent AN patients. This is encouraging because FBT relies to a great extent on parents taking a firm stance regarding weight restoration, and appears to suggest that this treatment is applicable to adolescents across the age range, even in manualized format. It is, however, unclear exactly what the upper age limit for the appropriateness of FBT might be. With some modifications, the approach might even be helpful to relatively young adults who are still living at home with parents; that said, results wherein adults as a whole were treated with FBT have been equivocal (Dare, Eisler, & Russell, 2001; Russell et al., 1987).

REFERENCES

American Psychiatric Association. (1993). Practice guidelines for eating disorders. *American Journal of Psychiatry, 150,* 207–228.

Couturier, J., & Lock, J. (2006). What is recovery in adolescent anorexia nervosa? *International Journal of Eating Disorders, 39,* 550–555.

Dare, C. (1983). Family therapy for families containing an anorectic youngster. In *Understanding anorexia nervosa and bulimia* (Report of the 4th Ross Conference on Medical Research, pp. 28–37). Columbus, OH: Ross Laboratories.

Dare, C., & Eisler, I. (1997). Family therapy for anorexia nervosa. In D. Garner & P. Garfinkel, *Handbook of treatment for eating disorders* (2nd ed., pp. 307–326). New York: Guilford Press.

Dare, C., Eisler, I., & Russell, G. (1990). The clinical and theoretical impact of controlled trial of family therapy in anorexia nervosa. *Journal of Marital and Family Therapy, 16,* 39–57.

Dare, C., Eisler, I., & Russell, G. (2001). Psychological therapies for adults with anorexia nervosa: Randomized controlled trial of out-patient treatments. *British Journal of Psychiatry, 178,* 216–221.

Dodge, E., Hodes, M., Eisler, I., & Dare, C. (1995). Family therapy for bulimia nervosa in adolescents: An exploratory study. *Journal of Family Therapy, 17,* 59–77.

Eisler, I., Dare, C., Hodes, M., Russell, G., Dodge, E., & Le Grange, D. (2000). Family therapy for adolescent anorexia nervosa: The results of a controlled comparison of two family interventions. *Journal of Child Psychology and Psychiatry, 41,* 727–736.

Eisler, I., Dare, C., Russell, G., Szmukler, G. I., Le Grange, D., & Dodge, E. (1997). Family and individual therapy in anorexia nervosa: A 5-year follow-up. *Archives of General Psychiatry, 54,* 1025–1030.

Eisler, I., Le Grange, D., & Asen, K. E. (2003). Family interventions. In J. Treasure, U. Schmidt, & E. van Furth (Eds.), *Handbook of eating disorders* (2nd ed., pp. 291–310). Hoboken, NJ: Wiley.

Eisler, I., Simic, M., Russell, G.F.M., & Dare C. (2007). A randomized controlled treatment trial of two forms of family therapy in adolescent anorexia nervosa: A five-year follow-up. *Journal of Child Psychology and Psychiatry and Allied Disciplines, 48,* 552–560.

Geist, R., Heineman, M., Stephens, D., Davis, R., & Katzman, D. K. (2000). Comparison of family therapy and family group psychoeducation in adolescents with anorexia nervosa. *Canadian Journal of Psychiatry, 45,* 173–178.

Krautter, T., & Lock, J. (2004). Is manualized family-based treatment for adolescent anorexia nervosa acceptable to parents? Patient satisfaction at the end of treatment. *Journal of Family Therapy, 26,* 66–82.

Le Grange, D., Binford, R., & Loeb, K. (2005). Manualized family-based treatment for anorexia nervosa: A case series. *Journal of American Academy of Child and Adolescent Psychiatry, 44,* 41–46.

Le Grange, D., Eisler, I., Dare, C., & Russell, G. (1992). Evaluation of family therapy in anorexia nervosa: A pilot study. *International Journal of Eating Disorders, 12,* 347–357.

Le Grange, D., & Lock, J. (2005). The dearth of psychological treatment studies for anorexia nervosa. *International Journal of Eating Disorders, 37,* 79–91.

Le Grange, D., & Lock, J. (2007). *Treating bulimia in adolescents: A family-based approach.* New York: Guilford Press.

Le Grange, D., Crosby, R.D., Rathouz, P.J., & Leventhal, B.L. (2007). A randomized controlled comparison of family-based treatment and supportive psychotherapy for adolescent bulimia nervosa. *Archives of General Psychiatry, 64,* 1049–1056.

Le Grange, D., Lock, J., & Dymek, M. (2003). Family-based therapy for adolescents with bulimia nervosa. *American Journal of Psychotherapy, 57,* 237–251.

Lim C. (2000). *A pilot study of families' experiences pf a multi-family group day treatment programme.* MSc Dissertation, Institute of Psychiatry, Kings College, University of London.

Lock, J., & Le Grange, D. (2001). Can family-based treatment of anorexia nervosa be manualized? *Journal of Psychotherapy Practice and Research, 10,* 253–261.

Lock, J., Agras, W.S., Bryson, S., & Kraemer, H.C. (2005). A comparison of short- and long-term family therapy for adolescent anorexia nervosa. *Journal of the American Academy of Child and Adolescent Psychiatry, 44,* 632–639.

Lock, J., Couturier, J., Agras, W.S. (2006). Comparison of long-term outcomes in adolescents with anorexia nervosa treated with family therapy. *Journal of the American Academy of Child and Adolescent Psychiatry, 45,* 666–672.

Lock, J., Le Grange, D., Agras, W. S., & Dare, C. (2001). *Treatment manual for anorexia nervosa: A family-based approach.* New York: Guilford Press.

Loeb, K.L., Walsh, B.T., Lock, J., Le Grange, D., Jones, J., Marcus, S., et al. (2007). Open Trial of Family-Based Treatment for Adolescent Anorexia Nervosa: Evidence of Successful Dissemination. *Journal of the American Academy of Child and Adolescent Psychiatry, 46,* 792–800.

Minuchin, S., Baker, L., Rosman, B. L., Liebman, R., Milman, L., & Todd, T. C. (1975). A conceptual model of psychosomatic illness in childhood. *Archives of General Psychiatry, 32,* 1031–1038.

Minuchin, S., Rosman, B. L., & Baker, L. (1978). *Psychosomatic families: Anorexia nervosa in context.* Cambridge, MA: Harvard University Press.

Morgan, H. G., & Russell, G. (1975). Value of family background and clinical features as predictors of long-term outcome in anorexia nervosa: Four-year follow-up study of 41 patients. *Psychological Medicine, 5,* 355–371.

Palazzoli, M. (1974). *Self-starvation: From the intrapsychic to the transpersonal approach to anorexia nervosa.* Oxford, England: Chaucer.

Robin, A. L., Siegel, P. T., Koepke, T., Moye, A. W., & Tice, S. (1994). Family therapy versus individual therapy for adolescent females with anorexia nervosa. *Journal of Developmental and Behavioral Pediatrics, 15,* 111–116.

Robin, A. L., Siegel, P. T., Moye, A. W., Gilroy, M., Dennis, A. B., & Sikand, A. (1999). A controlled comparison of family versus individual therapy for adolescents with anorexia nervosa. *Journal of the American Academy of Child Adolescent Psychiatry, 38,* 1482–1489.

Russell, G., Szmukler, G. I., Dare, C., & Eisler, I. (1987). An evaluation of family therapy in anorexia nervosa and bulimia nervosa. *Archives of General Psychiatry, 44,* 1047–1056.

Schmidt, U., Lee, S., Beecham, J., Perkins, S., Treasure, J., Yi, I., et al. (2007). A randomized controlled trial of family therapy and cognitive-behavioral guided self-care for adolescents with bulimia nervosa and related disorders. *American Journal of Psychiatry, 164,* 591–598.

Scholz, M., & Asen, E. (2001). Multiple family therapy with eating disordered adolescents: Concepts and preliminary results. *European Eating Disorder Review, 9,* 33–42.

Steinhausen, H. C. (2002). The outcome of anorexia nervosa in the 20th century. *American Journal of Psychiatry, 159,* 1284–1293.

Chapter 9

INCARCERATED FEMALE TEENS AND SUBSTANCE ABUSE

The Holistic Enrichment for At-Risk Teens (HEART) Program

AMELIA C. ROBERTS AND CHIQUITIA WELCH

The increasing criminalization of girls has changed the gender distribution in detention and youth development centers where girls are being detained and incarcerated at a growing rate. From 1988 to 1997, the number of cases in which girls were detained in a secure youth facility increased by 65%, from 36,300 cases to 60,000 (Office of Juvenile Justice and Delinquency Prevention [OJJDP], 2000). Much of this increase has been attributed to substance misuse, which is directly and indirectly related to female delinquency (Jackson & Knepper, 2003; Regoli & Hewitt, 2003; Senna & Siegel, 2001). For example, between 1993 and 2002, the number of girls arrested for liquor law violations increased by 37%.

To the same effect, the number of girls arrested for drug abuse violations increased by 120%, which was the largest increase for any offense category. Girls were arrested for a variety of drug abuse violations: using drugs, selling drugs, distributing drugs, and transporting drugs. Moreover, many juvenile female offenders commit illegal acts such as shoplifting, theft, or prostitution to aid their addiction.

Substance abuse has also been associated with serious delinquency and violent crimes among this population (Potter, 1999); arrests for violent crimes have been increasing steadily among girls. Research demonstrates that substance abuse is related to severe antisocial behavior among delinquent adolescents (McNamus, Alessi, Grapentine, & Brickman, 1984). And longitudinal research has shown

We would like to thank the staff of the North Carolina Department of Juvenile Justice and Delinquency Prevention for giving us the opportunity to partner with them in the design, development, and implementation of the HEART program. Specifically, we thank George Sweat, deputy secretary; Dr. Martin Pharr, director of clinical services; and Judy Julian, project director. Collectively, their vision and fervent desire to provide therapeutic treatment and services to girls involved in the North Carolina Juvenile Justice System are to be lauded. Additionally, the promising results of the HEART program could not have been achieved without the keen clinical skills of Pam Wiggins, program director, and Debra Eng Hunter, psychotherapist, and the staff members who transitioned successfully to the use of therapeuti approaches. Most important, the participants have played a key role in the success of the program. With their passion, dedication, and commitment to the therapeutic process and the therapeutic community they are the *heart* of the HEART program. (For a visit to HEART contact Pam Wiggins, at pam.wiggins@ncmail.net, or Judy Julian, at judy.julian@ncmail.net.)

Finally, we would like to thank the team members of the University of North Carolina at Chapel Hill: Dr. Raymond Kirk, Dr. Judith Meece, Diane Griffith, Sharon Parker, Dr. Ariana Wall, Ernestine Stone, and Cyrette Cotton-Fleming.

that the more serious the abuse, the more serious the youth's involvement in delinquency (Huizinga, Loeber, & Thornberry, 1994). This finding is consistent across gender, age, and race. Huizinga et al. (1994) findings also reveal that "prior changes in substance use are found to have a larger impact on subsequent changes in delinquency, while prior changes in delinquency have a somewhat smaller impact on subsequent drug use" (p. 11). Based on this finding, one could surmise that substance abuse treatment is critical to breaking the substance abuse-delinquency cycle.

The aforementioned statistics and findings indicate the need to develop effective interventions for adolescent female offenders with substance abuse disorders. Questions have been raised, however, about the adequacy of therapeutic models that have been designed with the needs of boys in mind. Thus, an issue of central importance is how best to treat adolescent female offenders, and those with substance abuse and co-occurring disorders in particular. Because knowledge about how best to intervene and treat girls involved in the juvenile justice system is limited, more research on female offenders is needed (Spatz-Widom, 2000). Insufficient knowledge regarding girls involved in the juvenile justice system has translated into inadequate resources and interventions. With few alternatives, a system has been "created that over-incarcerates young female offenders, often treating their social problems with ineffective correctional sanctions" (Owen & Bloom, 1997, p. 4). Consequently, youth development centers have become prime places to intervene in the lives of girls. Therefore, targeted interventions in institutional settings are needed to treat and address female offenders' substance abuse disorders and other multiply related and varied problems (Jenson, Potter, & Howard, 2001) that lead to their substance abuse and delinquent behaviors.

In this chapter, we provide an in-depth overview of the Holistic Enrichment for At-Risk Teens (HEART) program, a multicomponent intervention delivered in a residential therapeutic community at an all-female youth development center. We present a conceptual and theoretical overview of the HEART program. We also outline the interventions that comprise HEART, treatment strategies and approaches, and the evaluation design of the HEART program. First, however, we present an overview of the treatment needs of adolescent female offenders with substance abuse disorders.

TREATMENT NEEDS OF ADOLESCENT FEMALE OFFENDERS WITH SUBSTANCE ABUSE DISORDERS

Many girls are entering the juvenile correctional system with unaddressed substance abuse/dependence and comorbid disorders. It has been estimated that between 60% and 87% of girls committed to youth developmental centers or juvenile correctional facilities need substance abuse treatment at intake, and more than half are multiply addicted (Freitas & Chesney-Lind, 2001; Prescott, 1997). Co-occurring with substance use disorders are other forms of mental health disorders such as depression, anxiety, conduct disorder, and posttraumatic stress disorder (PTSD).

In addition to mental health and substance abuse problems, adolescent female offenders are entering juvenile correctional facilities with a confluence of complex, interrelated problems. For instance, many female offenders have been reared in fragmented families and unstable communities; have experienced academic failure; have lived in families and neighborhoods characterized by pervasive poverty (Acoca, 1999; American Bar Association & National Bar Association, 2001); and have histories of sexual, emotional, and physical victimization (Chesney-Lind, 1998). Moreover, a high percentage are mothers who face considerable challenges with parenting and other interpersonal relationships (National Mental Health Association, 2001). These experiences can "diminish a youth's life chance" (Lerner & Galambos, 1998, p. 420); and if left unaddressed, these factors may contribute to the female juvenile offender having poor outcomes in late adolescence and adulthood. Studies have shown that female juvenile offenders without intervention or treatment have high rates of psychiatric illnesses, substance abuse and dependency, domestic assaults and interpersonal violence, and arrests in adulthood (Snyder & Sickmund, 1999; Zocolilo & Rogers, 1991).

Research indicates that girls who are detained in juvenile correctional facilities exhibit higher levels of psychopathology than their male counterparts. They have higher levels of depression, anxiety (Goldstein et al., 2003; Kataoka et al., 2001) posttraumatic stress disorders (Cauffman, Feldman, Waterman, & Steiner, 1998; Royce-Baerger, Lyons, Quigley, & Griffin, 2001), abuse histories (McCabe, Lansing, Garland, & Hough, 2002; Royce-Baerger et al., 2001; Walrath et al., 2003), and suicidal ideation (Goldstein et al., 2003; Royce-Baerger et al., 2001). Moreover, with regard to substance abuse, research studies conducted with general and clinical samples of adolescents have shown pronounced distinctions between boys and girls revolving around physiological effects. For example, girls become addicted to drugs faster (Greenfield, 2002) and are more susceptible to drug and alcohol-induced brain damage (Hommer, Momenan, Kaiser, & Rawlings, 2001; Reneman et al., 2001). In addition to differing physiological effects, psychological effects and antecedents to substance misuse appear to be divergent. Girls have a higher prevalence of psychological comorbidity, particularly depression and anxiety disorders (Goldstein et al., 2003). Depression and other factors such as low self-esteem and concerns about weight and appearance, all of which are more prevalent in the female population, place girls on pathways to substance abuse (National Center on Addiction and Substance Abuse at Columbia University, 2003).

Accordingly, the need for specialized treatment approaches for adolescent females has been advocated. Comprehensive substance abuse treatment is an essential component of programming for female adolescent offenders, and should address the multiple underlying causes of substance abuse: physiological, psychological, physical, familial, relational, and structural (Molidor, Nissen, & Watkins, 2002). Substance abuse treatment, however, for the general population of girls and for girls who are incarcerated has been scarce. Historically, substance abuse/dependence and correctional programming have been designed and developed primarily for males. However, with advances in our knowledge on substance abuse and delinquency among adolescent females, a general consensus has emerged that a comprehensive continuum of female gender-specific, gender-sensitive, culturally competent, and developmentally appropriate prevention and intervention services need to be developed and tailored to address the distinct needs of girls (American Bar Association & National Bar Association, 2001; Guthrie & Flinchbaugh, 2001; Sondheimer, 2001; Weiler, 1999), and delinquent girls in particular (Bloom, Owen, Deschenes, & Rosenbaum, 2002; Calhoun, Jurgens, & Chen, 1993; Molidor et al., 2002).

Despite the growing knowledge base on female delinquency, substance abuse, and the interrelatedness between the two phenomena, substance-abuse interventions for adolescent females detained in juvenile correctional facilities remain scarce. A few promising female gender-specific programs have been developed to address the needs of adolescent female offenders, such as the Alternative Rehab Communities, Harriet Tubman Residential Center, Girls and Boys Town USA, and PACE Center for Girls. Taken as a whole, these programs provide individualized treatment plans, holistic services and interventions, substance abuse treatment, and specialized treatment interventions for female adolescent offenders. Yet no programs have been developed that provide comprehensive treatment to adolescent female offenders with co-occurring substance abuse and mental health disorders.

Conversely, in an effort to address the gap in services for incarcerated girls with co-occurring substance abuse and mental health disorders, the HEART program was developed. Similar to features of the aforementioned programs, HEART addresses the needs of its participants in an intense and individualized manner. Unlike the other programs, HEART provides comprehensive substance abuse and mental health treatment to incarcerated girls with substance abuse comorbidities and serious or chronic histories of delinquency. Additionally,

HEART blends an educational and treatment model. In the subsequent sections, we describe HEART and present some preliminary findings.

CONCEPTUAL OVERVIEW OF THE HOLISTIC ENRICHMENT FOR AT-RISK TEENS PROGRAM

Recognizing that incarcerated adolescent females with co-occurring substance abuse and mental health disorders were in dire need of treatment programming to address their comorbid disorders and delinquent behaviors, staff of the North Carolina Department of Juvenile Justice and Delinquency Prevention (DJJDP) collaborated with faculty and staff of the University of North Carolina at Chapel Hill's Schools of Social Work and Education to design, develop, and implement HEART. This gender-specific substance abuse intervention program targets females between the ages of 14 and 18 with a *DSM-IV-TR* diagnosis of substance abuse or substance dependency diagnosis, and with 6 to 12 months remaining on their sentence at a youth development center located in North Carolina. The time remaining on their sentences permits sufficient time in the treatment program to experience the full range of components of the intervention.

The holistic multimodal program, which uses modified therapeutic principles, cognitive-behavioral techniques, and a blended educational and treatment model, addresses the substance abuse, mental health, psychosocial, educational, and spiritual needs of incarcerated adolescent females, as well as physical, emotional, and sexual trauma, family and peer relationships, and racial and cultural identities. Because principles and methods of the therapeutic community modality underscore the intervention, treatment, activities, and services are carried out in a self-contained residential community, meaning participants reside in a separate cottage within the wider all female youth developmental facility, and have minimal contact with the wider population.

The unique features of HEART are its integrated intervention approaches that address substance abuse and comorbid mental health disorders, and its blended educational treatment model.

Goals and Guiding Principles of the Holistic Enrichment for At-Risk Teens Program

HEART is designed to address the lives of females holistically. With a broad rehabilitative approach, the multimodal program targets several outcomes: substance abuse, education, prosocial behaviors, and recidivism. As such, HEART has six specific goals:

1. Reduce substance use.
2. Enhance relapse prevention skills.
3. Enrich prosocial behaviors and attitudes.
4. Reengage students in the educational and learning process.
5. Aid students in the achievement and maintenance of positive and productive lifestyles upon and after community reentry.
6. Reduce recidivism.

Accompanying the goals are several principles guiding the HEART program:

- Listening to and valuing girls' voices.
- Assessing each girl's social environment, sociocultural realities, and internal experiences, which are integral to the therapeutic process.
- Recognizing the importance of relationships to girls' psychological growth and development.
- Allowing students to be active learners and empowered "knowers."
- Identifying and building strengths through the use of strengths-based approaches.
- Focusing on developing healthy relationships.
- Having positive expectations of a "you can do it" attitude.

Theoretical Frameworks of the Holistic Enrichment for At-Risk Teens Program

It has become quite clear that one theoretical or explanatory model is insufficient to address the complex needs of young girls with both substance abuse and delinquent histories. Multiple theoretical frameworks provide a multidimensional approach for addressing the interwoven factors of girls with interrelated substance abuse and delinquency histories. Hence, the HEART program is informed by the Bio-Psychosocial-Spiritual Model of addiction, relational theory, and cognitive and social learning theories.

Bio-Psychosocial-Spiritual Model of Addiction within a Developmental Context

The bio-psychosocial-spiritual perspective posits that many factors—biological, psychological, social, developmental, and spiritual—interact to produce or cause substance abuse and substance dependence:

- *Biological* factors include genetics, heritability, neurotransmitters, physiological susceptibility, pubertal maturation, and familial histories of alcohol or drug abuse.

- *Psychological* factors include individual characteristics such as temperament, mental health disorders, low self-esteem, suicidality, and personality.

- *Social* factors include environmental stressors such as poverty, racism, sexism, familial functioning, peer relationships, laws, and culture.

- *Spirituality* factors include the role of religion, theology, and faith as protective aspects in the substance abuse prevention and recovery process (Amey, Albrecht, & Miller, 1996; Hodge, Cardenas, & Montoya, 2001; Kutter & McDermott, 1997).

It is important that the Bio-Psychosocial-Spiritual Model of addiction be embedded within a developmental context because the course of addiction among adolescents differs from that of adults, and their developmental needs are vastly different. Adolescence is a period of robust maturation—physical, psychological, social, and moral. During this stage of development, girls experience hormonal changes brought on by puberty, and develop secondary physical characteristics. It is also a period during which girls are experimenting with different roles, exploring their burgeoning sexuality, attempting to integrate their newfound roles and sexuality into their personal schema, and exploring existentialism. Not only are their bodies changing, but the way they think and feel about their bodies are changing, too. Countering media images regarding aspects of beauty and physicality, which have an immense effect on girls' self-esteem and their view of themselves, is an important issue that is addressed by the staff of HEART. During this period of development, adolescents seek greater independence and strive to establish an identity outside of the family system. Accordingly, relationships with family members change during this stage of development.

The staff of HEART addresses these developmental issues sensitively, so that treatment approaches are tailored to the individual needs of each girl, and stalled or delayed development brought on by the abuse of substances and by other social-cultural factors is addressed.

Relational Theory

HEART's Relational Interconnectedness Model is informed by relational theory, which emphasizes the importance of connections and relationships in the lives of girls. Based on the model, connections are fundamental to the psychological growth and development of females; failure to form attachments and affiliations are underlying sources of anxiety, low self-esteem, and depression among females (Covington, 2003).

Relational theory counters traditional theories of development, which are based on male models of development and which emphasize autonomy, separation, and independence as key features of healthy development. Accordingly, it has been posited widely that traditional theories of development ignore the life experiences of many women, which include enhancing relationships, and developing intimacy and a sense of connectedness. These attributes have been viewed through the lens of a deficit framework, implying weakness and dependency.

Based on relational theory, it has been advocated that for treatment interventions to be successful with substance-abusing females, relational needs must be addressed (Finkelstein, Kennedy, Thomas, & Kearns, 1997). Therefore, promoting healthy relationships, which is essential to many female's psychological and emotional growth (Miller, 1986), is a cornerstone of the HEART program.

Cognitive, Behavioral, and Social Learning Theories

Cognitive theory posits that the moods, cognitions, and behavior of individuals can be changed when they learn how to examine and correct thinking patterns that may be distorted or adversely negative (Beck, Wright, Newman, & Liese, 1993). The central premise of cognitive theory is that thoughts affect emotions. Behavioral theory posits that behavior is conditioned and elicited by environmental stimuli and operant learning. Substance abuse disorders are developed and maintained through learned responses that are reinforced in a variety of ways; and, in order to change behavior, one must learn new behaviors. Social learning theory, which focuses on learning within social contexts, posits that individuals learn through observation and that cognition plays a role in the learning process. As such, according to Bandura (1977), "Most human behavior is learned observationally through modeling: from observing others one forms an idea of how new behaviors are performed, and on later occasions this coded information serves as a guide for action" (p. 22). These theories are combined to address one's thinking that influences one's behavior, and behavior and social learning influences one's thinking. These theories are combined into the cognitive-behavioral therapy.

TREATMENT MODELS OF THE HOLISTIC ENRICHMENT FOR AT-RISK TEENS PROGRAM

Modified Therapeutic Community Modality

The therapeutic community (TC) is an intensive, comprehensive residential treatment program that provides a highly structured, prosocial environment for the treatment of substance abuse/dependency. The TC was initially designed for adults but has been modified to treat adolescents with substance-use disorders (Department of Health and Human Services, 1993). One of the key features of the TC modality is that the *community* is conceptualized to be a key agent of change. The community comprises the social environment, peers, and the staff.

Therapeutic communities emphasize a holistic approach to treating substance abuse. Holistic approaches address practically every aspect of residents' lives, and emphasizes comprehensive lifestyle changes (Weinman & Dignam, 2002). Therapeutic communities rely on group processes and peer support to assist residents in addressing issues related to their substance abuse, delinquency/criminality, and family relationships. Participating in a TC of peers who are struggling with similar issues promotes rapid progress through stalled or delayed developmental stages.

Research demonstrates that this line of treatment has positive proximal and distal treatment effects (Condelli & Hubbard, 1994; DeLeon, 1984, 2000; Gerstein & Harwood, 1990). For example, therapeutic communities have been found to be effective in reducing drug use, increasing employment, and decreasing criminal behavior (Barr, 1986; DeLeon, 1993, 2000). In addition, this line of treatment has been shown to be effective with males, females, adolescents, and diverse racial and ethnic groups (Deitch, Carleton, Koutsenok, & Marsolais, 2002). Accordingly, the Therapeutic Community Model was selected for the HEART program because of its effectiveness with residents whose profiles are similar to the target population of HEART—a protracted history of substance abuse, serious and chronic involvement in the commission of delinquent or criminal acts, and a lack of marketable educational and vocational skills.

Levels System

Because the HEART program is based on principles and methods of the TC modality, a *levels system* is employed to gauge progress during treatment and to symbolize advancement and impute status within the community. The levels system used in the HEART program has been adopted from the Harriet Tubman Youth Development Center in New York and comprises four stages:

1. *Orientation* (the reluctant beginner),
2. *Adjustment* (the enthusiastic learner),
3. *Transition* (the cautious performer), and
4. *Honors* (the competent and committed performer).

Progress from each level to the next is based on behavioral changes and individual competencies and goals. Advancement from each level to the next is proclaimed and publicly acknowledged by community peers and staff. Each student is expected to proceed through each stage. To facilitate an understanding of the levels system used in the HEART program, we provide an overview of the orientation stage, which includes assumptions and behavioral requirements underlying the stage (see Table 9.1).

Cognitive-Behavioral Therapy

Cognitive-behavior therapy (CBT) is grounded in social learning theory, behaviorism, and cognitive psychology, and combines cognitive and behavioral approaches to alter and challenge faulty cognitions and maladaptive behaviors through cognitive restructuring. CBT is a research-based intervention that has empirical evidence supporting its efficacy in treating adolescents with substance abuse disorders (Carroll, 1998).

Staff members and participants of the HEART program are trained in the CBT model. Some of the areas of training include: problem solving, cognitive restructuring, self-control, social perception, and coping skills. Staff members receive initial training so that they have a basic understanding of CBT concepts and approaches and have the skills to integrate them into their therapeutic work with program participants. Subsequently, residents are trained in the use of CBT approaches so that they can begin to challenge their own and their peers' negative self-talk, irrational thoughts and beliefs, and distorted thinking patterns, and begin to recognize triggers and patterns that lead to anxiety, depression, and substance misuse. The training includes role-plays and the use of real-life scenarios to aid residents in exploring and discussing their cognitions, emotional responses, and behaviors. An example of a vignette used in one of the training sessions is provided here. The "If you think . . . how do you feel" scenarios allow participants to actively explore their thoughts, feelings, and behaviors.

> **Situation:** Your mother walks into your room with a really angry expression on her face.
>
> If you think, "What did I do now—she always blames me?" how do you feel?
>
> If you think, "She must have had another fight with my sister," how do you feel?
>
> If you think, "She just got off the phone with her boss—maybe she has a problem and wants me to listen," how do you feel?

Table 9.1   Example of Levels System 1—Orientation

Entry level (1): Orientation Stage—Curious Learner	During this stage, participants learn about the purpose and goals of the program and the expectations of participants. The orientation stage lasts a minimum of 14 days, with the anticipation that most participants will progress to Level II within 30 days. This stage is the most restrictive.
Entry level: Orientation Stage Assumptions	We believe that most participants want to succeed but have not had the environment or consistent support to take the necessary steps to do so. They may have very low expectations for personal, social, academic, and vocational success, but may have the desire to change their lives and succeed.
Placement in the juvenile system	Does not accept sentencing. Has no plans for future, except to "get out." Sees being at the facility as just "serving time."
Skills: social and group	Deficient in prosocial skills. May be weak in or lacking traditional educational skills. Likely to be lacking in independent living skills. Lacking in vocational skills.
Motivation and confidence level	Lacks commitment to this program, or may be excited about this transition. Lacks motivation to change. Lacks confidence in abilities. Lacks initiative.
Attitude and behaviors	Resistant to authority. Projects blame. Acts impulsively. Is influenced negatively by peers. Egocentric, concrete moral reasoning. Problems reoccur and are not resolved quickly. Physically or verbally aggressive; lacks internal control.
Responsibility for directing own behaviors/locus of control	Takes no responsibility for directing own behavior. Relies on external controls. Does not see or accept how her behavior impacts on others. Externalizes blame.
Leadership	Shows no positive leadership skills. Has difficulty accepting constructive advice from peers.
Team members' style	Directing: When using this style, team members are telling, not yelling. Directing means being concrete, consistent, and objective in your verbal statements to residents at this stage. Staff members are firm and task-focused, providing instruction and directions. They maintain close and continuous supervision. They supervise and evaluate resident performance without resident input.

(continued)

Table 9.1 *(Continued)*

Strengths	Observe positive behaviors. Look for these strengths: art, music, drama, verbal skills, critical thinking, humor, creativity, intelligent/smart kids, leadership, and loyalty bonds. Reframe negative behaviors: Manipulative—ability to scope out the environment and figure people out; stubborn—persistent, stick-to-itiveness; overly sensitive emotional antennae—can read others well, but needs to learn how to discriminate.
Entry Level Requirements	This resident is expected to demonstrate a general commitment to participate in this program and to learn and practice positive social skills. Comply with all facility behavioral expectations—with frequent reminders. Comply with instructions from the medical staff. Be familiar with behavior al expectations in each domain (education, counseling, living unit, dining room, etc.) of the program. Learn and follow daily schedules and routine (wake-up time, school time, etc.). Remain under close supervision. Get permission to talk with other residents who are at the entry level stage. Get permission to move by raising their hand. Participate in all psychoeducational programs. Follow directions and instructions from staff. Seek clarification from a team member if unclear about program expectations. Be familiar with problem-solving steps. Understand and explain the differences between short- and long-term goals. Participate in all program areas. Develop an awareness of one's own culture. Interact with all staff when necessary. Maintain good hygiene, including keeping self, room, and clothing clean. Participate in the educational plan and assessments.
Criteria from Moving from Entry-Level Orientation Stage to Adjustment Stage	Have no unresolved rule violations or restrictions. Be willing to become involved in treatment. Be willing to accept placement. Begin to demonstrate behavior control. Show preliminary understanding of the use and abuse of ATOD. Demonstrate willingness to learn from mistakes.

Table 9.1   *(Continued)*

	Participate in the competencies groups for this level.
	Respond appropriately to staff direction.
	Begin to demonstrate an awareness of cultural and gender differences.
	Seek clarification from staff about program expectations when questions or concerns arise.
	Seek staff assistance with problems and be receptive to staff helping to solve them.
	Complete educational assessments.
	Meet requirements of the orientation stage and begin to exhibit characteristics of the adjustment stage.
	Give presentation on knowledge of orientation stage to peers and team members.
Education and Treatment Interwoven	Give presentation of knowledge of the orientation stage to staff and peers, including a discussion of at least one of the competencies and one of the psychoeducational programs.
	Write two essays that will reflect the blending of education and treatment: (1) What makes it difficult or easy to make a commitment to participate in all aspects of the HEART treatment and educational programs? Share where you are in the process of commitment. (Use Stages of Change, DiClemente & Prochaska). This essay must be a minimum of one typewritten page, double-spaced, 12-pt font. (2) What are some of the reasons that led you to begin using and abusing alcohol and other drugs? This essay must be a minimum of one typewritten page, double-spaced, 12-pt font.

Moreover, because of the flexibility of the CBT intervention, it is integrated within a relational approach so that residents are provided with a corrective emotional experience as they relate to others. Additionally, the CBT model of treatment is incorporated into other treatment interventions of HEART, such as psychotherapy, psychoeducation, and psychopharmacology.

Blended Education and Treatment Model

Because the target population comprises adolescents who are still of school age, a "blended" educational model is employed in which the curriculum materials parallel the treatment materials. The Blended Education and Treatment Model combines educational and treatment services by integrating academic skills with life skills and social skills. The primary task of the Blended Education and Treatment Model is to reengage residents in the learning process through the use of individualized, innovative, and gender-specific educational practices. Learning activities not only have educational benefits, but they also promote social, emotional, and moral development. The dual focus of HEART's blended education and treatment approach is illustrated in Table 9.2.

The model is predicated on empirical evidence that illustrates that girls detained in juvenile justice facilities have relatively few academic successes in traditional educational programs (OJJDP, 1998; Robinson, Rowan, & Rapport, 1999; Weiler, 1999). Therefore, the Blended Education and Treatment Model includes the following salient features:

- Individualized academic plans with specific goals and timetables
- Specific attention to special learning needs

Table 9.2   Education and Treatment: Dual Focus of the HEART Program

Treatment Focus	Education Focus
Racism and cultural diversity	*History Module:* Participants learn about diverse cultures and the history of immigration in the United States and its influence on the landscape of the country. Participants also examine the issue of racism. The goal of this module is to aid students in understanding and celebrating their own cultural uniqueness so that their self-esteem may be enhanced.
Dual diagnosis—depression	*Health and Biology Module:* Participants are taught how to recognize and understand symptoms of depression. In addition, they learn about medication and other therapeutic strategies to treat depression.
Conflict resolution—competency	*Social Studies Module:* Conflict resolution is addressed from a national perspective (e.g., wars, social movements, terrorism) and then applied to interpersonal situations so that participants will learn how to resolve and manage interpersonal conflicts.
Playwriting	*English/Literature Module:* Through literary work and the use of drama, participants learn about the lives of contemporary and historical women. Participants use the tool of drama to explore aspects of their own lives and how they feel about themselves and their social contexts—family, peers, and community.

- Innovative mathematical, science, and computer literacy curricula
- Culturally relevant material focused on female interests and issues
- Group discussions of psychoeducational topics and health issues
- Life planning and vocational education
- Peer teamwork, collaboration, and cooperation

Another core feature of the HEART program is its focus on recreational, active, and experiential learning. Studies indicate that girls in institutional settings often have less access to recreational and athletic activities than do boys (Belknap, Holsinger, & Dunn, 1997). Yet these activities have important benefits for girls. Daily physical and recreational activities promote a sense of health and well-being (OJJDP, 1998). They provide opportunities for self-expression, creativity, leadership, and teamwork. Research has documented positive benefits of sports participation for academic achievement, self-esteem, confidence, and career aspirations (Weiler, 1999). Leisure and recreational activities also serve as an important protective factor in adolescents' lives (Eccles & Barber, 1999; Mahoney & Stattin, 2000). For example, adolescent girls who are involved in athletic programs and extracurricular activities are at lower risk for drug and alcohol abuse, as well as early sexual activity and pregnancy (Weiler, 1999). Girls who are physically active also report fewer self-image problems and eating disorders.

Community Reentry Model

Because all residents will eventually return to their communities, a comprehensive reintegration plan is developed well in advance of each resident's release date. The reintegration plan is based on the Community Reentry Model (Altschuler, Armstrong, & MacKenzie, 1999), which posits that successful community reintegration is a critical component of treatment, and integral to girls' success. Successful reintegration requires that residents are connected to community resources and educational institutions, have learned job-seeking and vocational skills, and have increased communication with family members. The Community Reintegration Model serves as a guideline to facilitate residents' transitional process. The transitional process consists of residents reconnect with their families and school system, plan for college, prepare for employment, connect with community resources, and develop relapse prevention skills. Thus, reintegration for the resident begins at the day of entry into the program.

TREATMENT INTERVENTIONS OF THE HOLISTIC ENRICHMENT FOR AT-RISK TEENS PROGRAM

Primary treatment addresses and assists girls in the resolution of psychological, physical, mental, social, and spiritual problems that may have lead to their substance abuse or dependency, and their delinquency. Psychotherapy, individual counseling, process groups, psychoeducational groups, psychopharmacotherapy, and 12-step programs (e.g., Women in Sobriety, traditional AA 12-Steps, and the 12-Steps for Children of Alcoholics), reflection groups, and family therapy sessions are the predominant forms of treatment interventions:

- *Psychotherapy:* Psychotherapy is provided weekly by a licensed (or provisionally licensed) clinician (e.g., social worker, psychologist). The duration of each session is 35 to 45 minutes. The psychotherapeutic sessions focus primarily on the resolution of psychological, family, interpersonal problems, and issues revolving around substance abuse and sexual, emotional, and physical trauma. CBT approaches are incorporated into the psychotherapeutic intervention to challenge participants' negative thinking, address their behavioral patterns, and to aid participants in learning new coping and problem-solving skills.

- *Counseling with counselor I and/or counselor II:* Individual counseling sessions occur 2 to 3 times per week for about 30 to 45 minutes with a counselor who has a 2-year or 4-year degree. Such sessions are behavioral focused. Accordingly, residents learn skills to improve their behavior. In addition, participants discuss their treatment goals and their progress in the program, and they are given an opportunity to talk about and process their experiences and feelings.

- *Process group:* Each day begins with a process group session entitled "Morning Affirmations and Goal Setting." During each session, participants set and discuss daily objectives, make morning pronouncements that guide them through the day, address behavioral challenges and successes; and they are given an opportunity to share their thoughts, feelings, and insights about particular events or experiences.

- *Psychoeducational group treatment sessions:* A variety of psychoeducational group sessions are held throughout the week for the purposes of building skills, enhancing knowledge, changing behaviors, and enriching participants' psychological development. Listed here are some of the psychoeducational topics that are addressed:

—Bio-Psychosocial-Spiritual Framework of Addiction (5 sessions)

—Alcohol, tobacco, and other drugs: implications for female teens

—Understanding our emotions

—Dual diagnosis: depression, anxiety, PTSD, and substance abuse—What does this mean for me? (4 sessions)

—Developing healthy boundaries: effects of physical, sexual, and emotional abuse (2 sessions)

—Recovering from grief and loss

—Adult children of alcoholics

—Understanding relapse prevention

—What does it mean to be a female: sexuality/sexual development (6 sessions)

—Healthy relationships with a partner

—Physical health issues for teen girls

—Appreciating differences and cultural diversity

- *Psychiatric and psychopharmacotherapy:* To address participants' mental health needs, psychiatric and psychopharmacotherapy services are provided. The psychiatrist assesses, evaluates, and monitors the emotional and psychological needs of participants, and in consultation with the program director and the clinical team of HEART, the psychiatrist prescribes and monitors participants' use of psychotropic drugs for emotional disorders.

- *Self-help groups via 12-step programs:* Participants are introduced to three types of 12-step programs: Women and Sobriety 12-Steps, traditional AA 12-Steps, and 12-Steps for Children of Alcoholics. The groups are held within surrounding communities, and many of them are composed of adult women who are recovering from substance misuse. On occasion, 12-step meetings are held at the youth development center.

- *Reflection group:* The purpose of this group is to provide participants with an opportunity to think critically about new educational materials learned in the classroom setting and psychoeducational group sessions.

- *Family therapy sessions:* Family therapy sessions are provided periodically so that families can learn about addiction, family roles, and adolescent development, and how best to support the participant in her recovery process. Additionally, sessions are designed to resolve past difficulties between participants and family members, address familial functioning, and open the channels of communication.

Other Group Interventions

In addition to the core therapeutic interventions, other group therapy sessions and meetings are conducted throughout the daily treatment regimen. Some of the groups and meetings are described briefly here.

Female Issues Groups

Female issues groups address topics and issues specific or sensitive to the needs of females, such as premenstrual symptoms, the female body, the bond of sisterhood, relational aggression, the female socialization processes, females and discrimination, and societal responses to female substance abuse.

The groups are designed to teach participants empowerment skills and how to have a healthy view of themselves and other females. Further, the groups are designed to equip participants with the knowledge, skills, and insight to make healthy behavioral, relational, and life choices. Empowerment, behavioral, and relational skills are taught through the use of poetry, literary work, and drama. Group leaders model how to read poems dramatically. Some of the poetic work that has been used to date includes *Phenomenal Woman* (Angelou, 1994), *I Am a Black Woman* (Evans, 1970), and *Because* (Hernandez, 1994, as cited in Roth, 1994).

Grief and Loss Group

The purpose of this group is to help girls who have experienced loss, through death or separation, address their grief and begin the healing process. The chaplain of the youth development center and a trained counselor cofacilitate the weekly grief and loss group. Photography and nature are mechanisms used to aid the healing process.

Spontaneous Group

The purpose of this ad hoc group is to divert crises or address specific behaviors or attitudes that could lead to crises. An example of a recent spontaneous group that was convened is presented here:

> L. was recently admitted to the HEART program. As a new resident, she had difficulty bonding with other residents, resulting in her exhibiting disruptive behaviors such as arguing and becoming aggressive with peers. Her behaviors exacted a toll on the community. Consequently, residents requested to convene a group meeting to discuss their concerns. The HEART residents were able to voice their frustration within a therapeutic forum, and L. was given an opportunity to respond and share her experiences. The residents were highly emotional, but respectful to L. During the last 15 minutes of the group session, staff asked for

volunteers to share their experiences regarding their adjustment processes when they were new to the HEART program. Residents shared their experiences and gave suggestions to L. At the end of the session, residents engaged in a group hug and several residents gave individual hugs to L.

Special Groups and Events

This feature provides participants with personal and social growth experiences away from the cottage setting. Some of the special events include:

- Spirituality sessions: twice a year an Epiphany weekend is held for the girls and led by the chaplain and community groups
- Worship services are available on Sundays
- Women-Only Breast Cancer 5K Walk/Run Benefit
- Crop Walk for Hunger
- Hiking
- Nature trips
- Theater
- Culinary events
- Sea Turtle Benefit

Treatment Team Meetings

Campuswide treatment team meetings are held weekly. The meetings are designed to address the clinical needs of all girls committed to the youth development center. The program director of HEART participates in the weekly meetings and discusses the clinical needs of the participants of HEART. In addition, monthly HEART treatment team meetings are held. At that time, selected members of the HEART staff meet with respective participants to review individualized treatment plans, discuss treatment progress, and, if needed, plan remedial or corrective measures.

Therapeutic Community Meetings

These meetings are convened every day at 1:00 P.M. Staff and participants convene to discuss daily progress and cottage events. Participants and staff are given an opportunity to express their ideas and opinions, and to comment on other participants' or team members' strengths. In addition, participants are apprised of program changes or upcoming events.

Family Meetings and Gatherings

Monthly Lunch and Learn series are held during the last Sunday of each month. Lunch and Learn series are designed to provide information to families in an informal setting, while sharing a meal, when parents come to visit their children. These brief (30 minutes) psychoeducational sessions provide information about substance abuse, family issues, boundaries, and a variety of other topics. Additionally, family members are encouraged to attend multi-family group meetings and take part in special events and celebrations pertaining to their child or family member who is a participant of HEART.

Summary

As a whole, these core and secondary interventions comprise the therapeutic milieu of the HEART program. To facilitate an understanding of the therapeutic milieu, we present a 5-day schedule, outlining the daily therapeutic regimen that occurred during the week of August 15 to 19, 2005 (Table 9.3).

Strengths-Based Approach

The therapeutic interventions are embedded in a strengths-based approach. By using a strengths-based approach, the staff of HEART can assess, recognize, and examine each participant's strengths. To assess strengths and assets, strengths-based questioning is used. This line of questioning takes the following form: Tell me about your friends? When you have solved problems successfully in the past, what was done? How did you feel? How do you cope with [a given situation]? In times of need or distress, whom do you contact? When you handle problems well, how do you do it? This form of questioning affords staff an opportunity to aid participants in identifying and building on their strengths. Additionally, by asking these types of strengths-based questions, staff is engaging in a treatment approach referred to as "Something So Strong Within" (Strantz & Welch, 1995).

EVALUATION COMPONENT OF THE HOLISTIC ENRICHMENT FOR AT-RISK TEENS PROGRAM

Having a strong evaluative component has been posited to be a hallmark of a good substance abuse treatment program (Weinman & Dignam, 2002). The HEART program has an evaluative component to assess its treatment effectiveness. A quasi-experimental design is used to address the primary research question: Did the HEART program improve the psychosocial outcomes of participants? To study the effects of the program, the participants (the treatment group) are compared to comparison and control groups on pre- and posttest measures. The comparison group receives less intensive substance abuse treatment,

Table 9.3   HEART Daily Schedule: Week of August 15–August 19, 2005*

Monday

7:45 A.M.	Affirmation/goal setting—student
8:00 A.M.	Breakfast
8:30 A.M.	Move to school
10:30 A.M.	Break and snack (snacks provided by cafeteria)
10:45 A.M.	Blended education
11:50 A.M.	Lunch
12:20 P.M.	Blended education
1:15 P.M.	Honor/transition student present essays/workshops (Gibson)
2:00 P.M.	Monroe's group (Life Skills)
3:00 P.M.	MPAC/outdoor exercise
4:00 P.M.	Shift change/report (swimming, if Kinney is here)
5:05 P.M.	Dinner
5:30 P.M.	Prepare for group
6:00 P.M.	Group activity (ACOA discussions) Kirby and Crump (divide the groups)
7:00 P.M.	Showers/cottage clean-up (Crump/Kirby) (NA-Townsend/Farnsworth)
8:00 P.M.	Free time/journaling/community closure groups
9:00 P.M.	In rooms/lights out shortly before 10:00 P.M.

Tuesday

1:15 P.M.	Heart Manual and Heart Rules review (Farnsworth)
2:00 P.M.	Howell's arts and crafts
3:00 P.M.	Gibson and Black's exercise group
4:00 P.M.	Shift change/report
4:15 P.M.	Kinney's swimming (if rain, MPAC)
5:00 P.M.	Dinner
5:30 P.M.	Group (women's issue) (Townsend)
6:30 P.M.	Spiritual wellness group (Chaplain Wicker and guest)
7:30 P.M.	Showers/chores
8:00 P.M.	Free time/journaling/community group closure (Herndon)
8:30 P.M.	Individual counseling/free time

Wednesday

1:15 P.M.	Trust group—Gibson (Honors and Transition) Covington (Adjustment and Orientation)
2:00 P.M.	Covington's substance abuse group

*This is a summer schedule, thus the additional outdoor activities.

(continued)

Table 9.3 *(Continued)*

3:00 P.M.	Recreation—large muscle outside (Black and Covington)
4:00 P.M.	Shift change—girls in rooms
4:15 P.M.	Kinney's swimming (if rain, MPAC) (hair shop)
5:00 P.M.	Dinner
5:30 P.M.	Healing and Grief group through photography (Toni Manus, Wicker, Kirby) Herndon's group/or Townsend's group
7:00 P.M.	Showers/chores (groups to run while others are in the shower)
8:00 P.M.	Free time/clean-up
8:30 P.M.	Individual counseling/free time

Thursday

1:15 P.M.	Arts and crafts (Howell)
2:00 P.M.	Monroe's female health group
3:00 P.M.	Large muscle recreation (Covington and Farnsworth)
4:00 P.M.	Shift change—girls in rooms
4:15 P.M.	Kinney's swimming (if rain, MPAC)
5:05 P.M.	Dinner
5:30 P.M.	Strategies for learning communications—"I" statements (Crump and students)
6:15 P.M.	Farnworth's group (Substance abuse topic)
7:00 P.M.	Showers/chores /or NA (Crump and Herndon)
8:00 P.M.	Free time/clean-up (Townsend/Farnsworth)
8:30 P.M.	Individual counseling/free time

Friday

1:15 P.M.	Black's substance abuse group
2:00 P.M.	Monroe's social skills group
3:00 P.M.	Outdoor yardwork/ Too hot/ Indoor exercise (Covington and Black)
4:00 P.M.	Shift change—girls in rooms
4:15 P.M.	Kinney's swimming (if rain, MPAC)
5:00 P.M.	Dinner
5:30 P.M.	Canteen
6:15 P.M.	Townsend's group (female issues group) TBA)
7:00 P.M.	Showers/chores (Herndon/Townsend) NA—Crump/Kirby/Farnsworth
8:00 P.M.	Treatment movie with processing activities (preapproved) intervention movie/or substitute.

and the control group receives substance abuse prevention services. In addition, psychosocial, recidivism, and substance use data are collected at 3-, 6-, and 12-month intervals (after discharge) to assess the effects of the program.

Preliminary Findings

We present preliminary findings on the cognitive, behavioral, psychosocial, and educational changes of HEART participants based on data gathered from focus groups, individual treatment sessions, and standardized assessments. Assessments are the primary mechanisms for monitoring treatment progress and treatment effectiveness.

Cognitive and Behavioral Changes

Data on cognitive and behavioral changes were gathered from focus groups and the URICA Modified Measure (McConnaughy, Prochaska, & Velicer, 1983), a standardized assessment tool used by HEART counselors to monitor and assess residents' behavioral and skill attainment and to determine whether a resident's request for progression to an advance level within the HEART's levels system is warranted. The following domains are assessed: cognitive concentration, overt aggression, social involvement, social competence, relational aggression, consequential thinking skills, critical thinking skills, goal-setting skills, problem-solving skills, self-monitoring skills, self-control skills, and prosocial skills. Initial findings from the standardized assessment indicated positive outcomes for each resident as she moved through the program's levels system.

Some of the marked cognitive and behavioral changes described by residents, via focus group, were how they viewed themselves and their respective situations; how they responded to situations, experiences, and people; and how they gained insight into their particular experiences. To illustrate these cognitive and behavioral changes, we present some of the residents' statements regarding what they learned and how they changed since being a resident of the HEART community:

Cognitive and Emotional Effects

I have learned about depression and how I can get help. I never knew why I always felt so sad.

It is good to know that I can get help. I found out I was not the only one that felt crazy!

I no longer think that people are talking about me when I see two or three girls whispering.

My relationship really improved with the other girls when we did the "ropes course" trip. I had to learn how to trust somebody else in order to finish that course.

I have learned that the entire family needs help. I wish we could stop blaming each other and start healing.

Behavioral Effects

I have learned that you don't always have to approach disagreements with fist-fighting. I used to think this was the only way to handle anger. I really thought everyone handled anger like that.

It has been more than a year since I stopped cutting myself. I have learned different ways of coping with my feelings instead of cutting my body.

I have learned how to recognize a feeling and deal with it, instead of "flipping."

I can tell with more treatment that my aggressive behaviors have decreased.

Taken together, the preliminary findings indicate that the cognitive-behavioral approaches and other treatment approaches used in the HEART program appear to be effective in the modulation of behavior and emotions among participants. Additionally, the treatment approaches appear to assist participants in having a healthy appraisal of themselves and the world, and in embracing and accepting their emotions.

Changes in Psychosocial and Mental Health Functioning

At discharge, preliminary findings indicated that participants of the HEART program had better psychosocial outcomes—as measured by the Multidimensional Adolescent Assessment Scale (MAAS; Mathiesen, Scottye, & Hudson, 2002)—than girls in the control and comparison groups. The MAAS is a self-report measurement tool that measures adolescents' personal, psychological, and social functioning. Scores are generated across 16 domains: depression, self-esteem, problems with mother, problems with father, personal stress, problems with friends, problems with school, aggression, family relationship problems, suicidal thoughts, feelings of guilt, confused thinking, disturbing thoughts, memory loss, alcohol abuse, and drug abuse.

Participants of the HEART program made significant and positive changes in all domains of psychosocial functioning. Conversely, in many domains, the level of psychosocial functioning of participants in the comparison and control group remained unchanged, and in some domains their level of psychosocial functioning decreased.

Educational Progress

As stated previously, reengagement in the learning process is one of the primary goals of the HEART program. Based on the 16 girls who have reentered the community, 10 students completed their GED (two with honors); three students enrolled in online community college courses; all students in seventh and eithth grades passed their end-of-grade tests; and all English I students passed their end-of-course exams.

CHALLENGES OF IMPLEMENTING THE HOLISTIC ENRICHMENT FOR AT-RISK TEENS PROGRAM

Although the participants of the HEART program have been demonstrating promising outcomes, the program has not been without its challenges and setbacks, specifically in the early part of the implementation phase. In the initial implementation phase, it was difficult for staff to make the transition from a correctional model to a treatment model. As expected, the change in modality was often met with a high level of skepticism. Staff had to be trained on the importance of transitioning from punitive approaches to therapeutic approaches and on understanding the differences between the two approaches in terms of process and outcomes. Training consisted of teaching staff to look for strengths rather than focus on deficits, responding to situations therapeutically, and integrating the new treatment model into the existing environment.

Existing challenges include engaging families in the treatment process and collecting follow-up data on girls who have graduated from the program. Engaging and involving families in the treatment process are integral to participants' recovery process. Staff members have aggressively reached out to family members and have had some success, but more families need to be involved in the treatment process. Difficulty engaging families arises from several factors:

- Strained or disruptive relationships between participants and family members
- Family difficulties that have contributed to the substance abuse and delinquent trajectories of participants
- Family resistance to treatment
- Physical distance—the youth development center is located in a rural remote area, which makes it difficult for families to visit residents, attend meetings and family therapeutic sessions, and take part in special celebrations.

Staff members are also aware that many participants have home environments that are not conducive to their recovery process.

In terms of collecting follow-up data, it has been difficult to maintain contact with HEART graduates to obtain follow-up data. Once girls have been discharged from Post-Release Supervision—a process during which they are monitored by the North Carolina Department of Juvenile Justice and Delinquency Prevention Court counselors for a minimal period of 3 months after release—it becomes increasingly difficult to locate girls because of residential changes, changes in phone numbers, or runaway status. Additionally, wraparound services, which are planned for each participant well in advance of reentry to the community, have occasionally been disrupted because of the mental health reform that is currently underway in the state of North Carolina. The state's mental health reform, which will most likely be more effective in the future, has resulted in changes in service delivery, which in turn has affected the delivery of services. Consequently, it has become difficult to deliver and provide aftercare services in an effective, efficient, and expeditious manner.

Moreover, as with other programs in correctional settings, the HEART program is not immune to staff turnovers, scarce resources, legislative mandates, and the mandates of the wider correctional facility. All these factors affect the implementation and evaluation of the HEART program.

CONCLUSIONS

By subscribing to a multimodal intervention approach, the HEART program appears to be improving the psychosocial functioning of incarcerated adolescents with co-occurring substance abuse and mental health disorders. Preliminary findings indicate that the HEART program is ameliorating some of the cognitive, behavioral, and psychosocial difficulties faced by its participants. It is hoped that the positive changes in psychosocial functioning and educational outcomes among participants will translate into long-term decreases in substance use and delinquency, and increases in prosocial behaviors and academic and vocational success.

Moreover, preliminary findings also support model efficacy. In essence, the HEART program seems to be a promising intervention for addressing the psychosocial needs of incarcerated girls with co-occurring substance abuse and mental health disorders and other related problems.

The HEART program is still in its infancy, thus, evolving. As such, we recognize that there is a need to integrate more specialized services to strengthen the existing therapeutic milieu. For example, an intensive HIV/AIDS group intervention is needed because girls with substance abuse disorders are at high risk of engaging in behaviors that make them highly susceptible to contracting HIV. Additionally, because a high proportion of girls at the youth development center have experienced sexual victimization and other forms of trauma, a more intensive specialized trauma-focused intervention is needed. With the inclusion of these specialized programs, the added support and engagement of families, and the consideration and analyses of challenges, the promising outcomes of the HEART program can be sustained.

REFERENCES

Acoca, L. (1999). Investing in girls: A 21st-century strategy. *Juvenile Justice, 6*(1), 3–13.

Altschuler, D. M., Armstrong, T. L., & MacKenzie, D. L. (1999). *Reintegration, supervised release, and intensive aftercare.* Washington, DC: Office of Juvenile Justice and Delinquency Prevention.

American Bar Association and National Bar Association. (2001). *Justice by gender: The lack of appropriate prevention, diversion, and treatment alternatives for girls in the juvenile justice system.* Washington, DC: Author.

Amey, C. H., Albrecht, S. L., & Miller, M. K. (1996). Racial differences in adolescent drug use: The impact of religion. *Substance Use and Misuse, 31,* 1311–1332.

Angelou, M. (1994). *Phenomenal woman: Four poems celebrating women.* New York: Random House.

Bandura, A. (1977). *Social learning theory.* New York: General Learning Press.

Barr, H. (1986). Outcome of drug abuse treatment on two modalities. In G. DeLeon & J. T. Ziegenfuss (Eds.), *Therapeutic communities for addictions* (pp. 66–79). Springfield, IL: Charles C Thomas.

Beck, A., Wright, F. D., Newman, C. F., & Liese, B. S. (1993). *Cognitive therapy of substance abuse.* New York: Guilford Press.

Belknap, J., Holsinger, K., & Dunn, M. (1997). Understanding incarcerated girls: The results of a focus group study. *Prison Journal, 77*(4), 381–404.

Bloom, B., Owen, B., Deschenes, E., & Rosenbaum, J. (2002). Improving juvenile justice for females: A statewide assessment in California. *Crime and Delinquency, 48*(4), 526–552.

Calhoun, G., Jurgens, J., & Chen, F. (1993). The neophyte female delinquent: A review of the literature. *Adolescent, 28*(110), 461–471.

Carroll, K. (1998). *A cognitive behavioral approach: Treating cocaine addiction.* Rockville, MD: National Institute on Drug Abuse.

Cauffman, E., Feldman, S., Waterman, J., & Steiner, H. (1998). Posttraumatic stress disorder among female juvenile offenders. *Child and Adolescent Psychiatry, 37*(11), 1209–1216.

Chesney-Lind, M. (1998). *Girls, delinquency, and juvenile justice* (3rd ed.). Belmont, CA: Wadsworth/Thomson Learning.

Condelli, W. S., & Hubbard, R. L. (1994). Client outcomes from therapeutic communities. In F. M. Tims, G. DeLeon, & N. Jainchill (Eds.), *Therapeutic community: Advances in research and application* (pp. 80–98). Washington, DC: U.S. Government printing office.

Covington, S. (2003). *Beyond trauma: A healing journey for women: Facilitator's guide.* Center City, MN: Hazelden.

Deitch, D., Carleton, S., Koutsenok, I., & Marsolais, K. (2002). Therapeutic community treatment in prisons. In C. Leufkield, F. Tims, & D. Farabee (Eds.), *Treatment of drug offenders* (pp. 127–137). New York: Springer.

DeLeon, G. (1984). Therapeutic communities for addictions: A theoretical framework. *International Journal of the Addictions, 30*(12), 1603–1645.

DeLeon, G. (1993). Modified therapeutic communities for dual disorders. In J. Solomon, S. Zimberg, & E. Shollar (Eds.), *Dual diagnosis: Evaluation, treatment, training, and program development* (pp. 5–18). New York: Plenum Medical Book.

DeLeon, G. (2000). *The therapeutic community: Theory, model, and method.* New York: Springer.

Department of Health and Human Services. (1993). *Treatment of adolescents with substance use.* Rockville, MD: Author.

Eccles, J., & Barber, B. (1999). Student council, volunteering, basketball, or marching band: What kind of extracurricular involvement matters? *Journal of Adolescent Research, 14*, 10–43.

Evans, M. (1970). *I am a Black woman.* New York: Morrow Company.

Finkelstein, N., Kennedy, C., Thomas, K., & Kearns, M. (1997). *Gender-specific substance abuse treatment.* Rockville, MD: Center for Substance Abuse Prevention.

Freitas, K., & Chesney-Lind, M. (2001). Differences doesn't mean difficult: Practitioners talk about working with girls. *Women, Girls, and Criminal Justice, 2,* 65–67.

Gerstein, D. R., & Harwood, H. J. (1990). *Treating drug problems.* Washington, DC: National Academy Press.

Goldstein, N., Arnold, D., Weil, J., Mesiarik, C., Peuschold, D., Grisso, T., et al. (2003). Co-morbid symptom patterns in female juvenile offenders. *International Journal of Law and Psychiatry, 26,* 565–582.

Greenfield, S. F. (2002). Women and alcohol use disorders. *Harvard Review of Psychiatry, 10*(2), 76–85.

Guthrie, B. J., & Flinchbaugh, L. (2001). Gender-specific substance prevention programming: Going beyond just focusing on girls. *Journal of Early Adolescence, 21*(3), 354–372.

Hodge, D. R., Cardenas, P., & Montoya, H. (2001). Substance use: Spirituality and religious participation as protective factors among rural youth. *Social Work Research, 25*(3), 153–161.

Hommer, D., Momenan, R., Kaiser, E., & Rawlings, R. (2001). Evidence for a gender-related effect of alcoholism on brain volumes. *American Journal of Psychiatry, 158,* 198–204.

Huizinga, D., Loeber, R., & Thornberry, T. P. (1994). *Urban delinquency and substance abuse: Initial findings research summary.* Washington, DC: Office of Juvenile Justice and Delinquency Prevention.

Jackson, M. S., & Knepper, P. (2003). *Delinquency and justice: A cultural perspective.* Boston: Pearson Education.

Jenson, J. M., Potter, C. C., & Howard, M. O. (2001). American juvenile justice: Recent trends and issues in youth offending. *Social Policy and Administration, 35,* 48–68.

Kataoka, S., Zima, T., Dupre, D., Moreno, K., Yang, X., & McCracken, J. (2001). Mental health problems and service use among female juvenile offenders: Their relationship to criminal history. *Journal of the American Academy of Child and Adolescent Psychiatry, 40,* 549–555.

Kutter, C. J., & McDermott, D. S. (1997). The role of the church in adolescent drug education. *Journal of Drug Education, 27*(3), 293–305.

Lerner, R. M., & Galambos, N. L. (1998). Adolescent development: Challenges and opportunities for research, programs, and policies. *Annual Review of Psychology, 49,* 413–446.

Mahoney, J. L., & Stattin, H. (2000, April 23). Leisure activities and adolescent antisocial behavioral role of structure and social context. *Journal of Adolescence, 23*(2), 113–127.

Mathiesen, S. G., Scottye, J. C., & Hudson, W. (2002). The multidimensional adolescent assessment scale: A validation study. *Research on Social Work Practice, 12,* 9–28.

McCabe, K., Lansing, A., Garland, A., & Hough, R. (2002). Gender differences in psychopathology, functional impairment, and familial risk factors among adjudicated delinquents. *Journal of the American Academy of Child and Adolescent Psychiatry, 41*(7), 860–867.

McConnaughy, E. A., Prochaska, J. O., & Velicer, W. F. (1983). Stages of change in psychotherapy: Measurement and sample profiles. *Psychotherapy: Theory, Research, and Practice, 20,* 368–375.

McNamus, M., Alessi, N. E., Grapentine, W. L., & Brickman, A. (1984). Psychiatric disturbance in serious delinquents. *Journal of the American Academy of Child Psychiatry, 23,* 602–615.

Miller, B. A. (1986). *Toward a new psychology of women.* Boston: Beacon Press.

Molidor, C. E., Nissen, L., & Watkins, R. (2002). The development of theory and treatment with substance abusing female juvenile offenders. *Child and Adolescent Social Work, 19*(3), 209–225.

National Center on Addiction and Substance Abuse at Columbia University. (2003). *The formative years: Pathways to substance abuse among girls and young women ages 8–22.* New York: Author.

National Mental Health Association. (2001). *Mental health and adolescent girls in the juvenile justice system.* Washington, DC: Author.

Office of Juvenile Justice and Delinquency Prevention. (1998). *Guiding principles for promising female programming: An inventory of best practices.* Washington, DC: Author.

Office of Juvenile Justice and Delinquency Prevention. (2000). *Detention in delinquency cases 1988–1997.* Washington, DC: Author.

Owen, B., & Bloom, B. (1997). *Profiling the needs of young female offenders: A protocol and pilot study.* Washington, DC: National Institute of Justice.

Potter, C. (1999). Violence and aggression in girls. In J. M. Jenson & M. O. Howard (Eds.), *Youth violence: Current research and recent practice innovations* (pp. 113–138). Washington, DC: National Association of Social Workers Press.

Prescott, L. (1997). *Adolescent girls with co-occurring disorders in the juvenile justice system.* Delmar, NY: GAINS Center.

Regoli, R. M., & Hewitt, J. (2003). *Delinquency in society* (5th ed.). New York: McGraw-Hill.

Reneman, L., Booij, J., de Bruin, K., Reitsma, J. B., de Wolff, F. A., Gunning, W. B., et al. (2001). Effects of dose, sex, and long-term abstention from use on toxic effects of MDMA (ecstasy) on brain serotonin neurons. *Lancet, 358*(9296), 1864–1869.

Robinson, T., Rowan, M., & Rapport, J. K. (1999). Providing special education in the juvenile justice system. *Remedial and Special Education, 20,* 19–35.

Roth, S. (Ed.). (1994). *Bridges: Bright fires creative writing program.* San Bernardino, CA. Unpublished manuscript.

Royce-Baerger, Lyons, J., Quigley, P., & Griffin, E. (2001). Responding to juvenile delinquency: Mental health service needs of males and female juvenile detainees. *Journal of the Center for Children and the Courts, 3,* 21–29.

Senna, J., & Siegel, L. (2001). *Essentials of criminal justice* (3rd ed.). Belmont, CA: Wadsworth.

Snyder, H., & Sickmund, M. (1999). *Juvenile offenders and victims: 1999 national report.* Washington, DC: Office of Juvenile Justice and Delinquency and Prevention.

Sondheimer, D. (2001, Winter). Young female offenders. *Gender Issues,* 79–90.

Spatz-Widom, C. (2000). Childhood victimization and the derailment of girls and women to the criminal justice system. In *Research on women and girls in the justice system: Plenary papers of the 1999 conference on criminal justice research and evaluation—Enhancing policy and practice through research* (Vol. 3, NCJ-180973). Washington, DC: U.S. Department of Justice, National Institute of Justice.

Strantz, I. H., & Welch, S. P. (1995). Postpartum women in outpatient drug abuse treatment: Correlates of retention/completion. *Journal of Psychoactive Drugs, 27,* 357–373.

Walrath, C., Ybarra, M., Holden, W., Manteuffel, B., Santiago, R., & Leaf, P. (2003). Female offenders referred for community-based mental health service as compared to other service-referred youth: Correlates of conviction. *Journal of Adolescence, 26,* 45–61.

Weiler, J. (1999). *Girls and violence.* New York: Institute for Urban and Minority Education. (ERIC Document Reproduction Service No. ED-99-CO-0035)

Weinman, B., & Dignam, J. (2002). Drug abuse treatment programs in the Federal Bureau past, present, and future directions. In C. Leufkield, F. Tims, & D. Farabee (Eds.), *Treatment of drug offenders* (pp. 91–104). New York: Springer.

Zocolilo, M., & Rogers, K. (1991). Characteristics and outcomes of hospitalized adolescent girls with conduct disorder. *Journal of the American Academy of Child and Adolescent Psychiatry, 30,* 973–981.

Chapter 10

EMPIRICALLY VALIDATED APPROACHES TO FAMILY TREATMENT FOR ADOLESCENT GIRLS

JACQUELINE CORCORAN AND JANE PHILLIPS

Female adolescents are at risk for several major health and mental health problems, including sexual abuse, eating disorders, and depression. They are also vulnerable to the disruptive behavior disorders and substance abuse. This chapter focuses on the impact of the family on these problems and of intervention through a family approach. Culled from this literature and the research on female adolescents, the chapter concludes with some guidelines for family treatment with teenage girls.

OVERVIEW OF PROBLEMS

Sexual Abuse

Sexual abuse occurs at high rates for females. A meta-analysis of prevalence studies conducted in North America has found that 30% to 40% of females have been abused, compared to 13% of their male counterparts (Bolen & Scannapieco, 1999). A particular risk factor for sexual abuse is when it occurs in the context of the family (Wolfe, 1998). A protective factor associated with recovery involves the nonoffending parent's support of the sexually abused child (Bolen, 2002). However, adolescent girls are particularly at risk of nonsupportiveness by mothers (Heriot, 1996). The mother of an adolescent may have difficulty believing her daughter's account of the abuse because of other problems she may be having with her; the mother may see the disclosure as another way the girl is making problems in the family, for purposes of attention seeking, manipulation, or retaliation for punishment. Some mothers may believe that their daughters played a role in the sexual involvement, and were "old enough to know better" (Heriot, 1996, p. 191). If the abuse involves the mother's partner, it may arouse jealousy and competitive feelings.

Treatment involving the nonoffending caregiver (typically the mother) has received empirical support (Corcoran, 2004). However, treatment samples have included only preschool and school-age children. No studies have been conducted with adolescents, despite the needs of teenage girls for maternal support and the risk that sexual abuse may play for the development of other problems, including depression (Brown, Cohen, Johnson, & Smailes, 1999; Fergusson, Horwood, & Lynskey, 1996), eating disorders (Yager et al., 2002), and conduct problems (Hubbard & Pratt, 2002).

Depression

Beginning in adolescence, rates of depression for females are double those for males (Lewinsohn & Essau, 2002). Reviews have indicated lifetime prevalence rates for adolescent depression ranging from 15% to 20% (Lewinsohn & Essau, 2002). Point prevalence rates for major depression in adolescent depression are estimated at between 4% and 8.3%; for dysthymia, point prevalence rates range from 2% to 5% (Birmaher, Ryan, Williamson, Brent, & Kaufman, 1996; Cottrell, Fonagy, Kurtz, Phillips, & Target, 2002). According to the 2003 Youth Risk Behavior Surveillance, adolescent girls (35.5%) were also significantly more likely than teen boys (21.9%) to report feeling sad and hopeless almost every day for 2 weeks or more (Centers for Disease Control and Prevention [CDC], 2004). In addition, they were significantly more likely to have thoughts about committing suicide (21.3% for females versus 12.8% for males), and attempted suicide (11.5% for females versus 5.4% for males).

Aside from abuse, other family factors can present risk for the development, maintenance, and relapse of depression in youth (Diamond, Reis, Diamond, Siqueland, & Isaacs, 2002). Several research reviews found that families with an adolescent who is depressed show the following (Diamond et al., 2002): weak attachment bonds (Sund & Wichstrom, 2002); criticism and hostility; parental psychopathology; ineffective parenting; enmeshed family relationships (Jewell & Stark, 2003); and greater family stress (Asarnow, Jaycox, & Tompson, 2001).

Depression in mothers is a particular risk factor (Beardslee, Versage, & Gladstone, 1998), for various psychosocial reasons (Duggal, Carlson, Sroufe, & Egeland, 2001; Goodman & Gotlib, 1999). Maternal needs for nurturing and care can interfere with a mother's ability to meet children's emotional and social needs. Mothers may be emotionally uninvolved, unavailable, and feel a sense of helplessness in the midst of parenting challenges. Parents may model depressive affect, thinking patterns, and behaviors for their children and then reinforce the presence of depressive behaviors in their children. Depressed parents also tend to see their children's behavior in a negative light, using low rates of reward and high rates of punishment, or responding indiscriminately to the child's behavior. Finally, women with depression often experience high rates of marital discord, which, in turn, exposes children to high levels of parental conflict (Goodman &

Gotlib, 1999). Marital problems are also associated with an increased risk for depression in children (Beardslee et al., 1998).

Despite the known links between family factors and depression in youth, few studies have explored family-based interventions. In a couple of studies, a parenting component was added to cognitive-behavioral group intervention for adolescents with depression, but no particular benefits were gained by doing so (Clarke, Rohde, Lewinsohn, Hops, & Seeley, 1999; Lewinsohn, Clarke, Hops, & Andrews, 1990). In a study of family therapy for depression in adolescents (about 75% of the sample was female), subjects were randomly assigned to 12 to 16 weeks of cognitive-behavioral therapy, systemic behavioral family therapy, or nondirective supportive therapy (Birmaher et al., 2000). At 2 years posttest, there were no statistically significant differences between the three groups, with the majority of subjects (80%) recovering from depression. Family conflict was one of the factors associated with lack of recovery. In an evidence-based review of assessment and treatment of depression in children and adolescents, Klein, Dougherty, and Olino (2005) conclude that family approaches are not recommended for adolescent depression.

Eating Disorders

Eating disorders, although not limited to females, primarily present in girls and women, starting in adolescence. A review of surveys conducted both in the United States and England indicates a prevalence rate for bulimia nervosa, purging type, of 1% to 3% of adult females. In the United States, a prevalence rate of 3% of high school females has been found (Compas, Haaga, Keefe, Leitenberg, & Williams, 1998). The prevalence of anorexia among females is approximately 0.5%. In addition to diagnosable disorders, widespread body dissatisfaction is found among female samples. According to the 2003 Youth Risk Behavior Surveillance (CDC, 2004), female high school students were significantly more likely than male students to consider themselves overweight (36.1% of females versus 23.5% of males), to try to lose weight (59.3% of females versus 29.1% of males), and to have fasted for at least 24 hours to lose weight (18.3% of females versus 8.5% of males).

Different causal processes within the family environment may be implicated in the development of eating disorders. A history of sexual abuse is found in 20% to 50% of individuals with eating disorders, and often this abuse occurs in the context of the family (Yager et al., 2002). Though no specific patterns have been identified, families in which eating disorders develop tend to be more hostile, conflicted, isolated, lacking in cohesion, enmeshed, and less supportive and nurturing (Mizes & Palermo, 1997). Another factor involving families is the transmission of the societal emphasis on weight and appearance (Streigel-Moore & Cachelin, 1999). For instance, when parents are excessively concerned about their own, as well as their children's, shape and size, they may tease or pressure the child to lose weight (Kotler, Cohen, Davies, Pine, & Walsh, 2001; Mizes & Palermo, 1997).

The research on family intervention with eating disorders lacks methodological rigor, so it is difficult to draw conclusions about family work. There is, however, a consensus among practitioners that family involvement should be part of the treatment plan, at least for younger adolescents with anorexia (Crisp et al., 1991; Robin, Siegel, & Moye, 1995; Robin et al., 1999). Family involvement means that parents can participate in either collateral (separate from the client) or conjoint sessions (with the client and/or the whole family). Critical comments from parents need to be brought under control before conjoint family work can take place, however, because these are associated with dropout (e.g., Szmukler & Dare, 1991) and poor outcome (e.g., Butzlaff & Hooley, 1998; Szmukler & Dare, 1991; Van Furth et al., 1996). Critical comments comprise one aspect of *expressed emotion,* a measure of the family's affective communication.

A methodologically rigorous study has been conducted more recently on family therapy with anorexia nervosa (Lock, Agras, Bryson, & Kraemer, 2005). The researchers found that short-term treatment (10 sessions over 6 months) was as efficacious as long-term treatment (20 sessions over 12 months). However, nonintact families responded more favorably to long-term treatment.

Externalizing Disorders

So far, this discussion has centered on disorders and problems that girls are more likely to experience than their male counterparts. We turn now to the disruptive disorders—oppositional defiant disorder (ODD), conduct disorder (CD), and attention-deficit/hyperactivity disorder (ADHD)—and substance use disorders. Although these disorders are more likely in males, they also have female representation. Indeed, rates of ODD are equal among genders after puberty (APA, 2000), possibly because females after that time tend to become involved with antisocial males as partners (Burke, Loeber, & Lahey, 2003; Moffit, Caspi, Rutter, & Silva, 2001). In addition, rates of CD are likely underdiagnosed in females. The female presentation of CD tends to be less noticeable because nonaggressive, covert behaviors are involved (Hinshaw & Anderson, 1996; Loeber, Burke, Lahey, Winters, & Zera, 2000).

While many of the identified risk factors for juvenile offending are similar for males and females, family relationships and a history of sexual and/or physical abuse play an attenuated role in the development of delinquency for girls (Hubbard & Pratt, 2002). When examining treatment, Brestan and Eyberg (1998) conducted a comprehensive literature review of the ODD/CD treatment literature and found a much larger proportion of boys than girls represented in studies, at a ratio of 5 to 1. The authors concluded, given the lack of study on differential male and female response to treatment, that little valid information exists to guide treatment decisions for girls. Clearly there is a need for research into gender-specific treatment outcomes because CD in girls may result in serious consequences such as antisocial personality disorder, involvement with an antisocial partner, and teen pregnancy, which in turn increase the risk for behavior problems in offspring (Loeber et al., 2000).

One family-based intervention, multisystemic treatment (MST), has been developed specifically for adolescents in the juvenile justice system. MST has been extensively studied; approximately 800 families have participated in the intervention (Henggeler, Schoenwald, Rowland, & Cunningham, 2002). Several prominent national organizations—including the National Institute of Mental Health, the National Institute on Drug Abuse, the Center for Substance Abuse Prevention, and the Office of Juvenile Justice and Delinquency Prevention—promote MST as a model community program because of its strong empirical support (Henggeler et al., 2002). However, a more recent, systematic analysis of the data indicates that treatment outcomes are not as strong as previously reported (Littell, Popa, & Forsythe, 2005). Indeed, among the various outcome measures across studies, only in number of arrests did the treatment group show significant reductions from "treatment as usual." Although samples in the MST studies are typically male, it appears that females do as well as their male counterparts when undergoing this treatment (Scott Henggeler, personal communication, August 1, 2005).

A meta-analysis was conducted on the impact of family treatment on juvenile offending (Latimer, 2001). Although treatment was more successful for females than for males, the author concluded that the overall support for family intervention was not "convincing."

A similar pattern—lack of knowledge regarding treatment for girls—exists in the area of ADHD. When examining family treatment for ADHD, studies have comprised mainly male samples, giving us little information on the family therapy models that might be effective for girls (Corcoran & Dattalo, 2006). In addition, recent reviews of ADHD in adolescence offered no particular guidelines for girls (Barkley, 2004; Wolraich et al., 2005).

Substance Abuse

Among youths aged 12 to 17, the rate of substance abuse and dependence among females (9%) is comparable to that of the rates of males (8.7%) (Substance Abuse and Mental Health Services Administration [SAMHSA], 2005). Family factors (such as parental substance abuse and unemployment; permissive attitudes toward teen substance use; harsh, inconsistent, and ineffective discipline strategies; lack of monitoring and supervision; impaired bonding; and child abuse) explain much of the proportion of variance of teen use (Hopfer, Stallings, Hewitt, & Crowley, 2003). For adolescent substance use treatment, family-based interventions have been highly recommended as outpatient approaches (Vaughn & Howard, 2004; Waldron, 1997; Williams, Chang, & Addiction Centre Adolescent Research Group, 2000). Research, however, has typically been limited to males. For example, two recent systematic reviews on substance abuse treatment for adolescents made no mention of treatment for girls (Austin, Macgowan, & Wagner, 2005; Vaughn & Howard, 2004).

GUIDELINES FOR FAMILY TREATMENT WITH ADOLESCENT GIRLS

The most obvious conclusion to draw from this literature is that little is known about empirically validated family treatment for adolescent girls. An additional review was conducted of the literature, using such search terms as: *family conflict (discord), communication skills training, and problem-solving (negotiation skills),* and *adolescent (teen/teenage) girls (females),* but no new information was located. An obvious research recommendation is that more study needs to be conducted on family intervention with adolescent girls. In addition, when research is conducted on both male and female subjects in studies, the impact of family treatment on outcome should be performed separately for gender groups.

As well as these research recommendations, the following clinical guidelines for family work with adolescent girls are tentatively offered:

- Family work is important, given the importance of relationships and connection for most adolescent girls (Jordan, 2005).
- Assess for sexual abuse and offer treatment involving the nonoffending parent. Given the high rates of sexual abuse for girls and the potentially deleterious impact of such abuse, abuse issues need to be targeted in treatment. Family treatment to include the nonoffending parent (typically, the mother) is critical so that maternal support can help girls' adjustment.

- When seeing teenage girls for clinical problems, the social worker should assess for and offer treatment and referrals for parental adjustment problems, especially depression, marital problems, and addictions. Any addiction patterns in the parents must be recognized and, if possible, treated. It is, of course, recognized, that parents are often resistant to focusing on their own problems when they bring in their teenagers for treatment. The clinician must use considerable finesse in addressing such problems, perhaps focusing on the child initially and then moving to parents' issues, and take nonthreatening approaches, such as motivational interviewing and solution-focused therapy.

- Offer families with teenage girls communication skills training to reduce criticism and hostility, which may be detrimental to treatment goals. In addition, mothers should be clear in their communications about certain issues. For example, the research indicates that parental disapproval of premarital sexuality needs to be conveyed directly to girls in order to impact their sexual behavior, and that it needs to occur in the context of a close mother-daughter relationship (Jaccard, Dittus, & Gordon, 1996).

- Teach appropriate boundaries and be clear about rules and consequences. Guidance and monitoring are necessary, particularly when it comes to dating relationships, because premature sexuality and pregnancy are possible concerns. In addition, the conduct problems literature indicates that female involvement with antisocial partners leads to possible antisocial behaviors in these girls (Burke et al., 2003; Moffit et al., 2001).

  Firm yet permeable boundaries between parents and children are important for all families so that the division between parental authority and children is clear. This is particularly important with single-parent families. One study, for example, indicated that when mothers rely on their daughters as confidantes about divorce, impaired teen girl adjustment is a result (Koerner, Wallace, Lehman, & Raymond, 2002). The clinician must also recognize that nonintact families may not respond as well (Corcoran & Dattalo, 2006; Fonagy & Kurtz, 2002) or as quickly (Lock et al., 2005) as intact families to treatment. Although this has not been systematically studied for adolescent girls, it appears from the available evidence that teens in single-parent families may need more intensive treatment to achieve comparable outcome to those in two-parent families.

- Due to widespread body dissatisfaction in females, which may present in some young women as clinical disorders, the weight problems and concerns of parents should be addressed. In addition, parents should be taught to refrain from teasing and making comments about girls' developing bodies.

CONCLUSIONS

This case scenario demonstrates how to work with families with adolescent girls around rules and monitoring in the context of keeping the relationships close while maintaining boundaries. Little is known, however, from an empirical perspective about the family treatment of adolescent girls. Although guidelines have been advanced in this chapter, more work needs to be conducted to understand the needs of adolescent girls, and how this might impact treatment and outcome.

Case Example

Marla Thomas, a 33-year-old African American woman, scheduled a session for her 14-year-old daughter, Whitney, at a community mental health clinic. Initially, Marla and Whitney were seen together. (*Note:* During the sessions, the therapist referred to Marla as "Ms. Thomas" or "Mom" in order to establish the mother's parental authority and to show her respect.)

Ms. Thomas reported that Whitney had been "cutting class" and "hanging out with the wrong kids," had had "an attitude" for the past few months, and was refusing to do household chores.

Ms. Thomas reported there are four people in the household: Ms. Thomas and her boyfriend of 2 years, Charles, their 15-month-old son, and Whitney. Charles is employed as an assemblyman at an aircraft manufacturing plant, and Ms. Thomas is currently employed part-time as a sales clerk at a local retail chain. Ms. Thomas told the social worker she needed Whitney to help babysit after school so she could work, but that Whitney was undependable, coming home late from school and leaving the toddler with an adult neighbor when she wanted to go out with friends. Additionally, after discovering that two of Whitney's friends recently dropped out of school due to pregnancy, Ms. Thomas expressed concern that Whitney might become sexually active.

Ms. Thomas told the social worker that her main discipline method was to yell at Whitney, but that "nothing changes." She said that she and her boyfriend had also been arguing lately about how to manage Whitney. He said that she should "whip her"; but Ms. Thomas felt like Whitney was "too big" for physical punishment. She then told the social worker, "I hope you can fix this."

The social worker acknowledged Ms. Thomas's concerns and educated her about the importance of working together to help Whitney, explaining that when mothers and daughters have close relationships, the daughter is less likely to have premarital sex. The social worker went on to explain that one effective way of improving relationships is to improve communication. Despite her initial insistence that Whitney was the cause of the problems in their household, Ms. Thomas responded to the therapist's statement that Ms. Thomas was the most important person in Whitney's life and agreed to work with the social worker to help Whitney.

When prompted, Ms. Thomas was able to focus on Whitney's strengths, noting that Whitney was "smart," a loyal friend, and, until recently, a good student. The social worker also encouraged Whitney to express concerns about her relationship with her mother, which she did, saying her mother "is always in my business and gets on my nerves." Initially, Ms. Thomas became defensive, but the social worker intervened to encourage an open stance, with a focus on reflective listening. The social worker educated Ms. Thomas and Whitney about the use of "I statements," which, as for most people, was a difficult technique to apply to their relationship. Ms. Thomas struggled with the concepts of reflective listening and "I" statements, stating that Whitney should just be able to "mind me" and "show respect." The therapist concurred that authoritative parenting, defined as having clear and consistent rules and monitoring children's whereabouts and activities, was important. At the same time, she emphasized that teen girls tend to value relationships, including those with their mothers, and have a need to feel "heard." Further, obeying is more likely when there is a close relationship.

To practice the technique, Whitney began by saying to her mother, "I feel like you hate me when you yell." The social worker encouraged her to focus on one-word descriptions of her own feelings: happy, sad, glad, angry, and versions of these, informing her that "I feel like you hate me" might seem like an attack and could make her mom defensive. Whitney tried again: "I feel sad when you yell at me."

Ms. Thomas was encouraged to respond reflectively to this. She said, "You expect me to let you get away with anything you want." The social worker encouraged Ms. Thomas to focus on the *feelings* Whitney was expressing. Ms. Thomas tried again: "You think I hate you." Whitney stepped in, saying, "No, I don't think you hate me. I don't like it when you yell." The social worker instructed

(continued)

Ms. Thomas to respond to the message she believed Whitney was trying to convey, and Ms. Thomas replied, "When I get onto you, you get sad." Whitney clarified further, saying, "I know you have to get onto me sometimes. It's just hard when you yell instead of talking to me."

The social worker continued to help them become more effective at these communication skills, and Ms. Thomas was able to tell Whitney that she wanted Whitney to delay sexual activity until she went to college—college being the goal she had for her daughter. Whitney said that although she was a little embarrassed to talk to her mother about sex, she was relieved that their relationship was improving and felt as if her mother "understands more than I thought she did."

During this time, the therapist talked to Ms. Thomas about her options for work, given the need to monitor Whitney's whereabouts after school and ensure that her homework was done. The therapist framed monitoring as a necessary part of parenting teens, rather than singling Whitney out as a problem. She also conveyed that caring for a 15-month-old child was a heavy burden for a young girl, even while she understood the need for Ms. Thomas to make money for the family.

Initially, Ms. Thomas was unable to see other options, but she agreed to talk with her supervisor. She was told she could work a couple of weekend shifts (when her boyfriend was available to care for their son) instead of always working in the afternoons. And on the afternoons when Whitney was to babysit her brother, Ms. Thomas agreed to pay her a small amount per hour to do so. She also showed her appreciation to Whitney in the therapy sessions, stating that without her help, she wouldn't be able to earn money for the household. This gave Whitney more of an incentive to be responsible for her younger brother after school. In exchange, Ms. Thomas allowed Whitney some freedom on the weekend to see her friends.

Whitney told her boyfriend that she wanted to delay sex until she was in college. According to Whitney, her boyfriend became angry and told her she was "being ridiculous," that "everyone does it." When she refused to give in, he broke up with her. Whitney went to her mother in tears. At first, her mother was matter-of-fact, saying, "See, I told you boys only want one thing," but the therapist helped Ms. Thomas provide more empathic listening and support so that Whitney could grieve the relationship and sustain her choice. With the boyfriend's exit from her life, Whitney stopped hanging around with what Ms. Thomas termed "the wrong crowd" and no longer cut class. She was able to maintain a B average for the semester.

During their final therapy session (after 6 sessions), Whitney and her mother both agreed that the relationship between them had improved; Whitney said she felt comfortable sharing with her mother her hopes and fears about the future because her mother now listened, providing helpful feedback, without passing judgment on her. Ms. Thomas agreed that gains had been made because, as they had grown closer, Whitney had become more willing to help around the house and was much more reliable in her commitments to babysit for her little brother.

REFERENCES

American Psychiatric Association (2000). *Diagnostic and statistical manual of mental disorders* (4th ed., text rev.). Washington, DC: Author.

Asarnow, J. R., Jaycox, L. H., & Tompson, M. C. (2001). Depression in youth: Psychosocial interventions. *Journal of Clinical Child Psychology, 30*(1), 33–47.

Austin, A., Macgowan, M., & Wagner, E. (2005). Effective family-based interventions for adolescents with substance use problems: A Systematic review. *Research on Social Work Practice, 15,* 67–83.

Barkley, R. A. (2004). Adolescents with attention-deficit/hyperactivity disorder: an overview of empirically based treatments. *Journal of Psychiatric Practice, 10,* 39–56.

Beardslee, W., Versage, E., & Gladstone, T. (1998). Children of affectively ill parents: A review of the past 10 years. *Journal of the American Academy of Child and Adolescent Psychiatry, 37,* 1134–1141.

Birmaher, B., Brent, D., Kolko, D., Baugher, M., Bridge, J., Holder, D., et al. (2000). Clinical outcome after short-term psychotherapy for adolescents with major depressive disorder. *Archives of General Psychiatry, 27,* 29–36.

Birmaher, B., Ryan, N., Williamson, D., Brent, D., & Kaufman, J. (1996). Childhood and adolescent depression: A review of the past 10 years (Pt. II). *Journal of the American Academy of Child and Adolescent Psychiatry, 35,* 1575–1583.

Bolen, R. (2002). Guardian support of sexually abused children: A definition in search of a construct. *Trauma, Violence, and Abuse, 3,* 40–67.

Bolen, R., & Scannapieco, M. (1999). Prevalence of child sexual abuse: A corrective meta-analysis. *Social Service Review, 73,* 281–313.

Brestan, E., & Eyberg, S. (1998). Effective psychological treatments of conduct-disordered children and adolescents: 29 years, 82 studies, and 5,272 kids. *Journal of Clinical Child Psychology, 27,* 180–189.

Brown, J., Cohen, P., Johnson, J. G., & Smailes, E. M. (1999). Childhood abuse and neglect: Specificity of effects on adolescent and young adult depression and suicidality. *Journal of the American Academy of Child and Adolescent Psychiatry, 38*(12), 1490–1496.

Burke, J., Loeber, R., Lahey, B. (2003). Course and outcomes. In C.A. Essau (Ed.), *Conduct and oppositional defiant disorders: epidemiology, risk factors, and treatment* (pp. 61–98). Mahwah, NJ: Erlbaum.

Butzlaff, R. L., & Hooley, J. M. (1998). Expressed emotion and psychiatric relapse. *Archives of General Psychiatry, 55,* 547–552.

Centers for Disease Control and Prevention. (2004). Youth risk behavior surveillance: Surveillance summaries. *Morbidity and Mortality Weekly Report, 53*(No. SS-2).

Clarke, G., Rohde, P., Lewinsohn, P., Hops, H., & Seeley, J. (1999). Cognitive-behavioral treatment of adolescent depression: Efficacy of acute group treatment and booster sessions. *Journal of the American Academy of Child and Adolescent Psychiatry, 38,* 272–279.

Compas, B., Haaga, D., Keefe, F., Leitenberg, H., & Williams, D. (1998). Sampling of empirically supported psychological treatments from health psychology: Smoking, chronic pain, cancer, and bulimia nervosa. *Journal of Consulting and Clinical Psychology, 66,* 89–112.

Corcoran, J. (2004). Treatment outcome research with the nonoffending parents of sexually abused children: A critical review. *Journal of Child Sexual Abuse, 13,* 59–84.

Corcoran, J., & Dattalo, P. (2006. Parent involvement in treatment for ADHD: A meta-analysis of the published studies. *Research in Social Work Practice, 16,* 561–570.

Cottrell, D., Fonagy, P., Kurtz, Z., Phillips, J., & Target, M. (2002). Depressive disorders. In P. Fonagy, M. Target, D. Cottrell, J. Phillips, & Z. Kurtz (Eds.), *What works for whom? A critical review of treatments for children and adolescents* (pp. 89–105). New York: Guilford Press.

Crisp, A. H., Norton, K., Gowers, S., Halek, C., Bowyer, C., Yeldham, D., et al. (1991). A controlled study of the effect of therapies aimed at adolescent and family psychopathology in anorexia nervosa. *British Journal of Psychiatry, 159,* 325–333.

Diamond, G. S., Reis, B. F., Diamond, G. M., Siqueland, L., & Isaacs, L. (2002). Attachment-based family therapy for depressed adolescents: A treatment development study. *Journal of the American Academy of Child and Adolescent Psychiatry, 41*(10), 1190–1197.

Duggal, S., Carlson, E. A., Sroufe, L. A., & Egeland, B. (2001). Depressive symptomatology in childhood and adolescence. *Development and Psychopathology, 13*(1), 143–164.

Fergusson, D., Horwood, L., & Lynskey, M. (1996). Childhood sexual abuse and psychiatric disorder in young adulthood: Pt. II. Psychiatric outcomes of childhood sexual abuse. *Journal of the American Academy of Child and Adolescent Psychiatry, 35,* 1365–1374.

Fonagy, P., & Kurtz, Z. (2002). Disturbance of conduct. In P. Fonagy, M. Target, D. Cottrell, J. Phillips, & Z. Kurtz (Eds.), *What works for whom? A critical review of treatments for children and adolescents* (pp. 106–192). New York: Guilford Press.

Goodman, S. H., & Gotlib, I. H. (1999). Risk for psychopathology in the children of depressed mothers: A developmental model for understanding mechanisms of transmission. *Psychological Review, 106,* 458–461.

Henggeler, S., Schoenwald, S., Rowland, M., & Cunningham, P. (2002). *Serious emotional disturbance in children and adolescence: Multisystemic therapy.* New York: Guilford Press.

Heriot, J. (1996). Maternal protectiveness following the disclosure of intrafamilial child sexual abuse. *Journal of Interpersonal Violence, 11,* 181–194.

Hinshaw, S., & Anderson, C. (1996). Conduct and oppositional defiant disorders. In E. Mash & R. Barkley (Eds.), *Child psychopathology* (pp. 113–149). New York: Guilford Press.

Hopfer, C. J., Stallings, M. C., Hewitt, J. K., & Crowley, T. J. (2003). Family transmission of marijuana use, abuse, and dependence. *Journal of the American Academy of Child Adolescent Psychiatry, 42,* 834–841.

Hubbard, D. J., & Pratt, T. (2002). A meta-analysis of the predictors of delinquency among girls. *Journal of Offender Rehabilitation, 34,* 1–13.

Jaccard, J., Dittus, P., & Gordon, V. (1996). Maternal correlates of adolescent sexual and contraceptive behavior. *Family Planning Perspectives, 28,* 159–165, 185.

Jewell, J. D., & Stark, K. D. (2003). Comparing the family environments of adolescents with conduct disorder or depression. *Journal of Child and Family Studies, 12,* 77–89.

Jordan, J. (2005). Relational resilience in girls. In S. Goldstein & R. Brooks (Eds.), *Handbook of resilience in children* (pp. 79–90). New York: Kluwer Academic/Plenum Press.

Klein, D., Dougherty, L., & Olino, T. (2005). Toward guidelines for evidence-based assessment of depression in children and adolescents. *Journal of Clinical Child and Adolescent Psychology, 34*(3), 412–432.

Koerner, S. S., Wallace, S., Lehman, S. J., & Raymond, M. (2002). Mother-to-daughter disclosure after divorce: A double-edged sword? *Journal of Child and Family Studies, 11,* 469–483.

Kotler, L. A., Cohen, P., Davies, M., Pine, D. S., & Walsh, B. D. (2001). Longitudinal relationships between childhood, adolescent, and adult eating disorders. *Journal of the American Academy of Child and Adolescent Psychiatry, 40,* 1434–1441.

Latimer, J. (2001). A meta-analytic examination of youth delinquency, family treatment, and recidivism. *Canadian Journal of Criminology, 43*(2), 237–253.

Lewinsohn, P., Clarke, G., Hops, H., & Andrews, J. (1990). Cognitive-behavioral treatment for depressed adolescents. *Behavior Therapy, 21,* 385–401.

Lewinsohn, P., & Essau, C. (2002). Depression in adolescents. In I. H. Gotlib & C. Hammen (Eds.), *Handbook of depression* (pp. 541–559). New York: Guilford Press.

Littell, J. H., Popa, M., & Forsythe, B. (2005). Multisystemic therapy for social, emotional, and behavioral problems in youth aged 10–17 (Cochrane Review). In *The Cochrane Library* (Issue 3). Chichester, West Sussex, England: Wiley.

Lock, J., Agras, W. S., Bryson, S., & Kraemer, H. (2005). A comparison of short- and long-term family therapy for adolescent anorexia nervosa. *Journal of the American Academy of Child and Adolescent Psychiatry, 44,* 632–639.

Loeber, R., Burke, J. D., Lahey, B. B., Winters, A., & Zera, M. (2000). Oppositional defiant and conduct disorder: A review of the past 10 years (Pt. I).

Journal of the American Academy of Child and Adolescent Psychiatry, 39(12), 1468–1484.

Mizes, J. S., & Palermo, T. M. (1997). Eating disorders. In R. T. Ammerman & M. Hersen (Eds.), *Handbook of prevention and treatment with children and adolescents: Intervention in the real-world context* (pp. 238–258). New York: Wiley.

Moffit, T., Caspi, A., Rutter, M., & Silva, P. (2001). *Sex differences in antisocial behavior: Conduct disorder, delinquency, and violence in the Dunedin longitudinal study.* Cambridge: Cambridge University Press.

Robin, A. L., Siegel, P. T., & Moye, A. (1995). Family versus individual therapy for anorexia: Impact on family conflict. *International Journal of Eating Disorders, 17*(4), 313–322.

Robin, A. L., Seigel, P. T., Moye, A. W., Gilroy, M., Barker Dennis, A., & Sikand, A. (1999). A controlled comparison of family versus individual therapy for adolescents with anorexia nervosa. *Journal of the American Academy of Child and Adolescent Psychiatry, 38,* 1482–1489.

Striegel-Moore, R. H., & Cachelin, F. M. (1999). Body image concerns and disordered eating in adolescent girls: Risk and protective factors. In N. G. Johnson, M. C. Roberts, & J. Worell (Eds.), *Beyond appearance: A new look at adolescent girls* (pp. 85–108). Washington, DC: American Psychiatric Association.

Substance Abuse and Mental Health Services Administration. (2005). *Results from the 2004 national survey on drug use and health: National findings.* Retrieved May 24, 2006, from http://oas.samhsa.gov/NSDUH/2k4NSDUH/2k4results/2k4results.htm#ch7/.

Sund, A. M., & Wichstrom, L. (2002). Insecure attachment as a risk factor for future depressive symptoms in early adolescence. *Journal of the American Academy of Child and Adolescent Psychiatry, 41*(12), 1478–1486.

Szmukler, G., & Dare, C. (1991). The Maudsley Hospital study of family therapy in anorexia nervosa and bulimia nervosa. In B. D. Woodside & L. Shekter-Wolfson (Eds.), *Family approaches in treatment of eating disorders: Clinical practice* (No. 15, pp. 1–21). Washington, DC: American Psychiatric Association.

Van Furth, E. F., van Strien, D. C., Martina, L. M. L., van Son, M. J. M., Hendrickx, J. J. P., & van Engeland, H. (1996). Expressed emotion and the predication of outcome in adolescent eating disorders. *International Journal of Eating Disorders, 20,* 19–31.

Vaughn, M., & Howard, M. (2004). Adolescent substance abuse treatment: A synthesis of controlled evaluations research on social work practice. *Research on Social Work Practice, 14,* 325–335.

Waldron, H. (1997). Adolescent substance abuse and family therapy outcome: A review of randomized trials. In T. H. Ollendick & R. J. Prinz (Eds.), *Advances in clinical child psychology* (Vol. 4, pp. 199–234). New York: Plenum Press.

Williams, R., Chang, S., & Addiction Centre Adolescent Research Group. (2000). A comprehensive and comparative review of adolescent substance abuse treatment outcome. *Clinical Psychology, Science, and Practice, 7,* 138–166.

Wolfe, V. V. (1998). Child sexual abuse. In E. J. Mash & R. A. Barkley (Eds.), *Treatment of childhood disorders* (2nd ed., pp. 545–597). New York: Guilford Press.

Wolraich, M. L., Wibbelsman, C. J., Brown, T. E., Evans, S. W., Gotlieb, E. M., Knight, J. R., et al. (2005). Attention-deficit/hyperactivity disorder among adolescents: a review of the diagnosis, treatment, and clinical implications. *Pediatrics, 115,* 1734–1747.

Yager, J., Anderson, A., Devlin, M., Egger, H., Herzog, D., Mitchell, J., et al. (2002). Practice guideline for the treatment of patients with eating disorders. In *American Psychiatric Association practice guidelines for the treatment of psychiatric disorders: Compendium, 2002* (2nd ed, pp. 697–766). Washington, DC: American Psychiatric Association.

Chapter 11

MENTORSHIP

The GirlPOWER! Program

DAVID L. DuBOIS, NAIDA SILVERTHORN,
JULIA PRYCE, ERIN REEVES, BERNADETTE SANCHEZ,
ADRIANA SILVA, AKUA ANIMA ANSU, SIMONA HAQQ,
AND JANET TAKEHARA

The concept of mentoring youth has a long history dating back nearly 3 millennia to its namesake character Mentor in Homer's *Odyssey*. Formal mentoring programs, too, have been part of the landscape of community-based efforts to foster positive youth development in this country for nearly a century (Baker & Maguire, 2005). Yet, their remarkable surge in popularity during recent times is clearly unprecedented. More than 4,500 agencies and programs in the United States now provide mentoring services for youth (Rhodes, 2002). A growing global dimension is evident as well, with programs and initiatives appearing in numerous other countries. The appeal of mentoring is anchored by the interest it has attracted from practitioners and scholars who regard it as emblematic of the principles of the emerging field of positive youth development (Kuperminc et al., 2005) and by the broader public's belief that supportive relationships with nonparental adults are a vital asset for young people (Scales, 2003). An impressive array of not-for-profit organizations, corporations, and legislative initiatives, in turn, have been instrumental in translating this enthusiasm into programs (Walker, 2005).

Mentoring programs for youth vary widely in their format and structure (Sipe, 2005). In the typical community-based program, each adult volunteer is screened for appropriateness and then is matched with a youth who has been referred to the program. Matches may be made based on factors such as similarity in interests and personalities, as well as logistical considerations such as geographic proximity. Mentors are expected to provide companionship and friendship to the young person through regularly occurring contact (e.g., 2 to 3 times a month) over some minimum specified period of time (e.g., 1 year), although relationships that extend beyond this time frame are generally supported and encouraged. Programs often provide some initial training to mentors as well as ongoing support through periodic contact with the mentor, youth, and the youth's parent(s) or guardian. The relative simplicity of the design of most mentoring programs

The authors express their appreciation to Big Brothers Big Sisters of Metropolitan Chicago for their invaluable support as collaborative partners in the design, implementation, and evaluation of the GirlPOWER! program. The writing of this chapter and the research described therein was supported by a grant to the first author from the National Institute of Mental Health (5 R21 MH069564-03).

(notwithstanding the reality of formidable challenges to implementation in areas such as volunteer recruitment and sustaining relationships over time; Weinberger, 2005), coupled with their appeal to widely held values such as volunteerism, has been pivotal in their rise to prominence in the realm of social policy (Walker, 2005). There is evidence, moreover, that mentoring programs "work" insofar as participation appears to benefit youth on a range of outcomes pertaining to their emotional, behavioral, social, academic, and career development (DuBois, Holloway, Valentine, & Cooper, 2002; Jekielek, Moore, & Hair, 2002).

Increasingly, however, there is recognition of the need for stronger linkage between practice and research to youth mentoring (DuBois & Karcher, 2005; DuBois & Rhodes, 2006; Rhodes, 2002). One key concern is that very few programs have been developed through a systematic, empirically guided approach (DuBois & Silverthorn, 2005). This would entail a progression through a series of steps or phases from basic research to program development to investigations of program efficacy and effectiveness and, ultimately, large-scale dissemination (Flay, 1986; Institute of Medicine, 1994; National Advisory Mental Health Council Workgroup on Mental Disorders Prevention Research, 2001). The process would enable the development of mentoring programs to benefit from insights gleaned from basic research as well as formative (i.e., process-oriented) evaluation studies. Once established, programs could be refined and improved through rigorous evaluations of their efficacy and effectiveness. The dissemination of programs to larger systems, furthermore, could be more judiciously limited by empirical evidence, and strategies for achieving diffusion could be carefully tested (DuBois, Doolittle, Yates, Silverthorn, & Tebes, 2006). In the absence of a systematic empirical foundation, mentoring programs may be falling well short of realizing their potential to benefit youth. Programs also may be more likely to inadvertently do harm, perhaps in ways not even detected (DuBois & Karcher, 2005; Rhodes, 2002). Collaboration between community-based mentoring agencies and researchers has been recommended as a strategy for addressing these concerns while simultaneously taking advantage of the strengths of existing program models (DuBois & Silverthorn, 2005).

A second important concern is that mentoring programs for youth have tended to be "one size fits all" rather than adapted to the needs and strengths of specific populations. The National Research Agenda for Youth Mentoring (Rhodes & DuBois, 2004) highlights the need in particular for development and evaluation of programs tailored to populations of youth defined by differing configurations of gender, ethnicity, and age. A recent review focusing specifically on gender, similarly concluded that girls and boys may experience and respond to mentoring relationships differently and that the merits of gender-specific programs should be investigated (Bogat & Liang, 2005).

With these issues as background, in this chapter we describe our ongoing efforts to use a systematic, empirically guided approach to develop and evaluate an innovative mentoring program for ethnic/minority, young adolescent girls called GirlPOWER! Empirically based frameworks emphasize four stages of activity that should be carried out in developing an intervention prior to conducting a full-scale controlled trial of the intervention's efficacy (Bartholomew, Parcel, Kok, & Gottlieb, 2001; Flay, 1986; Green & Kreuter, 1999; Institute of Medicine, 1994; National Advisory Mental Health Council Workgroup on Mental Disorders Prevention Research, 2001):

1. Reviewing relevant theoretical, empirical, and intervention literature,
2. Obtaining input from representatives of stakeholder groups,
3. Piloting intervention activities and materials with the target population, and
4. Conducting a piloting and feasibility study (i.e., implementing the full intervention within the context of a small-scale randomized control trial).

Our current efforts focus on completing these activities in the context of a 3-year project supported by a grant from the National Institutes of Mental Health. All phases of the project are being conducted in collaboration with Big Brothers Big Sisters of Metropolitan Chicago (BBBSMC). Prior to the project, BBBSMC had been implementing gender-specific mentoring programs for girls for several years. Participants in these programs were predominantly African American and Latina and in the age range of early adolescence. For the most part, the programs adhered to the same general model in terms of their structure and curriculum. In the spirit of the collaborative approach referred to earlier, we have utilized this existing program model as a foundation for the design of GirlPOWER!

In the following section, we briefly summarize our review of theoretical, empirical, and intervention literature that informed the development of the GirlPOWER! program (stage 1). In doing so, we highlight areas in which the agency's existing program model was found to align well with available literature as well as promising avenues for innovation that were identified. We then provide a detailed overview of the GirlPOWER! program. In doing so, we discuss the ways in which stakeholder input and piloting of activities contributed to program modifications and refinements (stages 2 and 3). We also describe further adjustments that have been made as the result of lessons learned when implementing the full program for the first time as part of the piloting and feasibility study that currently is in progress (stage 4). We conclude by considering future steps in the development of the GirlPOWER! program, including the small-scale randomized evaluation of its efficacy that is being undertaken as part of the piloting and feasibility study.

REVIEW OF THE LITERATURE

As noted previously, it appears that mentoring programs can promote positive outcomes for youth in several domains. In a recent meta-analysis (DuBois, Holloway, et al., 2002), however, these estimated impacts were found to be small in magnitude, thus suggesting only modest benefits for the typical youth participant. Findings from the few studies that included follow-up assessments similarly did not to reveal the types of broad, transformative effects on young people at later stages of their development that are central to the arguments of those advocating for investment in mentoring initiatives (Walker, 2005). Overall, available research thus underscores a need for innovations in mentoring programs to enhance their effectiveness and better realize their full potential for promoting youth development (DuBois, Holloway, et al., 2002).

Mentoring Relationship Quality

Not surprisingly, youth participating in programs have demonstrated the greatest gains when their relationships with mentors are of high quality (DuBois, Holloway, et al., 2002; Rhodes, 2002). Existing literature points toward several indicators of mentoring relationship quality (Barrera & Bonds, 2005; DuBois, Neville, Parra, & Pugh-Lilly, 2002; Keller, 2005; Nakkula & Harris, 2005; Rhodes, 2002, 2005; Sipe, 2005; Spencer & Rhodes, 2005):

- Perceptions by the mentor and youth that they are similar to or compatible with one another
- A regular/consistent pattern of contact
- Mutual feelings of closeness characterized by trust, empathy, and positive regard
- Collaborative efforts to set and work toward goals
- Activities and topics of discussion that address salient youth concerns and interests
- Provision of a broad range of support functions, including: instrumental and informational support to assist with learning and goal attainment; emo-

tional support, to facilitate exploration of feelings and coping; appraisal support (constructive feedback) to enhance self-esteem and guide self-evaluation; and companionship support in the form of time spent together in mutually enjoyable activities

- Introduction of the youth to new persons and resources through advocacy and connections to the mentor's social network
- Cultivation of ties between the mentor and important persons in the youth's life, such as parents and teachers.

There is also substantial evidence that relationships must be maintained for a significant length of time (e.g., 1 year or longer) for benefits to begin to be realized (Grossman & Rhodes, 2002; McLearn, Colasanto, & Schoen, 1998). Relationships that end prematurely (i.e., after only a few months), moreover, have been linked to declines in youth well-being and thus appear to have the potential to do harm (Grossman & Rhodes, 2002).

As noted by Bogat and Liang (2005), "Relational theory argues that the core component of girls' and women's identities is their orientation to interpersonal relationships" (p. 206). Because of this relational orientation, girls may have a distinctive capacity to form and benefit from high-quality mentoring ties. Yet, in the limited number of studies that address this possibility, it appears that girls were less likely than boys to experience enduring and rewarding relationships with the mentors to whom they were assigned in formal programs (Bogat & Liang, 2005). One possible explanation is that girls enter relationships with different needs based on their relational orientation. Girls, for example, have been found to hold expectations of greater levels of intimacy, self-disclosure, and empathy in their friendships than do boys (Clark & Ayers, 1993). They thus may require more emotional depth and intensity in their ties with program-assigned mentors than do boys in order to receive optimal benefits.

Implications for Program Design

Overall, available research indicates that programs should strive to facilitate the development of high-quality and long-term mentoring relationships. In the case of girls, there also should be sensitivity to their relational orientation and its implications for their needs within programs. Several features of the BBBSMC program model that we used as the foundation for GirlPOWER! were consistent with these goals. In this model, girls and their female mentors began their relationships by meeting regularly (e.g., once every 2 weeks) in a group with several other female mentoring pairs, usually over a period of a few months. Female agency staff served as facilitators of the sessions. The meta-analysis referred to earlier (DuBois, Holloway, et al., 2002) found that programs offering structured opportunities such as this for mentors and youth to spend time together produced greater positive effects. The group context, furthermore, capitalized on the relational orientation of females by providing an opportunity for mentors and girls to form meaningful bonds with other participants. Theoretically, an exclusively female group environment also may help to ensure that girls' voices are not overshadowed or inhibited, as can be the case in mixed-gender settings (Gilligan, 1982). Some empirical support for advantages of all-girl groups in prevention programs has been reported that is consistent with this possibility (Chaplin et al., 2006).

The existing BBBSMC program model was noteworthy, too, because it appeared likely to promote several of the literature-based indicators of mentoring relationship quality described previously. The group meetings, for example, provided a promising approach to ensuring regular contact between mentors and youth during the critical early phases of relationship development. Research suggests that cultivating a consistent pattern of interaction enhances relationship quality in other areas and reduces the risk for premature relationship termination (Parra, DuBois, Neville, Pugh-Lilly, & Povinelli, 2002). The program sessions themselves, furthermore, were designed to engage mentors and youth in meaningful activities and discussions. Both group projects and presentations from organizations in the surrounding community were used for this purpose. The content of the sessions also reflected tailoring to address issues with well-documented importance for young-adolescent, ethnic-minority girls. These include, for example, enhancement of self-esteem and body-image (American Association of University Women [AAUW], 1991; Harter, 1999; Zimmerman, Copeland, Shope, & Dielman, 1997), promoting cultural awareness and pride (DuBois, Burk-Braxton, Tevendale, Swenson, & Hardesty, et al., 2002; French, Seidman, Allen, & Aber, 2006), and exploration of career interests (AAUW, 1991).

Evaluation findings provided support for the BBBSMC program model as well. Both mentors and youth reported a high level of satisfaction with the group sessions, for example, and rated them as beneficial in intended areas such as relationship development and learning of new skills (BBBSMC, 2002). A pre- and postevaluation conducted with a small sample of 16 girls, furthermore, revealed a significant increase in their reported levels of self-esteem, as well as an increase in the proportion of girls who listed their mentors as key members of their support network (Davis, Paxton, & Robinson, 1997).

At the same time, our review of the literature highlighted promising avenues for enhancement of the BBBSMC program model. First, there were several topic areas important to the health and development of girls negotiating the transition to adolescence that did not receive focused attention in the program (National Council for Research on Women, 1998). These included academic success, health-promoting behaviors in the areas of exercise and nutrition, health-compromising behaviors in the areas of substance use and violence, and developmental concerns relating to peer relationships and dating. Expanding the program to encompass these additional areas thus became one of our priorities.

Second, based on research indicating that helping youth to set and work toward goals is beneficial within mentoring relationships (Balcazar, Keys, & Garate, 1995; Hamilton & Hamilton, 2005), we concluded that it would be useful to explore incorporating these activities into the program. The theoretical importance of role modeling within mentoring relationships (Rhodes, 2002), furthermore, suggested the value of engaging mentors in a parallel process of identifying and striving to reach goals of their own.

Third, although the value of mentors and youth learning about and developing ties with persons in each other's social networks has been discussed (Rhodes, 2002), the existing program model reflected only limited attention to this concern. Mentoring programs offering opportunities for parental involvement, in particular, have been found to be more effective (DuBois, Holloway, et al., 2002). Strategies to actively engage parents and encourage collaboration between them and mentors, therefore, was one direction for enhancement targeted in this area.

Fourth, the literature we reviewed suggested it would be beneficial to incorporate activities for mentors and youth to engage in on their own, outside of the group sessions that were central to the BBBSMC program model. We concluded that this type of individualized time could serve as a vehicle for fostering emotional depth in relationships, which as noted may be especially important for girls (Bogat & Liang, 2005). It also appeared that it could be useful for a variety of other purposes, such as supporting youth in their efforts to reach goals, cultivating ties with each other's social networks, and providing opportunities for reinforcement, modeling, and practice of skills introduced in group sessions. With relevance to the latter consideration, the evaluation referred to previously failed to find an increase in girls' knowledge of program content (Davis et al., 1997). We thus viewed it as important to explore innovations that could facilitate more substantial gains in this area.

Fifth, in view of evidence that sustaining relationships for at least 1 year is important (Grossman & Rhodes, 2002), we sought to do as much as possible within the structure of the program to ensure that this objective would be met. The existing program model, for example, did not include systematic provisions for communication among participants after the conclusion of the group sessions. Theory and research emphasizing the relational orientation of girls and women suggested that opportunities for participants to stay in contact and eventually reconnect as a group could be of significant value for ensuring that relationships remained intact.

Sixth, both mentor training and relationship supervision have been indicated to increase the effectiveness of mentoring programs for youth (DuBois, Holloway, et al., 2002). These practices thus represented further targets for potential enhancement. Available literature (Cavell & Hughes, 2000; Parra et al., 2002; Stukas & Tanti, 2005; Weinberger, 2005), for example, suggested that training procedures should be instilled in volunteers a sense of efficacy for meeting program goals and expectations with the youth they mentor. A related implication was that supervision should be structured to enhance mentor-youth engagement in different facets of the program and overcome any obstacles to participation.

Finally, because systematic monitoring of implementation is associated with greater program effectiveness (DuBois, Holloway, et al., 2002), this emerged as also meriting attention. One frequently recommended monitoring strategy is to have mentors maintain logs of their activities with youth. It may be equally important, however, to assess staff adherence to program guidelines in areas such as curriculum delivery and relationship supervision (DuBois et al., 2006) A comprehensive approach to program monitoring thus was deemed most promising.

GirlPOWER!

GirlPOWER! incorporates enhancements to the existing program model of BBB-SMC that are derived from the literature review summarized in the preceding section. It also reflects modifications made on the basis of input from stakeholder group representatives and the piloting of intervention activities and materials, as well as further refinements stemming from our experiences thus far implementing the full program for the first time as part of the piloting and feasibility study (described later in this chapter). Stakeholder input was obtained via:

- In-depth, semistructured interviews with girls ($n = 5$), parents ($n = 5$), and female mentors ($n = 6$) who were recipients of services from BBBSMC. In several instances, these individuals had participated in one of the programs that was a predecessor of GirlPOWER!
- Semistructured interviews with administrative staff of Big Brothers Big Sisters agencies other than BBBSMC ($n = 3$)
- Meetings with an advisory council of girls, parents, and female mentors who have received services through BBBSMC. The advisory council has a fluid membership of approximately 10 persons and serves as a mechanism for ongoing input on the design and implementation of the program.

Program activities and materials were piloted with 6 Matches (Big and Little Sister pairs) recruited from BBBSMC. (*Match* is a term used by Big Brothers Big Sisters agencies to refer to the relationship between a *Big Sister,* also referred to in this chapter as a "Big," and her *Little Sister,* also referred to in this chapter as a "Little.") These relationships involved youth between the ages of 9 and 13 years and had all been initiated within the past year. During piloting, process evaluation data were collected using the procedures and instrumentation for monitoring implementation of the GirlPOWER! program that are described later in this chapter. In addition, 1 to 2 female members of the research team attended each group session and recorded their observations using a form developed for this purpose.

Program Overview

The overarching goal of the GirlPOWER! program is to facilitate the development of strong and lasting mentoring relationships that empower girls to grow into healthy and successful women. Currently, the program is designed for implementation by agencies that are approved affiliates of Big Brothers Big Sisters of America. Big Brothers Big Sisters (BBBS) agencies must adhere to rigorous standards in the areas of volunteer recruitment and screening, matching of mentors and youth, and support of relationships once established. All of these practices are considered an integral part of the GirlPOWER! program.

At present, the target population for the program is ethnic-minority girls between 10 and 13 years old who have been matched with their mentors for 12 months or less. The lower end of the eligible age range is based on results of piloting, which suggested that some of the topics addressed in the program (e.g., dating) had limited relevance for youth less than 10 years of age. A further consideration is that GirlPOWER! is intended for girls who are able to engage in age-appropriate social interaction with peers and adults in a group context. For this reason, girls who have a recent history of aggressive or violent behavior are excluded when recruiting participants for the program.

The BBBSMC program model that preceded GirlPOWER! implemented exclusively with new Matches. The decision to expand eligibility criteria to include Matches already in existence for up to 1 year was in response largely to a pragmatic concern that recruitment for the program might otherwise prove to be an excessive burden for host agencies. Recruitment issues pose a significant challenge in many mentoring programs, and often end up consuming a great deal of staff time and agency resources (Stukas & Tanti, 2005; Weinberger, 2005). By allowing host agencies to draw on existing Matches for participants, the resources required for recruitment are substantially lessened. We will revisit our decisions in this area as data become available concerning the program experiences and outcomes that are associated with Matches of varying length. Anecdotally, however, we have observed that mentors in existing Matches are able to offer valuable advice and support to those in the program who have just started their relationships. There thus may be benefits to having relatively more experienced and new mentors participate together.

Based on our experiences thus far with our implementation of the full program, we also have adopted several additional eligibility criteria. Most notably, Bigs are now required to live close enough to both their Littles and the program site (i.e., location where group sessions are held) to be able to pick up their Littles and get to the site within approximately 40 minutes. This criterion was adopted based on difficulties encountered in session attendance that seemed be related to Matches needing to invest considerable time (up to 2 hours in some cases) traveling to and from sessions. To accommodate this criterion within a large metropolitan area such as Chicago, we have been more strategic in our choice of site for the second year of the program implementation (i.e., an area with a concentration of the targeted population of youth as well as a sizable pool of volunteers to recruit as mentors).

We also have adopted other criteria designed to help screen on factors that could compromise the ability of the Match to participate consistently in program sessions and sustain involvement for the entire program. These include the exclusion of Matches in which the Big or Little are likely to be moving in the coming year, as well as those who anticipate more than occasional difficulty with session attendance.

Finally, eligibility criteria for the program also now exclude youth who demonstrate marked limitations in cognitive development (e.g., as might be indicated by placement in a special education classroom). This modification is based on our observation that such youth experienced significant difficulties with comprehension of program activities and concepts in their current form.

The core of the GirlPOWER! program is 1 year in duration, after which regular group meetings conclude. A reunion session, which takes place 6 months after the formal end of the program (and which can be repeated at 6 month intervals thereafter), serves to promote continuation of relationships. Long-term relationships are encouraged and can be supported by the host agency while youth remain within the age range of eligibility for services. In BBBS agencies, Matches are supported until youth are 18 years old or graduate from high school.

The GirlPOWER! curriculum can accommodate a group as large as 15 Matches. The program originally was designed for only 5 to 7 Matches. As the amount of staff time required became apparent during the piloting process, however, concern arose that implementation of the program with this number of Matches would not be cost-efficient for many agencies. Cost can be a barrier to adoption of new programs (Offord, 1996) and thus could have significant implications for the goal of eventually disseminating the GirlPOWER! program throughout the network of several hundred BBBS agencies.* The modification to allow for a larger group size is consistent with feedback received from mentors and youth during piloting. Some youth noted, for example, that they would have liked to have had the opportunity to get to know a greater number of other girls through the program. We observed, too, that with only a few absences the number of participants was in danger of dropping below the "critical mass" required for successful implementation of group activities.

The unifying theme of the program is symbolized by the acronym POWER, which stands for Pride, Opportunity, Women-in-the-Making, Effort and Energy, and Relationships.

- *Pride* refers to "feeling proud of who you are and what you can do." GirlPOWER! activities are designed to help girls develop healthy self-esteem and feel good about being female.
- *Opportunity* refers to "taking advantage of chances to learn new things and earn recognition from others." Program activities are oriented toward helping girls develop new skills and talents that receive validation from others.
- *Women-in-the-Making* refers to "picturing a POWERful and healthly future for yourself and doing what you can now to make your dreams come true." GirlPOWER! activities promote a positive orientation toward the future as well as attitudes and behaviors that will help girls realize their aspirations.
- *Effort and Energy* refers to "working hard to learn new things and achieve your goals." Program activities encourage goal-oriented behavior and self-improvement.
- *Relationships* refers to "being caring and giving with others and cherishing the wisdom and companionship of those who are closest to us." GirlPOWER! activities are intended to cultivate strong relationships between Big Sisters and Little Sisters, among members of the GirlPOWER! group, and between group members and the important people in their lives.

The concepts associated with POWER are used to structure and link program activities. Participants also are encouraged to relate their experiences and

---

* It should be noted that the goals relating to dissemination to other agencies discussed in this chapter are those of the research team. The involvement of BBBSMC and Big Brothers Big Sisters of America in this process would be highly valuable for many reasons, but it has not yet been negotiated.

observations of other group members to these concepts. Within the curriculum, these reflections are referred to as POWERConnections.

At the initial session of the program, photographs are taken of each participant and Match. Using a commercial vendor, these pictures are used to create jigsaw puzzles that depict each girl as well as the overall group. These puzzles are referred to as POWERPictures within the curriculum. Throughout the program, participants have the opportunity to earn pieces of both their individual POWERPictures and the group POWERPicture. Puzzle pieces can be earned through session attendance, positive efforts during sessions, and completion of between-session activities. For example, a youth receives a piece of her individual POWERPicture for each between-session activity that she and her mentor complete; all Matches receive a piece of the group POWERPicture for every five activities that are completed by the group as a whole. In this way, the puzzles serve as an incentive for participation in program activities. At a perhaps deeper level, the puzzles also are intended to function as visual metaphor for the positive identities that the program seeks to foster for both girls and the group as a whole. This may be especially valuable for the age group of girls participating in the program, for at least two reasons. First, issues relating to identity and group affiliation are salient concerns during early adolescence (Steinberg, 1998). Second, youth at this stage of development are still in the process of transitioning to abstract modes of thought. They thus may find concepts such as self-image and identity to be more easily accessible when presented in a concrete format.

Each participant in the program (mentor, youth, parent) is provided with a binder containing relevant forms and resource materials. A calendar, for example, highlights the dates of group sessions and offers prompts for completion of between-session activities. A glossary defines program terminology and includes brief descriptions of key concepts and skills.

Periodically during the program, a newsletter is produced and mailed to participants. Matches are encouraged to contribute items to the newsletter, such as updates on recent activities or developments in their lives that they would like to share with the rest of the group. The newsletter may be continued after the formal end of the program as a vehicle for helping Matches to remain in contact.

In the remainder of this section, we describe the different parts of the GirlPOWER! program in greater detail, organized according to the following major components of the intervention:

- POWERSessions (i.e., group sessions)
- POWERBuilders (i.e., activities for mentors and youth to complete outside of group sessions)

- Parental involvement
- Training and supervision
- Program monitoring and evaluation

Following this overview of the program, we briefly consider its alignment with a conceptual framework from the broader field of positive youth development. Those interested in implementing the program should contact the first author of this chapter for more detailed information and necessary permissions.

POWERSessions

The central component of the GirlPOWER! program is the joint participation of mentors and youth in a series of group sessions that are referred to as POWERSessions. The aim of the POWERSessions is to enhance the development of mentoring relationships through experiential learning activities and a supportive group context. Each session takes place on a Saturday morning for 3 hours and is cofacilitated by two female BBBS staff members. As shown in Table 11.1, there are 12 POWERSessions, followed by the group reunion. The POWERSessions take place on a monthly basis over a 1-year period. This structure reflects a modification from the initial implementation of the full program in which the 12 sessions were concentrated over a briefer period that conformed to the calendar of the school year. A major impetus for the change, now being piloted during our second year of program implementation, is the desire to facilitate session attendance through a less demanding and more consistent schedule. Within the original framework, sessions often had to occur twice in the same month, and this was cited by mentors as a challenge both for attendance and completion of between-session-activities. As noted, the reunion session takes place 6 months after the final POWERSession. The reunion capitalizes on the group component of GirlPOWER! and provides an incentive for Matches to continue beyond the formal 1-year period of the program. Host agencies also are encouraged to hold further group reunions to help foster long-term relationships.

Both the stakeholders interviewed and the advisory council strongly endorsed the group component of the program. They viewed the sessions as a valuable opportunity for collaborative learning and skill building between mentors and youth. At the same time, it was stressed that activities should be highly interactive and engaging for youth. The importance of participatory and age-appropriate activities was underscored as well by process evaluation data collected by BBBSMC from Bigs and Littles in the programs that were predecessors to GirlPOWER! Our piloting of POWERSessions helped us to refine the structure and content of the sessions in several ways that are consistent with this goal.

Table 11.1   Overview of POWERSessions

Number and Title of Session	Goals	Session-Specific Content[a]
1. POWER Up: Learning about GirlPOWER!	To welcome participants and introduce them to each other and the GirlPOWER! program.	Facilitators provide overview of program goals, content, and schedule.
	To have participants make a commitment to the program and to becoming POWERful together.	Bigs, Littles, and parents share motivations for program participation.
	To prepare Matches for their first POWERBuilder.	Participants interview each other using the concepts of POWER.
		Participants are oriented to the major components of the program through a collaborative group activity.
		Bigs, Littles, and parents make commitments to fulfilling their roles and responsibilities in the program and share these as a group.
		The group practices the POWERRap.
		Facilitators introduce the first POWERBuilder activity.
2. Me and My Big = POWER[2]: Building Strong Match Relationships	To facilitate sharing between Bigs and Littles regarding their values, interests, and life experiences.	Bigs and Littles explore their similarities and differences in an activity in which they use goal steppingstones to cross an imaginary river.[b]
	To introduce girls to principles of effective goal setting.	Facilitators introduce characteristics of good goals using the SMART acronym (Specific, Measurable, Achievable—realistic, but challenging, Relevant to your interests and wishes, and Time-limited) and steppingstone metaphor for achieving goals.[c]
	To have each Match establish individual goals and a joint goal for their relationship.	Each Match completes an art project in which they display their POWERGoals (i.e., goals for the Little, Big, and Match relationship) as well as first steps for working on each goal.[c]
		Matches share their goals with each other and provide encouragement for reaching them.[c]

Table 11.1 *(Continued)*

Number and Title of Session	Goals	Session-Specific Content[a]
3. It's More Than Just the Two of Us: Getting to Know Matches, Friends, and Families	To introduce Bigs and Littles to family, friends, and other people who are important in their lives. To help participants learn and practice steps for obtaining support from others. To promote group unity and teambuilding.	Matches play POWERBasketball, a team-building game in which they must all work together to score baskets representing the letters of POWER.[b] Each Match completes an art project in which they draw and discuss their social networks (referred to as POWERNetworks).[c] The group learns support-seeking skills, then practices them in an interactive game.[c]
4. She's Got the POWER!: Promoting Healthy Self-Esteem	To help girls appreciate their unique and special qualities as POWERful young persons. To help girls learn about and practice choices that promote healthy self-esteem. To facilitate sharing between Bigs and Littles about healthy ways of building self-esteem.	Matches practice juggling to illustrate how self-esteem can influence the ways in which they cope with challenging tasks.[b] Facilitators introduce the concept of healthy self-esteem: "Feeling proud of yourself based on choices that are good for you, your future, and other people." The group practices and discusses healthy self-esteem choices by making "self-esteem movies."[c]
5. Celebrating Our Sameness & Our Differences: Cultural Diversity	To help girls develop a positive ethnic and racial identity. To engage Bigs and Littles in sharing their cultural backgrounds with each other. To help girls learn strategies for coping with prejudice and discrimination.	Matches play POWERBingo, a game in which they must identify group members who have different types of cultural experiences and beliefs.[b] Each Match spends time sharing their racial and ethnic identities and their experiences with prejudice/discrimination.[c] The group expresses solidarity for valuing and supporting their diversity through a poetry reading.[c]

(continued)

Table 11.1 *(Continued)*

Number and Title of Session	Goals	Session-Specific Content[a]
6. Keeping Our Bodies Healthy: Eating Right & Exercise	To increase girls knowledge about nutrition and exercise. To help girls learn how to set and achieve realistic goals for eating and physical activity. To help each Big and Little work as teams to maintain healthy lifestyles.	Matches either design their own dance routines or play a game in which they have to guess the names of fruits and vegetables that are placed on their backs.[b] Facilitators introduce the "ABCs to a Healthy Body" (Accurate knowledge, Be motivated, Create a plan), along with factual guidelines for healthy eating and exercise.[c] The group practices applying skills and knowledge for nutrition and physical activity in an interactive game that incorporates exercise.[c]
7. The Future's So Bright I Gotta Wear Shades: Academic Success & Careers	To help girls develop confidence in their ability to achieve academic and career goals. To encourage Bigs and Littles to explore academic and career issues in their relationships.	Participants play a game in which they match pictures of famous female role models from diverse ethnic backgrounds with descriptions of their accomplishments.[b] Matches play an interactive game in which they progress toward high school graduation by exploring choices that influence their success in school and ability to reach career goals.[c]
8. Making POWER! Choices: Staying Away from Drugs & Alcohol	To help girls learn and practice skills for making healthy choices about substance use. To facilitate communication between Littles and Bigs about drugs and alcohol.	Bigs and Littles attempt a series of activities while blindfolded to illustrate the impairment that can result from substance use.[b] Matches work in small groups to develop public service announcements (PSAs) to discourage drug and alcohol use by girls.[c] Facilitators introduce strategies for avoiding involvement with drugs or alcohol in the context of discussing the PSAs created by the group.[c]

Table 11.1 *(Continued)*

Number and Title of Session	Goals	Session-Specific Content[a]
9. Playin' It Safe: Avoiding Violence	To help Bigs and Littles share their experiences and concerns about violence. To help girls learn skills for avoiding violence and coping with its effects. To sensitize girls to the effects of negative behaviors toward other girls.	Matches play a brief game in which they respond to questions about safety and violence.[b] The group discusses different forms of violence, including relational aggression among girls.[c] The group develops a story of a girl affected by violence and explores problem-solving solutions for her situation.[c] Facilitators introduce problem-solving steps for avoiding and coping with violence in the context of a discussion of the group's approach to the story-telling exercise.
10. Everything You Always Wanted to Know about Dating: Healthy Romantic Relationships	To help girls learn how to differentiate among types of affection and relationships. To familiarize girls with their rights and responsibilities in the area of dating. To help Bigs and Littles share their experiences and ideas about dating.	The group makes a collage depicting different types of love.[b] Facilitators introduce concepts of rights and responsibilities in dating relationships.[c] The group practices applying dating rights and responsibilities in mock court cases that involve girls similar in age to Littles.[c]
11. Showin' Our Stuff: Preparing for GirlPOWER! Extravaganza	To help Littles and Bigs recognize how POWERful they have become individually, as Matches, and as a group. To help Matches collaborate to plan a project that highlights the group's talents and accomplishments.	Participants play a game that incorporates a review of the content of previous POWERSessions.[b] Participants collaboratively plan and practice a group performance for the talent show. Individual Matches plan and practice their separate contributions to the talent show. Participants prepare invitations to the talent show and graduation.

(continued)

343

Table 11.1   *(Continued)*

Number and Title of Session	Goals	Session-Specific Content[a]
12. Celebrating Our Success: Talent Show and Graduation	To recognize the accomplishments of program participants and the support of parents and other important people in their lives. To give Littles and Bigs an opportunity to share their talents. To prepare Matches and the group for the end of the program.	Participants and guests complete the group POWERPicture using pieces that Matches have earned throughout the program.[b] Participants perform talent show for guests, with Littles serving as emcees. A graduation ceremony recognizes the contributions and accomplishments of each Little and Big. The group discusses ways of continuing POWERful Match relationships and maintaining contact.
Group Reunion	To give Littles and Bigs an opportunity to reconnect and share their experiences and accomplishments since the end of the program.	The content of this session is currently in development.

[a] Each session also includes a segment facilitated by a community guest(s) that is focused on the topic of the session.
[b] This is the Mystery Activity for the session.
[c] This activity is part of the POWERPlay for the session.
Source: GirlPOWER! Program Manual, by D. L. DuBois and Big Brothers Big Sisters of Metropolitan Chicago, 2007, University of IL, Chicago. Reprinted with permission.

Common Components   The structure and basic components of each POWER-Session are shown in Table 11.2. The only exceptions to this format are the initial orientation session and the two concluding sessions that are focused on the talent show and graduation (see Table 11.1).

Each session begins with a Mystery Activity. These are designed to be fun activities that relate in some way to the topic of the POWERSession, although this connection may not become fully apparent to participants until later in the session. For example, for the session focused on self-esteem (She's Got the POWER!), Matches are asked to try to juggle three pieces of fruit (an apple, orange, and a lemon). Participant reactions to the activity are explored later in the session as examples of strategies for coping with situations that threaten self-esteem. Our experiences during piloting suggest that leaving the connection between the Mystery Activity and the topic of the session unspecified increases its allure for participants and encourages useful dialogue between participants and

Table 11.2   Overview of POWERSession Activities

Activity	Time* (Minutes)
Mystery activity	10
MatchBuilders	10
Introduction to topic	5
Community guest(s)	30
Lunch or snack	30
POWERBuilders	10
POWERPlay	40
POWERRap	5
POWERTalk	15
Wrap-up	10

*Times are approximate and may be modified at the discretion of the session facilitators.

Source: GirlPOWER! Program Manual, by D. L. DuBois and Big Brothers Big Sisters of Metropolitan Chicago, 2007, University of IL, Chicago. Reprinted with permission.

their mentors. From a practical standpoint, the activities are designed so that they can be initiated by each Match immediately upon arrival at the session. This serves to accommodate inevitable variability in participant arrival times. Because the activities are novel and engaging, they also may encourage punctuality in attendance. A brief description of the Mystery Activity for each POWER Session is provided in Table 11.1.

The remainder of the session commences with an activity referred to as Match-Builders. A volunteer Match (determined at the previous session) first briefly acts out a scripted vignette that depicts a situation arising within the relationship of a hypothetical mentor (Erika) and girl (Vanessa). The group then discusses how to respond to the situation, after which the volunteer Match portrays an ending of their choosing. The primary objective of this activity is to foster dialogue and reflection concerning challenging issues that can arise in mentoring relationships. In doing so, the aim is to enhance the capacity of Matches to address similar concerns in their own relationships. Each vignette is thematically tied to the topic of the session and thus is integrated with the curriculum. For example, in the session focused on substance use (Making POWER Choices), the issue of mentors being sensitive to their influence as role models for youth is addressed. In this vignette, Vanessa observes Erika making plans to go out with friends for a drink and then shares her desire to do this with her own friends. The emphasis is on ensuring that

Matches have fun in the activity and are able to express themselves creatively. With this goal in mind, costumes are provided for the actors, and they are encouraged to ad lib and reverse roles (i.e., the youth plays Erika and the mentor plays Vanessa).

A brief introduction to the topic of the POWERSession is next. In the context of this discussion, facilitators help the group identify linkages to the topics of prior sessions. The group's overall progress in the program is also charted visually using the characters of Erika and Vanessa.

A guest from the community with expertise relevant to the topic of the session facilitates the next segment of the POWERSession. This portion of the curriculum is drawn from the BBBSMC program model described previously. It is designed to capitalize on assets within the surrounding community (Kretzmann & McKnight, 1993). It also serves as a vehicle for mentors and youth to become aware of resources they can make use of in their own relationships. During piloting, participants responded very favorably to this portion of the sessions. This was particularly the case when there were ample opportunities for dialogue and interaction. In the session focused on academic success and careers (My Future's So Bright I Gotta' Wear Shades), for example, a female entrepreneur engaged the group in a lively discussion about jobs and professions for women and then led them through an exercise in which youth shared their future aspirations with their mentors. Written guidelines and expectations were subsequently developed for community guests, to encourage this type of interactive approach.

At approximately the midway point of each session, a nutritious lunch or snack is provided. Feedback obtained during piloting suggested that mentors and youth valued this part of sessions as "downtime" and an opportunity for formal socialization. Further feedback suggested, however, that the 20 minutes we had allotted for the break period was not sufficient for these purposes. We thus extended this part of the session to a full half hour.

Facilitators next lead Matches in a brief discussion of POWERBuilder activities. Completed POWERBuilders are logged on a large POWERRuler that is visible to the entire group, and pieces of individual and group POWERPictures are distributed accordingly. To set the stage for the next set of POWERBuilders, they are reviewed by the group. Each Match is encouraged to identify the activity of greatest interest to them and to discuss plans for completing it. As necessary, facilitators help the group problem solve ways to overcome obstacles to engaging in POWERBuilder activities. In doing so, Matches are invited to share suggestions with each other and to team up to complete activities where and when appropriate. Matches have responded quite positively to these types of opportunities for mutual support and involvement that are provided by the group format of the program. On several occasions, for example, Matches have arranged to get together as a group for activities such as ice-skating and potluck dinners. Bigs, furthermore, have spontaneously developed e-mail lists to keep in touch between sessions.

The POWERPlay, an extended multipart activity focused on the topic of the session, follows the discussion of POWERBuilders. (The content of the POWER-Play activity for each session is summarized in Table 11.1.) The activities introduce new skills or concepts using an experiential learning approach with a minimum of didactic instruction. This may involve individual Matches each completing a small project as well as participants working together in small or large groups. The utilization of these structures is varied both within and across sessions. The emphasis is on encouraging personally meaningful sharing among participants and ensuring that Bigs and Littles have a common base of experience with the relevant ideas and information. This portion of the session is thus intended both to foster group cohesion and to set the stage for new areas of discussion and guidance in Match relationships outside of sessions. To facilitate the latter process, a handout summarizing the skills or concepts that are introduced is provided as a resource to each Big and Little.

The group marks the completion of the POWERPlay by performing POWER-Rap (whose lyrics are reproduced here, with permission from DuBois and BBBSMC, 2005). The rap is used as a fun and age-appropriate strategy for keeping the concepts of POWER salient for participants and as a way of energizing the group through movement and creative expression. The rap also functions as a ritual that promotes cohesion and identification with the program among participants.

Pride

Pride (3 claps)
I'm proud to be who I am;
I'm unique and I am special.
Each part of me is a treasure,
way, way, way beyond measure.

Opportunity

Opp-Opp-Opp-or-tu-ni-ty (3 claps during "tu-ni-ty")
My eyes are open, my ears are sharp,
I'm ready to learn, ready to start!
Respect is mine to get and give,
I earn respect, that's how I live!

Women-in-the-Making

Women in the making (3 claps)
I am healthy, I am caring,
My future is bright and I mean *glaring*!
I work hard to guarantee that I become as good a ME as I can be.

Effort and Energy

Eff-ort (3 slow claps)
I am full of en-er-gy.
I'm moving forward, yes you see,
With strength and honesty and goals to meet,
Workin' hard today til my goal's complete!

Relationships

Relationships (3 claps)
I learn to be wise beyond compare,
I show my love! I show I care!
I need others and they need me,
We are strong together, power-fully!

Next, in POWERTalk, participants then have the opportunity to reflect on their experiences during the session. In doing so, they are encouraged to share POWERConnections as well as any other feelings or thoughts about the session. In response to pilot findings, the POWERTalk segment has evolved to be increasingly less structured and focused on session content. The more open-ended format has facilitated meaningful sharing among participants and helped them stay connected to each other's lives outside the group.

At the conclusion of the POWERSession, a brief note about the session is distributed for Littles to take home to their parents or guardians. Mentors and girl then each complete evaluation forms about the session.

As POWERSessions were piloted it became apparent that facilitators often were feeling rushed trying to complete all of the activities. Participants shared similar feelings and a desire to have more time to spend in more informal interaction. Keeping in mind relational theory, ensuring that sessions are not "overstuffed" with activities in a manner that compromises opportunities for rewarding interactions among participants may be especially important in a program designed for girls. Accordingly, during the program development and piloting process, we have made a number of revisions to the curriculum to reduce time pressures and manage session time more effectively. These modifications include, for example, reducing the number of discrete activities that are included in the POWERPlay portion of each session. As noted, we also have lengthened the break period and loosened the structure of the POWERTalk portion of sessions. Following these changes, both participants and facilitators have reported experiencing sessions as more relaxed and conducive to meaningful sharing and reflection.

Content   Table 11.1 provides an overview of the goals and content of each POWERSession. The topics addressed encompass the domains of health promotion (exercise, nutrition, self-esteem), risk behavior prevention (substance use, violence), education (academic success, career exploration), and positive youth development (social relationships, goal setting, problem solving, coping skills, cultural awareness, and pride). Several sessions (1, 2, 3, 11, and 12, and the group reunion) are geared primarily toward promoting the development of mentoring relationships and group cohesion.

Stakeholder group members who were interviewed, as well as the advisory council, endorsed our proposed content for the POWERSession curriculum as highly relevant to the health and well-being of the target population of young-adolescent, ethnic-minority girls. Several parents, however, did express concern about the appropriateness of a plan to address issues relating to sexual risk behavior. Based on this input, the relevant session was revised to focus instead on the more developmentally normative topics of dating and romantic relationships.

The curriculum is designed to be both culturally appropriate and gender-specific. Session 4 is devoted to the topics of cultural diversity, ethnic identity, and coping with prejudice and discrimination. Several other features of the curriculum also reflect sensitivity to the cultural backgrounds of the participants. These include the use of graphics depicting members of ethnic minority groups, activities that promote learning about ethnic minority role models, and skill-building vignettes that incorporate culturally relevant themes.

With respect to gender, two sessions (2 and 3) focus on promoting supportive interpersonal relationships, and thus capitalize on the relational orientation of females. Specific threats to the health and well-being of girls receive significant attention as well. These include risk factors at the individual level, such as low self-esteem; at the interpersonal level, such as relational aggression (i.e., manipulative or harmful behaviors that damage another girl's peer relationships or sense of social acceptance; Crick & Grotpeter, 1995); and at the societal level, such as pressures and stereotypes contributing to unhealthy diet. The materials and activities utilized throughout the curriculum, moreover, incorporate positive images of girls and women, and portray sensitivity to gender-relevant themes and a female perspective.

Recall that the literature review identified goal setting as a beneficial component of mentoring relationships. This topic is addressed in the first session (i.e., session 2) after orientation to the program. During this session, each Match decides on goals for the Little, the Big, and their relationship. Having the Big choose a goal for herself is designed to create the opportunity for her to model the process of setting and working toward goals with her Little throughout the program. It also increases opportunities for reciprocal exchanges of support within the mentoring relationship. The goal that each Match sets for their relationship ensures that attention is directed toward promoting the growth of the mentoring bond. It also provides further opportunity for mutual forms of support between the mentor and youth. Illustrative of this possibility, one Match set a goal of "trading skills with each other," in which the Big would teach the Little ice skating and the Little would teach the Big origami.

During initial piloting, goal setting occurred within the context of a supervision contact between the program facilitator and each individual Match. This process proved inefficient and time-consuming from an agency perspective, however, and did not provide the opportunity for Matches to become familiar with each other's goals. These considerations were the impetus for our decision to incorporate goal-setting activities into a POWERSession. As noted in Table 11.1, this session includes an activity during which Matches share their goals and offer each other support and encouragement for reaching them. When implemented as part of the piloting and feasibility study, the session has been very well received by both Littles and Bigs.

Sequence　The sessions that focus on development of the mentoring relationship and group cohesion (2 and 3) occur early in the curriculum, for several reasons. Because many Matches are likely to be new or established only recently, it is important to provide opportunities for Bigs and Littles simply to get to know one another at this stage of the program (Keller, 2005). It also is assumed that a solid foundation of trust and mutual positive regard will be required if Matches are to participate successfully in later portions of the curriculum that ask them to explore a range of sensitive and personal topics together (Rhodes, 2002, 2005). Similarly, by devoting attention to building cohesion among all participants, it is expected that the group is more likely to be experienced as a safe and supportive environment throughout the program. The topics addressed in the following sessions (4 and 5), self-esteem and cultural diversity, are interwoven into the remainder of the curriculum and thus also are introduced at a relatively early stage.

The sequencing of the next set of sessions (6 to 10) is informed by several considerations. The first of these sessions, which focuses on exercise and healthy eating, provides an opportunity for participants to begin to concentrate on health promotion in an area that is likely less sensitive and more accessible than those that are the focus of later sessions in this part of the curriculum. The next session (7) deals with achieving academic and career success. This session is strategically situated in the latter half of the curriculum to help ensure that participants do not misconstrue the program as overly focused on school-related concerns. Both stakeholder interviews and advisory council feedback suggested that such a message would detract from youth engagement with the program. The subsequent three sessions (8 to 10) address risk behaviors (e.g., substance use) and other sensitive issues (e.g., dating) that may be especially challenging to discuss within Matches and the group. These topics are concentrated in the latter stages of the curriculum to ensure that participants have developed the levels of trust and intimacy required for such concerns to be explored in ways that are beneficial.

POWERBuilders

POWERBuilders, the activities that mentors and youth complete outside of group sessions, are an integral part of the GirlPOWER! program. This portion of the program is intended to enrich the interactions that each Big and Little have when spending time together on their own. The activities involved are designed to help Matches further explore skills and concepts introduced in the POWERSessions. At each POWERSession, Matches are asked to complete one POWERBuilder relevant to the topic of that session prior to the next session.

Stakeholder interviews and advisory council input provided support for the general idea of providing activities for Matches to complete outside of group sessions. The feedback also informed the development of this portion of the program in several ways, as did suggestions provided by participants during piloting. Mentors in particular emphasized a desire for:

- Brief, user-friendly resource materials
- Practical and inexpensive activities
- Choice among different activity options

To address the first of these concerns, the description of each activity is limited to a single sheet of paper. The information provided follows a common format, which includes the goal of the activity, necessary materials, and step-by-step instructions for completion. A one-page overview orients participants to the set of POWERBuilders associated with each POWERSession and is coupled with a list of tips and suggestions to consider when completing these activities. To address feasibility, all activities have little or no associated costs. And within each set of POWERBuilders is at least one activity that can be completed by telephone. This option is designed to accommodate situations when the mentor and youth are unable to get together in person. A sample POWER-Builder is shown in Table 11.3.

To provide choice typically a set of five different POWERBuilder options are given for each POWERSession topic. Each of these activities is thematically

Table 11.3   Sample POWERBuilder

Accentuating the Positive

POWERSession: She's Got the POWER!:

Promoting Healthy Self-Esteem

P-O-W-E-R! Area: Pride

Goal: To help Little and Big become more aware of their positive qualities and how they are appreciated by others.

Materials Needed:

✓ Two 3′ × 6′ pieces of paper
✓ Markers and any other desired craft materials
✓ Magazines
✓ *My Self-Esteem and Me: Keepin' It Healthy* handout

Activity: Big and Little talk about each other's positive qualities and illustrate them in collages in the shape of their bodies.

- **Briefly review the handout** together to remind yourselves about ways of keeping your self-esteem healthy that you can be proud of.
- **Create silhouettes of each of your bodies** on the two large pieces of paper.
- **Decorate each silhouette with words, phrases, photographs, or magazine cutouts to display your positive qualities.** Take turns filling in each other's silhouettes to show positive qualities that you see in one another.
- **Talk about your collages.** Why did you decorate them the way that you did? How can your positive qualities help you make choices that keep your self-esteem healthy? How can you work as a team to stay positive and appreciate what makes you special as a person? Where would you like to display your collages?
- **Remember to update your Match Activity Log** to show this activity!

tied to a different letter of the POWER acronym and its associated concept. Those linked to R (Relationships), for example, may have the Match complete a project in which they offer each other support and validation in a given area (e.g., exercise). These activities, furthermore, frequently incorporate participation of people from the social networks of the Little and/or Big, such as the Little's parents. Linking multiple POWERBuilders to each session ensures that Matches have a large pool of potential activities to engage in after the formal end of the program. In our stakeholder interviews, BBBS agency staff emphasized the value of providing this type of resource.

To offer additional flexibility, Matches are encouraged to consider any activities they engage in outside of sessions as potential POWERBuilders. Matches are given the option of substituting such activities for those included in program materials. In doing so, they are asked to relate the activity to the concepts of POWER and the topics of one or more POWERSessions using a brief form developed for this purpose. This option addresses a concern expressed by both girls and mentors that Matches should be given ample opportunity to pursue their shared interests outside the more structured portions of the program.

To kick off the POWERBuilder portion of the program and promote group cohesion, all Matches complete the same activity between sessions 1 and 2. In this activity, they introduce each other to different parts of their lives by taking photographs together with a disposable camera. All Matches also complete the same POWERBuilder between sessions 2 and 3, to begin work on the goals they have set, and between sessions 11 and 12 to practice their acts for the talent show.

Both girls and mentors also recommended that POWERBuilders include activities that give Matches the chance to learn about and take advantage of resources in the surrounding community. Each set of POWERBuilders includes at least one activity with this type of emphasis. A POWERBuilder associated with the session that addresses cultural issues, for example, involves eating at a restaurant that serves food from the Little's ethnic group.

As noted, each set of POWERBuilders is designed to promote the objectives of an associated POWERSession. To reinforce the skills and concepts introduced in the session, most activities begin with the Match reviewing the handout that summarizes this information. Applications of the material are then incorporated into the activity. For example, guidelines for diet and exercise from the Keeping Our Bodies Healthy session are utilized as part of activities in which the Match cooks a nutritious meal or spends time practicing a sport. Prompts or dialogue and reflection are included within each activity to help enrich mentor-youth.

Each participant's program notebook includes tips and suggestions for getting the most out of the POWERBuilder activities. Obstacles that may arise when attempting to plan or implement these activities are addressed. Opportunities for ongoing integration of similar activities into the Match relationship are also highlighted as are potential connections to the goals that the Match is working on in the program.

Parental Involvement

The parents and guardians of Littles are actively involved in GirlPOWER! through four mechanisms:

1. Parents attend several of the POWERSessions. These include the orientation session (session 1), the talent show and graduation (session 12), each of which features activities to promote parental engagement with the program (see Table 11.1). Parents also are invited to a POWERSession midway through the program. This gives them an opportunity to observe a typical session firsthand and to review and discuss program-related issues with facilitators.

2. As mentioned previously, following each POWERSession, a note is sent home that summarizes the session and offers suggestions for parental reinforcement and support. The note is personalized by having the Little briefly share what she liked about the session and how her Big supported her participation.

3. Several of the POWERBuilder activities incorporate opportunities for parental involvement, as referred to previously. There is encouragement, furthermore, for Matches to discuss their activities with parents and to place completed projects in a visible location in the Little's home.

4. Supervision of each Match by program staff includes regular contact with the Little's parent or guardian. These contacts focus on promoting teamwork between the parent and mentor as well as on incorporating program ideas and concepts in the parent-child relationship. Staff also can use these contacts as an opportunity to address issues relating to the Little's home environment that may be interfering with her availability to attend POWERSessions or spend time with her mentor outside of sessions.

Training and Supervision

Agency staff members receive training to prepare them to effectively deliver all components of the GirlPOWER! program. A significant portion of this training focuses on ensuring staff readiness to implement the POWERSessions that are at the core of the program. A "teach, demonstrate, practice, and reflect" sequence is used to familiarize staff with each of the different types of session activities. Skills for group facilitation also are addressed. In the piloting of the program, staff training has been conducted by members of the research team; however, in the future, we envision a "train the trainer" model, in which we would prepare experienced GirlPOWER! facilitators to provide the training.

Mentors participate in a group training session lasting approximately 3 hours prior to the start of the program. The BBBS staff who will be facilitating the POWERSessions conduct the training. The goals of the training are twofold: (1) to provide an overview of the GirlPOWER! program and the roles and responsibilities of mentors within the program, and (2) to give mentors confidence that they can be effective in working with their Littles in the program. The importance of the latter aim is underscored by research in which the perceived quality of training predicted reports of stronger efficacy beliefs by mentors (Parra et al., 2002). Mentor self-efficacy, in turn, was linked to the establishment of higher-quality and longer-term relationships with youth.

Several strategies are used in the training to prepare Bigs to work successfully with their Littles in the program. These include instruction and practice in approaches for developing strong relationships within the framework of the POWER concepts. In accordance with the focus on ethnic-minority youth, sensitivity to cultural issues in mentoring relationships also is addressed (Sanchez & Colon, 2005). Bigs are invited throughout the training to share their ideas for effective mentoring so as to validate the experience and expertise that they bring to the program. Group discussions and collaborative activities are utilized as well to help foster cohesion and mutual support among the mentors.

In the second year of implementing the program, we also have added a training session for Littles. Along with preparing girls for their roles and responsibilities in the program, the training seeks to empower them to successfully negotiate different types of issues that may arise with their mentors or other group members while participating in the program. The training session for Littles is held conjointly with the session for Bigs. This serves to avoid logistical barriers to attendance and ensure that the training is a shared experience for Matches.

As part of the supervision component of the program, agency staff (GirlPOWER! program facilitators or BBBS Match Support Specialists) periodically make contact with the Big and Little in each Match and, as noted previously, the Little's parent or guardian. All three parties (Big, Little, and parent/guardian) are contacted during the first and final months of the program. Bigs continue to be contacted on a monthly basis throughout the program, whereas Littles and parents/guardians are contacted monthly on an alternating schedule. Both the frequency of these contacts and the involvement of the Big, Little, and parent/guardian are consistent with BBBS practice standards. Each supervision or Match support contact addresses certain topics that are required by BBBS guidelines, including child safety. Match supervision guidelines for GirlPOWER! ensure attention to several additional topics specific to the program. For Bigs, these include POWERSession attendance, completion of POWERBuilder activities, and progress on goals. In addition, Match activities and conversations that are relevant to the topics addressed in GirlPOWER! are reinforced, and opportunities to incorporate these topics into future interactions are explored. Staff members use the Match Activity Logs completed by Bigs (described in the following section) to inform these discussions.

Contacts with youth address similar issues, including their participation in POWERSessions and activities with their mentors outside of sessions. Girls also are encouraged to share any concerns they have regarding the program or their relationships with their mentors. Staff members focus on supporting girls in a process of identifying and taking steps to address such difficulties in a manner that is consistent with the underlying empowerment theme of the program. Support contacts with the Little's parent or guardian focus on issues pertinent to their participation in GirlPOWER! that were described previously.

Program Monitoring and Evaluation

Procedures for monitoring and evaluating implementation are incorporated into all components of the GirlPOWER! program. These procedures are designed to:

- Serve as aids to program staff and mentors as they carry out their different roles and responsibilities.
- Facilitate reflection among participants regarding their experiences in different activities.
- Provide data that can be used both to meet reporting requirements of funders and to enhance the agency's future implementations of the program.

Collectively, these processes provide a mechanism for ensuring accountability at multiple levels: individual participants, the program and agency, and community stakeholder groups such as funders (Coyne, Duffy, & Wandersman, 2005). This type of accountability may increase effectiveness as well as the capacity of agencies to implement the program on a sustained basis (Coyne et al., 2005). An overview of the different forms used for program monitoring and evaluation in GirlPOWER! is provided in Table 11.4.

Table 11.4   Overview of Program Monitoring and Evaluation Forms

Form	Description	Person(s) Completing	Schedule for Completion
Staff Training Evaluation Form	Ratings and comments regarding quality of training	Agency staff	End of staff-training sessions
Training Evaluation Form	Ratings and comments regarding quality of training	Big and Little	End of mentor and youth training sessions
GirlPOWER! Mentor Survey	Ratings of confidence for fulfilling roles and responsibilities as a mentor in the program, and expected benefits of participation; assessment of program knowledge	Big	End of program orientation (POWERSession 1)
Facilitator Self-Assessment Form	Checklist of preparation and implementation items for a POWERSession; ratings of participant engagement and quality of session facilitation	Agency staff	After each POWERSession
POWERSession Evaluation Form	Ratings and comments regarding experiences in a POWERSession	Little, Big, and parent/guardian (when applicable)	End of each POWERSession
POWER Questionnaire	Reports of experiences relating to concepts of POWER (e.g., feelings of pride, opportunities for learning); knowledge of skills and concepts introduced in program	Little	Beginning and end of the program
Match Activity Log	Report of contacts with Little outside of group sessions, including POWERBuilders checklist of Match activities and discussions relating to program topics	Big	Monthly
Match Support Reporting Form	Report of Match Support contacts with Bigs, Littles, and parents/guardians, including checklist of program topics discussed	Agency staff	After each contact
Staff Task and Expense Reporting Form	Report of staff time and other resources utilized for implementation of program	Agency staff	Monthly throughout program planning, recruitment, and implementation
GirlPOWER! Survey	Ratings and comments regarding experiences in the program	Little, Big, and parent/guardian	Midpoint and end of program

Source: GirlPOWER! Program Manual, by D. L. DuBois and Big Brothers Big Sisters of Metropolitan Chicago, 2007, University of IL, Chicago. Reprinted with permission.

Linkages between GirlPOWER! and Positive Youth Development

As noted previously, the rise in popularity of mentoring interventions has occurred in tandem with growth in the field of positive youth development (Kuperminc et al., 2005). It is useful, therefore, to consider how GirlPOWER! aligns with emerging models and approaches to fostering youth development. Kuperminc and colleagues described a conceptual framework linking different categories of activities common to youth development programs with the process and outcome domains likely to be of greatest concern for these types of programs. The GirlPOWER! program encompasses each of the major types of intervention activities included in the framework: didactic (e.g., teaching new skills through the POWERSessions and POWERBuilder activities), experiential (e.g., community-based activities within POWERBuilders), and relational (e.g., the emphasis throughout the program on fostering the development of the Match relationship, as well as positive connections to the larger group). The domains of processes and outcomes in the framework are similarly all addressed by the program: prevention/competence promotion outcomes (e.g., POWERSessions focusing on topics such as substance use, violence prevention, and school performance), self-definition (e.g., emphasis on positive identify formation through the core program concepts of pride/self-esteem and women in the making), and relatedness and social connections (e.g., activities that focus on building trust, communication, and intimacy within the Match relationship, as well as a sense of belonging and mutual support among group members). Overall, the strategy of integrating mentoring with other program activities in GirlPOWER! reflects a comprehensive orientation toward promoting youth development. The mechanisms through which the intervention may achieve desired outcomes thus include not only those directly attributable to mentoring, but also those that stem from the activities and supportive experiences to which relationships are linked through the program curriculum (Kuperminc et al., 2005).

CONCLUSIONS

Although growing in popularity, mentoring programs for youth, when rigorously evaluated, have been indicated to have only modest effects on participant outcomes. An important limitation of existing programs is that few have been developed and evaluated using an empirically based framework. Programs also have not been tailored to specific populations of youth, such as those representing different configurations of age, gender, and race/ethnicity.

In this chapter, we described the results to date of our efforts to develop a community-based mentoring program for ethnic/minority, young adolescent girls in accordance with recommended steps from empirically based frameworks for the design, evaluation, and dissemination of preventive interventions. Review of theoretical, empirical, and intervention literature informed the development of the program by providing support for several facets of an existing program model in use by the agency with which we are collaborating and by highlighting several promising avenues for innovation. Stakeholder input and piloting of activities, furthermore, proved invaluable as a basis for making significant modifications and refinements to all components of the program.

In accordance with the recommended steps outlined at the start of this chapter, the chief future need of the program is for its development to be further informed through the results obtained in a small-scale randomized evaluation of its efficacy (i.e., stage 4, piloting and feasibility study). This step, currently in progress, is allowing for piloting of program evaluation methodology, including random assignment procedures and assessment instrumentation, and, when completed, will provide preliminary estimates of program effects that may be used in planning a full-scale efficacy trial (Flay, 1986). The piloting and feasibility study also is yielding valuable process evaluation findings stemming from implementation of the program in its entirely for the first time. As described in this chapter, examination of these data already has prompted us to make several midcourse adaptations to the program.

In the piloting and feasibility study, BBBSMC Matches meeting eligibility criteria for the program have been randomly assigned either to participate in GirlPOWER! or to receive the agency's standard community-based mentoring services. An initial cohort of Matches ($N = 20$) has completed participation in the study, with 10 of those Matches having participated in GirlPOWER! Data collection for a second cohort of similar size is currently nearing completion. The additional cohort will increase the overall sample size of the study. It also is providing an opportunity to implement the program with the modifications made during the course of its initial implementation with the first cohort.

The process evaluation data for the study are being collected using the measures summarized in Table 11.4, as well as through agency records and observations of POWERSessions by members of the research team. Outcomes are being assessed using a multi-informant, multi-source strategy. These data include surveys completed by girls, their parents/guardians, and mentors in both the program and comparison groups on three occasions: start of the program, 3 months into the program, and at the end of the 1-year period of program participation. (A follow-up assessment at the time of the group reunion would be desirable, but the funding necessary to collect these additional data is not currently available.)

Further data are being collected via ratings obtained from participants' teachers at the beginning and end of the program and from agency, school, and the juvenile justice system records. The outcomes assessed are derived from a logic model for the GirlPOWER! program (DuBois & BBBSMC, 2005). These include relatively proximal (i.e., direct or immediate) effects of program participation on the duration and quality of mentoring relationships; intermediate impacts on youth resources, such as self-esteem and health attitudes and knowledge; and relatively distal, longer-term outcomes in areas such as health behavior and mental health. It also is anticipated that mentors may benefit from program participation. Accordingly, the survey completed by mentors includes measures of their outcomes in several of the same domains that are being assessed for youth (e.g., health behavior). These types of effects would be noteworthy in their own right and also could be important in moderating program impacts on youth.

As is evident from this chapter, the development of an intervention within an empirically based framework is a long-term endeavor that necessitates a significant investment of time, effort, and resources. Yet, it is equally apparent that this approach has proved invaluable in our work to date with the GirlPOWER! program. It is thus the continuation of the collaborative, empirically driven process we have initiated that offers the best prospect for ensuring that the program realizes its potential to empower girls for healthy futures through mentoring.

REFERENCES

American Association of University Women. (1991). *Shortchanging girls, short-changing America.* Washington, DC: Author.

Baker, D. B., & Maguire, C. P. (2005). Mentoring in historical perspective. In D. L. DuBois & M. J. Karcher (Eds.), *Handbook of youth mentoring* (pp. 14–29). Thousand Oaks, CA: Sage.

Balcazar, F., Keys, C., & Garate, J. (1995). Learning to recruit assistance to attain transition goals: A program for adjudicated youth with disabilities. *Remedial and Special Education, 16,* 237–246.

Barrera, M., & Bonds, D. D. (2005). Mentoring relationships and social support. In D. L. DuBois & M. J. Karcher (Eds.), *Handbook of youth mentoring* (pp. 133–142). Thousand Oaks, CA: Sage.

Bartholomew, L. K., Parcel, G. S., Kok, G., & Gottlieb, N. H. (2001). *Intervention mapping: Designing theory- and evidence-based health promotion programs.* London: Mayfield Publishing.

Big Brothers Big Sisters of Metropolitan Chicago. (2002). *Unpublished raw data, 1997–2002.* Chicago: Author.

Bogat, G. A., & Liang, B. (2005). Gender in mentoring relationships. In D. L. DuBois & M. J. Karcher (Eds.), *Handbook of youth mentoring* (pp. 205–217). Thousand Oaks, CA: Sage.

Cavell, T. A., & Hughes, J. N. (2000). Secondary prevention as context for assessing change processes in aggressive children. *Journal of School Psychology, 38,* 199–235.

Chaplin, T. M., Gillham, J. E., Reivich, K., Elkon, A. G. L., Samuels, B., Freres, D. R., et al. (2006). Depression prevention for early adolescent girls: A pilot study of all girls versus co-ed groups. *Journal of Early Adolescence, 26,* 110–126.

Clark, M. L., & Ayers, M. (1993). Friendship expectations and friendship evaluations: Reciprocity and gender effects. *Youth and Society, 24,* 299–313.

Coyne, S. M., Duffy, J. L., & Wandersman, A. (2005). Mentoring for results: Accountability at the individual, program, community, and policy levels. In D. L. DuBois & M. J. Karcher (Eds.), *Handbook of youth mentoring* (pp. 546–560). Thousand Oaks, CA: Sage.

Crick, N. R., & Grotpeter, J. K. (1995). Relational aggression, gender, and social-psychological adjustment. *Child Development, 66,* 710–722.

Davis, T., Paxton, K. C., & Robinson, L. (1997). *After-school action programs: Girl World Builders summary report.* Chicago: Authors.

DuBois, D. L., & Big Brothers Big Sisters of Metropolitan Chicago. (2007). *GirlPOWER! program manual.* University of Illinois, Chicago.

DuBois, D. L., Burk-Braxton, C., Tevendale, H. D., Swenson, L. P., & Hardesty, J. L. (2002). Race and gender influences on adjustment in early adolescence: Investigation of an integrative model. *Child Development, 73,* 1573–1592.

DuBois, D. L., Doolittle, F., Yates, B. T., Silverthorn, N., & Tebes, J. K. (2006). Research methodology and youth mentoring. *Journal of Community Psychology, 34,* 657–676.

DuBois, D. L., Holloway, B. E., Valentine, J. C., & Cooper, H. (2002). Effectiveness of mentoring programs for youth: A meta-analytic review. *American Journal of Community Psychology, 30,* 157–197.

DuBois, D. L., & Karcher, M. J. (2005). Youth mentoring: Theory, research, and practice. In D. L. DuBois & M. J. Karcher (Eds.), *Handbook of youth mentoring* (pp. 2–11). Thousand Oaks, CA: Sage.

DuBois, D. L., Neville, H. A., Parra, G. R., & Pugh-Lilly, A. O. (2002). Testing a new model of mentoring. In G. G. Noam (Editor-in-chief) & J. E. Rhodes (Ed.), *A critical view of youth mentoring* (New Directions for Youth Development: Theory, Research, and Practice, No. 93, pp. 21–57). San Francisco: Jossey-Bass.

DuBois, D. L., & Rhodes, J. E. (2006). Youth mentoring: Bridging science with practice. *Journal of Community Psychology, 34,* 647–655.

DuBois, D. L., & Silverthorn, N. (2005). Research methodology. In D. L. DuBois & M. J. Karcher (Eds.), *Handbook of youth mentoring* (pp. 44–64). Thousand Oaks, CA: Sage.

Flay, B. R. (1986). Efficacy and effectiveness trials (and other phases of research) in the development of health promotion programs. *Preventive Medicine, 15,* 451–474.

French, S. E., Seidman, E., Allen, L., & Aber, J. L. (2006). The development of ethnic identity during adolescence. *Developmental Psychology, 42,* 1–10.

Gilligan, C. (1982). *In a different voice.* Cambridge, MA: Harvard University Press.

Green, L. W., & Kreuter, M. W. (1999). *Health promotion planning: An educational and environmental approach* (2nd ed.). Mountain View, CA: Mayfield Publishing.

Grossman, J. B., & Rhodes, J. E. (2002). The test of time: Predictors and effects of duration in youth mentoring programs. *American Journal of Community Psychology, 30,* 199–219.

Hamilton, M. A., & Hamilton, S. F. (2005). Work and service-learning. In D. L. DuBois & M. J. Karcher (Eds.), *Handbook of youth mentoring* (pp. 348–363). Thousand Oaks, CA: Sage.

Harter, S. (1999). *The construction of the self: A developmental perspective.* New York: Guilford Press.

Institute of Medicine. (1994). *Reducing risks for mental disorders.* Washington, DC: National Academy Press.

Jekielek, S., Moore, K. A., & Hair, E. C. (2002). *Mentoring programs and youth development.* Washington, DC: Child Trends.

Keller, T. E. (2005). The stages and development of mentoring relationships. In D. L. DuBois & M. J. Karcher (Eds.), *Handbook of youth mentoring* (pp. 82–99). Thousand Oaks, CA: Sage.

Kretzmann, J. P., & McKnight, J. L. (1993). *Building communities from the inside out.* Evanston, IL: Asset-Based Community Development Institute, Northwestern University.

Kuperminc, G. P., Emshoff, J. G., Reiner, M. M., Secrest, L. A., Holditch Niolon, P., et al. (2005). Integration of mentoring with other programs and services. In D. L. DuBois & M. J. Karcher (Eds.), *Handbook of youth mentoring* (pp. 314–333). Thousand Oaks, CA: Sage.

McLearn, K. T., Colasanto, D., & Schoen, C. (1998). *Mentoring makes a difference: Findings from the Commonwealth Fund 1998 Survey of Adults Mentoring Young People.* New York: The Commonwealth Fund.

Nakkula, M. J., & Harris, J. T. (2005). Assessment of mentoring relationships. In D. L. DuBois & M. J. Karcher (Eds.), *Handbook of youth mentoring* (pp. 100–117). Thousand Oaks, CA: Sage.

National Advisory Mental Health Council Workgroup on Mental Disorders Prevention Research. (2001). Priorities for prevention research at NIMH. *Prevention and Treatment, 4,* Article 17. Retrieved July 14, 2004, from http://journals.apa.org/prevention/volume4/pre0040017a.html.

National Council for Research on Women. (1998). *The Girls Report: What we know and need to know about growing up female.* New York: Author.

Offord, D. R. (1996). The state of prevention of early intervention. In R. D. Peters & R. J. McMahon (Eds.), *Preventing childhood disorders, substance abuse, and delinquency* (pp. 329–344). Thousand Oaks, CA: Sage.

Parra, G. R., DuBois, D. L., Neville, H. A., Pugh-Lilly, A. O., & Povinelli, N. (2002). Mentoring relationships for youth: Investigation of a process-oriented model. *Journal of Community Psychology, 30,* 367–388.

Rhodes, J. (2002). *Stand by me: The risks and rewards of mentoring today's youth.* Cambridge, MA: Harvard University Press.

Rhodes, J. (2005). A model of youth mentoring. In D. L. DuBois & M. J. Karcher (Eds.), *Handbook of youth mentoring* (pp. 30–43). Thousand Oaks, CA: Sage.

Rhodes, J., & DuBois, D. (2004). *National research agenda for youth mentoring.* Alexandria, VA: MENTOR/National Mentoring Partnership. Retrieved July 14, 2004, from www.mentoring.org/research_corner/researchagenda.pdf.

Sanchez, B., & Colon, Y. (2005). Race, ethnicity, and culture in mentoring relationships. In D. L. DuBois & M. J. Karcher (Eds.), *Handbook of youth mentoring* (pp. 191–204). Thousand Oaks, CA: Sage.

Scales, P. C. (2003). *Other people's kids: Social expectations and American adults' involvement with children and adolescents.* New York: Kluwer Academic/Plenum Press.

Sipe, C. L. (2005). Toward a typology of mentoring. In D. L. DuBois & M. J. Karcher (Eds.), *Handbook of youth mentoring* (pp. 65–80). Thousand Oaks, CA: Sage.

Spencer, R., & Rhodes, J. E. (2005). A counseling and psychotherapy perspective on mentoring relationships. In D. L. DuBois & M. J. Karcher (Eds.), *Handbook of youth mentoring* (pp. 118–132). Thousand Oaks, CA: Sage.

Steinberg, L. (1998). *Adolescence* (5th ed.). New York: McGraw-Hill.

Stukas, A. A., & Tanti, C. (2005). Recruiting and sustaining volunteer mentors. In D. L. DuBois & M. J. Karcher (Eds.), *Handbook of youth mentoring* (pp. 235–250). Thousand Oaks, CA: Sage.

Walker, G. (2005). Youth mentoring and public policy. In D. L. DuBois & M. J. Karcher (Eds.), *Handbook of youth mentoring* (pp. 510–524). Thousand Oaks, CA: Sage.

Weinberger, S. G. (2005). Developing a mentoring program. In D. L. DuBois & M. J. Karcher (Eds.), *Handbook of youth mentoring* (pp. 220–233). Thousand Oaks, CA: Sage.

Zimmerman, M. A., Copeland, L. A., Shope, J. T., & Dielman, T. E. (1997). A longitudinal study of self-esteem: Implications for adolescent development. *Journal of Youth and Adolescence, 26,* 117–141.

Author Index

Subject Index

L.S. WASHINGTON LIB. - SUNO

3 6873 010 076 592